From Every People

A HANDBOOK OF TWO-THIRDS WORLD MISSIONS
WITH DIRECTORY/ HISTORIES/ANALYSIS

by Larry D. Pate

Introduction by
Lawrence E. Keyes

Foreword by
Edison Queiroz

MARC
919 W. Huntington Drive
Monrovia, California 91016

Larry D. Pate

From Every People

A HANDBOOK OF TWO-THIRDS WORLD
MISSIONS WITH DIRECTORY/HISTORIES/ANALYSIS

Copyright © 1989 by OC Ministries, Inc., 25 Corning Avenue, Milpitas, CA, USA 95035-5336, Telephone (408) 263-1101.

ISBN 0-912552-67-0 (MARC)

Co-published by MARC and OC Ministries. First printing, 2,500, May 1989. Cover design by Richard Sears. Typography and formatting with VENTURA PUBLISHER.

Missions Advanced Research and Communication Center (MARC) is a division of World Vision International, 919 W. Huntington Drive, Monrovia, CA, USA, 91016.

Dedicated to the
MISSIONARY MARTYRS
of the Two-Thirds World
Missionary Movement

Though they are scarcely known
outside the places and peoples
where they have fallen, they are
the true heroes of eternity!

84805

FOREWORD

by Edison Queiroz

WHEN I THINK ABOUT THE COUNTRIES OF AFRICA, ASIA, AND LATIN America, and the challenge they face in trying to evangelize the whole world, I remember the disciples in the book of Acts. They were without money, and without the technical ability to communicate that we have today. However, they still made a great advance in the task of world evangelization.

It renews my excitement to see that God is using the Church of the Two-Thirds World to reach the unreached in this generation. I believe in miracles and this is one area where they are happening.

The awakening that is happening in this part of the world reminds us of two very important principles: First, it is impossible to do effective missions work without the power of the Holy Spirit. Second, where the power of the Holy Spirit is displayed, there is also missionary vision.

For me, this is the basis for Christian service. The pattern of the Bible is that every church should be a missionary church. Every church should have an emphasis on cross-cultural preaching and a vision to evangelize the world. The local church can be used to identify, select, train and send its missionaries. This is what is happening in Latin America.

My church was sending a couple to reach the Marubo Indians in the Amazon jungle. During the commissioning service, I gave this couple a solemn charge: "I give you two years to introduce me to the first Indian with a missionary calling." They were startled until I explained that they must plant a "missionary" church among the Amazon Indians.

Some time later I received a letter from them with this report, "One of the Indian converts was filled with a desire to start a work in another part of the tribe." They were starting a new church! I was happy because this missionary was following the biblical pattern.

Today God is moving the Church of the Two-Thirds World to missions. When I think about this, I see tremendous latent potential. God in His sovereignty, grace and power is moving the Church to accomplish the task to preach the gospel to every nation.

The Church of the Two-Thirds World is trusting in miracles. For such needs God is a specialist. In the face of formidable hurdles in economics, politics, and social instability, we can see God working in supernatural ways. A church in that strife-torn Central American country of El Salvador is surmounting its own difficulties to send a missionary couple to Spain. If God can move the church in El Salvador, what can stop the rest of His Church from making similar thrusts around the world?

In this book we have three case histories to serve as inspiration to help us advance in the work of missions. The directory of missions will be a tremendous tool to help us work in partnership with our brothers and sisters in Christ. My prayer is that this book will promote greater cooperation not only among the churches, but also between the missions of the West and the missions of the Two-Thirds World.

We know that many doors are closed for missionaries from the West, but those same doors are open to missionaries from other parts of the world. We need to work in cooperation and unity to coordinate our efforts to reach the unreached. Remember what the Apostle Paul said in Romans 15:20:

> **"It has always been my ambition to preach the gospel where Christ was not known." (NIV)**

This book comes to us in the midst of God's great activity. I praise God for all our brothers and sisters who have worked on it. I especially commend Larry Pate who coordinated all the effort that produced these materials.

May God use this book to help each one of us accomplish the task.

The Reverend Edison Quieroz *is a Brazilian Baptist pastor with a missionary heart. He presided over the Congreso Misionero Ibero-Americano '87, better known as COMIBAM, and continues to chair its ongoing structure.*

ACKNOWLEDGMENTS

A BOOK LIKE THIS REQUIRES FAR MORE WORK than can be accomplished by any one individual. This one is the result of numerous people's efforts who deserve more recognition than space allows here. Several organizations and dozens of individuals have participated in this project, either with their labors or their finances.

The people

One of the most difficult parts of this project has been the collection of data in various languages around the world. About 50% of the data was collected using English as the communications medium and directly through our Emerging Missions office at OC Ministries' headquarters in Milpitas, California. The rest was gathered in many languages through the efforts of a number of coordinators and consultants. Those people include:

Coordinators

- INDONESIA: Greg Gripentrog and Paulus Wibowo
- PHILIPPINES: Met Castillo, Coordinator, and Philippine Crusades team
- TAIWAN: Rahn Strickler
- JAPAN: Marvin L. Eyler
- SOUTH KOREA: Marlin L. Nelson
- BURMA: Simon P. K. Enno
- KENYA: Donna Downes
- NIGERIA: Niyi Gbade
- BRAZIL: Jim Kemp, Ted Limpic and Larry Kraft
- ARGENTINA: Donald Fults, Steven Griswell, and Steven Johnson
- COLOMBIA: Ric Escobar
- ECUADOR: Robert A. Hatch
- MEXICO: Moises Lopez
- GUATEMALA: Tim Halls

Consultants

- ARGENTINA: Federico Bertuzzi

- GHANA: Ross Campbell
- LATIN AMERICA: Robert A. Hatch
- SINGAPORE: Peck Hock Cheng

General Consultants

- C. Peter Wagner
- David Barrett
- Lawrence E. Keyes

Communications Consultant

- Viggo Søgaard

Computer Consultant

- Bill Shumaker
- James Simon

Many of the above named coordinators have conducted extensive country-wide surveys in even greater detail than needed for this survey. These were designed to benefit the missions movements in those countries. The results may already be published in those particular countries. In some cases, the results of those studies do not completely agree with our data here. This is because we had additional data besides that which was collected by those national research projects. In every case, the data from those projects is included in our data.

Also in every case, we are very grateful for the significant contribution of these coordinators and consultants. This work would have been impossible to complete without their dedicated involvement.

Another group of people who made this work possible are those who have worked closely with me in our Emerging Missions office. Those include Jim Santee, Computer and Data Manager; Merritt Capossela, Projects Coordinator; Bonnie Bagley, my Administrative Assistant who has helped in ways too numerous to mention; and data input volunteers Paul Neumann, Joseph Kitur, Keith Brown, and Char Brown.

Finally, I must thank Paul Yaggy and his research staff at OC Ministries, who have lent their expertise and helping hands during the last two months of this project. Dave Nesmith helped sort and merge previous data and assisted with computer programming. Roy Wingerd greatly assisted by refining data in the target peoples files and by programming important parts of the database. Clara Nesmith expertly refined, checked and inputted data during the critical final stages of the project.

I am proud to be associated with the people named above. Their dedication and determined efforts are what really made this project possible. To whatever degree we have succeeded in our stated objectives, the primary credit belongs to them. To whatever degree there are shortcomings in this project, I alone must bear the responsibility.

The organizations

I was first approached about this project by John Robb. Representing the *Strategy Working Group of the Lausanne Committee for World Evangelism*, and its director, Edward R. Dayton, John asked me to include this project as a part of my research and dissertation at the School of World Mission, Fuller Theological Seminary. Since the whole research project was too large to complete in time, we decided to split the project into two phases so this book could be released in conjunction with the Lausanne II Congress. Both Ed Dayton and John Robb are working with the *Missions Advanced Research & Communication Center (MARC)*, a ministry of *World Vision International*, with Dayton serving as the director. Because the Strategy Working Group and MARC provided the initial funding for the non-personnel costs of this research, I will long be grateful. I also appreciate the encouragement and help of these men.

I must also express gratitude to the leadership of the *Missions Commission* of the *World Evangelical Fellowship*. They have provided a significant portion of the funding for this project. I especially want to thank the commission's Chairman, Theodore Williams, and the Executive Secretary, William Taylor, for their invaluable encouragement.

Globalink Ministries of Waynesboro, Virginia should also be commended for their financial assistance to this project. Their unselfish efforts to raise funds for this project are very unusual and much appreciated.

I wish also to thank the leadership and staff of *OC Ministries, Inc.* who have encouraged and assisted in this project in many ways. Particularly, I would like to thank OC President Lawrence E. Keyes for his personal encouragement and understanding throughout the completion of this project.

A final word

I also wish to thank my family for giving up their husband and father for too many hours of the night so this work could be accomplished. My wife, Mary, in particular, deserves more credit than she will ever receive for her many sacrifices in this regard.

All of us owe a special debt of gratitude to those missionary leaders of Latin America, Africa, Asia and Oceania who have shared their labors and their lives with us through the pages of this book. It is our prayer that this handbook will be a means of encouragement and a strategic source of information for them. If only in a small way, may it be a resource to increase their fruitfulness in the harvest fields of the world.

Larry D. Pate
Milpitas, California
April 1989

TABLE OF CONTENTS

CASE HISTORIES : *Missions in the Two-Thirds World*

DIRECTORY *of Two-Thirds World Mission Agencies*

FIGURES

PREFACE
Please Read This First

by Larry D. Pate

THIS BOOK IS BASED UPON THE FIRST PHASE of a two-phase survey of Two-Thirds World missions. It is a handbook of the missionary activities of the churches in Latin America, Africa, Asia and Oceania. It is also designed to be a guidebook to give understanding of the scope, nature and potential of this burgeoning non-Western missionary movement.

On the shoulders of others

There are some pioneers in the area of researching the non-Western missions movement who have provided the foundational works upon which this study is built. James Wong, Peter Larsen and Dwight Pentecost teamed together to accomplish the first world survey of non-Western missions. Their 1972 study reported in the book, *Missions from the Third World*, was an eye-opener concerning the new force for missions which was arising in Latin America, Africa and Asia. (1)

The next worldwide research project on this subject was conducted by Dr. Lawrence E. Keyes, who is currently President of OC Ministries, the major sponsor of this current research project. Keyes' excellent 1980 study demonstrated increasing growth of this movement and was published as *The Last Age of Missions*. (2)

There have been two other significant regional studies on Asia since 1972. The first was conducted by Dr. Marlin L. Nelson, and was entitled, *The How and Why of Third World Missions*. (3) This excellent study was the first serious effort to classify the missionary activities of Asian missionaries. This present study builds on that practice. Our second-phase research intends to use some of the same classifications applied by Nelson.

The second Asian study was that which I conducted in 1985. The results were reported in a special edition of "Bridging Peoples." (4) This study confirmed the continuing growth of the movement and suggested some possible implications for missions as a whole.

This study owes a great deal to those who have pioneered in this field. Their work required an admirable amount of determination and perseverance to be successfully completed.

Part of the credit for their encouragement should go to Dr. C. Peter Wagner, Professor of Church Growth at the School of World Mission, Fuller Theological Seminary. In every study mentioned above except my own, he served as academic mentor to the research projects and dissertations involved. In fact, he is now serving as my own mentor for a dissertation project of which this present research is a part.

The above research and books will be referred to often in the analysis of the data in this book.

The Analysis

The first chapter contains a summary analysis of the movement as a whole, together with analyses by continent and country. It tracks the most significant trends revealed by the survey data and suggests some possible implications for world missions. The purpose of this chapter is to lend perspective and definition so the reader can make best use of the material which follows.

In a very real sense, this first chapter is the heart of the book. What follows illustrates and documents the contents of the first chapter.

Those who are serious students of the missionary movement outside the Western world will want to pay close attention to the footnotes and explanations which document the conclusions in the text. But, in an effort to make the material more readable, lengthy explanations are avoided in the text of the chapter. Nevertheless, even the casual reader who intends to quote from the material, and those who intend to use it for strategy or planning, should not fail to read the comments and explanations in the footnotes.

The Histories

This book contains three case histories. Two are the stories of missionary organizations in India and Malawi and the leaders who established them. The third is about the Argentine missions movement and the visionary leaders who are catalyzing it.

These are stories about men of faith and vision, and the mission organizations they established as vehicles to bridge the gospel into unreached peoples and areas. These accounts are told in enough detail to let the reader sense the heroic nature of the faith of these leaders and the nature of the barriers they overcame. But they are also detailed accounts of the success of their missionary organizations. There is an introduction to these stories at the beginning of that section of the book.

The Directory

This section lists the mission agencies of the Two-Thirds World together with their addresses and summary information about their missionaries and their ministry. They are listed alphabetically by country and category within each continent. It is important to read the explanations and codes which appear at the beginning of the directory section.

A word about definitions

We have chosen to use the term "Two-Thirds World Missions" to depict the missions movement which is the subject of this book. The rationale for doing this can be found in the analysis section of the book. A more precise definition also appears there. "Non-Western Missions" and "Emerging Missions" will also be used as synonyms for this term. All these terms refer to the missionary activities of the Protestant churches of Africa, Asia, Latin America and Oceania.

In order to be classified as a "mission agency," and therefore be included in this study, an organization must meet the following requirements:

- It must send missionaries and/or resources across significant cultural and/or geographic boundaries,
- The agency is led and administered by indigenous, non-Western leaders,
- Their missionaries go across significant cultural and/or geographic boundaries,

OR

- Their missionaries are supported across significant cultural and/or geographic boundaries,
- They are at least partially funded from non-Western sources. Generally, at least 25% of funding must come from non-Western sources.

We are using a definition which includes all those groups who are sending workers and/or funding across significant cultural and/or geographical boundaries. This means a church or agency which supports workers to plant another church among its own people within its own area WILL NOT here be considered a mission agency. But a church or agency which supports a worker to plant churches outside its own geographical or cultural boundaries will be considered a mission agency.

Seeking to define a "missionary"

Many internationalized Western agencies include missionaries on their teams who work in their own countries on full missionary status as a part of an international team. In the same way, a team of missionaries may come from several states in India to work in the state of Orissa. If the team also includes missionaries who come from Orissa, they are also counted as missionaries. In a case like this, the missionary is supported from a base outside his own people and territory. This is an exact parallel to the international Western agency which includes an international status missionary working in his own country on their own missionary rosters. This is an example of what is meant when we stipulate that a missionary must be sent and/or supported across significant cultural and/or geographic boundaries to be included in this study.

Some may think this is a significant broadening of the definitions given by previous researchers. It is really more clearly defining the research which has preceded this study. In studying the source documents of Keyes' 1980 study (mentioned below), I found this definition best fits the data he used. In fact, we have dropped from the list a considerable number of agencies listed in his study because it was demonstrated they failed to meet the criteria listed above.

Funds also cross borders

There are two areas in which there is a measurable difference in the criteria of this study and that of Keyes. In this study, we made the minimum funding level from indigenous sources to be 25%, rather than 50% as Keyes used. We did this because of the increasing proliferation of international support for the emerging missions, a development which Keyes advocated in his work. There are a few legitimate, indigenously founded and administered agencies who now receive a little more than half their support from outside their own countries, though that was not the case before. Rather than exclude them because of an arbitrary minimum limit, we decided to change the limit to better allow for the increasing partnerships being developed.

A second area where we have deviated from Keyes' study is in the types of mission organizations we list. We list some agencies which are not sending missionaries, but which perform a specialized supportive role or task which directly contributes to the sending of missionaries. This is explained more fully in the introduction to the directory.

4

In some cases, we have also listed individual churches as sending organizations. Church-based sending is on the rise, though it would require another study to discover just how much. This is true in Malaysia and Singapore and many parts of Latin America. Since these churches function like what Westerners think of as mission agencies, we could not justify excluding them.

More precise categories

A final distinction between Keyes' study and this one relates to the "International Sending" category (see the introduction to the directory). Keyes did not classify the agencies as we have done here, but he did include the local branches of those types of agencies in various countries. For instance, he included the local branches of Overseas Missionary Fellowship in a number of countries. (5) These figures ONLY include the non-Western missionaries working on those international teams.

We have continued that practice of including international mission organizations who report the non-Western missionaries on their teams. They are all classified as "International Sending" and included in this study. More information on this is contained in the introduction to the directory section.

The definitions related to the terminology in the directory portion of this book also appear at the beginning of the directory section.

Why study the Two-Thirds World Missions movement?

It may not have been seriously considered by many who read this, but world missions is changing rapidly. The restriction or revocation of Western missionary visas continues to grow, even in countries which were previously wide open. Militant religion is on the upswing. Political and economic developments in many parts of the world portend some ominous signs concerning the acceptability of many types of current Western missionary efforts.

Such a gloomy picture is counterbalanced by the burgeoning growth of missions by Christians in the Two-Thirds World. That is the subject of this book.

Such factors as these, when combined, demonstrate that a large part of the future of missions belongs to the missionaries of Latin America, Africa, Asia and Oceania. The Christian world should be intensely interested in the developments related to that movement. The missionary efforts of every denomination, church and mission agency will increasingly be affected by that movement. A significant share of the future of world evangelization will depend upon it!

FOOTNOTES

(1) Wong, James, *et al.*; *Missions From the Third World*; Singapore, Church Growth Study Center; 1972.

(2) Keyes, Lawrence E.; *The Last Age of Missions*; Pasadena, William Carey Library; 1983.

(3) Nelson, Marlin L.; *The How and Why of Third World Missions*; Pasadena, William Carey Library, 1976.

(4) Pate, Larry D.; "Asian Missions: Growth, Problems and Partnership;" in BRIDGING PEOPLES, Vol 5, N. 4, Oct. 1986.

(5) Keyes, *op. cit.*, pp. 156, 185.

INTRODUCTION

by Lawrence E. Keyes

S INCE 1980, WHEN THE WORLDWIDE SURVEY of Third-World missionary outreach was completed for the book, *The Last Age of Missions,*
major activity has continued in all regions of global Christianity. A few illustrations will demonstrate the kinds of development we have seen during the last decade.

Land of the Rising Sun

In Japan, emerging missions growth has been surprisingly significant.

The Reverend Minoru Okuyama is General Secretary of the *Asian
Missions Association, Antioch Mission* and Principal of the *Missions
Training Center* in Tochigi Prefecture. He says the growth of Japanese
missions demonstrates a new momentum in world mission. From 130
missionaries in 1979 to 291 in 1988, the number grew by 124%.

During the same period, according to Okuyama, the number of sending agencies increased 31%, from 48 to 63. The number of countries im-
pacted by these missionaries increased 50%, from 24 nations to 36 today.
Certainly, if such an increase in missionary involvement continues, Japan
will become a significant force in world evangelization.

Seventy percent of the 291 reported missionaries referred to above are
involved in cross-cultural evangelism. The Japanese church has sent
workers to minister in every continent of the world.

Mission advance in Africa

In Lilongwe, Malawi, in 1981, the 4th General Assembly of the *Association of Evangelicals of Africa and Madagascar (AEAM),* created a new
Mission Commission. Labeled the *"Evangelism and Mission Commission
of AEAM,"* some of its purposes were to: 1) identify emerging or indigenous mission agencies in Africa, 2) motivate churches and mission organizations toward evangelism and cross-cultural mission, 3) serve as a
liaison between missionary sending agencies and receiving fields, and 4)
coordinate the research work on unreached peoples in Africa.

Thus far, this Commission has helped to sponsor several missionary
conferences, provide valuable information on emerging missions
throughout Africa, and assist in the formation of the *Nigerian Evangeli-*

cal *Missions Association (NEMA)*. This Commission is also planning a major *All-Africa Congress on Missions* in 1991. The Reverend Panya Baba is the Commission's secretary.

From Japan to Malawi and beyond, these examples are illustrations of God's handiwork in missions development. He continues to bring into being strong and effective mission agencies in countries which histori-cally have been labeled "mission fields."

Thousands of new missionaries

Since the 1980 Emerging Missions survey, dozens of new societies have been formed in Africa, Asia, Oceania and Latin America. Thousands of new missionaries have been recruited, trained and deployed for cross-cultural ministry. And, the peak of this growth has not yet been seen!

Because of the explosive increase in this vital area of world evangeli-zation, a new study was needed to update facts and provide greater clar-ity. The research contained in this book provides the results of this newest study. This book will help to strengthen our missionary efforts, present a clearer understanding of God's harvest force in the non-West-ern world, and encourage all of us toward new dimensions of partner-ship as we work to complete the Great Commission.

A balanced perspective

The Reverend Larry Pate, director of this research project, is a compe-tent, experienced missionary. He is an educator, author and strategist in the field of non-Western missions development. His vision for emerging missions is balanced. He recognizes the significant growth and evangelis-tic impact inherent in the growing missions movement in the Two-Thirds World. But he also knows that many of these missionaries need addi-tional support systems and training. Therefore, Pate ministers on every continent of the world, working toward strengthening the effectiveness of these new missionaries and the organizations that send them.

This research project is part of a broader ministry we call Emerging Missions, a division of the International Ministry Team of *OC Ministries*. This service assists indigenous, homebred mission agencies in Latin America, Africa and Asia in their efforts to develop their own missionary training programs, motivational conferences, strategies and partnerships. Larry Pate is the coordinator of these Emerging Missions ministries.

Inspiration for the century's last decade

We all owe Pate a debt of gratitude for this fine publication. I trust the information contained in these pages will help you in your own missionary work as we enter the last decade of the twentieth century.

God bless you! May this book bring us all closer to the ultimate fulfillment of Psalms 67:2-5:

> *May your ways be known on earth,*
> *your salvation among all nations.*
> *May the peoples praise you, O God;*
> *may all the peoples praise you.*
> *May the nations be glad and sing for joy,*
> *for you rule the peoples justly*
> *and guide the nations of the earth*
> *May the peoples praise you, O God;*
> *may all the peoples praise you.*

Dr. Lawrence E. Keyes *is President of O.C. Ministries, Inc.; Editor, BRIDGING PEOPLES newsletter; Author of* **The Last Age of Missions;** *and LCWE Associate for Emerging Missions.*

ANALYSIS
of Two-Thirds World Missions

And they sang a new song:
You are worthy to take the scroll
and to open its seals,
because you were slain,
And with your blood
you purchased men for God
From every tribe and language and
people and nation. (Rev. 5:9 NIV)

THE COMMUNICATIONS REVOLUTION MAKES THE WORLD seem smaller every year. Far from becoming a global community, however, human events appear more as a kaleidoscopic swirl of opposing forces unleashing their own brands of fury.

Political ideology may have become watered down in the economic realities of the world's dwindling resources. But history's greatest fuel for conflict, religious militancy, is on the rise! From India to Nigeria, Mindanao to Iran, religion is becoming nationalistic, leaving war and religious martyrdom in its vortex. Change-whipped winds of religious zeal make the missionary message of the cross harder to hear when spoken from Western lips.

That is why the Scripture above is so comforting. We have the assurance that people from every tribe, language, people and nation will one day join in praise to the Lamb of God. The question remains how that will come to pass when so much of the world seems reactive rather than receptive to the gospel. In the minds of many missiologists, a major portion of the answer to that question will involve the missionary movement on the rise in Latin America, Africa, Asia and Oceania.

The *Evangelical Missions Quarterly* asked two well-known missionary statesmen what they considered to be the most important trend in world missions during the last 20 years. Jack Frizen, Executive Director, Interdenominational Foreign Missions Association, said, "My choice is the renewed focus on unreached people groups and penetrating the frontiers still remaining." Wade Coggins, Executive Director of the Evangelical

Foreign Missions Association, also identified the unreached people movement, but as a second choice. As his first choice, Coggins pointed to "the rise of mission agencies and missionaries in Africa, Asia and Latin America" as the most significant trend in the last 20 years. (1)

The fact that Coggins and Frizen (along with other missions leaders) together cited the need to reach unreached peoples and the rise of missions in the Two-Thirds World is significant. According to the results of this present study, there are almost 36,000 non-Western missionaries targeting at least 2,425 people groups located in at least 118 countries of the world as of the end of 1988. It is very probable that the Lord of the harvest is raising up such a significant force for missions from Latin America, Africa and Asia that a major portion of those from "every tribe, language, people and nation" who populate heaven will be there as a result of missionary activity from the Two-Thirds World.

Why "Two-Thirds World" Missions?

Some may wonder why we have chosen to use the term "Two-Thirds World Missions" to depict the missions movement which is the subject of this book. To be honest, this term won out by default. There is no widely accepted term which fully conveys the exact definition of the phenomenon this book describes.

"Third World Missions" has historically been the most widely accepted term for our subject. Wong, Larsen and Pentecost's study, *Missions From the Third World*, did much to popularize this appellation. (2) Marlin Nelson's *The How and Why of Third World Missions: An Asian Case Study and Readings in Third World Missions* did much to continue this popularity. (3)

"Third World" has historically been associated with the economically less developed countries of the world. It has been contrasted with the politically polarized and economically more developed Western Bloc nations (First World) and Eastern Bloc nations (Second World). As historically useful as the term has been, it is no longer an acceptable one. The peoples of Latin America, Africa and Asia have rightly questioned the Western World's right to designate them "Third" while calling themselves "First." This is especially an appropriate criticism today, when the economic vitality of some countries of the "Third World" surpasses most countries in the "First World."

Other terms have also been used to depict this movement. "Non-Western Missions" is still often used. It works well in countries of Asia and the West, but this term makes African countries appear an afterthought, and the peoples of Latin America consider themselves just as "Western" as the "gringos" of North America.

The terms "Northern Missions" and "Missions from the South," plus similar derivatives, have been proposed. (4) This terminology derives from the "North-South" dialogues between the rich (North) nations and the economically disadvantaged nations (South) of the Southern Hemisphere. This term is also unacceptable for two reasons. First it capitalizes (pun intended), or focuses, on economic disparities as a basis for defining the parts of the world we are trying to describe. But as indicated above, some of the countries to which we are referring represent some of the most economically powerful nations in today's world. Second, and even more important, 71% of Two-Thirds World mission organizations are in the Northern Hemisphere.

"Emerging Missions" is a term which has been used more recently. It was especially popularized by Lawrence E. Keyes in *The Last Age of Missions*, which has been the most authoritative study on this movement to date. (5) Keyes documents the fact that there have been some missionaries sent from the Two-Thirds World which predate almost all such activity from the West. But then he documents the rapid growth of the movement which has occurred mostly in the last three decades. In that sense, the Two-Thirds World missions movement could be characterized as "Emerging." In my own writings and speaking, I have typically used this as the favored term.

But is it accurate any longer to characterize a movement which now comprises approximately 30% of the total Protestant missionary force as "Emerging?" (5) Furthermore, for some people it is too easy for the term to connote "inferior," or "less developed," in contrast to a more experienced, "superior" Western mission force. As this book documents, the term "Emerging Missions" is no longer fully acceptable because the Two-Thirds World missions movement has already emerged! While it is true there are more new missions arising in non-Western countries than in the West, the movement has grown to a point where it is a major force in world evangelization. It no longer deserves to be called "emerging."

The question may arise, why make any distinction at all between missions in one part of the world and missions in another part of the world? Why not just use African missions, Asian missions, etc? The answer is, that for the foreseeable future, people will be interested in the missions movement arising in countries which have traditionally been seen as receiving countries. As long as people are interested in this movement, they will give it a name so they can talk about it. And books like this will continue to be published.

"Two-Thirds World" does appear to be the least offensive and most accurate term. It accurately implies a majority of the world's peoples and land mass. The countries of Latin America, Africa, Asia and Oceania comprise approximately two-thirds of the inhabited land mass of the earth and even a greater percentage of the world's population. Furthermore, the term "Two-Thirds World" is not offensive to any specific portion of the world to which it refers. It is probably the best term available until somebody thinks of a better one.

What specifically, then, do we mean when we say, "missions from the Two-Thirds World?" The term represents the existing and newly forming missionary sending organizations among non-Western Christians, located primarily in Africa, Asia, Latin America and Oceania. They may be little more than the missions committee of a local church sending missionaries independently, or they may be denominational or interdenominational organizations representing hundreds of missionaries each. While primarily located in the non-Western world, they may also be formed by emigrant communities in Western countries.

The terms "non-Western missions" and "missions of Asia, Africa and Latin America" will be used synonymously throughout this book. For our purposes here, they should be considered identical to the term "Two-Thirds World" missions and carry the same definition.

Distinctives of this study

The missionary movement in the Two-Thirds World is growing rapidly and reaching considerable size. One purpose of both phases of this research is to establish a computerized database on this movement which can be updated periodically. It is intended that this database be updated and shared with those Christian mission organizations who have need of its information.

Because of the size of the movement and the complexity of establishing the database, it is no longer possible for one person to individually research this movement effectively. Accordingly, a team of field researchers, consultants and computer specialists has been mobilized to accomplish this project up to this point (see "Acknowledgments"). While the results of this study should still be classified as somewhat temporary, pending the completion of the second phase, it can still be convincingly stated that this is the most complete and accurate study to date.

One accusation which has been leveled at previous research on this subject follows a line of reasoning like this:

> Those of you who are researching the non-Western missions movement say you are seeing rapid growth. All you may be doing, however, is simply discovering more mission agencies than were discovered in previous research. You list those new agencies, but then you calculate your growth rates based on the increases represented by the newly discovered agencies which may also have existed previously. This yields an overly optimistic set of growth rates and an inflated picture of the future of non-Western missions.

The main problem I have with this accusation is that it is at least partially true!

For this present study, we have worked hard to overcome that criticism. The primary method for doing this involves using data received in this study to *revise* the data in Keyes' 1980 study. We asked each reporting agency to list not only their present number of missionaries, but those they had in previous years. As a general rule, we did not change Keyes' figures for agencies that reported data to him. We considered them to be more authoritative because they were reported closer to the 1980 date. But we did uncover and receive information from many agencies which existed when Keyes did his study but were not discovered by his research. When they reported data in 1980, we used it to revise overall totals for countries and continents for that year (see Figure A-1).

We also had access to the source documents of Keyes' studies. Comparing the information received in his study with information on the same organizations reporting in our study, we were able to determine that there were several dozen agencies he reported which are clearly evangelistic organizations, rather than mission agencies. Those have been deleted from the lists of mission agencies and the missionary totals revised accordingly. (6)

The net result of all these refinements is more accurate data for 1980. We followed similar procedures for estimating data for non-reporting agencies in 1988. This will be explained further in the final portion of this chapter. This whole procedure has yielded the most accurate statistics possible for 1980 and 1988. These figures have been used as a basis for measuring growth rates and making projections for the future. With these refinements in mind, it is safe to say that the projections made as a part of this study are more accurate than those made in the past. (7)

FIGURE A-1
TWO-THIRDS WORLD MISSION AGENCIES

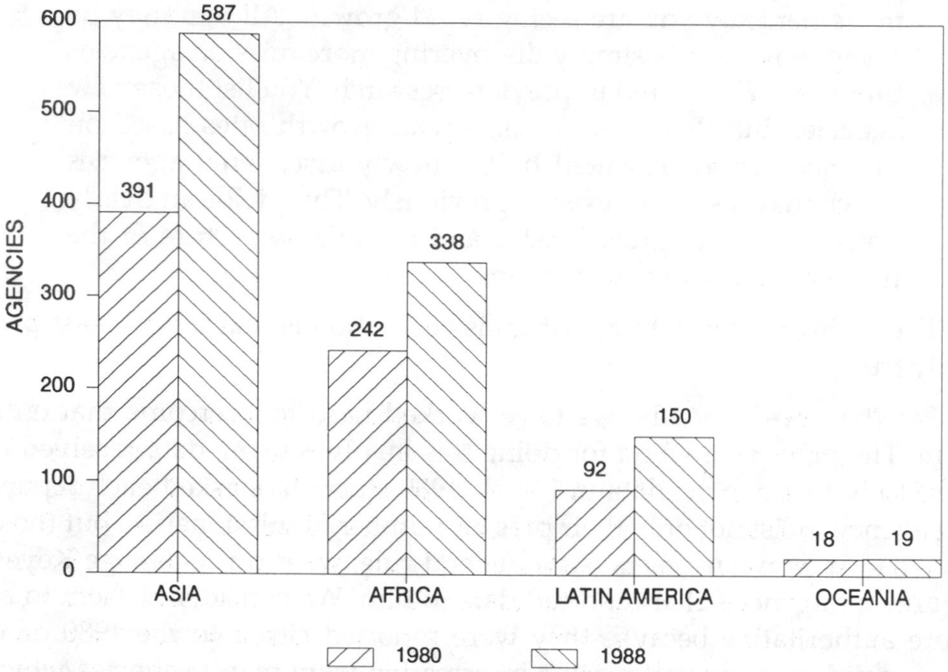

Portrait of a movement

Much is being said today about the growth of the church in the non-Western world. The majority of that growth is among evangelical churches. In the year 1900, only 10% of evangelicals were from non-Western countries. By 1985, fully 66% of evangelical Christians were from the Two-Thirds World. (8) Evangelical Christianity in the Western countries grew an average of 1.3% annually from 1975-1985. In the Two-Thirds World (not including China), the growth rate was 6.7% annually. (9) There can be little doubt that a large part of the future growth of Christianity will take place as a result of the ministry of evangelical Christians in the Two-Thirds World.

This means the growth and vitality of the missions movement of the Two-Thirds World church is of vital importance. Our research demonstrates that the non-Western missions movement is growing at 13.29% per year. This is much faster than even the 6.7% growth of non-Western evangelical churches. This amounts to a phenomenal increase of 248% every ten years! (10)

Figure A-1 pictures the overall growth of Two-Thirds World missionaries by continent from 1980 to 1988. The missionary total for 1980 is 13,238, with 35,924 for 1988. This is a net gain of 22,686 missionaries in just eight years! This very high rate of growth promises to change the picture of world missions well into the future. (11)

The number of mission agencies and sending groups has also seen a large increase, though not nearly as dramatic as the numbers of missionaries. Figure A-2 depicts this growth by continent from 1980 to 1988. In 1980, there were 743 agencies and sending groups. In 1988, there were 1,094, a gain of 351 agencies in eight years! (11) This is a rate of 4.96% per year and 62% per decade.

These figures indicate there was an average of 33 missionaries per sending agency in 1988. This compares to an average of 17 missionaries per agency in 1980. The average ratio of North American missionaries to mission agencies was 88 in 1985. (12) The low ratio of missionaries to

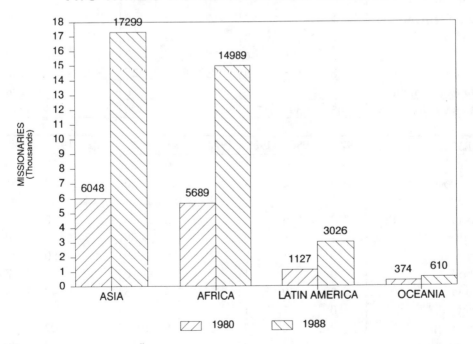

FIGURE A-2
TWO-THIRDS WORLD ESTIMATED MISSIONARIES

agencies in the Two-Thirds World indicates it is likely to continue its rapid growth well into the future.

FIGURE A-3
HISTORICAL SUMMARY OF MISSIONARIES AND AGENCIES

ASIA	Active Agencies (A)			Reported Missionaries (RM)			Estimated Missionaries (EM)		
	1972	1980	1988	1972	1980	1988	1972	1980	1988
AGAMA*		1	1		82	500		82	500
Bangladesh	0	1	1		4	5		4	5
Burma	2	17	22		1010	1797	10	1010	2560
Hong Kong	6	17	19	26	120	92	31	120	191
India	26	140	184	543	3328	6841	598	3328	8905
Indonesia	1	20	25	13	381	896	5	381	1114
Japan	32	50	74	97	125	288	137	125	291
Korea	7	31	104	33	199	1004	38	199	1184
Malaysia	2	6	10	2	24	87	5	24	92
Nepal	1	1	1		0	8	5	0	8
Pakistan	0	5	7		61	88		61	96
Philippines	13	37	54	155	586	1125	170	586	1814
Singapore	4	52	67	10	116	517	10	116	646
South Vietnam	1	0	0	2	0	0	2	0	0
Sri Lanka	2	2	3		5	37	13	5	37
Taiwan	3	6	6	26	7	3	31	7	10
Thailand	3	5	9	3	0	127	8	0	132
Asia Adjustments						-286			-286
Totals for Asia	**103**	**391**	**587**	**905**	**6048**	**13129**		**6048**	**17299**

AFRICA	1972	1980	1988	1972	1980	1988	1972	1980	1988
Benin	0	1	1		0	0		0	0
Cameroon	0	4	4		23	0		23	51
Chad	1			4			4		
Central African Rep.	0	5	6		0	6		0	6
Egypt	2	3	3		101	59	5	101	170
Ethiopia	0	1	2		50	9		50	34
Gabon	0	1	1		29	0		29	7
Ghana	0	30	46		843	523		843	1545
Israel	0	1	1		0	6		0	6
Kenya	2	36	62	10	68	1966	15	1002	2242
Liberia	1	2	3		0	280	5	0	280

	1972	1980	1988	1972	1980	1988	1972	1980	1988
Madagascar	2	4	4	30	30	128	35	30	166
Malawi	2	10	13		117	436	10	117	436
Namibia	0	1	1		9	13	0	9	13
Nigeria	4	63	84	810	1141	2489	820	1141	2959
Sierra Leone	0	1	3		41	78		41	103
South Africa	6	10	11	59	617	125	84	617	999
Swaziland	1	1	1		4	28	5	4	28
Tanzania	0	5	8		54	165		54	168
Uganda	1	6	11		47	777	5	47	1113
Zaire	3	37	44	4	990	436	9	990	2731
Zambia	0	10	15		95	289		95	392
Zimbabwe	0	10	14		496	1464		496	1540
Totals for Africa	**27**	**242**	**338**	**917**	**4755**	**9277**	**1007**	**5689**	**14989**

LATIN AMERICA	1972	1980	1988	1972	1980	1988	1972	1980	1988
Argentina	7	9	19	30	0	56	30	0	70
Belize	0	1	1		0	10		0	10
Bolivia	0	1	3		0	47		0	47
Brazil	26	40	57	495	791	1167	595	791	2040
Chile	2	1	1		0	0	10	0	0
Colombia	2	9	9	2	22	169	7	22	192
Costa Rica	3	1	1	1	0	3	11	0	3
Dominican Republic	0	1	1		0	0		0	0
Ecuador	1	3	3	11	12	0	11	12	36
El Salvador	0	1	4		2	18		2	21
Guatemala	3	6	16	3	27	45	8	27	90
Haiti	0	1	1		0	0		0	0
Honduras	0	1	2		0	7		0	17
Jamaica	3			4			14		
Mexico	5	11	24	64	24	182	69	24	224
Peru	0	2	4	3	144	164	8	144	164
Puerto Rico	2	1	1	20	36	0	30	36	45
Trinidad	3			5			5		
Spain	1	1	1		0	10		0	10
Uruguay	1			15			15		
Venezuela	2	2	2	2	69	0	7	69	64
Latin America Adjustments						-7			-7
Totals for Latin America	**61**	**92**	**150**	**655**	**1127**	**1871**	**820**	**1127**	**3026**

OCEANIA	1972	1980	1988	1972	1980	1988	1972	1980	1988
American Samoa	1	1	1		0	18	5	0	18
Fiji	2	3	3	22	153	22	22	153	202
Guam	0	3	3		0	0		0	0
Papua New Guinea	0	7	8		81	14		81	102
Solomon Islands	1	2	2	22	130	0	22	130	254
Tonga	1	1	1	12	0	14	12	0	14
Western Samoa	0	1	1		10	0		10	20
Totals for Oceania	**5**	**18**	**19**	**56**	**374**	**68**	**61**	**374**	**610**

Assemblies of God Asian Mission Association, an association of national Assemblies of God mission agencies for ten Asian countries.

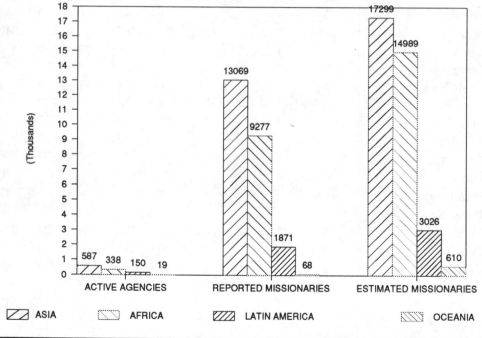

FIGURE A-4
TWO-THIRDS WORLD SUMMARY
Agencies and Missionaries

Missionary totals for each country

Figures A-3 and A-4 display the totals for mission agencies and missionaries by country, continent and year. Asia is the largest missionary sending continent in the Two-Thirds World, with an estimated total of

17,299 missionaries. Africa has an estimated total of 14,989 missionaries. The estimated total for Latin America is 3,026. Oceania's total is estimated at 610 missionaries.

Notice that the number of mission agencies for each region corresponds fairly well to the number of missionaries. Asia has 587 mission agencies, by far the largest number. This is followed by Africa, with 338 agencies; Latin America, with 150 agencies, and Oceania, with 19 known agencies. These are all agencies which have been confirmed in some way. They are not estimates.

It is important to explain here that these figures are calculated conservatively. The reason they are more than the figures in the "reported missionaries" column is a result of the reporting procedure. Eighty-three percent of the agencies listed in the directory have reported data at least once from 1972 to 1980. Of those, approximately 93% reported data in 1988. For those which did not report data in 1988, a projection was made based upon their growth history to determine the probable number of missionaries for each agency in 1988. (13) While they may not be accurate for each agency, they should, on average, yield accurate projections for each country as a whole. Those projected figures were then added to the figures of "Reported Missionaries" for each country.

There were a few adjustments to these figures, which apply especially to Asia and Latin America. There were two international non-Western missionary sending agencies. The first is the *Assemblies of God Asian Mission Association* (AGAMA). It acts as an association of national Assemblies of God mission agencies for ten Asian countries. But it also targets certain countries, projects and regions for joint effort by its member agencies. Because it belongs to no particular Asian country and counts its missionaries from all the countries combined, it is listed separately under "Asia" in the country column of Asia. In order to avoid duplication, an "Adjustments" line has been added to the Asia chart to subtract for Assemblies of God mission agencies reported for each country.

A similar problem exists with *Project Magreb,* a mission agency in Latin America. Though this agency draws its missionaries and its support from the countries of Mexico, Central America and South America, Project Magreb is headquartered in Spain. It, too, is an international non-Western mission agency. Because of this, the total figures reported for this agency are listed for Spain, but they are also duplicated in those countries of Latin America which have their local Project Magreb division. All are legitimate, indigenous agencies and are listed as such in each country. This also explains why Spain is listed under Latin America, though it is a European country. As in the case of AGAMA in Asia, there is an adjustment line to make up for this duplication for Latin America.

It is necessary here also to provide one more explanation related to Figure A-3. There is a large difference between the number of missionaries reported and the number of missionaries estimated for 1980 as listed for the country of Kenya in Africa. This is due to the fact that the information received from Kenya was the result of a special survey conducted by African Ministries Resources in that country toward the end of 1988. (14)

While the survey was an excellent study, it did not include growth histories for the various mission agencies. Furthermore, this study revealed that many of the agencies listed in Keyes' 1980 study for Kenya did not fit the definition of a mission agency used in this book. Accordingly, such agencies were deleted from the 1980 figures. With no 1980 figures reported on the agencies in the 1988 survey, this left a very low (68 missionaries) total of reported missionaries for 1980. Because we know that many agencies reported in 1988 also existed in 1980, we have an estimated 1980 figure for Kenya which is much higher. (15)

Comparisons with previous data

It is interesting to make some comparisons between data reported in 1988 with that reported previously. The first thing which should be said is that Keyes' estimate of 1980 total missionaries was a very accurate estimate, and even a bit conservative. He listed a total of 10,841 reported missionaries and estimated a total of 13,000. Our present study's figures for 1980 list a total of 12,304 reported missionaries, and an estimated total of 13,238.

Figure A-5 lists 1980 figures for both Keyes' study and this present study. The reason the figures are different lies in our method of compiling the information, which was explained earlier in this chapter.

FIGURE A-5
ADJUSTMENTS TO 1980 DATA

ASIA	Active Agencies (A)		Reported Missionaries (RM)		Estimated Missionaries (EM)	
	1980 LAM*	1980 REV**	1980 LAM	1980 REV	1980 LAM	1980 REV
		1		82		82
Bangladesh	1	1		4		4
Burma	5	17	988	1010	988	1010
Hong Kong	9	17	57	120	57	120
India	66	140	1667	3328	2277	3328
Indonesia	13	20	131	381	201	381
Japan	27	50	130	125	184	125
Korea	22	31	112	199	499	199
Malaysia	3	6	10	24	15	24
Nepal	1	1		0		0
Pakistan	5	5		61		61
Philippines	30	37	364	586	544	586
Singapore	7	52	127	116	172	116
Soouth Vietnam		0		0	0	0
Sri Lanka	8	2		5		5
Taiwan	7	6	29	7	43	7
Thailand	3	5		0		0
Totals for Asia	**207**	**391**	**3615**	**6048**	**4980**	**6048**

AFRICA	1980 LAM	1980 REV	1980 LAM	1980 REV	1980 LAM	1980 REV
Benin	1	1	0	0	0	0
Cameroon	2	4	23	23	28	23
Central African Rep	0	5		0		0
Egypt	2	3	22	101	22	101
Ethiopia	1	1	50	50	50	50
Gabon	1	1	40	29	40	29
Ghana	23	30	827	843	1127	843
Israel	0	1		0		0
Kenya	16	36	827	68	1002	68
Liberia	1	2		0	2	0
Madagascar	2	4	30	30	30	30
Malawi	1	10	1	117	2	117
Namibia	0	1		9		9
Nigeria	16	63	2350	1141	2500	1141
Sierra Leone	0	1		41		41

23

South Africa	6	10	569	617	579	617
Swaziland	1	1		4	2	4
Tanzania	3	5	2	54	6	54
Uganda	1	6	22	47	22	47
Zaire	14	37	284	990	334	990
Zambia	6	10	88	95	88	95
Zimbabwe	8	10	40	496	50	496
Totals for Africa	**104**	**242**	**5175**	**4755**	**5884**	**4755**

LATIN AMERICA	1980 LAM	1980 REV	1980 LAM	1980 REV	1980 LAM	1980 REV
Argentina	3	9	4	0	24	0
Belize	0	1		0		0
Bolivia	1	1	4	0	4	0
Brazil	29	40	649	791	693	791
Chile	0	1	2	0	8	0
Colombia	5	9	12	22	30	22
Costa Rica	0	1	2	0	2	0
Dominican Rep.	1	1		0	2	0
Ecuador	3	3	12	12	18	12
El Salvador	0	1	4	2	4	2
Guatemala	7	6	28	27	43	27
Haiti	0	1		0		0
Honduras	0	1		0		0
Jamaica	2		26		30	
Mexico	2	11	16	24	26	24
Panama			10		10	
Peru	2	2	41	144	46	144
Puerto Rico	0	1		36	2	36
Trinidad	0				4	
Spain	0	1		0		0
Uruguay	0				2	
Venezuela	1	2		69	4	69
Totals for Latin America	**56**	**92**	**810**	**1127**	**952**	**1127**

OCEANIA	1980 LAM	1980 REV	1980 LAM	1980 REV	1980 LAM	1980 REV
American Samoa	2	1	35	0	35	0
Fiji	3	3	38	153	48	153
Guam	3	3	2	0	2	0
Papua New Guinea	5	7	486	81	491	81
Solomon Islands	2	2	130	130	130	130

Tonga	1	1		0		0
Western Samoa	0	1		10		10
Totals for Oceania	**16**	**18**	**691**	**374**	**706**	**374**

*LAM: figures from "Last Age of Missions" by Larry Keyes
**REV: Revised 1980 figures

There is a significant difference between Keyes' figures and our fig-ures insofar as the number of mission agencies for 1980 are concerned. We report a total of 743 agencies in 1980, whereas Keyes records 368 agencies. The large difference lies in the fact that we have included those agencies newly discovered through our study which existed in 1980 as a part of the 1980 totals. In effect, this procedure allows us not only to up-date the status of the Two-Thirds World missionary movement as of 1988, it also allows us to update the 1980 figures. This makes our picture of the progress of the movement much more complete. It also makes our growth projections much more accurate.

Another area of interesting comparisons is the relative percentage of missionaries and agencies by region. While the largest missionary send-

FIGURE A-6
TOTAL MISSIONARIES BY REGION 1980

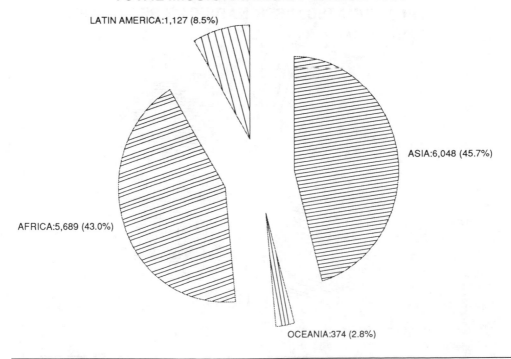

LATIN AMERICA:1,127 (8.5%)

ASIA:6,048 (45.7%)

AFRICA:5,689 (43.0%)

OCEANIA:374 (2.8%)

ing region has traditionally been Asia, it is significant to note that the percentage of Asian missionaries in relation to the total is also on the rise. In 1980, 46% of all Two-Thirds World missionaries were Asian; 43% were African, 9% were Latin American and 3% were from Oceania. In 1988, 48% were Asian; 42% were African; 8% were Latin American; and 2% were from Oceania (see Figures A-6 and A-7).

This growth is also reflected in a comparison of the figures for mission agency growth (see Figures A-8 and A-9). In 1980, 53% of total mission agencies were Asian; 33% African; 12% Latin American; and 2% from Oceania. In 1988, 54% were Asian, 31% African, 14% Latin American; and again, 2% were from Oceania.

My research in 1985 demonstrated a rising percentage of Asian missionaries and agencies. At that time, I estimated that Asia would comprise 50% of the total non-Western missionary force before the year 2000. (16) Asia's rise to 48% of the total missionaries and 54% of the total agencies in 1988 confirms this trend once again.

This trend is also reflected in the percentage of gain for each region (see Figure A-1). From 1980 to 1988, estimated Asian missionaries grew by 11,251, a decadal (ten year) growth rate of 272%. Africa grew by 9,300

FIGURE A-7

TOTAL ESTIMATED MISSIONARIES BY REGION 1988

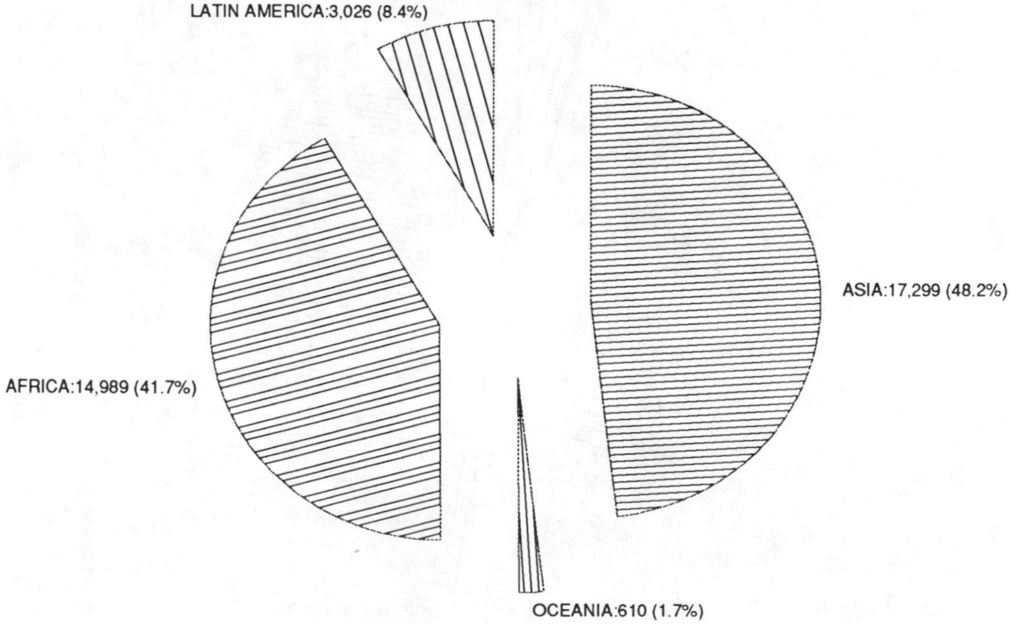

LATIN AMERICA:3,026 (8.4%)

ASIA:17,299 (48.2%)

AFRICA:14,989 (41.7%)

OCEANIA:610 (1.7%)

FIGURE A-8
TOTAL MISSION AGENCIES BY REGION 1980

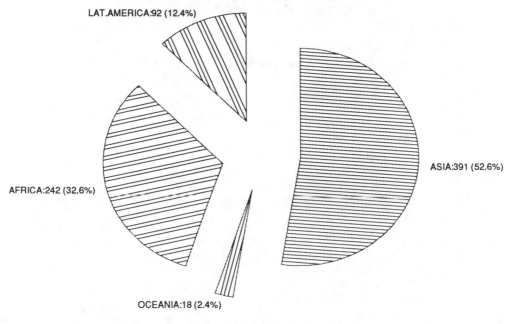

LAT.AMERICA:92 (12.4%)

ASIA:391 (52.6%)

AFRICA:242 (32.6%)

OCEANIA:18 (2.4%)

FIGURE A-9
TOTAL MISSION AGENCIES BY REGION 1988

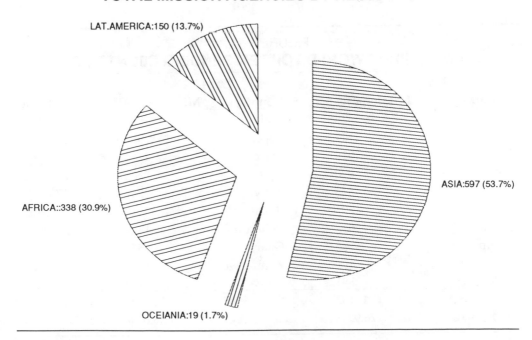

LAT.AMERICA:150 (13.7%)

ASIA:597 (53.7%)

AFRICA::338 (30.9%)

OCEIANIA:19 (1.7%)

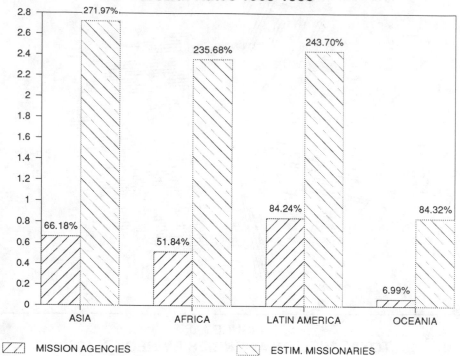

FIGURE A-10
AGENCIES AND MISSIONARIES
Growth Rates 1980-1988

ASIA: MISSION AGENCIES 66.18%, ESTIM. MISSIONARIES 271.97%
AFRICA: MISSION AGENCIES 51.84%, ESTIM. MISSIONARIES 235.68%
LATIN AMERICA: MISSION AGENCIES 84.24%, ESTIM. MISSIONARIES 243.70%
OCEANIA: MISSION AGENCIES 6.99%, ESTIM. MISSIONARIES 84.32%

FIGURE A-11
TWO-THIRDS WORLD TOP TEN SENDING COUNTRIES

1980		1988		
Country	Missionaries	Country	Missionaries	DGR
India	3328	India	8905	242.23%
Nigeria	1141	Nigeria	2959	229.10%
Burma	1010	Zaire	2731	255.52%
Zaire	990	Burma	2560	219.81%
Ghana	843	Kenya	2242	173.66%
Brazil	791	Brazil	2040	226.83%
South Africa	617	Philippines	1814	310.61%
Philippines	586	Ghana	1545	113.24%
Zimbabwe	496	Zimbabwe	1540	312.14%
Indonesia	381	Korea	1184	829.23%
TOTALS	10183		27520	246.51%
% of total	76.92%		76.61%	

28

missionaries, a decadal growth rate (DGR) of 235%. Latin America grew by 1,899 missionaries, a DGR of 243%. Oceania grew by 236 missionaries, a DGR of 84%. (17) As mentioned above, the overall decadal growth rate for all regions is 248% (see Figure A-10).

The largest sending countries

Figure A-11 depicts the top ten sending countries for both 1980 and 1988. Notice that India remains at the top of the list, with 3,328 missionaries in 1980 and 8,905 missionaries in 1988. This represents a decadal growth rate (DGR) of over 242%. In both years, Nigeria remains the second largest sending country. But with a DGR of 255.52%, Zaire overtook Burma as the third largest sending country in 1988. Notice also that Kenya and Korea have replaced South Africa and Indonesia in the top ten for 1988. In both years, there are five countries from Africa, four from Asia and Brazil, representing Latin America.

The largest sending agencies

The top ten missionary sending agencies for 1988 are listed in Figure A-12. The Burma Baptist Convention heads the list, with 1440 missionaries in 1988, up from 887 in 1980. The Diocesan Missionary Association, of the Church of the Province of Kenya (Anglican), is second with a total of 1,283 missionaries. Notice that while the very largest agencies are from various countries of Africa, five agencies of the top ten are from the single country of India. This demonstrates the breadth of the Indian missions movement.

FIGURE A-12
TOP TEN SENDING AGENCIES, ALL REGIONS

Agency	Country	Missionaries in 1988
Burma Baptist Convention	Burma	1440
Diocesan Missionary Association (CPK)	Kenya	1283
Forward in Faith Ministries	Zimbabwe	1275
Evangelical Missionary Society	Nigeria	729
Fellowship of Pentecostal Churches of God	India	560
Indian Evangelical Team	India	559
Friends Missionary Prayer Band	India	439
Zoram Baptist Mission	India	408
Gospel Mission of Uganda	Uganda	406
All India Prayer Fellowship	India	403
TOTALS		7502
% of overall total (of 35,924)		20.88%

Target countries of Two-Thirds World Missions

Figure A-13 lists each country which is the recipient of missionaries from the Two-Thirds World. In each case, these Figures *include* those missionaries sent from within the receiving country as well as those sent from other countries. Here are explanations for each column of Figure A-13:

Target Country: This is the country which receives missionaries listed on that line. Those marked with an asterisk are regions, rather than countries. For reasons of their own, some agencies listed their target countries by region, rather than by the name of the country where their missionaries are actually located.

Sending Countries: Lists the number of countries from which missionaries have been sent to the target country from the Two-Thirds World.

Sending Agencies: Lists the number of agencies from all sending countries which are sending missionaries to the target country.

Target Peoples: Lists the total number of tribal, ethnic, linguistic, or cultural groups being targeted by the missionaries sent.

Missionaries: Lists the total number of missionaries working in the target country from the Two-Thirds World.

Home Missionaries: Lists the total number of missionaries working in the target country which have been sent by agencies within that country.

Foreign Missionaries: Lists the total number of missionaries which have been sent to the target country by Two-Thirds World mission agencies outside the target country.

FIGURE A-13
TARGET COUNTRIES AND PEOPLES OF
TWO-THIRDS WORLD MISSIONS

Target Country	Sending Countries	Sending Agencies	Target Peoples	# of Miss.	Home Miss.	Foreign Miss.
Africa*	5	11	7	23		23
American Samoa	1	1	1	18	18	0
Angola	3	10	6	19		19
Argentina	4	25	11	87	29	58
Asia*	3	3	8	38		38
Australia	11	24	17	58		58
Austria	2	2	1	5		5

Target Country	Sending Countries	Sending Agencies	Target Peoples	# of Miss.	Home Miss.	Foreign Miss.
Bangladesh	5	16	9	35	11	24
Belgium	3	5	3	11		11
Belize	3	3	2	6		6
Benin	2	6	7	19		19
Bhutan	1	10	5	31		31
Bolivia	7	20	14	105	43	62
Botswana	1	1	1	3		3
Brazil	7	28	50	762	710	52
Brunei	1	1	1	4		4
Burkina Faso	2	3	4	5		5
Burma	4	29	39	2175	2150	25
Cameroon	3	11	12	36		36
Canada	6	8	7	55		55
Central African Rep.	2	2	4	9	6	3
Chad	1	1	4	13		13
Chile	3	7	7	25		25
China	2	2	2	3		3
Colombia	6	9	16	76	55	21
Congo	1	1	1	2		2
Costa Rica	3	3	2	4		4
Cyprus	2	2	2	3		3
Dominican Republic	7	11	4	38		38
Egypt	4	7	3	126	117	9
El Salvador	1	1	1	7	7	0
Equitorial Guinea	1	2	1	2		2
Ethiopia	2	2	3	60	59	1
Europe*	2	2	2	5		5
Fiji	1	1				0
France	8	9	5	26		26
Gabon	1	1	2	2		2
Gambia	5	7	6	16		16
Germany, West	5	14	7	144		144
Ghana	6	45	45	475	449	26
Guam	1	1		1		1
Guatemala	3	6	5	11	4	7
Guinea Bissau	1	2	2	4		4
Honduras	3	5	5	21	15	6
Hong Kong	7	28	12	76	8	68
India	8	141	260	5120	5019	101

Target Country	Sending Countries	Sending Agencies	Target Peoples	# of Miss.	Home Miss.	Foreign Miss.
Indonesia	9	56	964	964	834	130
Iran	1	3	2	10		10
Israel	4	4	3	4		4
Italy	5	6	5	8		8
Ivory Coast	4	15	13	36		36
Jamaica	2	2	2	3		3
Japan	8	27	8	118	4	114
Jordan	3	3	3	5		5
Kenya	10	72	72	588	531	57
Korea, South	5	6	3	10	4	6
Liberia	6	17	21	212	160	52
Libya	1	2	2	2		2
Macau	3	6	3	12		12
Madagascar	1	1	2	128	128	0
Malawi	6	14	15	220	197	23
Malaysia	8	27	19	98	32	66
Mali	1	1	1	2		2
Malta	1	1	3	3		3
Mexico	5	21	42	187	174	13
Morocco	2	3	3	10		10
Mozambique	7	16	22	111		111
Namibia	4	4	9	12	8	4
Nepal	7	22	7	83	8	75
Netherlands	6	6	6	15		15
New Zealand	3	5	4	11		11
Nicaragua	3	3	2	4		4
Niger	3	4	2	11		11
Nigeria	7	61	139	1799	1761	38
North Africa*	2	2		2		2
Pakistan	10	24	12	234	210	24
Palau	1	1	1	2		2
Panama	4	4	2	6		6
Papua New Guinea	9	15	14	85	41	44
Paraguay	5	18	5	84		84
Peru	8	16	9	50	19	31
Philippines	6	71	89	1467	1348	119
Portugal	4	10	6	41		41
Saudi Arabia	1	2	2	12		12
Senegal	2	2		2		2

Target Country	Sending Countries	Sending Agencies	Target Peoples	# of Miss.	Home Miss.	Foreign Miss.
Sierra Leone	3	8	9	112	104	8
Singapore	7	32	6	97	74	23
Somalia	2	2		3		3
South Africa	9	14	14	97	74	23
South America*	1	1		1		1
South East Africa	1	1		2		2
South East Asia	1	1	2	1		1
Spain	9	16	7	48		48
Sri Lanka	3	6	4	34	31	3
St. Vincent	1	1	1	1		1
Sudan	1	1	1	6		6
Swaziland	3	3	2	13	6	7
Sweden	3	4	4	6		6
Switzerland	2	2	2	4		4
Taiwan	5	31	18	81		81
Tanzania	7	34	15	180	119	61
Thailand	9	41	17	177	41	136
Togo	1	10	8	22		22
Turkey	2	3	2	7		7
United States	16	41	21	363		363
USSR	1	1	11	15		15
Uganda	5	34	38	685	586	99
United Arab Emirates	3	3	3	8		8
United Kingdom	13	27	16	75		75
Uruguay	2	6	3	37		37
Venezuela	3	3	3	9	3	6
West Africa*	2	3	2	4		4
Western Samoa	1	1	1	9		9
Yugoslavia	1	1	1	1		1
Zaire	8	32	45	995	964	31
Zambia	10	30	33	203	175	28
Zimbabwe	9	21	13	166	143	23
Total for all Countries				19877	16479	3398

Exact locations withheld at request of sending agencies

Note that not all mission agencies reported the locations of their missionaries. Others reported the locations of only some of their missionaries. Also, most agencies have administrative personnel who reside in the country of the sending agency. Such personnel are usually not listed along with target information. These factors account for the fact that of a total of 24,285 reported missionaries, 19,877 are listed in relation to the people and places where they work.

Two-Thirds World missionaries serve in a total of at least 118 countries and six regions. They work among a total of 2,425 target peoples. Notice that 20.6% of all Two-Thirds World missionaries reported are foreign missionaries. There are many countries whose governments do not allow funds to be sent outside the country. The missionary activity from such countries is often confined within its own borders. Fortunately, in many of those countries, such as India, that is where the missionaries are most needed anyway.

Two-Thirds World missionaries are sent mostly to target peoples in the non-Western world. But of the total reported, 715 missionaries were working in 11 countries among 77 target cultures. The rest (19,162 of those reported) or 96.4% of the total, were working among in 107 countries throughout Latin America, Africa, Asia, and Oceania. This demonstrates the tremendous complexity and diversity of the Two-Thirds World missions movement.

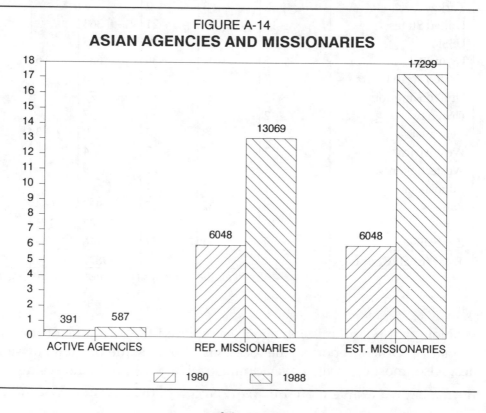

FIGURE A-14
ASIAN AGENCIES AND MISSIONARIES

Focus on Asia

Asia is the rapidly growing giant of non-Western missions. In every country listed, growth from 1980 to 1988 has been significant. Figure A-14 displays the growth of Asian mission agencies, reported missionaries and estimated missionaries from 1980 to 1988. (18) Active mission agencies grew at a decadal rate of 66% during that period. Reported agencies grew at a 162% DGR and estimated agencies grew at a 272% rate. (19) For both reported and estimated missionaries, these are the highest rates of growth in the Two-Thirds World.

Notice there were approximately the same number of Asian missionaries reported in 1988 (13,069) as there were total missionaries for the whole Two-Thirds World (13,238) in 1980.

According to the *World Christian Encyclopedia*, Christianity in Asia was growing at a 37% decadal rate in 1985. This is just behind the growth of Christians in Africa, which stood at 38% for the period 1980 to 1985. (20) Because of the rapid growth of the church in China and Indonesia during this decade, however, it is likely that the growth of Christianity in Asia is considerably higher, perhaps as high as 127%! (21) With this in mind, it is little wonder the missions movement in Asia is rising faster than in any other part of the world. Asia promises to play an ever increasing role in world missions in the future.

Figure A-15 displays the top five countries in Asian missionary sending and their growth from 1980 to 1988. Figure A-14 summarizes the growth of Asian mission agencies and missionaries together. India is by far the largest sending country in Asia; indeed in the Two-Thirds World. In spite of the large size of India's missionary movement, she still continues to grow at a rapid 242% per decade rate. This demonstrates that India will likely sustain a high rate of growth well into the future. Already India has an amazing 51.5% of the Asian estimated missionaries total, and 24.8% of the Two-Thirds World missionary total!

India continues to increase the number of mission agencies as well. We have discovered 44 mission agencies in India which did not exist in 1980. The total agencies were up from 140 in 1980 to 184 in 1988. This is an average of 48 missionaries per agency, which is considerably higher than average of 33 missionaries per agency for the entire Two-Thirds World.

Burma is the second largest sending country in Asia and the fourth largest in the Two-Thirds World. This is due in great measure to the Burma Baptist Convention (BBC), the largest of the 22 mission agencies in

FIGURE A-15
ESTIMATED ASIAN MISSIONARIES
Top Five Countries

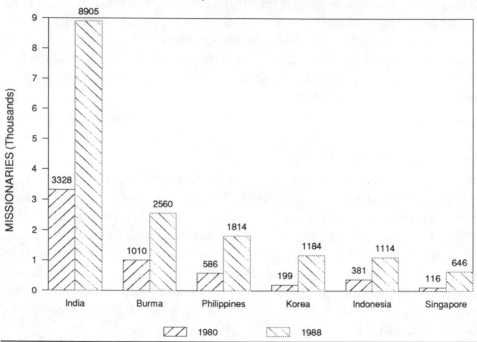

| | 1980 | | 1988 |

Burma. The Reverend Simon P. K. Enno, Associate General Secretary of BBC, reports the number of BBC missionaries grew from 887 in 1980 to 1,440 in 1988. This makes BBC's missionary outreach the largest mission agency in the Two-Thirds World. This missionary team represents the 435,999 Christians of the BBC who live primarily in Northern Burma. During the past eight years, these missionaries have seen 16,330 conversions among ten people groups in Burma and surrounding countries. Adoniram Judson, who founded the Burma Baptists, would be very proud!

Focus on Africa

Africa also has a rapidly developing missionary movement, but it is also the most difficult to measure. More than in any other region, Africa turns the definitions of words like "church," "evangelist," and "missionary" into a multitudinous mixture of meanings which are often very difficult to distinguish from one another. For some groups in Africa, "elders" are really missionaries according to our definition. For other groups, "missionaries" are migrating families of lay Christians who are commissioned to move to a new area, earn their own living and start churches cross-culturally. (22)

Because of this difficulty in discerning true missionary activity, several dozen African agencies previously thought to be missionary, and listed as such in Keyes' 1980 study, have been deleted in this study. This was because further investigation revealed they did not fit our definition of missionary agencies.

On the other hand, there were many new and old agencies discovered in this study which more than made up for those deletions. Figure A-16 reveals the five African countries with the highest number of mission agencies in 1988. Figure A-17 displays the five top missionary sending countries.

Nigeria leads all other nations in Africa, both in terms of missionary sending (2,959 missionaries) and missionary agencies (84). Largest among its agencies by far is the *Evangelical Missionary Society* (EMS) headquartered in Jos, Northern Nigeria, with Reverend Mai Kudi Kure serving as Acting Director. EMS sends 729 missionaries to 21 people groups

FIGURE A-16
AFRICAN MISSION AGENCY GROWTH
Top Five Countries

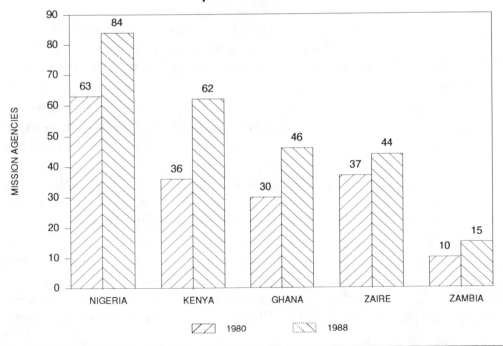

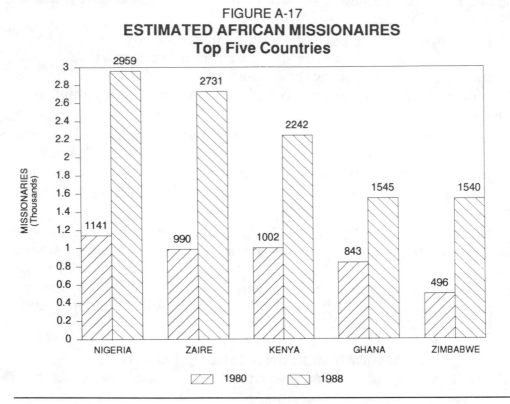

FIGURE A-17
ESTIMATED AFRICAN MISSIONAIRES
Top Five Countries

in Northern Nigeria and neighboring countries. Several hundred churches have been planted by this highly successful missionary team. EMS is the missionary arm of the Evangelical Church of West Africa (ECWA).

It is important to note that the second largest sending country, in terms of missionaries, is the country of Zaire. As a rule, missionary activities have not developed in African Francophone countries as much as they have in Anglophone countries. The exception is Zaire. Zaire's missionary movement is one of the more mature of African missionary movements. With 44 agencies and 2,731 missionaries, Zaire holds promise to stimulate missionary activity in other Francophone countries.

Zimbabwe is a country with explosive missionary potential. Not only are the 14 mission agencies reaching out to other tribes within their own country, they are successfully planting churches in most of the surrounding countries as well. One such agency is the *Forward In Faith Ministries* of the Zimbabwe Assemblies of God-Africa, an independent denomination led by Ezekiel Guti. This group has fielded 1,275 missionaries who minister in 20 African countries.

One important area of study which is needed to complete the picture of the African missionary movement relates to the African Instituted Churches movement (AIC). These are independently established African denominations. They often are started by a dynamic African Christian leader who breaks away from his own denomination to start another. Nobody knows exactly how many such newly-formed denominations there are in Africa, estimates range upwards of 4,000 separate AIC denominations. Perhaps the best conservative estimate is by Professor Dean S. Gilliland, of Fuller Theological Seminary, who estimates there are 5,770 AIC denominations in Africa.

The problem in measuring the missionary activities of these groups is that many of them are very syncretistic, even to the point of not being Christian by any reasonably Scriptural standard. On the other hand, there are many which are both doctrinally and practically well within the spectrum of Christian teachings generally accepted in other parts of the world.

What is needed first of all is a method to determine which groups are so syncretistic that they should be considered an object of missionary activity, and which groups should be considered part of the missionary force. That is no small task. Having determined some method for measuring such groups and estimating the number of groups which can be considered genuinely Christian, it would then remain to estimate the extent of their missionary activity.

Because the AIC movement is growing so rapidly, any truly comprehensive assessment of African missionary activity must address these questions and arrive at some measurable conclusions. Such a task is far beyond the scope and time limitations of this study, but it is hoped this can be attempted as a part of Phase Two of this research project.

Focus on Latin America

Interest in missions in Latin America is rising rapidly. Figure A-18 displays the growth of agencies, reported missionaries and estimated missionaries from 1980 to 1988. Active agencies grew from 92 to 150 during that period, raising the percentage of Latin American agencies from 12% to 14% of Two-Thirds World totals (Figure A-19). The number of Latin American mission agencies rose at a decadal rate of 84%, higher than any other region.(23)

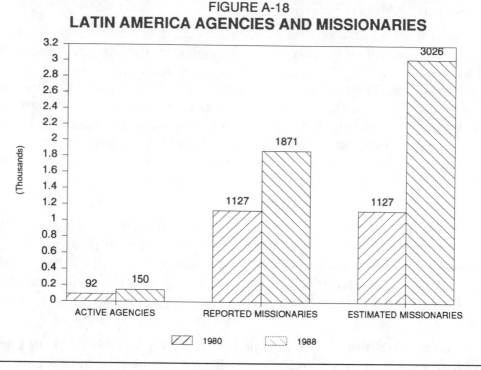

FIGURE A-18
LATIN AMERICA AGENCIES AND MISSIONARIES

The number of Latin American missionaries also increased rapidly, from 1,127 in 1980 to 3,026 in 1988. This represents a DGR of 243%, which is second only to Asia (272%) in the rate of growth for estimated missionaries.

Figure A-20 pictures the top five sending countries of Latin America. Brazil continues to lead the way in Latin American missions, accounting for more missionaries (2,040) than all other Latin countries combined. Nevertheless, rapid growth is very apparent in the other top five Latin countries as well. Mexico, which was not even in the top five in 1980, moved rapidly up to second place for all of Latin America. Colombia and Guatemala also experienced phenomenal growth.

Much of the credit for increasing missionary activity in Latin America belongs to the COMIBAM movement. COMIBAM stands for the "Ibero-American Congress on Missions." Organized in Mexico City in December 1984, COMIBAM formed national interdenominational committees in each Latin country to stimulate meetings, conferences and regional congresses on missions. This led to an international continent-wide congress called "COMIBAM '87" which convened in November 1987 in Sao Paulo, Brazil. Over 2,900 delegates from every Latin American country, plus

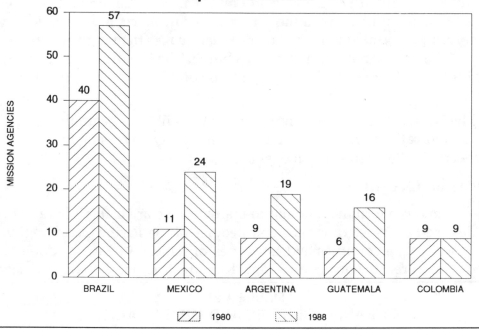

FIGURE A-19
LATIN AMERICAN MISSION AGENCIES
Top Five Countries

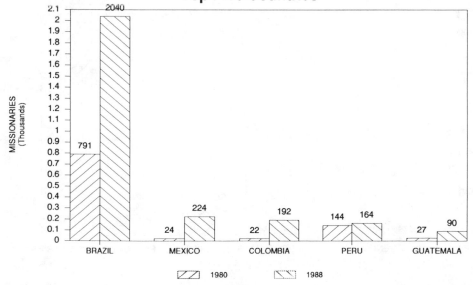

FIGURE A-20
ESTIMATED LATIN AMERICAN MISSIONARIES
Top Five Countries

some 300 guests from around the world, met for one week to focus on the cross-cultural missionary responsibility of the Latin American church.

This congress, and the processes leading up to it, has done more to stimulate the growth of missions in Latin America than any other effort to date. In conjunction with the congress, for instance, more missionary literature was printed in Latin American languages than in the entire history of the Latin American Protestant church. The COMIBAM movement continues under the able leadership of Edison Quieroz, Executive Director.

The Latin American missions movement is still in its beginning stages, but all indications are that it will become a rapidly increasing force in the Two-Thirds World missions movement.

Focus on Oceania

Oceania is a term not familiar to many. As we are using it here, it includes the non-Western islands and peoples of the Pacific Ocean region. Specifically, the countries and territories of American Samoa, Cook Islands, Fiji, French Polynesia, Guam, Kiribati, Micronesia, Nauru, New

FIGURE A-21
OCEANIA AGENCIES AND MISSIONARIES

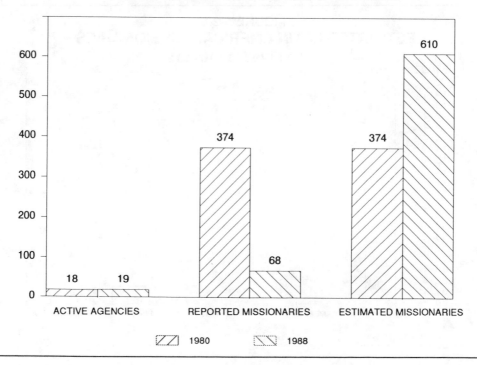

Caledonia, Papua New Guinea, Samoa, Solomon Islands, Tonga, Tuvalu, Vanuatu, Wallis and Futuna are included in Oceania. These archipelagoes consist of thousands of islands which dot the Western Pacific region. There are over 1,200 ethnolinguistic groups in Oceania.

Oceania can boast some of the earliest and most dynamic missions movements, such as the Melanesian Brotherhood, which sent missionaries to many islands and swept many into Christianity in the nineteenth century. Because of such missionary activity, large percentages of many countries in Oceania are at least nominal Christians. In fact, nominality has become a problem. Recognizing this, there are leaders in Oceania who are setting forth plans to revive the missionary movement of the nineteenth century. It is too early to tell how successful these efforts will be.

Figure A-21 summarizes the 1980 and 1988 data on agencies and missionaries from Oceania. Notice there were only 68 missionaries reported as part of this current study. One of the reasons for this is that one organization listed in the 1980 study which had many missionaries was dropped from the current study. It was determined that this

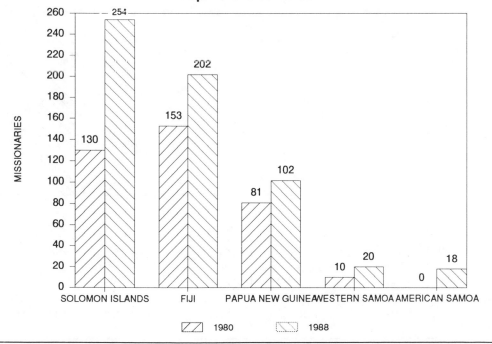

FIGURE A-22
ESTIMATED OCEANIA MISSIONARIES
Top Five Countries

organization's "missionaries" did not fit the definition of this study. This is a major reason for a low number of reported missionaries and a lower estimate for missionaries in Oceania than was reported in Keye's 1980 research. (24)

Figure A-22 displays the top five sending countries in Oceania for both 1980 and 1988 data. The estimated 254 missionaries from the Solomon Islands and the 202 from the Island of Fiji comprise 75% of the total estimated missionaries from Oceania.

It is hoped that the efforts under way to stir a renewed missionariy vision in Oceania will be successful. Not only is there a need to renew existing churches and nominal Christians in the islands, there are still unevangelized people groups in Oceania. The Indian population on the island of Fiji is the largest unreached people group of Oceania. (25) If the current efforts to revive earlier missionary activity by Oceanian Christians are successful, we may see some new models and methods of missionary activity focused on both the unreached peoples of the area and the nominal Christian areas as well.

FIGURE A-23
TWO-THIRDS WORLD MISSIONARIES
Totals and Projections

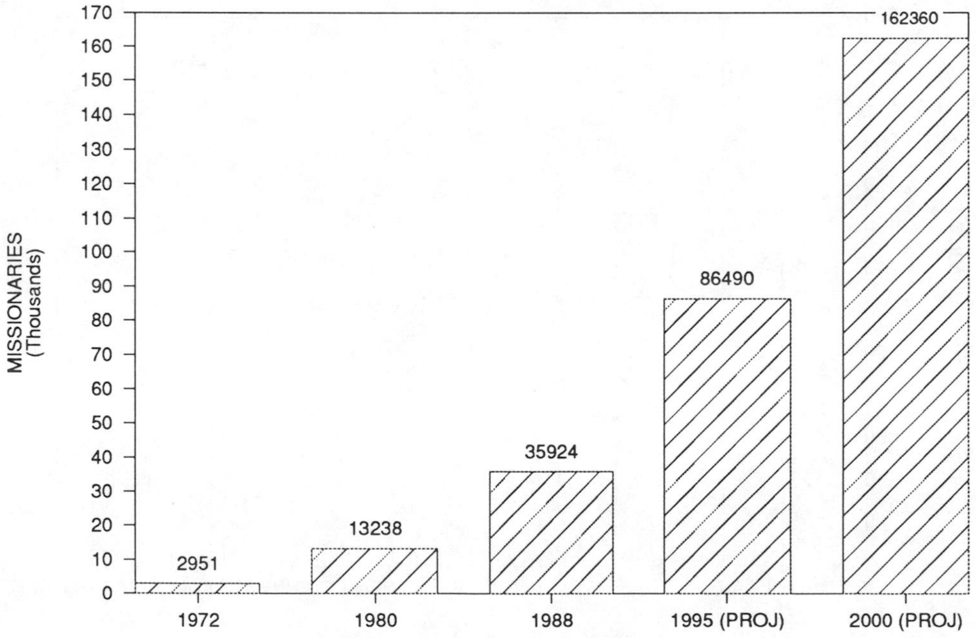

The future of the Two-thirds World missions movement

The Two-Thirds World missions movement is growing at a phenomenal pace. Our data indicates that the non-Western missions movement increased by an estimated 22,686 missionaries from 1980 to 1988. This reflects an average annual growth of 13.39%, which is 248% per decade. From 1979 to 1980, the Western missionary movement grew at an annual rate of 4.0, or 48% per decade. This means the Two-Thirds World mission movement has grown approximately five times faster than the Western missions movement during the last ten years! (26) Not only does this have great statistical significance for the future of global missions, it carries many important implications for the world missionary enterprise and for the global Church itself.

Figure A-23 shows the total number of estimated missionaries projected to the year 2000. According to the best available soujrces, there were 2,951 missionaries in 1972, 13,238 missionaries in 1980, (27) and 35,924 in 1988. If the Two-Thirds World missionary movement continues

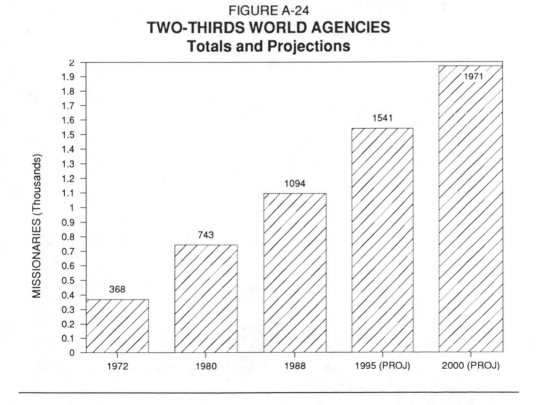

FIGURE A-24
TWO-THIRDS WORLD AGENCIES
Totals and Projections

at its its present rate of growth, there will be an estimated total of 86,490 non-Western missionaries in 1995 and 162,360 by the year 2000! (28)

While not so dramatic, the growth in the number of mission agencies is also very substantial. Figure A-24 depicts the total mission agencies from 1972 to 1988 plus the projected agencies to the year 2000. There were 368 agencies in existence in 1972, 743 agencies in 1980 and 1,094 agencies in 1988. This reflects a decadal growth rate (DGR) of 98% over the entire 16-year period. The growth rate from 1980 to 1988 was 62% (DGR). The projections for 1995 and 2000 are based upon this latter growth rate. Therefore, if the growth of mission agencies in the Two-Thirds World continues as it is, there will be 1,541 non-Western mission agencies in 1995 and 1,971 such agencies in the year 2000.

These projections can be broken down by region to gain insight on the future geographic trends in Two-Thirds World missions. Figures A-25, A-26, A-27 and A-28 display the confirmed and projected growth of Asian, African, Latin American and Oceanian missionary sending, re-spectively.

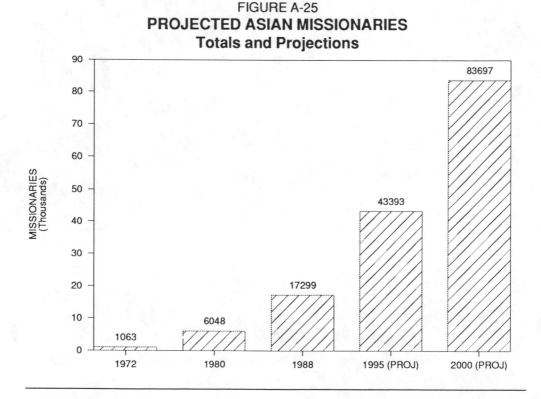

FIGURE A-25
PROJECTED ASIAN MISSIONARIES
Totals and Projections

FIGURE A-26
PROJECTED AFRICAN MISSIONARIES
Totals and Projections

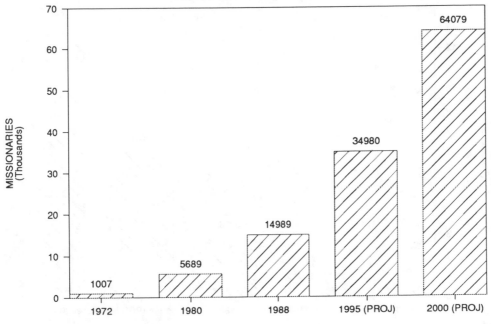

From 1980 to 1988, Asian missions is growing at an annual rate of 14.04% (DGR=272%). If it continues at this rate, there will be 43,393 Asian missionaries in 1995 and 83,697 in the year 2000.

African missions grew at an annual rate of 12.87 (DGR=235%) from 1980 to 1988. If African growth continues at this rate, there will be 34,980 African missionaries by 1995 and 64,079 missionaries by 2000.

During the same period, the Latin American missionary movement grew at an annual rate of 13.14% (DGR=243%). If Latin America continues at this pace, there will be 7,181 Latin American missionaries by 1995 and 13,313 by 2000.

During the same eight years, estimated growth for Oceania was 6.31% annually (DGR=84%). If Oceania continues its growth at that rate, there will be 936 Oceanian missionaries in 1995 and 1,271 in 2000.

Will the growth continue at this rate?

It is important to remember that a projection is not a prediction! Growth rates change from year to year in various regions of the world. External factors, such as economics, politics, changes in religious toler-

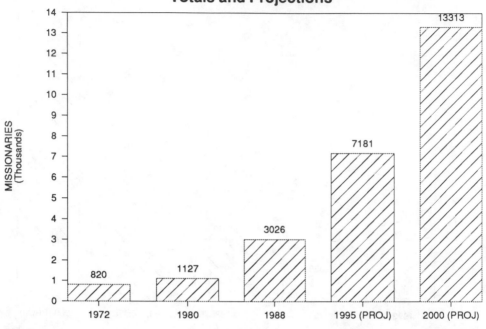

FIGURE A-27
PROJECTED LATIN AMERICAN MISSIONARIES
Totals and Projections

ance, financial exchange rates, and various changes in government regulations can dramatically affect the rates of growth in a given country. It is impossible to accurately predict what the true growth rates of Two-Thirds World missions will be in the future. The best we can do is project on the basis of what has happened in the past.

Projections can, and often do, prove to be unreliable. But to allow that fact to keep us from making projections is irresponsible. In the absence of crystal ball knowledge of the future, projections are our best means for preparing for the future.

The question remains: How reliable are the projections of this study? There are some hints which help answer that question embedded within the data itself. Figure A-11 contains two such important indicators. Notice that the top ten sending countries sent out approximately 77% of the total missionaries for *both* 1980 and 1988. Since the ten top countries represent such a large percentage of the total, whatever trends are discovered for them will greatly reflect trends in the whole movement.

FIGURE A-28
PROJECTED OCEANIAN MISSIONARIES
Totals and Projections

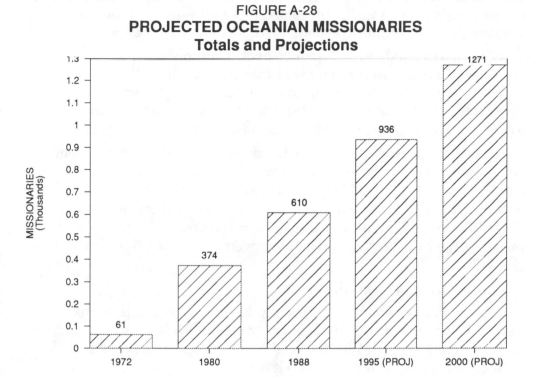

The significant point here is that the percentage of the totals for the top ten countries did not decline from 1980 to 1988. Had it done so, that would have been an indicator that the larger missionary sending countries had reached the height of their growth rates and that other countries were beginning to account for more of Two-Thirds World missions growth. Because the percentage stayed virtually the same, this indicates that growth in the ten top countries promises to continue well into the future.

A more direct indicator of the same conclusion is the fact that the overall rate of growth for the ten top countries is almost the same as the growth rate for the entire Two-Thirds World missions movement. The top ten countries grew at DGR 246.51% from 1980 to 1988, compared to 248.28% for the movement as a whole. As a missions movement grows larger in a country, it becomes increasingly more difficult to maintain the rate of growth. The actual numbers of missionaries added each year may continue to grow, but the *rate* of growth is very difficult to maintain. The fact that the top ten countries grew at a rate almost identical to the growth of the movement as a whole indicates those countries will continue to grow for some years into the future. Since they account for 77% of the non-Western missionary totals, this indicates the movement as a whole will also continue to experience this kind of rapid growth.

With this in mind, it would not be overly optimistic to expect the present rates of growth to continue well into the middle of the next decade. Not only are the largest sending countries continuing to grow at remarkable rates, but there are many other countries, particularly in Latin America, which are beginning to pick up the missionary vision in earnest.

Even if the growth of the Two-Thirds World missions movement declines somewhat by the year 2000, that decline is not likely to be a very large one. Even in the unlikely event that the growth declined to average only 175% DGR from 1988 to 2000, that means there would still be 121,000 Two-Thirds World missionaries in the year 2000! This would still be larger than the Western missions movement by that time (see discussion below)!

On comparing "apples with apples"

A number of researchers, including this one, have made comparisons between the number of missionaries from the Western world and the numbers from the non-Western world. In one sense, it is valid to make such comparisons, in another sense it is not.

It is generally not valid to make exact comparisons between Western and non-Western missionary figures because Western missionary totals do not usually contain the number of cross-cultural missionaries working within the countries that send them. There are North American missionaries, for instance, who work among many of the estimated 600 ethnic groups living in North America. Nobody knows how many there are. Such figures are hard to obtain because that type of ministry is often not distinguished from other kinds of "home missions" by many denominations. Western home missionaries work mono-culturally as well as cross-culturally. As in the non-Western world, it is difficult to distinguish cross-cultural "home" missionaries from extension church planters in the West!

But in the case of non-Western missionary figures, they do include those working as missionaries within their own countries. Since approximately 80% of non-Western missionaries are working within their own countries (a far greater percentage than in the West), it would be of little value to simply measure foreign missionaries in the Two-Thirds World.

The number of cross-cultural home missionaries from the West is unknown, but is a relatively low percentage of the total. However, it is instructive to make comparisons based upon the number of Western foreign missionaries alone. While such comparisons are not entirely legitimate because they do not include Western cross-cultural home missionaries, they are legitimate in terms of the object of their ministries, which is to reach peoples who live mostly outside the Western world. Both Western and non-Western missionaries are working largely outside the Western world. In fact, 96.4% of non-Western missionaries work outside the Western world. Accordingly, it is legitimate to compare their numbers in order to measure the force for the evangelization of those parts of the world, and the relative strength of both movements.

Based upon the current figures being published in the 14th edition of MARC's *Mission Handbook* for North America, and upon interviews with leading authorities for Europe and Australia/New Zealand, there were approximately 85,000 Western missionaries as of the end of 1988. At least 32,000 of these were short-term missionaries, with the remainder working as career missionaries. (29)

This means that there is a total of approximately 121,000 Protestant missionaries in the world. (30) The 35,924 Two-Thirds World missionaries represent 29.7% of that total. In making such a comparison, it is important to state that an ever-increasing share of Western missionaries work on a short-term basis. In 1988, for instance, 31,387 North American missionaries were short term, working at least one month on the field, but not as career missionaries. This is 42% of the North American total. On the other hand, while we do not yet have accurate statistics, a much larger share of non-Western missionaries are career missionaries. So in terms of actual ministry on the field, the percentage of Two-Thirds World missionary activity would be considerably higher.

If both the Western missionary force and the Two-Thirds World missionary force continue to grow at their current rates, figure A-29 demonstrates that the majority of Protestant missionaries will be from the non-Western world. The number of Two-Thirds World missionaries would overtake the number of Western missionaries sometime in 1998. By 2000, Western missionaries would be approximately 136,000, and Two-Thirds World missionaries would number over 162,000! This would make the non-Western missionary force 54.4% of the total Protestant missionaries.

Implications for the future

There can be little question that the size and growth of the Two-Thirds World missions movement will have an increasingly greater im-

FIGURE A-29
PROJECTED MISSIONARIES
Western and Two-Thirds World

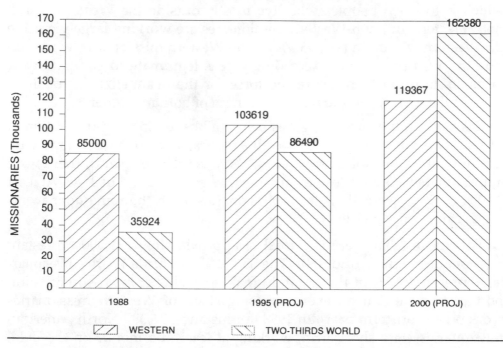

pact on both the church and world evangelism in the future. Exactly what kind of impact is more difficult to ascertain. Even though there is not enough space here to enter a full discussion of the subject, it may be worth the effort to briefly suggest some of what may appear over the horizon, in the light of information revealed in this study.

If there is any thought that this study should underscore, it is *change* — rapid changes are coming in world missions. Here are some questions to ponder concerning possible changes which will impact the global missionary activities of the church:

1. **As the Western missionary steps aside** to make room for the non-Western counterpart who has rapidly come alongside, how will his/her role change? Will the missionary continue to gravitate away from pioneer ministries toward institutional activities as in recent years? Or will the institutions presently directed by the missionary come under the full control of local churches and denominations; and will he/she be replaced by a local counterpart who is just as well-trained and qualified for the position? Will more Western missionaries

52

move once again into pioneer missionary activity? Will they link to-gether with their non-Western counterparts in meaningful partner-ship? In what roles will Western churches be willing to support Western missionaries in the future?

2. **How will partnership patterns develop** in areas such as missionary support, internationalization and international cooperative efforts? Will partnerships of the future be based more upon tasks to be per-formed than upon denominational affiliation or national origin? Will Western churches opt to support Two-Thirds World missionaries as inexpensive surrogates, instead of sending their own sons and daugh-ters? Will non-Western churches also support Western missionaries? (31) Will international Christian organizations truly become interna-tional, or will most continue to be dominated by Western agendas and personnel?

3. **What kind of missionary training patterns** will emerge in the global missionary enterprise? Will international missionary training opportu-nities arise in the Two-Thirds World? Will Western missionaries gain part of their training under non-Western missionary trainers in places like Sao Paulo, Jos, New Delhi, Singapore and Seoul? Will non-West-erners also gain part of their training close to the target of their minis-try? Will interdenominational missionary training continue to gain ground in the Two-Thirds World to conserve resources and make the best use of indigenous trainers?

4. **Will missiology become globalized?** Will Western missiology be in-formed by the theory and methods of the non-Western missions movement, as well as vice versa? What new models of missionary ac-tivity are developing, and what sending structures will emerge in the Two-Thirds World? How will our definitions for missionary activity expand or contract? As missionary activity expands around the globe, will it become more international or more regionalized?

5. **How will the changes brought on by the Two-Thirds World missions movement** affect the whole church's understanding of itself and of its collective role in world evangelization? Will churches labeled "na-tional" and "indigenous" and "autonomous" too often continue to mean "nationalistic" and "ethnocentric" and "sectarian?" Will West-ern missions and Two-Thirds World missions ever become just sim-ply, *GLOBAL MISSIONS*?

These are important questions; too important to be treated lightly or superficially. There is not space to give them the attention they deserve here. It is anticipated that questions such as these will be given a much fairer treatment when the results of the second phase of this research is published.

Conclusion

Denominational and missionary leaders around the world would do well to consider the implications of the growing missions movement in the Two-Thirds World. It is approximately 30% of the world Protestant missionary total. It is growing at a rate 5 times faster than the Western missionary movement. The number of Two-Thirds World missionaries holds the very real promise of surpassing the number of Western missionaries by the year 2000.

The Two-Thirds World missions movement will doubtless play a very significant role in bringing representatives of "every tribe and language and people and nation" to Christ. How effective they will be and how rapidly that goal is accomplished may very well depend upon how today's Christian leaders grasp the fact that, for the first time in history, the Good News is truly becoming a gospel FROM EVERY PEOPLE!

FOOTNOTES

(1) *Evangelical Missions Quarterly* 20, no. 2 (April 1984): 127; 122.

(2) James Wong, et. al.; *Missions From the Third World: A World Survey of Non-Western Missions in Asia, Africa and Latin America;* Singapore, Church Growth Study Center; 1973.

(3) Marlin L. Nelson; *The How and Why of Third World Missions: An Asian Case Study;* Pasadena, William Carey Library; 1976; _____ , *Readings in Third World Missions;* Pasadena, William Carey Library; 1976.

(4) Harvie M. Conn; "Response to the Article by Pate and Keyes"; in *International Bulletin of Missionary Research 10,* no.4 (Oct 1986), 163-164.

(5) See below, note 28.

(6) Do not misunderstand the value of Keyes' study on this point. My close contact with his data has given me a great appreciation for the mammoth task he completed. Furthermore, some organizational leaders may misunderstand some questions, or report their data in a manner which they think you want to see, rather than as you asked. Whenever there is more information on a particular agency, it will give further insight into the true nature of its ministry. It will not be surprising if the second phase of our research reveals that some of the agencies we have listed need also to be dropped. This is simply the nature of this kind of research. The only alternative would be for the same person to spend considerable time with each agency in each country in order to identify the nature of its work accurately and according to the same criteria.

(7) Larry D. Pate, "Asian Missions: Growth, Problems and Partnership;" BRIDGING PEOPLES 5, no.4 (Oct 1986).

(8) David J. Hesselgrave; *Today's Choices For Tomorrow's Mission;* Grand Rapids, Zondervan; p. 189.

(9) Patrick Johnstone; *Operation World;* Pasadena, William Carey Library; 1986; p. 35.

(10) These should be considered conservative figures. Every effort throughout this book has been made to select methods for calculations which do not inflate the figures.

(11) The 1980 figures do not agree with those of Lawrence E. Keyes' *The Last Age of Missions* (Pasadena, William Carey Library; 1983) because we revised them to reflect newly discovered agencies which also existed in 1980, but were not then discovered by Keyes' research. See figure A-5.

(12) Samuel Wilson & John Siewert, Eds.; *Mission Handbook: North American Protestant Ministries Overseas;* Monrovia, Missions Advanced Research & Communication Center (MARC), 1986; pp 562-563.

(13) When there was adequate growth history, we used projections based upon the actual data of each agency. In some cases, there was an insufficient amount of data to make an accurate projection. For instance, if a newer agency reported two missionaries in 1980 and ten in 1985, the growth rate would be unreasonably high and impossible to sustain. In all cases where the growth rate reached or ex-

ceeded 12% annually, we reviewed that particular agency. If there was insufficient data to make an accurate long-term projection, we used the overall growth
rate for the country to project for the agency in question. This kept the rates of
growth conservative and more reasonable. Only those agencies which had a
demonstrated track of data were allowed to remain at 12% annual growth or
greater.

(14) Compiled by D. R. Downes; "Directory of Kenya's Missionary- Sending Ministries;" Nairobi, African Ministry Resources, 1988.

(15) We used Keyes' (*op. cit*, p. 64) estimated figure for 1980.

(16) Pate, *op. cit.*

(17) It would not be appropriate to compare these growth rates to those from 1972-
1980 data reported in earlier studies because our method of calculation includes
the data for agencies which existed in 1980 where the 1980 study did not follow
the same procedure for 1972 data.

(18) The majority of the information from Korea was compiled by Marlin L. Nelson
and his students and assistant researchers, Stephen Choi and Han Chi-Won.
Their research was scheduled for publication as *The Directory of Korean Missionaries and Mission Societies*, by Basilae-Com Ltd., Seoul, at the time this book went to
press.

(19) Since virtually all agencies from which we have data from any source reported
1980 data, (with the exception of those in Kenya), we made no higher estimates
than those reported for 1980 data.

(20) cf. Pate, op. cit. and David B. Barrett, Ed.; *World Christian Encyclopedia;* New York,
Oxford University Press, 1982; p 778.

(21) That is the rate of growth I calculated, based upon expert estimates of the true
size of the church in China as 50 million (source: Jonathon Chao) and the true
size of the church in Indonesia at 36.8 million (source: Census Bureau of Indonesia, unofficial figures, 1985).

(22) Before we hastily judge this method as something other than missionary sending,
let us remember it was precisely this method employed by the Moravians in the
18th century which made theirs one of the greatest missionary movements in
Western church history!

(23) Asian, African and Oceanian mission agency growth was 66%, 52% and 7%, re-
spectively.

(24) Keyes, *op. cit.*, p 65.

(25) Johnstone, *op. cit.*, p 76.

(26) This is based upon figures from the 12th and 14th editions of the North American
MISSION HANDBOOK (Monrovia, MARC). The 12th edition figures have been
revised from more recent data to 52,622 total of North American missionaries
for 1979. The 14th edition total of 74,964 was a prepublication total. This Western missionary growth rate assumes the same growth rate for Western Europe
and Australia/New Zealand as for North America (which comprises approximately 89% of the Western total). This also assumes a growth rate for domestic,

cross-cultural Western missions which does not exceed that rate. These unknown rates could be lower, but are most likely to be higher. Total estimated Western missionaries for 1988 is 85,000 (see Footnote 29).

(27) Figures for 1972 and 1980 are not our estimates. They reflect data on our records of reported missionaries. That is why they do not agree exactly with previous estimates for those years in the 1972 study by Wang, *et al.(op. cit.)*, and the 1980 study by Keyes (*op. cit.*).

(28) In spite of the high numbers, these estimates should be considered conservative for the reasons explained in note 13.

(29) Based upon figures obtained as in note 26, plus figures obtained by telephone interviews with knowledgeable leaders familiar with figures tabulated or estimated for other parts of the Western World.

(30) Excluding Western cross-cultural missionaries working in their own countries (with the exception of U.K.), which do not include such missionaries in their figures.

(31) The author is a "faith" missionary whose largest supporting church is in Malaysia, a Muslim country!

Case Histories

CASE HISTORIES
from Missions in
the Two-Thirds World

WHEN PEOPLE THINK OF MISSIONARIES in the Two-Thirds World, many are tempted to romanticize their organizations and their effectiveness. Westerners in particular tend to assume that non-Western missionaries almost automatically succeed and have less difficulty in presenting the gospel than do cross-cultural workers from the West.

Both my research and experience convince me that this is a myth which does not serve our understanding of the realities of the missionary movements in the countries of the Two-Thirds world. No missionary movement in any country has a corner on either success or failure. Brilliant strategy is just as likely to come through an inspired missionary leader from India as it is from leaders in Singapore or Japan. But strategic methodological blunders may as easily appear in the work of a Brazilian or a Korean missionary as in the history of Western missionary activity.

Non-Western missionaries must face as many obstacles as Western missionaries face, and sometimes more. They may not always need passports and visas, but they may be denied adequate training, financial resources or education for their children. The obstacles may differ, but they do not disappear. Overcoming barriers is central to the nature of missionary work itself!

The case histories in this book tell three stories about leaders who are overcoming barriers successfully. They have been selected because they are somewhat typical of the types of missionary activity existing in their part of the world. They have also been selected because they are unusual in their success.

The first is the story of the Evangelical Church of Malawi and its dynamic leader, the Reverend Matthias Munyewe. He is leading a spiritually powerful missionary thrust among the large, unreached Yao Muslim tribe of that country. The details of how this is being accomplished are instructive concerning the nature of missionary activities in Africa as a whole.

The second story is not only that of a mission agency, but of a national missions movement in Argentina. It is the story of Federico Bertuzzi and

Misiones Mundiales. The missions movement in most of Latin America is really at its earliest stages. This story presents a model of how the churches of a whole nation can be mobilized toward missions. It is also a demonstration of the unity in the midst of diversity which is possible for the Body of Christ when it marches under the flag of missions.

The final story is from India. India represents one of the most widely developing missionary movements in the world. To do effective missionary work in India requires visionary, exemplary leadership. The Reverend P. G. Vargis, founder and director of the Indian Evangelical Team (IET) is such a leader. His example of faith and self-sacrifice has been instrumental in building one of the largest and most successful missionary ministries in India. The success is not evident in the cash flow statements, but in the missionary statistics of that organization. IET gives much insight into the nature of the India missions movement and the struggles of those missionaries who labor as part of it.

A PEOPLE TO WIN

The Story of the Evangelical
Baptist Church of Malawi

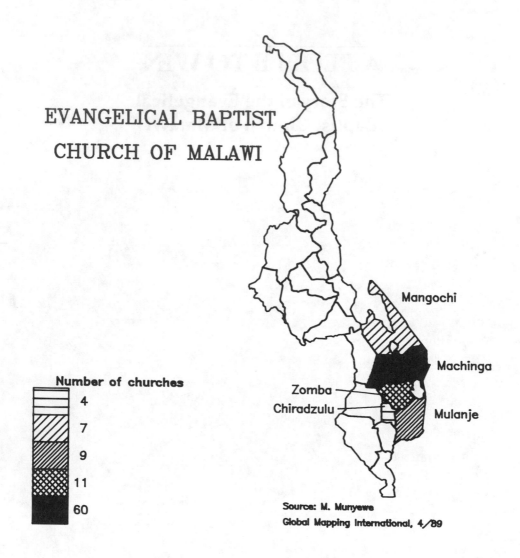

EVANGELICAL BAPTIST
CHURCH OF MALAWI

Mangochi

Machinga

Number of churches

4

7

9

11

60

Zomba

Chiradzulu

Mulanje

Source: M. Munyewe
Global Mapping International, 4/89

A PEOPLE TO WIN
The Story of the Evangelical Baptist Church of Malawi

THE MISSIONARY WAS HAPPY TO BE HOME. He had been in the Liwonde area of Malawi obtaining tracts, Bibles and literature to carry back into war-torn Mozambique. He was back home with his wife and children in a village of northwestern Mozambique. They had planted a church there.

The country's economy was in a shambles. The tug of war between the Marxist government and the guerrilla resistance movement made daily existence an ordeal. Life was cheap. But it also made people spiritually hungry and the missionary was gratified with the rapid success of his church planting efforts.

They hadn't really fallen asleep when the soldiers came. The missionary and his wife were beaten savagely. The soldiers accused them of being spies. Their savage rage knew no limits. They torched the house and the thatch roof burned like a beacon in the night sky. As the children watched on in horror, the soldiers committed horrible atrocities against their parents. The ordeal seemed to last an eternity and the atrocities were unspeakable. When it was finally over, the mother lay bruised and bleeding, convulsing beside the disemboweled body of her husband. The children couldn't cry any more.

With what strength she could find, the missionary mother escaped back to Malawi with her children where she collapsed from the physical and emotional ordeal she had endured. It took six months for her to recover enough to function even partially. It is doubtful she would have ever recovered except for the loving support and care she received from her church. She and her husband were missionaries of the Evangelical Baptist Church of Malawi (EBC).

The Yao people

The Yao people receive their name from a hill in East Africa from which they migrated to various points of the compass over a period of centuries. David Livingston reported meeting one of their chiefs east of

Lake Nyassa. He reported them as slave traders and said there was a strong Arab influence in their culture. (1)

The Yao people speak the Chiyao language. Though they actually consist of ten separate tribes, their language and Muslim religion tie them together. During a time of widespread famine in the mid-19th century, four of those tribes moved into what is today the country of Malawi in the southeast portion of Central Africa. They moved into the area just south of Lake Malawi and they form the largest portion of the population in the northern portion of Southern Malawi. Abdallah lists these four tribes, which generally take their names from the prominent hill in their areas:

- **Amakale** of Chief Katuli in Mangochi District, or Achisi, Yao.
- **Amasinga** of Chief Makanjira in Mangochi District.
- **Amangochi** of Mangochi Hill in Mangochi District.
- **Amachinga** of Chief Jalasi, Mponda Msamala, Kawinga and Liwonde, Machinga District. (2)

Though Arabs influenced the Yaos a great deal over the centuries, there were no widespread mass conversions to Islam until early in the 20th century in Malawi. In the latter half of the 19th century, three chiefs (Makanjira, Mponda and Mataka) were so impressed by what the Arabs could do technically, they asked that teachers (Mwalimu) be sent to teach their people. The first chief to embrace Islam was Makanjira in 1870. Yao chiefs generally followed him and joined the Islamic faith.

Though the chiefs turned to Islam, the scattered Yao remained pagan until the first decade of this century. In 1910, Sir Alfred Sharp wrote:

> Twenty years ago when I first knew Nyasaland, Mohammedanism was almost non-existent, except at one or two spots where it had been brought by Arabs. Since, it has spread greatly, particularly during the last eight or ten years. The Yaos are the tribe who have taken to Muslim teaching mostly. On the other hand, among the tribes to the West of Lake Nyassa (present day Lake Malawi), there is hardly any Mohammedan. All through the Yao land — that is to say, from Lake Nyassa to the East Coast, there is in most villages a mosque and a Mwalimu. (3)

The Yao people were very receptive to Islam because it welcomed their traditional dances and practice of circumcision. The Christian missionaries rejected both as heathenism. A simple adaptation of Islamic ceremonies into their traditional dances and circumcision rites was all that was necessary. This was not difficult because the Islamic circumcision ceremony, "dando," was very similar to the "lupanda" ceremony of the Yao.

By 1976, government statistics reported 480,000 Muslims in Malawi. By 1986, the number had leaped to 1.1 million. (4) At least 950,000 of them are Yao.

There are various estimates as to what percentage of Yao have become Christians since the tribe moved into Malawi. According to the *Unreached Peoples '84* handbook, there were reported the following figures for the five largest denominations with Yao work:

- **Anglican Church**, since 1900: 500 members
- **Roman Catholic Church**, since 1920: 500 members
- **Presbyterian Church**, since 1920: 500 members
- **Baptist Church**, since 1950: 100 members
- **Lutheran Church**, since 1960: 50 members (5)

Even discounting the fact that many of those listed as Christians among the Yao are very nominal, these results of the last 60 years seem dismal when compared to the hundreds of thousands of converts to Islam in this century. That is why the story of the Evangelical Baptist Church is all the more important and amazing!

The unknown fruit

In 1973, two young evangelists came to the village of Mowere in the Machinga District of Malawi. They preached the gospel faithfully but had little visible results. Unknown to them however, was that 25 of their hearers were converted in their hearts. They did not openly declare their faith for fear of their neighbors and friends, who were Muslims. Five of them began to meet for Bible study and they began to grow in their faith, even though they had no one to teach them.

"Since we have become Christians, we should start a Christian church in this place," they concluded. That was the beginning of the Evangelical Baptist Church (EBC) of Malawi. A group of secretly converted ex-Muslims formed the first EBC church. (6) Even though the churches which resulted would not clearly focus on the evangelization of Muslims for another ten years, this beginning accounts for the root of the EBC desire to reach Muslims which would blossom later.

The initial rejection of the new Christians by the Muslim community made life difficult for the 25 members of the first EBC church. They were forced to move their families to the town of Mbere in the same district.

Furthermore, Christian leaders were not trained in Chiyao but in Chichewa, the national language of Malawi. Services were conducted in Chichewa. This further distanced the congregation from the Muslim community. Four new EBC churches were started from 1974 to 1979. Though some of their converts were Yao, the worship services were still conducted in the national language.

This all caused a process whereby the EBC churches became more and more like the other Christian churches, adopting Christian music in the national language and becoming more distanced from the majority Muslim population around them. This did not begin to change significantly until after the Reverend Matthias Munyewe assumed the leadership of EBC in 1979.

A chosen vessel

Matthias Munyewe was raised in an unusual family. Half of them were Muslims, the other half were Christians. As a child, Matthias was exposed to the teachings of both Christianity and Islam. Even though Matthias had a grandfather who was a Mwalimu (Muslim teacher), part of his heritage was Christian. Matthias' father became a believer and committed himself to Christ as a part of the original 25 converts in Mowere. Matthias received an opportunity to attend seminary in Zambia. While there, he also became a believer in Christ. Munyewe relates his family background and conversion:

> Though they were Christians, they were nominal in their faith. I did not know the Lord until I went to the Bible Seminary. I studied there for three years. Then I came and worked for the Lutheran Church for two years to fulfill my contract. After that I resigned and accepted a call to the Evangelical Baptist Church. (7)

Munyewe began seminary in 1973, about the same time the first EBC church had been established. He became the chairman, or chief officer, of EBC in early 1979. He brought with him a vision to evangelize the Muslim Yao. Concerning his call to EBC, Munyewe said:

> When I received the call to the Evangelical Baptist Church in 1979, it was really very small. But when I realized I had opportunity to reach the Yao, I said that is the right call because I was raised in the Yao Muslim background. I knew that these people need Christ very much more than other unreached peoples in Central Africa. (8)

When Munyewe assumed the leadership of EBC in 1979, he faced a formidable challenge. As a people, the Yao had embraced Islam almost completely. Those who were Christians, were almost completely nominal descendants of Yao, who had turned to Christianity early in this century. There was virtually no vital group of believers among the Yao people.

But Munyewe knew the hearts of the Yao. He sensed intuitively that Islam had never penetrated deeply into the world view and daily lives of the Yao. He knew that Islam was little more than a thin veneer of religion covering a deep folk religion of animistic practices. Though Islam retained the outward loyalty of the Yao, those loyalties were based as much on tribal identification as they were upon Islamic faith. He knew the hearts of the Yao were hungry for a more vital and fulfilling religion.

Growth of the Evangelical Baptist Churches of Malawi

When Munyewe assumed the leadership of EBC, there were only four EBC churches with a combined membership of slightly more than 400. It had been three years since a new church had been planted. It did not seem like the kind of beginning which would lead to the EBC becoming one of the fastest growing churches in Central Africa. Yet Munyewe came with a vision for Muslims and a passion to evangelize the lost. Within the next ten years, he was destined to lead the Evangelical Baptist Churches of Malawi to plant a total of 91 churches with a combined membership of more than 8,000. By that time, the EBC would also have begun what appears to be the most significant penetration of the Yao people in the history of that Muslim tribe.

The early years: clarifying the vision

In the six years prior to the beginning of Munyewe's leadership, only four churches had been planted. Nevertheless, those churches had been effective in outreach among the receptive Chichewa-speaking majority in the country. They had grown from 98 believers in 1974 to 400 by the end of 1978, or an average of 42% per year (Figure EBC-1). That is excellent growth, even for a new group of churches. But their effectiveness in winning converts did not readily translate into planting new churches.

Even when Matthias assumed EBC leadership, there was not a great emphasis placed upon church planting. Evangelization and soul-winning was stressed above all else. The result was an even greater numerical increase in converts. Under Munyewe's inspirational leadership, membership increased from 400 in 1978 to 1,401 by the end of 1983, a growth of 350% (Figure EBC-2). During this same period of time, however, only five new churches were planted, a growth of only 225%.

FIGURE EBC - 1
EBC MEMBERSHIP

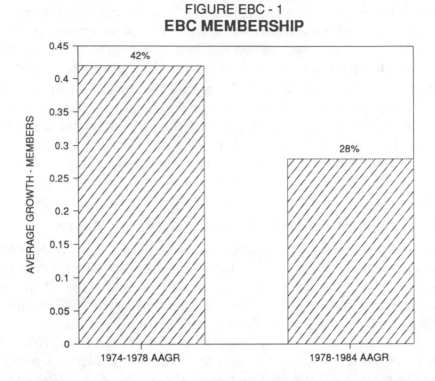

The disparity between the growth of EBC membership and the plant-ing of new churches began to build pressure against continued rapid membership growth. There was only a limited amount of space to hold new converts in each church. As the number of members per church con-tinued to rise, the number of new converts began to decline steadily. Fig-ure EBC-3 dramatically demonstrates this phenomenon. As the average number of believers in each EBC church rose, there was a corresponding decline in annual *rates* of growth. Just after the average member per church reached its peak in 1983 (190 per church), EBC experienced its slowest rate of growth (2% in 1984). There was a clear need to begin planting more and more churches, if EBC was to continue its rapid growth.

A vision for the Yao

In 1983, Matthias Munyewe became concerned about the slowing of growth among EBC churches. He prayerfully began to consider what God wanted his nine churches to do in ministry for Him. It was at that time Matthias came to believe that God wanted EBC to concentrate on winning Muslim Yao to Christ. His churches were situated in the center of the Muslim parts of Southern Malawi. Like himself, there were a number of converts and leaders who had at least some background with Yao Muslims. With 1.1 million Muslims, the Yao represented the largest unreached tribe in Central Africa. After much prayer, Matthias concluded that EBC had been given a special mandate to evangelize the Yao.

Gospel of love

The EBC churches are located in one of the most impoverished areas of Central Africa. It is not a cash economy. When EBC churches first began to reach out to the Yao, their total annual offerings were only a few hundred dollars for all the churches combined. Most donations were in produce. So the people gave what they had to the Yao Muslims — the gospel, their food, *and a lot of love.*

The fighting in nearby Mozambique was still driving thousands of refugees across the border into Malawi. Though most Yao live in Malawi, 200,000 live in Mozambique. The EBC Christians began to reach out in love and compassion to those Yao refugees pouring across their borders. Many had fled their homes with scarcely more than the clothes on their back. EBC believers fed and sheltered them as best they could, though

FIGURE EBC - 2
EBC MEMBERSHIP GROWTH 1973-1984

71

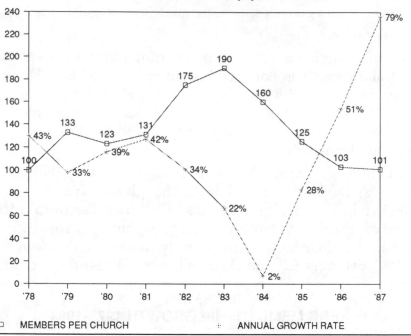

FIGURE EBC - 3
EBC ANNUAL GROWTH
Compared to Membership per Church

☐ MEMBERS PER CHURCH   ⁛ ANNUAL GROWTH RATE

they were very poor themselves. At one point, a shipment of used clothing donated for poor EBC church members arrived from Canada. Rather than use the clothing for themselves, the churches decided to give it to the Mozambican refugees who needed it even more. This demonstrates the practical love of EBC people for the Yao. This practical and vibrant faith has done much to bring Muslims to Christ through EBC churches.

"Practical" also means praying for the sick. One Muslim, named Kawerama, was in much pain and his arm was paralyzed. He had worn the special amulets with the Koranic verses contained inside for years. He had consulted Muslim herbal healers, but the pain increased. After prayer by EBC believers one night, Kawerama went to bed. During the night, his arm returned to normal and stopped hurting. He awakened at 5:00 A.M., realizing he was healed and that he had slept through the night. "That is the first time I have slept through the night in five years," he exclaimed. Kawerama became a Christian and led many others to do the same.

In 1983, the son of a well-known Muslim teacher became a Christian. This infuriated his father, who employed the services of Muslim shamans to place a curse upon the pastor to kill him. The Christians prayed and the shamans practiced their sorcery. Many people were interested to see what would happen. When they observed that the pastor was not harmed, but rather seemed to be even more blessed, many people became Christians. After a few years, the famous Muslim teacher also became a Christian. He is a leader in the EBC churches today. (9)

Missionaries for the Yao

Munyewe began to direct the efforts of his churches and "evangelists" toward the Yao tribe. The practical effect was to turn his "evangelists" into missionaries. The Yao people speak the national language, Chichewa. This was the language used primarily in the earlier days of outreach to the Yao. Not only did this facilitate communication for missionaries, it allowed many pastors, elders and local church believers to reach out to the Yao in practical ways. They welcomed them into their congregations, a few of which began to have a significant contingent of Yao converts.

The intensified outreach to the Yao tribe began to swell the ranks of new converts. Even though more Yao Muslims began to turn to Christianity, Chichewa-speaking non-Yao also became believers in larger numbers. The EBC was increasing its momentum and its vision at the same time.

Two new churches were planted in 1984, and seven were planted in 1985. The slowing of growth reversed, shooting up to 22% for 1985. As the number of believers per church declined, the number of new members increased even more dramatically (see Figure EBC-3).

A team is formed

By 1985, Munyewe realized more converts were coming from the Yao tribe than any other. This prompted him to do two important things. First, he decided to train and deploy ten more missionaries to the Yao by the end of 1987. Second, he also decided to plant more churches, especially in Yao areas. In addition, he decided to continue an emphasis upon Yao ministries through existing local churches.

I received a letter from Munyewe in 1985 in which he wrote:

> The Lord laid a burden to win Muslims in our area...we are waiting on the Lord in prayer and fasting to see the great day when we will harvest many... As the chairman of this church,

73

> I would like to know if you could kindly direct our church to a ministry to send a man who can come and teach our church, so that we can be self-reliant, and reach our goal of sending ten missionaries to the Yao from today to 1987.

Munyewe also reported that many hundreds of Muslims had already become Christians. Later investigation showed there were almost 1,100 Muslim converts who were members of EBC churches by that time. They already had four missionaries, and had a goal to send ten more within two-and-a-half years.

Needless to say, the letter made an impression upon me. The Yao were an unreached people group obviously receptive to the gospel. Some groups have worked among Muslims for 100 years in some countries without seeing that number of converts! EBC Christians were just as obviously committed to missionary ministry to the Yao. I decided to find a way to train their churches so they could send their ten missionaries to the Yao. We began to encourage their ministry.

It wasn't until May, 1987 that I was finally able to be in Malawi for a cross-cultural training seminar for EBC leaders. I was thrilled to see they had already grown to 3,600 believers in 36 churches by that time (see Figure EBC-2).

Chairman Munyewe had done a fine job in leading his churches to growth and outreach to the Yao. Their zeal and love for the lost had already given them an excellent reputation in many villages and towns. After analyzing their growth patterns with Munyewe, we outlined a number of important principles which should help them grow even faster and become even more effective in their work among the Yao. Some of the more important ones were:

Increase church planting efforts: The relationship between increasing average membership per church and declining rates of growth was discovered. The only solution was to plant many more churches, using the larger churches as mother churches.

Use the Yao language: Because the Yao converts understood the national language, Chichewa, worship services were almost entirely in that language. This was true even though some of the leaders were capable in Chiyao, the language of the Muslim converts. A decision was taken to make services bilingual in as many churches as possible, where there was a sufficient number of Yao converts to justify doing so. It was also decided to emphasize the planting of churches in Yao villages, using the Chiyao language for witness and worship.

Expand the leadership base: Without a rapid increase in capable leadership, more rapid growth could not be sustained. By kerosene lantern, we planned an extension training program which would train pastors, elders and missionaries. It was to be very low budget so it could sustain itself within seven to ten years, after sufficient growth had taken place. Until then, partners would need to be found to subsidize this training.

On the last day of the seminar, EBC leaders committed themselves to following such principles. At the last session, each of six district leaders stood to announce their district goals.

The first said, "Last year, we planted five churches in our district. Next year, we believe God will help us plant 20 churches."

The second leader said, "Last year we planted eight churches. This year, by God's grace, we intend to plant 25 new churches!"

After hearing that, I was becoming concerned. I said to Munyewe, "Don't you think they may be setting goals which are too high? Can they expand leadership to handle all those new churches that fast?"

"Don't worry," he replied, "If they say they will plant 25 new churches, they will do it."

I didn't say anything more. After all six district leaders had related their goals, they had pledged to plant 67 new churches in one year! I was thinking, "Thirty-six churches to plant 67 new churches in one year? They will probably never make it! But if they even come close to half that many, it could mean the beginnings of a real people movement toward Christianity among the Yao!"

I confess I did not have much faith that EBC leaders could reach their goal. But I decided to wait and see what would happen in 12 months, by May 1988. What I didn't understand was that EBC leaders were not making a 12-month goal!

I began to receive letters from Munyewe with excerpts like this one:

> What fire of the Holy Spirit has been started by you has really burned far beyond what we expected. The Holy Spirit really used you to challenge the elders here to know their role. The very week you went, I received word that small churches of 15-18 people were started here in Liwonde. Today, I have heard that 20 of these churches have been started! The urgency to spread the word has really burned into their hearts! (10)

To make a long story a short one, I received a letter from Munyewe in December 1987. He wrote:

> I am happy to report that all our districts have reached their goals. All the churches have been started. The district leaders have now been asking what their next goals should be. (11)

They had planted all 67 churches not in 12 months, but in seven months! I was amazed! Also within that year, EBC had exceeded its goal to send missionaries, fielding a total of 13 new missionaries. This was more than all the previous years combined! Just as important, it wasn't just the missionaries who were participating in the outreach toward the Yao. All the EBC churches had been mobilized to become involved directly in evangelizing Yao Muslims.

Consolidation

As it turned out, I was not altogether unwise in my original concern about the feasibility of such rapid growth. Though many new churches were planted, all of them could not be sustained without being combined with others because of lack of qualified local leadership. When all the

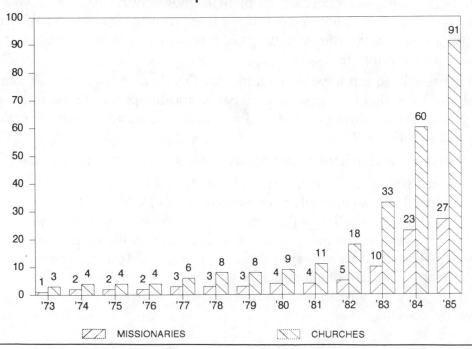

FIGURE EBC - 4
EBC MISSIONARIES AND CHURCHES
Comparison of Growth

FIGURE EBC - 5
EBC CHURCHES
Annual Growth Rates

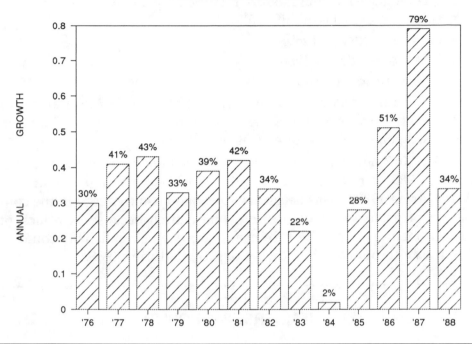

combinations over the past two years are taken into account, the net gain in new churches which remain is 27 new churches for 1987 (Figure EBC-4). That was four times the gain of two years earlier and almost twice the gain of a year earlier (Figure EBC-5).

This need for consolidation does point to the continuing need to train new leaders rapidly. With that in mind, a comprehensive proposal for an extension training system has been established. Some initial funding subsidy has been provided through OC Ministries in cooperation with Globalink Ministries of Waynesboro, Virginia, U.S.A. Emmanuel International of Ottawa, Canada will soon be sending a specialist, Reverend Jim Cannon, for 18 months to help EBC initiate the training program. If additional start-up funding can be obtained, the training program should be well under way in the near future.

The fruit of the vision

The growth of EBC churches, membership, leaders and missionaries increased dramatically from 1984 to 1988. An examination of that growth can be as instructive as much as inspiring. It is especially a testimony to the leadership of Matthias Munyewe and the dedication of the EBC churches to evangelize the Yao.

After having experienced only 2% growth in membership in 1984, for each succeeding year through 1987, membership increased by increasingly greater numbers (Figure EBC-6):

- 486 were added in 1985
- 1154 were added in 1986
- 2666 were added in 1987

The 1987 figures reflect the highest rate of growth (79%) for any year since 1975 and are a reflection of the cross-cultural ministry seminar and the increased goals which resulted (see Figure EBC-5).

In 1988, 2,057 new members were added. While this was not as much as during 1987, it reflected a 34% gain which is very high for annual growth. During 1988, it was necessary to expend some energy in the consolidation of groups of churches into one church because of a lack of enough trained leaders to be responsible for each church. This could at least partially account for the slowing of growth during 1988.

FIGURE EBC - 6
EBC MEMBERSHIP GROWTH

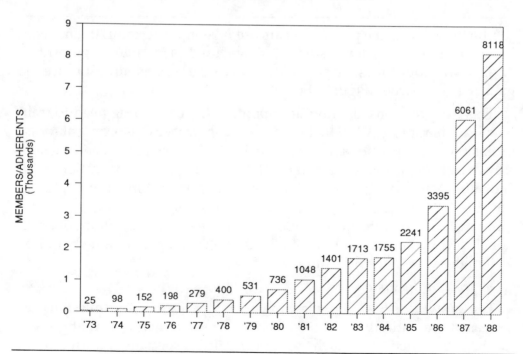

FIGURE EBC - 7
EBC MEMBERSHIP
Average Anuual Growth

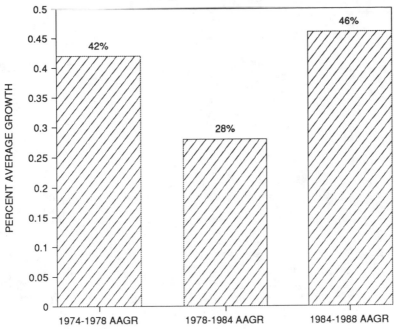

One thing is clear, however. The growth rates of the 1984-1988 period significantly exceeded the previous periods. It even surpassed the rapid growth of the early years, which is unusual. Usually, as denominations grow older, their rates of growth slow down. (12) That is why EBC's average annual growth of 46% from 1984 to 1988 is so significant (see Figure EBC-7). If that growth can be sustained, EBC membership will rise to 36,884 by 1992!

Leadership growth

An important factor for continued growth will be to find a way to rapidly reproduce new leaders while they are still active in ministry. Figure EBC-8 shows the total number of gospel workers for each year. This includes pastors, elders and missionaries. Figure EBC-9 compares the average annual growth in leadership with the average annual growth in membership. There is a direct correlation between the two. This means EBC's plan to expand its leadership base is critical to its continued growth.

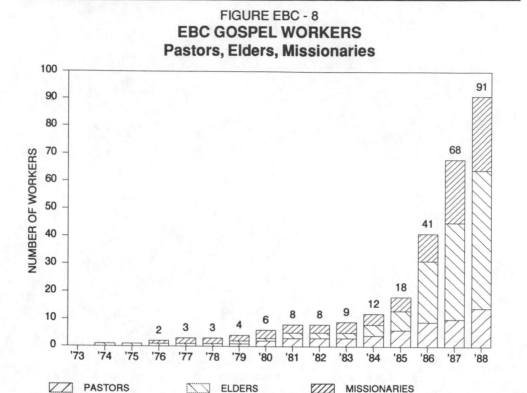

FIGURE EBC - 8
EBC GOSPEL WORKERS
Pastors, Elders, Missionaries

NUMBER OF WORKERS

PASTORS   ELDERS   MISSIONARIES

There are already indications that growth has been hindered by a lack of growth in the number of trained leaders. The 14 leaders given the title of "pastor" actually are overseers of an average of six or seven churches each. The "elders" actually are in charge of a single local church. The number of churches under each pastor's care cannot continue to expand much more. There must be more pastors trained.

Furthermore, had there been enough leaders at the elder level, it is likely there would have been no need to consolidate the 47 churches which had already been planted in 1987. Were those churches to have continued with adequate leadership, EBC would have at least 138 churches by now and a considerably higher membership. A method for rapidly reproducing leaders is a must for the future growth of EBC.

Church planting

Growth in the rate of church planting has increased even more rapidly than average annual membership growth (Figure EBC-10). Rates of growth were similar for 1974 to 1978 and 1978 to 1984. But the more rapid rate of growth for churches planted (70%) for 1984 to 1988 represents a greater potential for future evangelism. This is because there remains greater evanelism potential when the churches do not have a high average membership. This demonstrates the direct relationship between planting new churches and gaining new members for EBC. Church planting must remain a very high priority if rapid growth is to continue.

Growth of missionary team

Another factor which was very significant in the growth of EBC is the increase in their missionaries. The number of missionaries rose in similar proportion to growth in churches (see Figure EBC-4). This indicates it will be important to continue to expand the number of missionaries to unreached Yao areas in order to facilitate the planting of churches. This is especially true in order for EBC to succeed in their desire to evangelize the Yao.

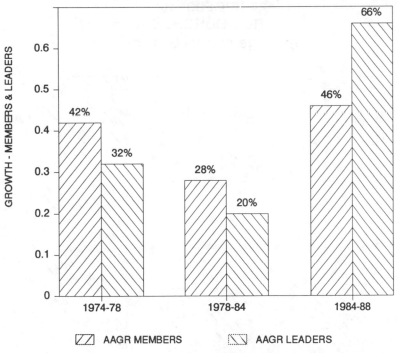

FIGURE EBC - 9
EBC GROWTH OF LEADERSHIP
Compared to Growth of Membership

Evangelism of Yao Muslims

Figure 11 shows the present percentage of EBC membership from animistic backgrounds, nominal Christian backgrounds, and from the Yao Muslim background. By the end of 1989, 46% of the total, or 3,735 members, were from the Yao Muslim background.

By the end of 1988, there were a total of 50 EBC churches in Yao villages. All of them worship in the Yao language. In addition, another 25 churches (usually in towns) are a mixture of Yao and Chichewa or Yao and Lomwe tribes. Ministry and worship are now bilingual. All of this has greatly contributed to the evangelism of the Yao. Together, this means a total of 75 of the 91 EBC churches have at least a significant percentage of their membership who are converted Yao Muslims! (see Figure EBC-12)

This phenomenal growth means EBC has far more Yao churches and members than any other denomination in Central Africa. There is great potential for EBC to evangelize a large percentage of Yao in the future. It

FIGURE EBC - 10
EBC CHURCHES
Average Annual Growth

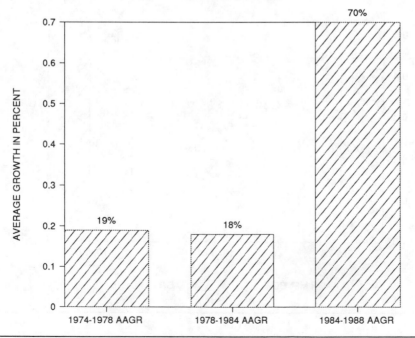

82

is our prayer that EBC will receive all the spiritual, human and financial resources necessary to make this vision a reality!

EBC partnerships

Nobody will probably ever know the full extent of the sacrificial service of EBC Christians and their leader, Matthias Munyewe. Their zeal, love and reaching out to the people of Malawi and the Yao Tribe, in particular, will probably not be known very far and wide. That commitment, together with the inspirational, dynamic leadership of Munyewe is the major reason they have been such a blessing to others and effective in their work.

But there have been a few others besides me who have recognized the potential of EBC. For the most part, these people have chosen to work in partnership with them in some valuable but unobtrusive ways. Perhaps the one who recognized EBC potential first was the Reverend Terry Orchard of Emmanuel International of Ottawa, Canada. Orchard visited Malawi on two occasions in 1983 and 1984. He taught leaders, preached

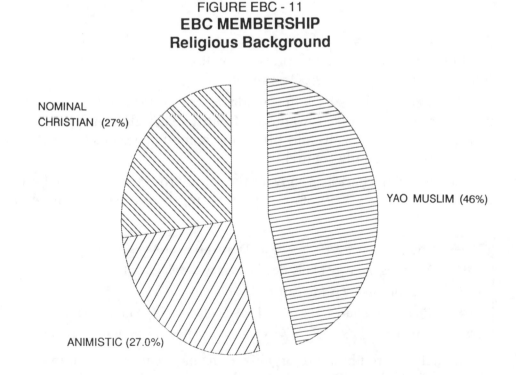

FIGURE EBC - 11
EBC MEMBERSHIP
Religious Background

NOMINAL CHRISTIAN (27%)

YAO MUSLIM (46%)

ANIMISTIC (27.0%)

FIGURE EBC - 12
EBC CHURCHES
By Language Group

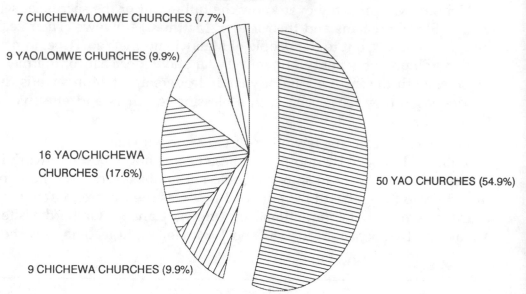

7 CHICHEWA/LOMWE CHURCHES (7.7%)

9 YAO/LOMWE CHURCHES (9.9%)

16 YAO/CHICHEWA CHURCHES (17.6%)

50 YAO CHURCHES (54.9%)

9 CHICHEWA CHURCHES (9.9%)

in churches and was highly praised for his abilities and willingness to live and work among the EBC members.

Although now he is back in Canada, he continues to expend considerable energy to help EBC through EIM. Since 1987, EIM has provided resources for digging wells and providing some village health services in poor areas through EBC churches.

The following chart lists some of the other groups which have become involved with the EBC in its ministry, noting when they began helping and what they contribute:

Dates	Organization	Description of Assistance
1984	Preparing the Way Ministries	Literacy development
1988	Preparing the Way Ministries	Audio tapes
1988	Kings Way Church, U.K.	US $11,000 to help build six churches
1989	Tear Fund, U.K.	Assumed funding for literacy program

The help offered by these organizations has been very valuable to encourage EBC in their outreach into the communities where they serve.

Because these organizations have entrusted those programs to EBC leadership, they have been effective in helping many people in some areas where EBC ministers. Equally important is the enhanced receptivity to the gospel which has resulted from this community assistance.

As can readily be seen from the above information, the vast majority of human and material resources for EBC comes from the membership themselves. This is especially true when it comes to the spread of the gospel. Pastors, elders and missionaries are supported by indigenous resources. This is a testimony to the zeal and commitment of EBC to evangelism, church planting and reaching the Yao people.

Significant characteristics of EBC

The Evangelical Baptist Church of Malawi is both a denomination and a mission agency at the same time. It is holistic in its approach to evangelism and church planting. Unlike most Western denominational mission agencies, there is no department or organizational division that distinguishes outreach to the Yao from outreach to the other peoples of Malawi. This holistic approach does not stop missionaries from specializing in their efforts to reach the Yao, as in other mission agencies. But it does encourage the rest of EBC leadership and membership to participate directly in that outreach and in the incorporation of converts into the churches. Let us briefly discuss some other important characteristics of EBC.

Leadership is reproducible

EBC uses an extensive system of lay leadership. Only 14 of the 91 leaders are considered pastors, yet all those leaders together have managed to increase the number of EBC churches from 11 to 91, or 827 percent in the last five years! There is a multi-level system of ministry responsibility, ranging from elders who are in charge of a single local church to missionaries, to pastors, to Chairman Munyewe. The important element is that each higher level of ministry responsibility is based more upon what ministry a leader has accomplished than upon what formal training he has completed. While there is a strong need and desire for more training at all levels of leadership, position is based upon ministry fruitfulness. This allows leadership to rise to the top as a result of giftedness. Such leaders are followed. Such a system is very reproducible.

Generosity and joy!

Rarely have I witnessed a more generous, loving people than those in the EBC churches. They have shared everything from food to housing with those who need it, even though they are very poor themselves. Their generosity is only exceeded by their joy in worship. Their lively, rhythmic syncopated singing is captivating and their worship is heartfelt. This generosity and enthusiasm has proven to be a powerful attraction to unbelievers.

Love for the lost

Perhaps the most important, though immeasurable characteristic of EBC membership, is their love for the lost. Their Christian faith is at the center of their lives. They are genuinely committed to the evangelization of the lost. This commitment supersedes tribal and family loyalties which are very strong in Africa.

Committed, capable leadership

Without question, the individual most responsible for the growth of EBC has been its chairman, Reverend Matthias Munyewe. His excellent, intelligent leadership is combined with a rare commitment and personal integrity. Because of these qualities, he has the complete loyalty of EBC leaders and churches alike, though he is only 34 years old.

Munyewe keeps meticulous records, both in finances and numerical growth of churches, leaders and members. He uses this information to make plans and adjust tactics. He is becoming a master at training and encouraging leaders who develop under him. He works tirelessly as an example to others.

To a large degree, it is the zeal and passion of Matthias Munyewe, multiplied in the hearts of EBC members and leaders, which accounts for the wonderful growth of EBC. The following quote, from an interview just after the cross-cultural training seminar in 1987, reveals the heart of Munyewe:

> As I have already admitted, there was a time when we were not growing much because we were making too many mistakes. We have corrected those mistakes now, and we now have many souls who are seeking and coming to the Lord. If we cause any problems today — if we make any more mistakes — that will mean that thousands and thousands of souls will go to hell. We must not do that. (13)

Such is the zeal and vision of Matthias Munyewe.

Conclusion

The work of EBC, though unusual in its successful outreach to the Yao Muslims, does reflect some characteristics which are common to the missions movement in many parts of Africa. Like EBC, the movement is more holistic and ecclesiocentric than missions movements in some parts of the world, notably the West. Missionary activity is less an activity *outside* the churches and more an activity *through* the churches. The African missionary outreach involves both missionaries and church members in its activities. Because of this holistic approach, there are very few African parachurch missionary ministries.

Another characteristic of EBC missionary ministry common in Africa is the deployment of lay people for missionary purposes. In EBC outreach, some non-paid lay families move to new areas to assist in the establishment of a new work. They assume major responsibilities in the establishment of the new works. This also is a common practice in the more missionary-minded churches of many parts of Africa. It is this mobilization of the laity, even in missionary activity, which accounts for much of the spread of Christianity in Africa from tribe to tribe.

Direct lay involvement in missionary activity is one important aspect of African missions which often makes analysis of the movement by Western categories difficult. If we categorize as missionaries only those who are regularly supported by sending churches or organizations, then we must remove many of the missionaries from the history of Western missions.

The Moravians, for instance, represent one of the most dynamic missionary sending forces in 18th-century Western missions. But they were sent with passage in hand, and little else, to many parts of the world at a phenomenal rate. But after they arrived, they made their living where they were.

Many African missionary outreaches follow a pattern more similar to the Moravians than to present Western models. But does that make them less missionary? I think not! They successfully plant churches and evangelize in previously unreached, or minimally reached areas. They sacrifice homeland, and often family and people, to go to their place of calling. While this often keeps them from our Western missionary statistics, I doubt if it keeps them out of the annals of missionary ministry being written in heaven!

It is hoped the example of EBC will inspire other groups to reach out toward the Yao and other Muslim tribes of Central Africa. The *Unreached Peoples '84* handbook contains a description of the Yao people of Malawi. In it there is a statement concerning the need for increased Christian witness among the Yao:

As the Yao rub shoulders with the Christians in the cities and towns, they have opportunity to receive a personal word of testimony from fellow countrymen. There is no concerted effort to reach Muslims who live in the remote villages of Malawi. Those who live in the cities have the opportunity to hear of Christ's love, but they rarely receive a personal invitation to receive Christ. (14)

Because of the work and dedication of the Evangelical Baptist Churches of Malawi, the above statement is no longer true. The missionary outreach of EBC is making the gospel abundantly available to Yao Muslims in many towns and villages in southern Malawi. It is hoped that the work of EBC among the Yao will prove to be only the beginning of a people movement among the Yao which will bring many thousands to Christ.

FOOTNOTES

(1) Munyewe, Matthias; "Reaching Muslims for Christ," Unpublished paper, January 1989, p. 2.

(2) *Ibid*.

(3) *Ibid*, p. 3.

(4) *Ibid*, p. 4.

(5) Dayton, Edward R., Wilson, Samuel, Eds.; *Unreached Peoples '84*; Monrovia, MARC (Missions Advanced Research & Communication Center), 1984; p. 4.

(6) From the ms. of an interview with Matthias Munyewe conducted in Blantyre, Malawi, May 10, 1987; p. 4.

(7) *Ibid*.

(8) *Ibid*.

(9) Reported in a telephone conversation with the Rev. Terry Orchard on March 14, 1989.

(10) Reported in a letter from Matthias Munyewe to Larry D. Pate, June 9, 1987.

(11) Reported in a letter from Matthias Munyewe to Larry D. Pate, dated December 12, 1987.

(12) It is important to measure the rate of growth as well as the actual numerical growth, because *rates* of growth measure actual reproduction. It is common for numerical growth to increase while rates of growth decline because rates are the percentage of growth based upon the difference between (usually the last) two data points. For instance, if a church started with 100 members and grew numerically by 100 members each year, its rate of growth would follow this pattern:

100%, 50%, 33.4%, 25%, etc. Rates of growth measure the degree of reproduction of each previous year's membership.

(13) *Op. cit.*, Interview, (6), May 10, 1987, p. 6.

(14) Dayton, *op. cit.*, p. 344.

From Every People

BIRTH OF A MISSIONS MOVEMENT

ARGENTINA

BIRTH OF A MISSIONS MOVEMENT

by Jonathan Lewis with Larry D. Pate

Introduction

What does it take to generate a missions movement in a country which has been a missionary receiving nation for over 100 years? A simple answer is that it takes vision plus an acute awareness of each church's responsibility to make disciples of all nations. But how does the national church come to the point of being able to accept that vision? And, once the vision is implanted, how does it manage the awesome logistics involved in sending missionaries? The following emerging missions story centers on how one country is overcoming missions inertia and moving a generation of Christians towards full participation in the Great Commission.

Europe in Latin America

Argentina is a land rich in natural wealth. Geographically, it is the eighth largest nation in the world. During the last two centuries, fertile soils attracted settlers from Europe in several large migratory waves. This influx established its character as a European society on Latin territory. Eighty-five percent of its 30 million inhabitants are of pure European descent. The other 15% are mixed Indian and pure Indian races.

The immigrants brought their religion with them. Until recently, Catholicism has had an unquestioned hold on the country, both socially and politically. The flow of immigrants included Protestant groups from Germany, Great Britain and Russia who maintained their religious traditions. But the total proportion of evangelical Christians remained well under 1% of the population until recently.

Missions to Argentina

The first missionary outreaches to Argentina were initiated during the last half of the 19th century by the Methodists and the Baptists. During the first part of this century, the need for railroad construction crews brought another wave of immigrants who were followed by European missionaries. Plymouth Brethren came from Great Britain. Swedish and Italian Pentecostal missionaries also arrived in small numbers.

During the 1930s and 1940s, solid mission efforts were also initiated by denominational groups from North America. These included the Assemblies of God, the Church of God, the Southern Baptists and the Christian and Missionary Alliance. Currently, there are approximately 590 missionaries to Argentina, representing 58 denominations. (1)

In spite of these concentrated mission efforts, the Protestant church in Argentina remained an extremely small and somewhat persecuted minority. This, in part, explains why the concept of sending missionaries to other countries was a totally novel idea to the general Christian population when it was first suggested.

Within this context, "missions" had always been the term used for efforts to initiate new works in unevangelized neighborhoods and towns within Argentina and, to this day, remains the primary outreach focus of most churches. I have often heard the accusation that missionaries failed to teach the Argentine church her responsibility for sending missionaries to the unreached peoples of the world and this may well be. Nevertheless, it is consistent with the Great Commission to assume that because thousands of communities remain without a permanent Christian witness within Argentina, the church should make a concerted effort to evangelize its own nation. But it is also consistent with the Great Commission to infuse a vision for the whole world into the hearts of Argentine believers. That concept should be allowed to mature simultaneously with the church, something missionaries from outside the country have usually failed to do.

First signs of missions interest

When does the church in one nation show signs of "coming of age," demonstrating the capability to generate its own missionary movement? One indicator seems to be the presence of rapid church growth. As a general rule, it is safe to say that most of the national churches actively involved in sending missionaries cross-culturally have experienced, or are currently experiencing, dynamic quantitative growth. Through numeric strength, these churches have reached a point of "critical mass" which allows them not only to attend to normal evangelistic activities but to also occupy themselves with cross-cultural and foreign mission efforts.

Argentina is no exception to this rule. Having been recognized by leading missiologists as a "flashpoint" of church growth, the evangelical community has experienced a phenomenal quantitative increase in the last few years. In 1982 it was estimated that less than 3% of the general population of Argentina was evangelical. In 1986, information from a poll taken by a secular agency concluded that those identified with the evangelical church comprised 6% of the total population. Current estimates, two years later, put the figure at around 8%.

These figures reflect the numbers of people who have made some commitment to Christ through evangelistic efforts, but not necessarily those who have been incorporated into the evangelical church. A recent census of the major denominations indicates that these growth figures are not reflected in membership statistics.(2) Consolidation of the harvest is, perhaps, the church's most critical task at this time.

If the present levels of evangelism are maintained, we can calculate that 20% of the Argentine population will have made an initial commitment to Christ by the year 2000.

This encouraging growth, which some are calling a genuine revival, can be attributed to many factors. In simplest terms, it is the result of intense hunger for spiritual reality caused by the social and economic upheaval the country has undergone in recent years. In 1982, through peaceful means, Argentines overthrew a repressive military dictatorship which had led the country into a fruitless war with Great Britain and left the nation saddled with a $50 billion debt. The fledgling democracy inherited economic problems that they have not been able to solve. Spiraling inflation combined with recessionary tendencies have caused the standard of living to drop significantly. In the midst of crumbling economic hopes and aspirations, people have faced deeper spiritual issues and many are finding new meaning in a personal relationship with Christ.

This unprecedented interest in spiritual matters, combined with a general recognition of the spiritual bankruptcy of the traditional religion, has created a vacuum which the Gospel has been able to fill for many people. Aggressive mass evangelistic ministries, led by some key men God has raised up, has stimulated the evangelistic fervor of the church in general, and almost all congregations have experienced growth.

Local churches with memberships numbering in the thousands are not uncommon. One which initiated its activities five years ago in the city of Cordoba draws 8,000 adherents to its principal meeting on Sundays.

Crowds of 40,000 have stood night after night in open fields to hear native evangelist Carlos Anacondia, and as many as 50,000 decisions for Christ have been registered in a single city during one of his campaigns. Pastor Omar Cabrera has adopted the approach of a single congregation which has divisions in many locations. He travels continually to minister to the estimated 140,000 followers of his message. In the midst of this great harvest, the Spirit has manifested His power continually through miracles of healings, deliverance and changed lives.

Giving birth is not easy

In 1982, shortly after the current Argentine harvest had begun, MEI, an indigenous interdenominational church organization, sponsored a national pastors' conference. One of the invited speakers was Luis Palau, a native son who is a well-known international evangelist. During one of the plenary sessions, Palau, who bases his ministry in the United States, exhorted the 900 participants of the congress to consider the possibility of sending Argentines throughout Latin America and the world. He said the unique personality and cultural traits of Argentine Christians could be used to good advantage in the cause of the Gospel. Palau's own success as well as that of several other Argentines who have reached positions of international Christian leadership, bears testimony to the appropriateness of his admonition.

Among those at the conference who heard Palau's challenge was a pastor from Santa Fe, Federico Bertuzzi. This unique young man is the son of a second-generation Italian immigrant. His mother was a recent arrival from Germany. He accepted Christ as a teenager through the ministry of a Baptist church in his home town. His father died when he was only two, leaving Federico's mother little with which to raise her two sons.

Shortly after his conversion, Federico traveled to Germany with his mother where he pursued studies in art and later at the Brake Bible School. While in Germany, he also came into contact with Operation Mobilization. Through their ministries, Federico had his eyes opened to the needs of the unreached peoples of the world. Returning with his mother to Argentina in 1968, he enrolled in the Buenos Aires Bible Institute and, after graduation, accepted the pastorate in the same church where he had first heard the Gospel.

As he listened to Palau's exhortation in 1982, he felt that a unique opportunity was presenting itself to discuss the challenge of world missions with those assembled, something that was very close to his heart. After the meeting, an impromptu session was held for those interested in exploring the implications of sending Argentine missionaries to foreign fields. About 100 pastors and leaders attended. As an outcome of that encounter, it was decided that an organization should be formed to promote this vision in Argentina. This entity was simply called "Misiones Mundiales" (World Missions) and its elected director was Federico Bertuzzi. In the years to come, when the history of the Argentine missions is written, it is very likely that Bertuzzi will come to be known as the father of that movement.

Growing involvement

Three years passed in which the fledgling organization was little more than an archive in Federico's filing cabinet. Pastoring a growing church was an all-consuming task. That, together with extremely limited resources, restricted the activities of Misiones Mundiales to little more than a few mailings sent to a swelling number of missions enthusiasts.

This publication work, as well as an increasing demand for Federico as a missions speaker, eventually led him to a crisis point in his ministry. He would have to choose between full-time commitment to raising the vision for world evangelization in Argentina, or commitment to the pastorate. He could not do both. In September of 1985, after much prayer and waiting on the Lord, Federico resigned his 11-year-old pastorate with the full blessing and financial support of his church. He began dedicating himself completely to the task of growing a missions movement in Argentina.

A strategy for strength

From the outset, Federico's strategy was to win over the churches' leadership to Christ's global cause. At first he was uncertain how to proceed. He thought about making Misiones Mundiales a model sending agency, then encourage other groups to organize their own mission efforts. Finally, he decided it would be best for Misiones Mundiales to play a catalytic role, encouraging many groups to send missionaries. By not becoming a sending agency, he would not be competing for the resources of churches. This would make his message less of a threat and Misiones Mundiales could be a resource agency to serve all the churches.

Using his remarkable gifting in "public relations" to best advantage, Bertuzzi began building a network of relationships within the evangelical community. He soon gained the confidence of many church leaders because he never asked for anything and was always willing to use his time and limited resources sacrificially in serving others.

Bertuzzi describes the role of Misiones Mundiales as "the starter motor for world missions in Argentina." His non-threatening approach worked very well in bringing together evangelicals from a great many denominations, under the banner of world evangelization. The main vehicle for spreading the missionary vision has been missions consultations for pastors and other leaders, organized by Misiones Mundiales.

In 1986, I received an invitation from Misiones Mundiales and ACIERA to join Federico in his work. I traveled to Argentina with my family in May of that year. Having been born in Argentina of missionary parents, I have the unique advantage of enjoying dual citizenship. It was a unique invitation to work within this "indigenous" mission organization. I had already served as a missionary in Peru and spent the previous three years developing a missions course in Spanish. So I welcomed the opportunity to work with Misiones Mundiales, particularly in the development of missionary training programs.

Our immediate objective upon arrival in Argentina was the publication of our three volume missionary training manuals entitled *Mision Mundial*. (3) These were to be introduced at "Mission '86" the annual pastors' conference sponsored again by MEI, this time on the theme of world missions.

First National Missions Conference

In 1986, MEI decided to sponsor its annual pastors' conference under the theme of missions. This marked one more significant step in the progress of the Argentine missions movement.

Mission '86 was a major victory for the cause of world evangelization in Argentina. For the first time ever, this theme was given a national platform. Paul Smith of Toronto's People's Church, Edison Queiroz, current director of COMIBAM, and John White, internationally-known author, were among the world class speakers who challenged the hearts of the pastors and leaders who attended the conference.

Many of those assembled were being confronted with missions for the very first time. Dozens of workshops were offered during the afternoons. On Saturday, the conference ranks were swelled by youth from churches around the country. Over 150 of these young people committed their lives for mission service at the end of the rally that evening.

There is a saying in Spanish that (roughly translated) states, "Between the intention and the fact, there's a long path." Motivating people to make a commitment to mission service apparently was not going to be tough in Argentina. Getting them to the mission field was another matter! Without the support of leaders and pastors at every level from the local church to denominational headquarters, the emerging mission spirit would be suppressed. This fact was soon to be born out in the lives of many young people. Having made an initial commitment to missions, they found themselves totally frustrated by the lack of support from their churches and pastors. There was a discouraging scarcity of opportunity to be trained or sent by mission organizations. Only the few who have received encouragement from their churches are reaching their goal.

One such person is Bibiana, a young doctor who received her "calling" while specializing in tropical medicine in Brazil. She came to Mission '86 looking for specific guidance on where to serve as a missionary. What she got instead was a practical dose of advice on the importance of Biblical preparation and involvement in the local church.

Undaunted by the prospect of several years of additional preparation, she enrolled in a local Bible school. With the support of the elders of her church in Buenos Aires, she pioneered the organization of a functional missions committee and worked diligently in developing its program. One of their first activities was to sponsor an inter-church missions seminar over the course of two weekends for which Misiones Mundiales provided the program and lecturers.

Bibiana's missiological training has come primarily by working through the self-instructional course we introduced at Mission '86. She also took an intensive course offered in January of '88 by Misiones Mundiales. In addition to this theoretical preparation, in October of '88 she had the opportunity to travel to Haiti where her heart was captured by the physical and spiritual needs of the people. Her medical skills were also put to good use.

At this writing, her church is on the eve of their third missionary conference and is working out the logistics for sending Bibiana back to Haiti for a longer term. In this whole process, three other young people from her church have emerged with a strong commitment to foreign mission service. As part of their practical training, they are involved together in an outreach to the nearby delta region of the Parana River, an area accessible only by hours of river travel in small craft.

Bibiana's story is a bright spot in the emerging missions picture. Unfortunately, there are many like Bibiana who have responded in their hearts to God's call, but unlike her, have not been given a nurturing environment to develop that calling.

The knowledge that without committed leadership, the latent potential in the hundreds of young missions volunteers would not be realized continued to drive Federico in his zeal to win the nation's evangelical leadership to the cause of world missions.

A proliferation of conferences

In November of 1986 the first national leaders' mission consultation was held in a retreat center near the capital city of Buenos Aires. This "by invitation only gathering" was attended by some 80 top evangelical leaders. The consultation, which adopted a seminar approach, allowed for the presentation of papers on mission themes with a discussion following. During the prayer time after one such exposition, a spirit of repentance manifested itself, and tears were shed for having neglected the world mission task which is so explicit in Scriptures. Needless to say, this consultation proved to be a spiritual landmark for the emerging mission movement in Argentina.

Soon after Federico took full-time responsibilities for Misiones Mundiales he was also asked to serve as regional coordinator for COMIBAM '87 (Congreso Misionero Iberoamericano). This is an indigenous movement toward developing missions throughout Latin America. It culminated in an international missions conference for the whole of the Spanish- and Portuguese-speaking world, held in Sao Paulo, Brazil in November of 1987.

The work of serving on the organizing committee and promoting this conference not only in Argentina, but in several neighboring countries as well, was the primary thrust of Federico's activities that year. It also put Federico in contact with leading missionary thinkers in Latin America and other parts of the world. Consistent with his philosophy, he aimed at getting as many pastors and leaders to COMIBAM '87 as possible.

In order to promote the conference and build on the spirit of the national mission consultation, several regional leaders' consultations were organized that year. Each of these took on its own character, but prayer for the unreached nations was always an integral part of the event.

During one of these times, after praying in twos and threes for nations of the world as the Spirit led, the moderator asked if anyone had been burdened for any country in particular. Instantly a voice rang out "Italia," followed by a whole chorus of "Italia," "Italia," "Italia!" Italy, the motherland for many Argentines whose fathers and grandfathers had migrated from there, has become a prime target for this generation's hopeful missionaries. Spain and the North of Africa also have begun to emerge as objective mission fields.

The interest in Spain and Italy can be attributed to the racial links with these countries but the interest in North Africa is not so easily traced. It is true that the 800-year domination of Spain by the Moors has produced significant racial and cultural affinity. Many Argentines' physiological features and coloring bear resemblance to those of North Africans. There are an estimated 6,000 Spanish words derived from Arabic root sources as well. Cultural similarities have also been noted in the area of relationships and time values, but this in itself does not satisfactorily explain the emerging focus on Muslim evangelism. The only motivating factor that adequately clarifies this phenomenon is the work of the Holy Spirit in drawing Latins to this tremendous challenge in world evangelization. This is demonstrated by that fact that fully 33% of the missionaries being sent outside the country by the emerging Argentine missions movement are being sent to Muslims in Africa and Pakistan. (4)

Misiones Mundiales becomes a hub

By 1987 Misiones Mundiales had become the central hub of missionary activity in Argentina. Both ACIERA and CEP (Confraternidad Evangelica Pentecostal) looked to Misiones Mundiales and to Bertuzzi to coordinate the activities of this growing movement.

The newly installed computer at Misiones Mundiales worked overtime during 1987. The database cranked out letters and labels for mailings concerning the consultation and COMIBAM. Federico had also agreed to publish two books for the COMIBAM congress in Brazil. Eventually, two more computers were added for word processing and a laser printer for publication work.

The organization's staff also grew quickly. A full-time secretary came on to manage correspondence and word processing. A half-time assistant was added to handle shipping and other office tasks. Both women were supported through donations to the organization and Federico's church maintained his full support. As a matter of policy, he had decided that Misiones Mundiales must be financed solely by the Argentine evangelical community if it was going to live the message that it preached. Bertuzzi firmly believed that Argentina could and must become a sending nation.

COMIBAM '87 brought together over 3,000 participants from every Spanish- and Portuguese-speaking country of the world and many observers from other nations. The five-day conference was packed to the limit with plenary sessions, teaching times and dozens of workshops. The impressive roster of speakers and lecturers included many of Latin America's most prominent pastors and veteran missionaries as well as emerging mission leaders from other continents. Among those attending were some 280 delegates from Argentina.

A significant event occurred at COMIBAM when the Argentine delegates met together in an afternoon meeting. They voted unanimously to work toward the establishment of a national, interdenominational missionary sending agency.

The impact of this conference on the overall development of the mission movement from Latin America is still to be measured, but the observable results in the lives of those with whom we are personally acquainted has been remarkable. Infused with a bright vision of Latin involvement in the Great Commission, they have returned to Argentina to work diligently at making this a reality in their own sphere of influence.

One evidence of this zeal was three regional missions conferences conducted in Argentina during 1988. They were organized largely by COMIBAM delegates with the assistance of Misiones Mundiales. Patterned after the great conference in Brazil, each of these three events drew from 300 to 500 full delegates and many more participants to the evening meetings. As a result of these meetings, hundreds of young people and leaders signed cards manifesting their desire to be directly involved in taking the Gospel to the unreached peoples of the world. The vision was spreading more rapidly!

Unity in missions

One of the most remarkable side benefits of the consultations and conferences is the spirit of unity with which they have been implemented. Argentina, like most mission fields of the world, has allowed denominational rivalries to divide its evangelical community. But world missions has proven to be an excellent banner under which to rally Christians from across the spectrum of evangelically-oriented persuasions. When the magnitude of the unfinished task is clearly understood, interdenominational squabbling fades to insignificance.

To foster this kind of unity in missions was part of the goal of Misiones Mundiales from the outset. Its national Board of Reference was chosen carefully to represent the widest denominational spectrum. All the consultations and conferences were organized and carried out by committees that also reflected the broadest representation possible. Likewise, a denominational balance was always sought in selecting the speakers and moderators for each event.

This careful approach has resulted in evangelicals from many backgrounds sharing common times of blessing and fellowship through the consultations and conferences. It has also produced some long-range commitments to work together. In Cordoba, for example, a committee has been organized that is sponsoring city-wide mission related events on a monthly basis and has as its long-term goal to function as a missionary channeling agency for churches in its area.

Practical issues

Once the missions flame had been lighted in these hundreds of hearts, pastors and leaders began to struggle with the practical issues of training and sending. Since the Argentine church has had little experience in either area, getting these structures into place is a major hurdle. Consistent with its policy of not competing with existing organizations, Misiones Mundiales has aimed at stimulating churches and denominations to create their own structures and programs necessary to carry out these tasks. Part of this work has been accomplished through additional national consultations.

Missionary training

In August of 1987, missions professors and directors from the major Bible institutes and seminaries in Argentina met together to discuss the critical lack of missions education in theological institutions. Most of the schools had no course on missions. Only one, an interdenominational seminary in Buenos Aires — SEIT, had any program for those with vocational (tentmaking) missionary interests.

Stimulated by this consultation, many schools are now offering, or are planning to offer, courses in missiology. There are currently two full, tertiary level training programs available through theological institutions, a four-year bachelors degree program at SEIT and a three-year certificate program at the Cordoba Bible Institute (IBC). Operation Mobilization and Youth With a Mission are also initiating year-long programs with a missionary training focus.

FLET, a theological education by extension program, introduced a self-instructional, one-year certificate course in its curriculum, thus making missions study available in many areas throughout the country.

One of the earliest attempts to provide mission education on a popular level was an intensive, one-week course sponsored by Misiones

Mundiales in January of 1988. Forty hours of instruction were offered in a camp setting and this proved to be a tremendous blessing to those who attended. The course was offered again in February of 1989 in another part of the country and, again, enjoyed great success. Current plans are to shift the location of the camp each year and, in this manner, cover the country.

Virtually all the programs to provide missionary training in Argentina have been initiated within the last two years. This development does much to insure that the Argentine missions movement will continue to expand.

Training Trainers

Most of those involved in training missionaries at this time are either foreign missionaries to Argentina or self-taught nationals who have had no actual missionary experience. One exception to this rule is Marcelo Abel, 20-year missionary veteran to the Tobas of northern Argentina. His extensive knowledge of cross-cultural mission and many anecdotes have been the highlight of the afore-mentioned summer courses. But he is one of the few Argentines whose knowledge of missions goes beyond the theoretical. This shortage of qualified missionary trainers is a critical problem currently facing the Argentine missions movement.

As a partial solution to this problem, missionary trainers and potential trainers are being encouraged to be involved in short-term, intensive cross-cultural experiences. These are organized by Misiones Mundiales in conjunction with Marcelo Abel and the Toba tribe of northern Argentina. The Toba tribe has largely been evangelized and approximately 50% are Christians. They have willingly provided what amounts to an excellent cross-cultural laboratory right in Argentina. Missions teachers, such as Juana de Lavateli and Rogelio Castillo of the Cordoba Bible Institute (IBC), have been able to spend two weeks at a time living with Toba families. This brings to life what was only understood in theory.

In addition to this practical experience, missions professors at the institute are currently enrolled in graduate level courses offered by extension through the Latin American Institute of Missiology in Costa Rica (IMDELA). The long-range goal in this relationship is to have IBC function as an extension center of IMDELA in the south.

Missionary support

Although a great deal of measurable progress has been made toward launching the Argentine missions movement, there are still many hurdles to overcome. Unless one lives in a country experiencing severe recessionary inflation, it is difficult to imagine the economic pressures brought to bear on its citizens. The question of missionary support is one which has not been addressed adequately.

It has yet to be demonstrated that the typical North American and European model of church-based support is a solution for funding the Argentine missions movement. Those churches which have made dollar commitments to outgoing missionaries during the past year have found that inflation has priced dollars out of their reach. The result has been economic distress on the part of the missionaries and discouragement for the supporting base.

Self-support or "tentmaking" may be one important alternative model. A small number of professional tentmakers are already among Argentine missionaries overseas.

Partnerships may also be part of the answer. International sending organizations like Operation Mobilization and Youth With a Mission have already established partnership ties in Argentina. However, inter-church or inter-agency partnerships have yet to develop. Denominations could partner with their counterparts in other parts of the world to send and maintain Argentine missionaries on the field.

These approaches are not new, but they have yet to become a significant factor in Argentine support models. Until prototypes are created and successfully tested, it is unlikely that large numbers of Argentine missionaries will find their way to the field. Solving the problems related to funding missionaries in spite of international currency fluctuations is a critical need for the Argentine missions movement.

Sending structures

An even larger hurdle to cross than that of training is the issue of sending. Most of the denominations do not have any active mechanism for sending missionaries. There are some foreign based para-church organizations such as Campus Crusade for Christ and Youth With A Mission. Because of the scarcity of sending organizations, there have been few agencies to which aspiring missionaries can apply.

A good number of Latin American agencies are beginning to emerge, however, and there is promise that this situation will eventually be remedied. One of these agencies is Project Magreb, which aims at Muslim evangelism in northern Africa and the Middle East. Currently, there are six Argentine missionaries serving in this mission.

In July of 1988, a second national leaders' consultation was convened in the capital to discuss the issue of sending. Denominations were invited to send their top leaders to consider how they could start their own sending agencies. Some 55 denominational leaders from around the country attended. During the two days of meetings, Larry Pate, of Overseas Crusades' Emerging Missions Department, led the group through a step-by-step consideration of the whole process of establishing missionary-sending organizations. The objective was not to prescribe a particular method or type of organization for sending missionaries. Rather, each leader was encouraged to think through important principles, issues and questions related to organizing a sending organization.

A unique sending model

Partly as a result of this event, a national assembly of Christian leaders was convened in the capital in September of 1988 to discuss the possibility of establishing the national interdenominational mission agency which had first been proposed at COMIBAM. At this meeting, it was decided to make Misiones Mundiales the umbrella organization for establishing such a national agency.

Until such a national agency is fully established, it was decided that Misiones Mundiales will expand its role to assist churches and newer mission organizations in the logistics of sending their missionaries. This assistance is to be focused primarily on logistical tasks which would be difficult for churches or smaller agencies to accomplish themselves. Such tasks include researching government regulations, obtaining visas, networking with existing mission efforts in the target countries, and channeling funds outside Argentina. A committee was elected from those present to study the legal entity best suited to this purpose and draw up its statutes and internal regulations for later approval by the general assembly.

The establishment of this national Argentine mission agency is virtually without parallel anywhere in the world. To our knowledge, there is no other country where a national, interdenominational sending agency has been established to service the sending needs of such a wide spectrum of churches and denominations. Perhaps the closest parallel is the Philippines Mission Association (PMA), directed by Dr. Met Castillo. Though it is not a sending agency per se, PMA does *function* in a manner similar to the Argentine model being developed.

Though this national sending agency is presently under the umbrella of Misiones Mundiales, it has yet to take its final organizational form.

However, it will function as a service agency through which churches and denominations can send their own missionaries, as described above. It was decided to initiate its ministries under the umbrella of Misiones Mundiales because of the broad base of acceptance and trust developed by that organization. Functionally, this means even a local church, or a group of local churches, can band together to send missionaries through the national agency. Since Argentine ministries are very strongly church-based, this promises to open the door much wider to Argentine missions sending.

First fruits

In spite of the difficulties involved, there have been encouraging signs. Prior to 1988, most of the Argentines who were serving overseas were "self-starters" who had gone to the U.S. and from there based their ministries, or been sent to other Latin countries to head up denominational projects.

By marked contrast, during 1988 local churches united to send missionaries to nine other countries. It is notable that three of the persons sent out are doctors, indicating the potential inherent in the relatively

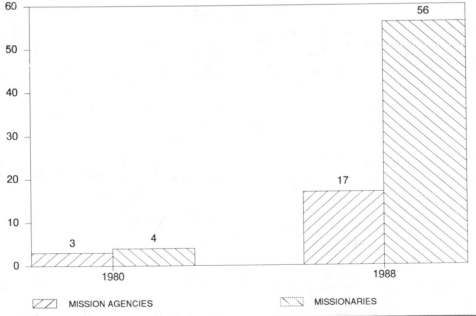

FIGURE ARG-1
REPORTED ARGENTINA MISSIONS
Agencies and Missionaries

large evangelical professional class. This initial contingent of cross-cultural missionaries is the "first-fruits" of what hopefully will become a significant tributary in the stream of the global missions movement.

Presently, 17 churches and mission organizations have reported sending at least 56 Argentine missionaries to ten countries. This compares very favorably with three reporting missionary agencies who confirmed sending four missionaries in 1980 (see Figure ARG-1). (5) Target countries and regions of reported Argentine missionaries are as follows:

Country	# of Missionaries
Bolivia	1
Dominican Republic	1
Italy	2
Pakistan	1
Paraguay	6
Peru	2
Spain	3
Zaire	4
North Africa	7
Argentina	29

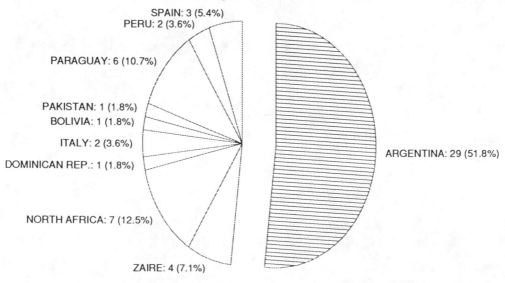

FIGURE ARG-2
ARGENTINA MISSIONARIES
Target Countries

SPAIN: 3 (5.4%)
PERU: 2 (3.6%)
PARAGUAY: 6 (10.7%)
PAKISTAN: 1 (1.8%)
BOLIVIA: 1 (1.8%)
ITALY: 2 (3.6%)
DOMINICAN REP.: 1 (1.8%)
ARGENTINA: 29 (51.8%)
NORTH AFRICA: 7 (12.5%)
ZAIRE: 4 (7.1%)

Forty-eight percent of these missionaries work in at least nine countries outside Argentina (Figure ARG-2). While all these missionaries receive support from Argentina, a number of them also receive some of their support from sources within their target countries. (6)

Fully one-third of these foreign missionaries are working among Muslims. Even though the Argentine missions movement is just getting started, this is still a phenomenal percentage of Muslim missionaries. There is no other country in the world whose foreign missionary force even comes close to that percentage of missionaries to Muslims! This demonstrates the strategic potential of the Argentine missions movement.

Most Argentine missionary-sending organizations are at the beginning of their ministries. The largest is the Evangelical Baptist Convention of Argentina, which has a total of 15 missionaries. Two are in Peru and 13 work among four tribal groups in Argentina. The largest foreign missionary team from Argentina is the six people who work to reach Muslims through Project Magreb.

Another encouraging development in recent years has been an increase in the targeting of people groups within Argentina itself. Argentine churches have sent missionaries to tribal groups for a number of years, though in much smaller numbers than those from other countries. In one notable case, the Toba church sent a missionary team to the unreached Quechua tribe in another province. This effort was initiated soon after a Toba musical group had been asked to sing in two of the regional missions conferences!

The 29 Argentine missionaries who work within Argentina are serving among six different people groups as follows:

Location/department	Target People	Missionaries
Buenos Aires	Laotian Immigrants	2
Chaco	Guarani	2
Chaco	Toba	6
Formosa	Toba	8
Formosa	Guarani	3
Formosa	Mataco	2
Neuquen	Mapuche	4
Santiago Del Estero	Quechua	2

All four missionaries reported in 1980 were sent to people groups within Argentina. The growth in missionary sending, both foreign and domestic, is an indication of the rising interest in missions by the Argentine churches.

A dynamic potential

Although the initial enthusiasm and response to world missions is encouraging, the challenges faced by the Argentine church in the next few years will demand innovative and disciplined action on the part of all those who are committed to the development of this movement. Recognizing that they are not alone in this challenge, Misiones Mundiales is looking to leaders of other emerging mission bases for counsel and encouragement.

As part of this effort, an international missions conference for the southern cone of the continent, "Mission '89," is being planned for November of 1989 featuring India's Dr. Theodore Williams. His leadership in the World Evangelical Fellowship and his firsthand experience in organizing one of India's most successful mission organizations should be of great help and inspiration to those struggling with practical missionary issues in Argentina.

Conclusion

Argentina is on its way toward building a significant missionary movement. The tremendous spiritual capital arising through the Argentine revival promises to spill over into a potentially powerful missionary movement. That spiritual zeal is the greatest asset any country can possess. May it not be dissipated within Argentine borders. May it be channeled into a dynamic stream of missionary sending which will touch the ends of the earth!

Although this story focuses on one Argentine organization's role as a catalytic agent for world evangelization, credit must also be given to the hundreds of individuals who, having picked up the torch of missions, are sustaining this movement through their efforts, prayers and united support.

Still, the Argentine missionary movement is gaining momentum rapidly due in large part to the united efforts of a few key individuals and organizations. This includes the two national evangelical fellowships, ACIERA, (headed by Pr. Juan Terranova), and CEP (headed by Pr. Juan Passuelo). Both are making missions a priority on their present and future agendas. Federico Bertuzzi and Misiones Mundiales have helped to spread the vision into every region of the country. The unity displayed in the recent establishment of a national sending agency promises great hope for every church or denomination which wants to send missionaries.

As leadership works to overcome the serious problems related to finances, training and organization, Argentina promises to be one of the most dynamic and unified missionary movements in the world.

Lord, let it happen!

Jonathan Lewis (M.A.) *is an Argentine-born son of missionary parents. An Argentine citizen, he has served as a missionary in Peru, Venezuela and Argentina.*

FOOTNOTES

(1) Johnstone, Patrick, *Operation World*, 1986, William Carey Library Publishers, pp. 91.

(2) Conducted jointly by ACIERA and Misiones Mundiales. ACIERA (Alianca Cristiana Eglesias Evangelica Republica Argentina) is a national interdenominational association of churches established in 1982. It currently involves about 1,500 churches. Its main function is to promote unity as a primary voice for the evangelical community before the government and the press. It also sponsors interdenominational activities at a national level.

(3) These are an edited, condensed version of *Perspectives on the World Christian Movement*, (Ralph D. Winter and Steven C. Hawthorne, Eds; Pasadena, William Carey Library, 1981).

(4) Based upon statistics gathered as a part of the research for this book.

(5) An astute observer will note that James Long, Peter Larson and Edward Pentecost reported 30 missionaries in 7 agencies for Argentina in 1972, *Missions From the Third World* (Church Growth Study Center, Singapore; 1973). An analysis of the source documents for those figures reveals that only 18 missionaries and 5 agencies fit the criteria used in the present study. Nevertheless, it does seem to indicate there was an earlier interest in missions in Argentina which declined considerably until recent years. Therefore a long-term study of the Argentine missions movement is in order to discover the reasons for the decline of both sending agencies and number of missionaries during the period 1972 to 1984. It is safe to say, however, that the Argentine missions movement is now moving ahead more rapidly than ever before.

(6) This practice is somewhat common in missionary activity throughout many parts of Latin America, Africa and Asia. Support may come from churches established by missionaries in the field, by Christians in the target area, or by tentmaking activities.

REACH THE UNREACHED AT ANY COST

The Story of the Indian Evangelical Team

INDIA EVANGELICAL TEAM
CHURCHES

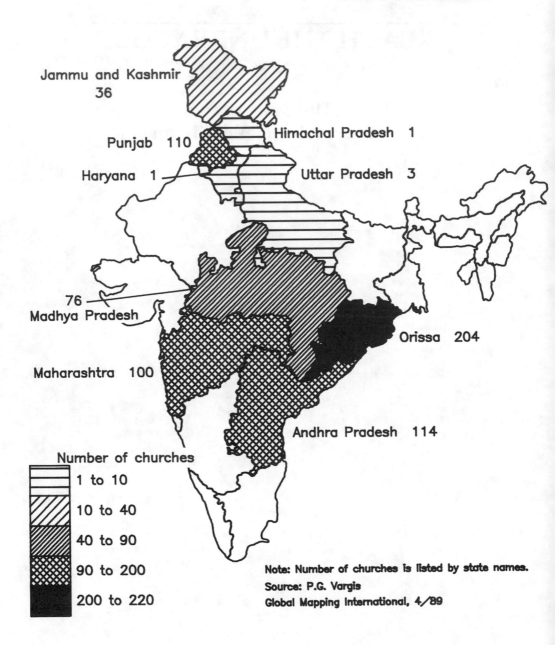

Jammu and Kashmir
36

Himachal Pradesh 1

Punjab 110

Haryana 1

Uttar Pradesh 3

76
Madhya Pradesh

Orissa 204

Maharashtra 100

Andhra Pradesh 114

Number of churches

1 to 10

10 to 40

40 to 90

90 to 200

200 to 220

Note: Number of churches is listed by state names.
Source: P.G. Vargis
Global Mapping International, 4/89

REACH THE UNREACHED AT ANY COST
The Story of the Indian Evangelical Team

by Larry D. Pate

O FFICER P. G. VARGIS WAS ABOUT TO CONCLUDE his day's work. He was one of 1,900 soldiers stationed in Udhampur, Kashmir, the northernmost state of India. It was the first day of October, 1971. Vargis handed over the keys to his army office to the duty officer, starting to leave the base. At that moment he noticed a magazine "Light of My Life" lying on the table.

That magazine "caused me to examine my life and to make a new decision...," Vargis would later write. He decided to follow Christ as Lord of his life. He started to witness to other soldiers. He even traveled to surrounding areas to witness to soldiers on other army bases. After three months, the 29-year-old Vargis felt a call to full-time Christian service. He did not hesitate. He resigned his job. His wife, Lily, also rejected her teacher's position and joined Vargis in Kashmir.

Concerning this time, it would later be written:

> They gave all they had for the gospel work. With an empty pocket and the faith that the Lord would provide, they went with their 10-month-old child to Katra, a Hindu pilgrim center in Kashmir, where there was no Christian.

In Katra, Vargis spent much of his time on the mountains of Jammu Kashmir. When he wasn't preaching, he spent much time in Bible study, prayer, and in studying the lives of great missionaries. On November 28, while in the mountain village of Ser Sund, Vargis received a vision to organize a faith mission to support missionaries to reach the lost. He had been reading *The Story of My Life* by Oswald J. Smith. He wrote on the last page of the book:

> I rededicate myself for the Lord's work faithfully. Though my bones will lie in some unknown valley of Kashmir, my wife

115

will become a widow in her twenties, my son an orphan in his childhood, nothing will turn me back. I will go ahead with my Master, who saved me and bestowed blessings; to evangelize the unevangelized.

That dedication began to yield spiritual fruit right away. Within the first year, the "Katra Church of Christ" had baptized 100 new believers, which was very unusual in North India. Soon, this church in a center of Hinduism had 150 members. Within five years it had become one of the leading churches in this highly unchurched area of North India. (1)

A team is formed

Vargis' zeal to reach the lost could not be contained within one location. Vargis began to envision the planting of other churches in the area. Just after committing himself to support more workers by faith, two volunteers showed up from the south. Upon hearing Vargis' vision for missionary outreach, they joined him in the task. Together, they became known as the "Kashmir Evangelical Team." They agreed to share everything they received for the work, a practice which continues to this day.

Katra is surrounded by mountains whose valleys are heavily populated. Vargis and his team began to plant churches in those mountains. "Reach the unreached at any cost" became the motto of the team. That vision and a zeal to carry it out became the foundation for success in the face of many obstacles.

The work was not easy. In addition to help from the Katra church, support for this missionary outreach was pledged from churches and believers in South India. But the support did not always arrive on time, if at all. One of these early missionaries reported:

It wasn't easy to start a church among caste Hindus, especially in an area where Hinduism was so strong. There was a lot of persecution. We fasted and prayed a lot. Sometimes we fasted because we didn't receive promised offerings from South India and there was nothing to eat. But God was good to us anyway and the churches were established for His glory. (2)

This success did not go unchallenged. There was much persecution and many obstacles, but God vindicated His Word with power. Signs and wonders were a common occurrence during the establishment of these churches. Within two years after founding the Katra church, 12 new churches had been founded in the surrounding mountains.

"Reach the unreached at any cost" was proving to be more than just words. It was a motto backed by the lives of Vargis and his coworkers. The faith and dedication of these missionaries, not to mention their success, began to captivate the imagination of other believers hungry to serve God as missionaries. As more workers joined the work, the ministry extended into Punjab, another largely unreached state of North India. That was when "Kashmir Evangelical Team" became INDIAN EVANGELICAL TEAM!

Expanding vision

By the time INDIAN EVANGELICAL TEAM (IET) conducted their annual training and prayer conference in 1979, the work had spread to three states—Kashmir, Punjab and Himachal Pradesh. By this time the team had grown to 36 missionaries.

Special guest for that annual conference was Dr. Roger E. Hedlund of the Church Growth Association of India. Hedlund challenged IET missionaries with principles to expand their effectiveness and vision. Church planting became a central focus. Before the conference was over, IET committed itself to the goal of establishing 200 churches by 1989. At the beginning of 1979, there were 23 churches and 20 mission stations (Figure IET-1). This focus upon church planting and a healthy faith goal set the stage for a decade of fruitful harvest.

Expanding growth

In 1979, the goal to plant a total of 200 churches loomed as a great challenge for the still small, weakly-financed IET. As it turned out, the goal itself proved to be too small! Only four years later, before the end of 1984, the 200th church was started! This was an average annual growth rate of 54%, a phenomenal rate of growth! By the end of 1984, the number of missionaries had already shot up to 258, an average growth rate of over 48% per year! By then, they were working out of 107 stations in eight states (see Figure IET-2).

After reaching their goal in only five years, IET leaders and team members set a new goal. They decided to start a total of 200 stations by 1989.

IET mission stations do not resemble the "mission stations" of the colonial era. They are not elaborate compounds complete with churches, schools and clinics. Usually, they are simply rented quarters for two or three missionary families located in a strategic place central to the target area. It is a church planting base. The workers target a certain area and

FIGURE IET - 1
IET CHURCHES

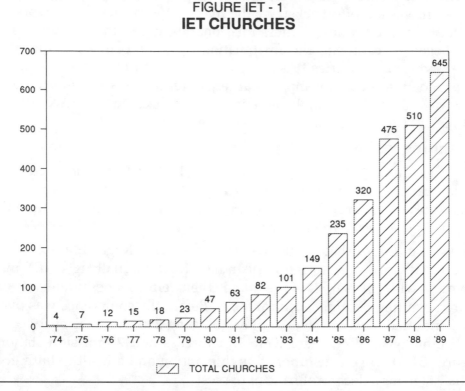

people. The "station" serves as their main living quarters, tract ware-house, training center, etc.

Between one and 12 churches are planted for each station. (3) Multi-plying stations was recognized as an effective means of pioneering new churches within the IET vision. The challenge to establish 200 new bases by 1989 was a real step of faith. As we shall see, IET was destined to reach that goal ahead of target also!

A decade of growth

Like churches, mission agencies may experience a high rate of initial growth. A fast-growing mission agency may increase its numbers more and more each year, but still have a slowing *rate* of growth. That is be-cause growth rates are calculated as a percentage of the previous year's totals. (4) For this reason, it is more useful to measure growth rates over a longer period of time, such as ten years. Ten-year growth rates, or deca-dal growth rates, measure the amount of growth at a ten-year rate. This is true no matter whether the period of growth is six years, 12 years, or ac-

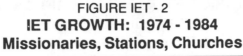

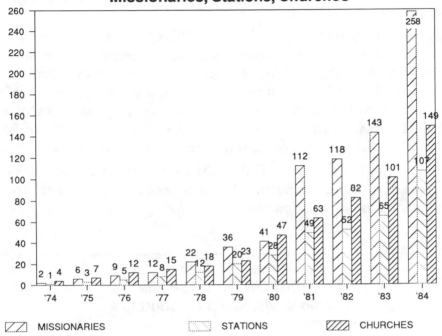

FIGURE IET - 2
IET GROWTH: 1974 - 1984
Missionaries, Stations, Churches

MISSIONARIES   STATIONS   CHURCHES

tually ten years. Decadal growth rates tell us how much an organization would grow in ten years at present rates.

The Indian Evangelical Team has experienced phenomenal growth during the past ten years (Figure IET-3). The missionary team itself increased from 36 to 559, a decadal growth of 1,453%! The number of stations increased from 20 to 303, a growth of 1,415%. The number of pioneer churches planted increased from 47 to 645, a decadal growth of 1,272%.

Though the work of IET was originally confined to one state, it eventually spread to a total of 12 by 1987 (Figure IET-4). A decision was taken in 1988 to confine ministries to the northernmost states of India because it was believed that is where the greatest need for IET ministries exist. Accordingly, the number of states of IET ministry was cut back to ten. As Figure IET-3 demonstrates, however, this did not diminish IET growth in any category.

IET reached its goal of establishing 200 mission stations by the middle of 1987, two years ahead of its goal. Now IET has a new goal, "2000 CHURCHES BY 2000 A.D." They intend to plant a total of 2000 churches within the next 11 years. If they continue at the rate they are going, they will reach that goal by 1996!

This type of dramatic growth is unusually high, but it is not unlike the growth which other mission agencies have experienced in India. The Friends Missionary Prayer Band of India, for instance, grew from 16 missionaries in 1972 to 170 missionaries in 1980, a decadal growth rate of 963%. Similarly, the Indian Evangelical Mission grew from 14 missionaries in 1972 to 300 missionaries in 1989, a decadal growth rate of 507%. The overall decadal growth of the Indian missions movement is 242%.

This even higher growth of IET ministries is dramatic evidence of the grace of God upon IET ministries. It is also evidence of the zeal and vision of its leaders and missionaries.

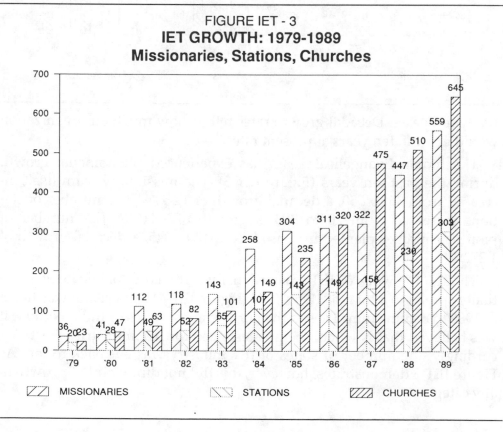

FIGURE IET - 3
IET GROWTH: 1979-1989
Missionaries, Stations, Churches

FIGURE IET - 4
STATES WHERE IET MISSIONARIES WORK

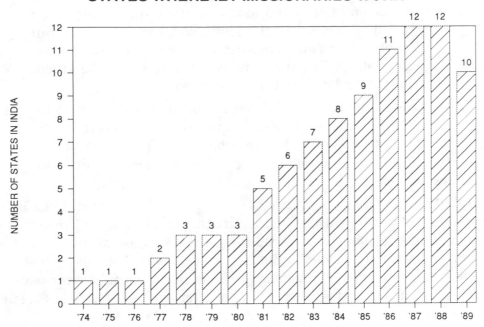

Not without cost

The successes of the Indian Evangelical Team have not been achieved without considerable sacrifice and external pressures. But these obstacles only appear to have strengthened the resolve of IET leaders and missionaries. In virtually every respect, IET has managed to sustain a very high rate of growth in spite of these obstacles.

The following story is representative of both the fruitfulness of IET and the obstacles they face in state after state:

> Brother P. G. Vargis and C. K. George visited Maharashtra and had three crusades. People came to hear about Jesus and for prayer for healing.

> God did great things and several hundred people made decisions to follow Christ. At three places, we could conduct baptism services. All together, 501 people were baptized. A few hundred more are on the waiting list. We are planning to have another one-week Bible class for these new babes.

As soon as the baptism was over, the Hindu militants came to know about it through someone who is jealous of our work. They surrounded the house and orphanage of Brother Dupte. They made an inquiry and took everything in writing. They searched the houses and the few belongings they had, but could not get anything against our brothers. The people wanted to attack Dupte and he was threatened to be killed. The news was all in the local newspapers.

Witnessing to the non-Christians is prohibited by the police now. The police went with Dupte to several villages and talked to the people who were baptized. The police found that the allegations made by the people are baseless. Even so, the inquiry is still in progress and we need your prayers. (5)

Militant religion is on the rise in many parts of the world. India is no exception. Sikh nationalism, Hindu and Muslim militancy, all are a threat to Indian missionaries who spread the gospel. Because of IET's determination to spread the gospel in the face of whatever obstacles or costs involved, it is not unusual for their missionaries to encounter opposition. That is the subject of this excerpt from a letter by P. G. Vargis to his supporters:

There is a great future for the gospel work in India. Many souls are given to those who work hard. The devil knows this very well. That is why organizations like Arya Samaj, Hindu Mahasabha, R.S.S., who were previously divided, are now coming together to work against Christian missionary efforts.

Anti-conversion bills have already passed in Madhya Pradesh and Orissa. They are being presented in many other states. Government laws are used to convert low sect (caste) Hindu-background Christians. Newspapers and magazines, especially from outside Kerala, are owned by Hindus and are accustomed to bring out articles and news against Christianity.

In a nutshell, all the powers in all the spectrum in India are very active against gospel preaching. Inquirers are ordered anywhere in case non-Christians accept Christianity. Missionary-evangelists who work there will be sent to jail. Foreign support will be stopped.

Yes, all the powers including the Indian government are against gospelization. They know that we are advancing. I see

122

that not only in my imagination, but I see it in the field with our team. 1,700 people were baptized by the team in 1987. Double that will be baptized in 1988. (6)

Persecution is not new to missionaries and gospel workers in India. To continue working among unreached groups in North India, missionaries must come to a definite decision to make "whatever the cost" more than just a slogan. This brief story by IET missionary Joseph L. Dupte is not unusual:

I was working with the team near Parli and distributing tracts in a festival place. Many youths got angry with me and they compelled me to go away from that place. They caught hold of me and destroyed the tracts and they tortured me black and blue.

"You may break my hand or neck, but I will preach about Jesus until I am dead," I said. Many people called me "mad." Then I returned home in the evening and narrated the events to my wife. Though she felt sad, she encouraged me. We both sang together and praised the Lord. (7)

The passage of anti-conversion laws may have a definite effect on the fruitfulness of IET ministries in the future, but it had not diminished their success up until the time of writing this report. For example, the work in "Bastar Division" of Madhya Pradesh, which passed anti-conversion laws as mentioned by Vargis above, was only begun in December 1987. By October 1988, ten missionaries had planted six new churches with a total of 138 new believers. Hopefully, the anti-conversion laws will increase interest in the gospel. They are certain to bring more difficulties to the missionaries.

IET Ministries

IET is active in many forms of ministry besides church planting and evangelism. While that remains the primary thrust, other ministries have come into being as a result of the needs and opportunities which have arisen.

Missionary Training

Figure IET-5 shows the growth of the IET missionary team. This rapid growth has been sustained in large part by the IET missionary training program, directed by Reverend Josh P. Kallimel. It consists of both long-term and short-term training.

FIGURE IET - 5
IET MISSIONARIES

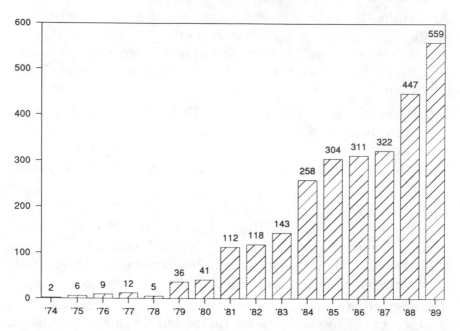

A missionary training center is maintained at Pathonkot, Punjab. It is busy year around with both three-month and six-month training sessions. Each session typically involves 20-30 missionary candidates. Completion of training does not guarantee a position with IET. About 70-80% of candidates are accepted into IET teams after their training. There are plans to make the training center a degree-level Bible college using Hindi as its language medium.

Because IET ministries are expanding over an increasingly wider area, it has been necessary to offer candidate training over a wider geographical area. IET had a goal of conducting five missionary training institutes in 1988.

In addition to the training base at Pathonkot, candidate training was offered in Jahadalpur, Madhya Pradesh; Nagapur, Maharashtra; and Navarangpur, Orissa.

In addition to the long-term training, three-day seminars are periodically offered to missionaries on location. These seminars provide the initial training for missionaries-in-training and enrichment to veterans.

Radio Ministry

IET founder, P. G. Vargis, has produced a regular radio program for several years. He believes this is an important tool for reaching into as yet unreached areas and peoples.

Crusade Ministry

Some of the leaders of IET, including Vargis himself, regularly conduct evangelistic crusades in key unreached areas. Each year, hundreds of new converts are baptized as a result of these crusades. IET team members assigned to the regions of the crusades follow-up on the converts, forming them into churches.

Institutes on Evangelism

These institutes are conducted in a number of centers each year to train and encourage new converts in evangelism. In 1988, five such training institutes were conducted in various states.

Literature Ministry

IET conducts a sizable literature ministry which produces tracts, books and magazines in several languages, including Hindi, Tamil, Malayalam and English. *The Key To Miracles*, *Jesus Will Set You Free*, and *The Life of Abraham - A Study*, are examples of book titles.

Children's Homes

IET operates three children's homes, caring for a total of 52 children. They are located in Nowrangpur, Orissa; Parli, Maharashtra; and Hoshangabad, Madhya Pradesh. These are primarily children who are orphaned or whose parents are unable to care for them.

Benevolence Ministries

In a few cases, such as for orphaned children or widows, special care or child support is provided for basic needs. For instance, livestock have been provided for poor widows, soap for lepers and blankets for the poor. Though IET is primarily a church-planting missionary organization, it does respond to specific needs of destitute people who come under team care, for one reason or another.

Bible Seminars

Bible seminars are conducted regularly to train and inspire missionaries in the field. These are usually three days to a week in duration. As with all IET training ministries, the Bible seminars are under the direction of Josh P. Kallimel, (M. Div.), IET Director of Training.

As the size and effectiveness of IET ministries have grown, so have the types of ministry in which it is engaged. Each type of ministry arose in response to obvious need which could not be ignored. Yet the vision for the evangelization of India has never waned in the hearts of the leaders. For many years, a motto has appeared on the letterhead of Founder/President Vargis: *"From Kashmir to Cape Comerin, India Shall Be Saved."*

Are they really missionaries?

Some people who are accustomed to thinking of missionaries as those who carry out gospel work outside their own country have a problem seeing those doing evangelism within their own country as missionaries. To them, IET missionaries might appear more like evangelists than missionaries.

But IET team members are genuine missionaries in the truest sense of the word. They are also typical of the estimated Indian missionaries working throughout India. To emphasize this point, consider the following:

- All IET missionaries are sent to work outside their own state.
- 59 minister in entirely different regions, using languages of those regions.
- 580 of the total 645 missionaries use languages other than Hindi, the language used at the sending base.
- IET plants churches in unreached people groups, including numerous scheduled castes, scheduled tribes, lower castes, and mixed groups. (8)
- The majority of IET's financial support comes from India, making their ministry a legitimate missionary ministry of the supporting churches and individuals of India.
- 92% of IET missionaries work to establish churches in unreached areas of North India. (9) They work to establish churches with their own local pastors.

India is a vast mosaic of peoples and languages. Though there are some 15 officially recognized national languages, there are some 1,600 other languages. India's nearly 800 million inhabitants are divided into over 3,000 castes, tribes and people groups. IET missionaries are supported across both cultural and geographical barriers and target unreached groups and areas. Though they minister within their own country, they are missionaries in every sense of the word!

Outstanding characteristics of IET

A number of Indian mission agencies have experienced rapid growth, even to the point of fielding teams of several hundred missionaries. But IET's sustained rapid rate of growth, together with its outstanding success in church planting, make IET one of the best kept secrets in Indian missions. There are several distinctives which may account for this success.

Zeal and vision

While it is not possible to measure the effect of personal zeal and commitment on the growth of IET, there can be no doubt they have played a major role in IET success. The faith and vision of P. G. Vargis and his top leaders has been instrumental in every aspect of IET ministry.

High commitment to team

The practice of "living by faith" and sharing what is provided has been a faith-building practice which inspires team members to commitment. It has inspired a willingness to sacrifice which is a testimony to believers and unbelievers alike.

The commitment of IET leadership has been a large part of the reason team members have been inspired to personal sacrifice. Typically, team members use bicycles for transportation in their ministries. On one occasion, the founder, P.G. Vargis, was given a jeep for transport. After using it for a few years, he gave it to one of his regional directors. On another occasion he was given a small motor scooter. That was donated to still another team member. In each case, Vargis went back to riding a bicycle or taking public transport. It is this kind of example which has inspired other IET missionaries to serve sacrificially.

Demonstrated accountability

There appears to be a relationship between the sense of accountability missionary leaders feel toward their task and their willingness to be accountable to their supporters. IET keeps a completely open set of financial books which are audited every year by an outside auditor. This sense of responsibility toward God for the resources He provides carries over into open and honest accountability with supporters. This increases supporter confidence and yields even more support. This has proven to be an important factor in the growth of IET ministries.

Decentralized leadership and individual initiative

A high level of autonomy is given to state and district coordinators. Leaders in headquarters often serve more to facilitate field leaders' success than to tell them what to do.

Individual initiative is acclaimed and leadership is recognized on the basis of proven ministry. Successful church planting is still the path to greater responsibilities, rather than simply the amount of formal training one has received.

There is a definite minimum standard for acceptance as an IET missionary. One may serve as an "experimental missionary" for some time before being accepted for missionary training in Pathonkot. These are really missionaries-in-training attached to a local IET church and its outreach ministries. The idea for this type of missionary ministry came to Vargis in 1985. He realized the need to test the potential of missionaries before expending the resources to fully train them as IET missionaries.

Experimental missionaries receive training in a three-day seminar after which they are expected to evangelize in a local area and serve as elders in a local church. If they are successful in this ministry, they are approved for six months' more training. If they are successful, they will be approved as full IET missionaries and sent to another state or region. Vargis reports these "experimental missionaries" are often very effective in their evangelistic efforts. This system provides an excellent method for placing new missionaries on probation until they have proven their ministries and taken adequate training.

Since this program started in 1985, the number of missionaries in this category has varied. The figures by year are:

- 1985: 10
- 1986: 161
- 1987: 249
- 1988: 354
- 1989: 193

This missionary-in-training system has greatly increased the quality and productivity of the whole IET missionary team. Each missionary is trained, but his acceptance is on the basis of proven ministry, not just the training.

All these factors combined serve to equip IET missionaries better than many of their counterparts in other Indian mission societies. While there are plans for continuing to improve their preparation, the system which has developed in IET's 16 years of ministry has proven to be very successful.

Indigenous support

From the outset, IET has emphasized faith in God for support, and that support has primarily been provided from churches and individuals in India. Up until recent years, over 90% of support came from sources in India. As IET ministries have come to be more widely known and trusted, some support has been sent from other countries. Currently, IET reports that 70% of its income is still derived from within India.

This indigenous support and prayer base has been a major factor in the success of IET. There have always been many more needs than there have been resources to meet them. Believers in India have often given sacrificially to support the ministries of IET. This has heightened each missionary's sense of responsibility for funds received, and it has heightened the value of the message they bear in the minds of those they are sent to reach.

Signs and wonders ministry

From the outset, IET missionaries have been men and women of faith and practical Christianity. Their primary objectives are bringing people to trust in Christ for salvation and forming them into local congregations of believers. But healing for the sick and exorcism of demons is also very much a part of their "full-gospel" ministry.

This type of faith ministry should not be dismissed lightly. It has proven to be an important factor in the growth of IET ministry.

C. Zechariah, in a doctoral study designed to elicit the primary reasons people in India turn from Hinduism to Christianity, documented that 61% do so because they, or someone close to them, was healed through the prayers of Christians. Another 20% became Christians through the exorcism of demons, either from themselves or from someone close to them. That is a total of 81% who became Christians as a result of the very ministry of signs and wonders, which is so much an integral part of IET ministry. (10)

The following accounts are not unusual in IET ministries:

> On the 3rd of January 1985, I reached Rowkela and Brother
> Samuel Idka was waiting for me. A meeting was conducted
> in the room of a Malayali Brother. The next night also many
> people came. I preached to them and prayed. Many Adivasis
> keenly listened to the Gospel. A born-deaf young man was

prayed for and God instantly healed him. The people applauded and praised God. (11)
— *P. G. Vargis*

I am staying in Madhya Pradesh and Orissa—and taking the gospel to 18 villages. I was once a Methodist Pastor, but they dismissed me after I took water baptism and was filled with the Holy Ghost. One day I will go for stone work, and the next four days I will preach the gospel. One night a young man took us to his house where a young woman was rolling on the ground by the attack of devils. I preached about Jesus and His deliverance. We prayed and the woman was immediately delivered. Many people received the Lord as their Saviour and five were baptized in water. Now there are 39 baptized members worshipping the Lord. (12)
— *Team Missionary Maddi Charan*

Whatever one's theological predisposition or suppositions, the positive role of "signs and wonders" ministry by IET missionaries should not be denied. It has been an important factor in their effectiveness. (13)

The Indian Evangelical Team is an example of the power and the vitality of the Indian missions movement. IET has established a record of faithfulness and commitment to its motto, "Reach the Unreached at Any Cost." The complexities of India's cultural mosaic has erected formidable historic barriers to the penetration of the gospel in Northern and Central India. IET was born in the midst of that mosaic and has formed its ministries in the struggle to cross those barriers.

May we learn from their sacrifice, as well as their success. May their motto become the motto of us all: "REACH THE UNREACHED AT ANY COST."

FOOTNOTES

(1) Indian Evangelical Team (IET) brochure, New Delhi, January 1, 1988.

(2) IET brochure, New Delhi, January, 1983.

(3) Personal conversation with Josh P. Kallimel in Seoul, Korea, January 1986.

(4) IET brochure, New Delhi, March 1, 1987.

(5) *Prayer Bulletin of Indian Evangelical Team*, December 1, 1987.

(6) *Indian Missionary Messenger (IMM)*, news bulletin of Indian Evangelical Team, New Delhi, October 1988, p. 2.

(7)   IMM, *op. cit.*, July-August 1986.

(8)   Gleaned from reports in numerous editions of the *Indian Missionary Messenger, op. cit.*

(9)   Reported by P. G. Vargis as a response to my questionnaire, November 25, 1988.

(10) Reported by P. G. Vargis in a phone conversation, March 16, 1989.

(11) Zechariah, Chelliah; *Missiological Strategy for the Assemblies of God in Tamil Nadu;* Doctor of Missiology dissertation for the School of World Mission, Fuller Theological Seminary, Pasadena, CA, April 1981, p. 208.

(12) IMM, *op. cit.*, May 1985.

(13) IMM, *op. cit*, December 1985.

Directory

INTRODUCTION
Two-Thirds World
Missions Directory

T HIS DIRECTORY LISTS MISSION AGENCIES FROM AFRICA, Asia, Latin
America and Oceania. It also includes information about their missionaries, location of their work, and the target peoples they have reported to be working among. Some comments about each item of the
directory and the manner in which it is organized are in order.

Organization Name

Missionary activity in the non-Western world is not organized into the
categories most common in the Western world. Those doing missionary
work carry a wide variety of organizational names. Some of them seem
to denote something other than missionary activity. Evangelism and missions, for instance, are often used interchangeably among the non-Western missions. Yet, sometimes those which call themselves "missions" are
really church denominations without any missionary activity. On the
other hand, many organizations which have the term, "evangelism" or
"evangelistic" in their title are engaged in genuine missionary ministry.

The old adage, *"Don't judge a book by its cover,"* can be adapted here:
"Don't judge a mission agency by its name!" Each of the mission agencies
listed here has demonstrated evidence of genuine missionary activity according to the definition discussed in the preface.

Address

This is the last known mailing address of the organization listed. In
about 20% of the cases, the agencies either did not report, or at least we
did not receive, data for this current survey. Therefore, it is possible that
some of these addresses are outdated. We have updated every address
possible.

Chief Officer

The name which appears immediately below the address is the top
leader of the organization listed. In most cases this is the name of the
leader of the actual missionary effort. In some cases, according to cultural
custom, the leader listed may be the head of a denomination who also
acts as titular head over the missionary activity.

135

Date Organized

In most cases this is the date the missionary activity of an organization began. In some cases, again according to cultural norms, there is little distinction in the minds of the respondents between the beginning of a denomination and the beginning of their missionary activity. To them, missionary work is not a distinct activity separate from evangelistic activity. In such cases, those leaders may have reported the beginning of the denomination, rather than the actual beginning of their missionary activity.

Missionaries Reported

This lists the number of missionaries since 1972 reported from any source. Whenever there have been conflicting reports, the more conservative figures were usually adopted. In some cases, reports came to us from organizations which listed many more missionaries than we have reported here. That is because the evidence indicated that some of those listed as missionaries did not fit the definitions of this study for being missionaries. This in no way reflects negatively on the validity of the ministry of those we have not included.

Estimated Figures

Those figures followed by an asterisk (*) in the 1988 column are an estimate based upon the average annual growth rate (AAGR) of the agency listed. These agencies reported no data for 1988. The estimated figure is based directly on the AAGR figure listed immediately below it.

Average Annual Growth Rate

This figure reflects the average of how much the listed agency has grown on an annual basis during the period of years for which data has been available. It is calculated based upon the first and last years of reported data.

In some cases, data was reported for only one year. In such cases, the symbol "N/A", (for "not available"), appears in the AAGR section. When this occurs and there is an asterisk (*) appearing beside 1988 data, the estimated figure has been calculated based upon an overall AAGR for the country under which the agency is listed.

Foreign Missionaries

This lists the number of missionaries among those reported above whose primary ministry is outside the country where the listed agency is based. This figure is as of the end of 1988. If the figure for 1988 is an estimated figure, as indicated by an asterisk, the words "not reported" appear on this line.

Fields of Service

This is a summary of the countries, states or provinces, and target peoples or locations of the listed agencies' missionary activity. This information directly reflects what was reported to us on question 14 of the Questionnaire (Appendix A).

The responses for "Target People, Tribe or Language Group" varied widely by type. They can be divided into seven classifications: 1) Tribe, such as the "Lisu" of Northern Burma; 2) Language, such as "Chichewa" (Malawi), which is spoken by more than one tribe; 3) Religion, such as "Hindus and Muslims;" 4) Occupation, such as "fishermen"; 5) Class, such as "Scheduled Castes" in India; 6) Location, such as "Filipinos," which is more a location than a people group; and 7) Ministry, which refers to responses such as "medical work" and "literacy work".

Sometimes more than one type of response is combined, such as "medical work among the Sweepers" (combining #4 and #7).

The work of some agencies is so extensive, they reported its targets only in general terms. Others reported incomplete or sketchy data here. In any case, what was reported is listed; first by country, then state or province, then target people.

Organization of Agencies listed

The agencies are listed alphabetically by country and category for each continent. Agencies classified as "Sending Agencies" are listed first. These comprise the bulk of those reported. This is followed by a section entitled "Other Agencies," which includes those classified as "Training Agencies," "Service Agencies," "Networking Agencies," and "Auxiliary Agencies." The third section lists "International Sending Agencies" which send non-Western missionaries as part of their international teams. A final section for each continent lists agencies for which there is no reported data. A descriptive definition for each of these classifications is in order.

Sending Agencies

These are indigenous mission agencies or organizations whose primary missionary aim is to send missionaries. Regardless of the form or title they take, in one way or another, they organize and supervise means for missionary sending.

Training Agencies

These are organizations whose missionary purpose is primarily related to training missionaries from their own countries. They may train only missionaries, or in a few cases, they may also have a wider theological training task of which missionary training is a part. Ordinarily, these organizations do not send missionaries. If they do, such missionaries are listed with other information concerning them. If they do not send missionaries, they reflect no figures among the total missionaries from their country. But they are legitimate agencies of missionary endeavor because they have a missionary purpose.

While it has not been our primary purpose for this phase of research to collect all the names of such non-Western missionary training agencies, it does fit within our long-range goals. We hope to develop a comprehensive list of such training agencies. At this point, we are simply listing those which have reported to us as a part of this survey and have been classified primarily as training agencies.

Service Agencies

These are agencies which ordinarily send missionaries whose ministries focus primarily on service to the target peoples and communities as a whole. Though they may participate in evangelistic ministries, that is not their primary focus. Examples of such ministries would include: medical and dental clinics, efforts to provide general education, and community development projects. Agencies of this type comprise a small percentage of the mission agencies in the Two-Thirds World.

Networking Agencies

These are non-Western agencies whose primary focus of ministry is to network people and organizations to accomplish a particular kind of missionary task. This would include missionary associations like the *Nigerian Evangelical Missions Association (NEMA)* and the *Korean Missions Association (KMA)*. NEMA sponsors an interdenominational missionary training institute in Jos, Nigeria as one of its missionary tasks. KMA sponsors a missiological journal.

This category also includes non-Western organizations which focus on a specialized missionary task, such as research, publishing, radio or missionary activity on behalf of a closed country. An example is the *Chinese Coordination Center of World Evangelism* in Hong Kong, which does research on China and mobilizes resources for evangelism of that country. The *Kansai Missions Research Center* in Japan is another example. So is

Misiones Mundiales of Argentina. These organizations often do deploy missionaries, though they may not be located permanently in a target country or area. When such organizations report their missionary personnel, they are included in the totals of this study.

Auxiliary Agencies

These agencies do not send missionaries themselves. However, their primary role is supportive to those denominations or agencies with which they cooperate who do send missionaries. A number of the mission agencies in Korea, for example, are auxiliary agencies. They generally perform some practical service to the missionaries and missionary-sending organizations. Examples are the *Institute of Mission Development* and the *End of the Earth Mission*, both in Seoul. Because these organizations do not send missionaries as a rule, their personnel are not reflected in the totals for their countries. They are counted as legitimate missionary agencies, however.

International Sending Agencies

These are international missionary organizations whose headquarters may be in a Western or non-Western country who field missionaries from the Two-Thirds World as a part of their international teams. These non-Western missionaries may be a majority or a minority of the teams deployed. Examples of such international organizations are *Operation Mobilization, Youth With A Mission,* and *SIM International.*

Figures reported for these organizations reflect only the non-Western missionaries on their teams. When the international headquarters of these organizations are listed, the total non-Western missionaries on their teams from all countries are listed. Some of those same missionaries may be listed also in individual country branches of those international agencies. When this occurs, the overall totals of non-Western missionaries are adjusted accordingly. In the first chapter analysis of the data, this adjustment appears on the line "International Adjustments."

Once again, the development of this category was not the primary objective of this phase of the research. It is a long-term objective, however. Those international agencies who include non-Westerners on their missionary teams may wish to write to us to report the number of Two-Thirds World missionaries on their teams, together with their total number of missionaries.

To do so, please write: Larry D. Pate, Emerging Missions, 25 Corning Avenue, Milpitas, CA 95035, USA. More complete data on this category will be reported through the second phase of our research.

Non-Reporting Agencies

This section lists the names and last known addresses of those agencies which we believe participate in missionary activity, but who have never reported data. There are hundreds of organizations to which we have sent questionnaires or have contacted who are not included in this directory. Many who have responded to those questionnaires are not in this directory because their reports do not give sufficient evidence of missionary activity based on the definition of this study. Others are not in this report simply because they did not respond.

Those listed in this "Non-Reporting" section did not respond either. But they have not been dropped because there is some kind of indication they are mission agencies. We have investigated scores of such agencies, confirming some and dropping others. In the country of Ghana, for instance, we have dropped 24 agencies which were included in Dr. Keyes' list of agencies in Ghana. We only dropped such agencies, however, if we had concrete evidence they were *not* participating in missionary activity.

Up to this point, we have been unable to confirm or deny the agencies listed in this section as genuine mission agencies. Until such time as we are able to do so, we will continue to keep them in our records. The reader who has concrete information concerning these agencies or their current addresses is invited to use the response form in Appendix B to share that information with us. Though these agencies are included in the total number of agencies, the possible number of missionaries they represent are not included in any estimates or totals.

One point already made in the Preface bears repeating. The agencies listed in this directory and the information concerning them is derived from the first phase of a two-part research project. We have endeavored to check and recheck the information as thoroughly as possible within the limitations of that which has been reported to us and the deadlines for publication. Among the many thousands of pieces of information which go to make up a study of this sort there are bound to be errors, for one reason or another. This information is as accurate and authoritative as has ever been compiled. Nevertheless, we welcome corrections and additions from interested readers so our next effort can be even more accurate.

Your help and use of the response form for that purpose will be appreciated.

ASIA

BANGLADESH

Evangelical Christian Church

PO Bandarban 4600, Bandarban Hill Tracts, BANGLADESH

Rev. Pakshim B. Tlung
Organized: 1918   Evangelical
MISSIONARIES IN SERVICE
(1980) 4   (1985) 2   (1988) 5
AAGR =   3%
Foreign missionaries in 1988:   0
FIELDS OF SERVICE
Bangladesh
 Mrokhiang Tripura
 Chimbok Area Mru
 Dubachari Khiang
 Rowangchari Chakma
 Tindu Area Khumi, Mru

BURMA

Assemblies of God of Burma

PO Box 1112 GPO, Rangoon, BURMA

Rev. U. Myo Chit
Organized: 1930   Assemblies of God
MISSIONARIES IN SERVICE
(1985) 120   (1988) 144*
AAGR = N/A
Foreign misionaries in 1988: NR
FIELDS OF SERVICE
Burma
 All 14 States All Racial Groups

Bethany Baptist Evangelical Ministry
Thamaing Post Office, PO Box 612
Rangoon, BURMA

U. Frisco
Organized: 1985   Evangelical
MISSIONARIES IN SERVICE
(1985) 8   (1988) 10*
AAGR = N/A
Foreign missionaries in 1988: Not reported.
FIELDS OF SERVICE
Burma
 Rangoon Division Burmese, Karen

Burma Baptist Convention
PO Box 506, Rangoon, BURMA

Rev. Aye Mya Kyaw
Organized: 1864   Baptist
MISSIONARIES IN SERVICE
(1980) 884   (1988) 1440
AAGR =   6%
Foreign missionaries in 1988:   0
FIELDS OF SERVICE
Burma
 Plain State Buddhists
 Kachin State Naga, Palaung, Chin, Kachin
 Shan State Akha
 Karen State Karen

Burma Christ Baptist Convention
Tedim-Tonzang Road,
Sakollam, Tedim, BURMA

Rev. Neng Khaw Vung
Organized: 1975   Baptist
MISSIONARIES IN SERVICE
(1980) 8   (1985) 8   (1988) 8
AAGR = 0%

Foreign missionaries in 1988:   0

FIELDS OF SERVICE

Burma

Chin State Zomi
Sagaing Division Zomi, Burmese,
Lushai

Churches of Christ

PO Box 299, Rangoon, BURMA

Mr. Joshua Leme
Organized: 1968   Nondenominational

MISSIONARIES IN SERVICE

(1972) 14   (1975) 16   (1978) 16
(1980) 30   (1988) 64*
AAGR = N/A
Missionaries in 1988: Not reported.

FIELDS OF SERVICE

Not reported.

Evangelical Baptist Conference

PO Box 1339, Rangoon, BURMA

Rev. Go Za Kham
Organized: 1974   Evangelical

MISSIONARIES IN SERVICE

(1988) 28
AAGR = N/A
Foreign missionaries in 1988:   7

FIELDS OF SERVICE

Burma

Magwe Division Burmese, Chin
Rangoon Division Burmese, Karen
Sagaing Division Thado, Shan
Chin State Tiddim, Chin
Kachin State Kachin

Evangelical Fellowship of Burma

PO Box 1301, Rangoon, BURMA

Robin H. Seia
Organized: 1978   Nazarene

MISSIONARIES IN SERVICE

(1972) 3   (1980) 3   (1982) 3
(1984) 7   (1985) 6   (1988) 9

AAGR =   7%
Foreign missionaries in 1988:   0

FIELDS OF SERVICE

Burma

Chin State Dhai Tribe

Evangelical Free Church of Burma

Tahan, Kalemyo, BURMA

Rev. Ronald Lalthanliana
Organized: 1955   Evangelical

MISSIONARIES IN SERVICE

(1985) 120   (1988) 144*
AAGR = N/A
Foreign missionaries in 1988: Not
reported.

FIELDS OF SERVICE

Burma

Chin State Chin, Animists
Sagaing Division Burmese, Buddhists
mostly Burmese
Rangoon Division Burmese, Buddhists

Evangelical Presbyterian Church of Burma

PO Box 531, Rangoon, BURMA

Rev. Nun Pum
Organized: 1983   Evangelical

MISSIONARIES IN SERVICE

(1985) 21   (1988) 25*
AAGR = N/A
Missionaries in 1988: Not reported.

FIELDS OF SERVICE

Burma

Rangoon Division Burmese, Buddhists

Full Gospel Business Men's Fellowship

PO Box 602, Rangoon, BURMA

Kenneth Kham Go Mang
Organized: 1984   Charismatic

MISSIONARIES IN SERVICE

(1985) 16   (1988) 19*
AAGR = N/A

Missionaries in 1988: Not reported.

FIELDS OF SERVICE

Burma

All 14 States All Racial Groups,
Burmese, Mobile TEAM

Fundamental Baptist Churches of Burma

Falam 03031, BURMA

Rev. Paul Dar Nei Sum
Organized: 1979   Baptist

MISSIONARIES IN SERVICE

(1988) 16
AAGR = N/A
Foreign missionaries in 1988:   0

FIELDS OF SERVICE

Burma

Sagaing Division Burmese, Buddhists
Chin State Chin, Animists

Uganda

Mukono Kkome Island, Buvuma
Tororo Bagwere, Banyore
Arua Lugubra, Madi, Lulu
Kabalore Rhanda Refuge Camp
Ssese Island Ssese People
Kasese Bakonjo

Independent Church of Burma

PO Box 446, Rangoon, BURMA

Rev. Lal Kap Zau
Organized: 1938   Independent

MISSIONARIES IN SERVICE

(1985) 72   (1988) 86*
AAGR = N/A
Missionaries in 1988: Not reported.

FIELDS OF SERVICE

Burma

Sagaing Division Burmese, Buddhists,
Animists, Other Dialects
Chin State Chin

Kenya

Nairobi   English, Swahili, Nominal
Christians

Nigeria

Oyo State Villages, Farmers, Yoruba
Oyo State Students, English
Kaduna State Villages, Muslims,
Hausa
Kaduna State Traders, Hausa
Kwara State Urban Poor, Ibariba
Tribe
Benue State Unreached People

India

Southern India Hindus

Layman Evangelist Mission (L.E.M.)

PO Box 158 GPO, Rangoon, BURMA

Pau Za Mung
Organized: 1983   Baptist

MISSIONARIES IN SERVICE

(1985) 7   (1988) 7
AAGR = 0%
Foreign missionaries in 1988:   0

FIELDS OF SERVICE

Burma

Arakan State Arkanese, Asho, Chin
Rangoon Division Burmese, Chin
Chin State Chin

Methodist Church Home Mission Committee

PO Tahan, Kalemyo, BURMA

Rev. Tlangdailova
Organized: 1966   Methodist

MISSIONARIES IN SERVICE

(1972) 10	(1975) 14	(1978) 25
(1980) 11	(1984) 10	(1985) 12
(1988) 13		

AAGR = 2%
Foreign missionaries in 1988:   0

FIELDS OF SERVICE

Burma

Chin State Dhai Tribe

Missionary Evangelistic Crusade

437 Dukahtong, Myitkyina, BURMA

Hkamung Gam

Organized: Not reported.
Church of God World Mission
MISSIONARIES IN SERVICE
(1980) 8   (1985) 13   (1988) 17
AAGR = 10%
Foreign missionaries in 1988:   0
FIELDS OF SERVICE
Burma
  Gatshanyane Kachin, Marv
  Waingmaw   Marv, Shan, Chinese,
    Lashi
  Myithyina Burmese, Chinese, Kachin
  Shwezet Marv, Lisu

New Apostolic Church
PO Box 420, Rangoon, BURMA

Rev. David Kap Cin Thang
Organized: 1979   Apostlic Faith
MISSIONARIES IN SERVICE
(1988) 48
AAGR = N/A
Foreign missionaries in 1988:   0
FIELDS OF SERVICE
Burma
  All 14 States Burmese, Chin, Karen,
    Kachin
Malawi
  Southern Region Chichewa, English
  Central Region Chichewa, English
Mozambique Portuguese
Zambia Bemba, English

Presbyterian Church of Burma
Tahan, Kalemyo, BURMA

Rev. L.R. Bawla
Organized: 1956   Presbyterian
MISSIONARIES IN SERVICE
(1972) 8   (1975) 23   (1978) 29
(1980) 33   (1988) 58
AAGR = 13%
Foreign missionaries in 1988:   0
FIELDS OF SERVICE
Burma
  Naga Hills Naga

  Arakan State Meo, Arrankanes
  Chindwin Area Shan, Burmese
  Chin State Chin

Self Supporting Karen Baptist Church
82 Sin yekanlan, Ahlone
Rangoon, BURMA

Rev. Mahn Ba Khin
Organized: 1912   Baptist
MISSIONARIES IN SERVICE
(1985) 10   (1988) 12*
AAGR = N/A
Foreign missionaries in 1988: Not
reported.
FIELDS OF SERVICE
Burma
  Rangoon Division Burmese
  Irrawady Division Burmese
  Karen State Karen

Seventh Day Adventist Mission
PO Box 977, U Wisara Road
Rangoon, BURMA

U. Thein Swe
Organized: 1904   Adventist
MISSIONARIES IN SERVICE
(1985) 160   (1988) 192*
AAGR = N/A
Missionaries in 1988: Not reported.
FIELDS OF SERVICE
Burma
  All 14 States All Racial Groups

Witnessing for Christ
PO Box 220, Rangoon, BURMA

Ronnie U Khin Maung Tun
Organized: 1973
Evangelical Brethren
MISSIONARIES IN SERVICE
(1985) 56   (1988) 67*
AAGR = N/A
Missionaries in 1988: Not reported.

FIELDS OF SERVICE
Burma
All 14 States All Racial Groups

HONG KONG

CCC Wanchai Church, Joint Mission Committee
Chuk Kui Terrace, W77 Spring Garden Lane, Wanchai, HONG KONG

Rev. Choy Yee-Hung
Organized: 1967   Church of Christ

MISSIONARIES IN SERVICE
(1972)	3	(1975)	3	(1978)	5
(1980)	6	(1984)	5	(1985)	3
(1988)	4				

AAGR = 2%
Foreign missionaries in 1988:   3

FIELDS OF SERVICE
Pakistan
Hong Kong   Local Church
Southeast Asia   Young people, English

China Evangelistic Mission
Flat B 10, 29 Parkes St.,
Kowloon, HONG KONG

Rev. Cheng Yee Sum
Organized: 1975   Evangelical

MISSIONARIES IN SERVICE
(1975)	1	(1978)	1	(1980)	4
(1984)	3	(1985)	5	(1988)	4

AAGR = 11%
Foreign missionaries in 1988:   4

FIELDS OF SERVICE
Thailand
Chiang Mai Chinese, Thai, Lahu

Christian Evangelical Centre
Hong Shun Bldg., 166-172 Woosung St.,
Kowloon, HONG KONG

Dr. K.K. Ho
Organized: 1979   Nondenominational

MISSIONARIES IN SERVICE
(1984)	5	(1985)	4	(1988) 4

AAGR = -4%
Foreign missionaries in 1988:   4

FIELDS OF SERVICE
Thailand
Golden Triangle Chinese refugees
Kenya

Christian Missionary Alliance Hebron Mission
4/F 20 Austin Ave, Rm. 401
Kowloon, HONG KONG

Rev. Jerry Hak Kun Wong
Organized: 1972   Alliance

MISSIONARIES IN SERVICE
(1972)	2	(1980)	11	(1985) 9
(1988)	17			

AAGR = 14%
Foreign missionaries in 1988:   8

FIELDS OF SERVICE
Australia
Western Australia (Perth) Cantonese, English, Mandarin
France
Paris Cantonese, French
Macau   Chinese
Taiwan   Chinese
Malaysia
Sarawak State Mandarin

Evangelical Lutheran Church of Hong Kong, Overseas Mission Committee
50 A Waterloo Road
Kowloon, HONG KONG

Fu Ming Kung
Organized: 1987   Lutheran

MISSIONARIES IN SERVICE
(1988)   1
AAGR = N/A
Foreign missionaries in 1988:   1

FIELDS OF SERVICE

Thailand
  Bangkok Thai

Foreign Missionary Society of CC&MA of Hong Kong

PO Box 34902
King's Road Post Office, HONG KONG

Rev. Wu Chin
Organized: 1973   Alliance

MISSIONARIES IN SERVICE

(1972) 11   (1975) 13   (1978) 13
(1980) 15   (1982) 16   (1984) 15
(1985) 16   (1988) 17
AAGR =   3%
Foreign missionaries in 1988:   8

FIELDS OF SERVICE

Peru
  Lima Department Peruvians
Liberia
  Todee Gola people
Thailand
  North Eastern Region Thai
Indonesia
  Sumatra Region Indonesian

Hebron Evangelical Association

20 Austin Ave., 1/F
Kowloon, HONG KONG

Dr. Philemon Choi
Organized: 1971

MISSIONARIES IN SERVICE

(1980) 14   (1988) 20*
AAGR = N/A
Foreign missionaries in 1988: Not reported.

FIELDS OF SERVICE

Not reported.

Hong Kong Baptist Church

50-56 Caine Road, HONG KONG

Rev. Timothy Lau Siu-Hong

Organized: 1901   Baptist

MISSIONARIES IN SERVICE

(1975) 1   (1978) 4   (1980) 2
(1984) 3   (1985) 2   (1988) 1
AAGR =   0%
Foreign missionaries in 1988:   1

FIELDS OF SERVICE

Liberia
  Flumpa

Hong Kong Overseas Mission

GPO Box 3976, Kowloon, HONG KONG

Ms. Esther Yu Chin Jung
Organized: 1962   Nondenominational

MISSIONARIES IN SERVICE

(1972) 2   (1975) 2   (1978) 1
(1980) 2   (1984) 2   (1985) 2
(1988) 4
AAGR =   4%
Foreign missionaries in 1988:   4

FIELDS OF SERVICE

Canada
  British Columbia Chinese
USA
  California Chinese
Taiwan   Mandarin

Hong Kong Swatow Christian Church Mission

23 Prat Ave, Tsimslatsui, HONG KONG

Rev. David Chu
Organized: 1971   Denominational

MISSIONARIES IN SERVICE

(1980) 4   (1988) 6*
AAGR = N/A
Foreign missionaries in 1988: Not reported.

FIELDS OF SERVICE

Not reported.

Kowloon Canaan Mission

215 G/F Sai Yee Street, Mongkok,
Kowloon, HONG KONG

Rev. Tang Chok Leung, Leader
Organized: 1966

MISSIONARIES IN SERVICE
(1980) 1   (1983) 1   (1984) 5
(1985) 5   (1988) 13*
AAGR = N/A
Foreign missionaries in 1988: Not
reported.

FIELDS OF SERVICE
Not reported.

Kowloon City Evangelical Church
71 Fuk Lo Tsun Road, Third Floor
Kowloon, HONG KONG

Lawrence Tsang Tsay Lour
Organized: 1978   Nondenominational

MISSIONARIES IN SERVICE
(1978) 1   (1980) 4   (1988) 6*
AAGR = N/A
Foreign missionaries in 1988: Not
reported.

FIELDS OF SERVICE
Not reported.

Overseas Missionary Fellowship, Hong Kong Council
PO Box 70505, Kowloon Central PO
Kowloon, HONG KONG

Rev. Kenneth Lo
Organized: 1966   Nondemoninational

MISSIONARIES IN SERVICE
(1972) 2   (1975) 2   (1978) 3
(1980) 3   (1984) 7   (1985) 8
(1988) 11
AAGR = 11%
Foreign missionaries in 1988: 11

FIELDS OF SERVICE
Japan
  Hokkaido Province Japanese
  Honshu Japanese
Pakistan
  Philippines

  Luzon Region Filipinos
Taiwan
  Tainan County Industry Workers
Thailand
  Muang Sakon Nakhon Thai

Ping An Christian Church, Mission Department
43-47 Man Cheong Bldg. 2/F Ferry
Point, Kowloon, HONG KONG

Miss Rita Fan
Organized: 1982   Evangelical

MISSIONARIES IN SERVICE
(1984) 3   (1985) 2   (1988) 4
AAGR = 7%
Foreign missionaries in 1988:   2

FIELDS OF SERVICE
Hong Kong
  Kowloon Chinese Hospital Patients
United Kingdom
  England (Manchester) Overseas
    Chinese (Students and Local
    Chinese)

World Outreach, Inc.
88 Robinson Rd., Solon House 1/B
HONG KONG

W.N. Molenkamp
Organized: 1932   Pentecostal

MISSIONARIES IN SERVICE
(1980) 46   (1984) 50   (1988) 54*
AAGR = N/A
Foreign missionaries in 1988: Not
reported.

FIELDS OF SERVICE
Thailand	**Bangladesh**
Singapore	**Papau New Guinea**
Spain	**South Africa**
Philippines	**Tanzania**
Fiji	**Indonesia**
Malawi	**Zimbabwe**
Kenya	**Japan**
Korea South	**Egypt**
India	**Hong Kong**
Chile	

INDIA

All India Prayer Fellowship
Q-3 Green Park Extension
New Delhi 110 016, INDIA

Dr. P.N. Kurien
Organized: 1957   Nondenominational
MISSIONARIES IN SERVICE
(1980) 227   (1982) 235   (1984) 248
(1985) 334   (1988) 403
AAGR = 7%
Foreign missionaries in 1988:   12
FIELDS OF SERVICE
India
  Tripura Chakma, Riang, Riang Lang,
    Darlong
  Assam Karbi
  Orissa Munda, Oraon
  Nagaland Naga Yimchungru
  Manipur Meithei, Paite, Vaiphei, Hmar
  West Bengal
Nepal

Alliance Ministries
INDIA

Organized: Not reported.
MISSIONARIES IN SERVICE
(1988) 6
AAGR = N/A
Foreign missionaries in 1988:   0
FIELDS OF SERVICE
India
  Maharashtra Marathi, Gujarati

Alpha Missionary Movement
PO Box 2039, Fatehgunt
Baroda 390 002, INDIA

Rev. Mathews Cherian
Organized: 1965   Pentecostal
MISSIONARIES IN SERVICE
(1972) 5   (1980) 9   (1985) 11
(1988) 12
AAGR = 6%

Foreign missionaries in 1988:   0
FIELDS OF SERVICE
India
  Gujarat Hindi, Gujarati, Tamil,
    Malayalam
  Kerala Malayalam

Amar Jyoti India
PO Box 27, Sutahat
Cuttack 753 001, INDIA

Mr. Ashok Patrot
Organized: 1979   Nondenominational
MISSIONARIES IN SERVICE
(1980) 7   (1985) 19   (1988) 41
AAGR = 25%
Foreign missionaries in 1988:   0
FIELDS OF SERVICE
Not reported.

Ao Baptist Churches Association
Impur 798 615, Nagaland, INDIA

Rev. K. Lanumeren Ao
Organized: Not reported.
MISSIONARIES IN SERVICE
(1972) 2   (1975) 5   (1978) 8
(1980) 10   (1984) 13   (1988) 24*
AAGR = N/A
Foreign missionaries in 1988: Not
reported.
FIELDS OF SERVICE
India
  Assam Assamese
  Arunachal Pradesh Territory Tangla,
    Wanchu, Nokdi
Bhutan   Hindi

Asia Evangelistic Fellowship
6 Farida Villa, TPSIU Rd. No. 1, Bandra,
Bombay 400 050, INDIA

K.J. Joseph
Organized: 1959   Nondenominational
MISSIONARIES IN SERVICE
(1975) 8   (1978) 10   (1980) 12

(1982) 13   (1988) 20*
AAGR = N/A
Foreign missionaries in 1988: Not
reported.

FIELDS OF SERVICE

Not reported.

Association for Garhwal's Advancement, Prosperity & Evangelism

173 C Rajpur Rd., Dehradun
Uttar Pradesh, INDIA

Rev. Vachan S. Bhandari
Organized: 1980   Evangelical

MISSIONARIES IN SERVICE

(1980) 3   (1985) 11   (1988) 15
AAGR = 22%
Foreign missionaries in 1988:   0

FIELDS OF SERVICE

India
  Uttar Pradesh Garhwali, Plain People,
  Jaunsari

Banjara Mission Development Trust

PO Box 459, Madras 600 006, INDIA

Rev. William Scott
Organized: Not reported.

MISSIONARIES IN SERVICE

(1988) 11
AAGR = N/A
Foreign missionaries in 1988:   0

FIELDS OF SERVICE

India

Bethel Bible College, Home Missionary Council

Punalur 691 305, INDIA

Rev. P.N. Zachariah
Organized: Not reported.

MISSIONARIES IN SERVICE

(1988) 6
AAGR = N/A
Foreign missionaries in 1988:   0

FIELDS OF SERVICE

India
  Kerala State Malayalam

Bethel Assembly

West Godavari District
Tadepalligudem 543 101
Andhra Pradesh, INDIA

Rev. G. Israel
Organized: 1963   Independent

MISSIONARIES IN SERVICE

(1988) 4
AAGR = N/A
Foreign missionaries in 1988:   0

FIELDS OF SERVICE

India
  Andhra Pradesh Telugu, Tribal

Blessing Youth Mission

Post Bag 609, Vellore 632 006
Tamil Nadu, INDIA

R. Stanley
Organized: 1971   Charismatic

MISSIONARIES IN SERVICE

(1988) 110
AAGR = N/A
Foreign missionaries in 1988:   0

FIELDS OF SERVICE

India
  Rajasthan Rajasthani
  Orissa Oriya
  Tamil Nadu Tamil
  Karnataka Kannada
  Maharashtra Marathi
  Madhya Pradesh Hindi

Bombay Revival and Prayer Band

PO Box 16774, Sion East
Bombay 400 022, INDIA

Jaya Thasiah
Organized: 1979   Nondenominational

MISSIONARIES IN SERVICE

(1980) 14   (1985) 18   (1988) 24

AAGR = 7%
Foreign missionaries in 1988: 0
FIELDS OF SERVICE
India
Maharashtra (Bombay) Slum dwellers

Carmel Pioneer Evangelical Mission
PO Box 476, Jullundur City 144 004
Punjab, INDIA

Rev. Sam George
Organized: 1980   Pentecostal
MISSIONARIES IN SERVICE
(1985) 10   (1988) 11
AAGR = 3%
Foreign missionaries in 1988: 0
FIELDS OF SERVICE
India
Punjab Poor, Illiterate
Haryana Poor, Illiterate

Christ for India Movement
CFIM Prayer Centre, Post Bag No 2
Nagpur 440 013, INDIA

Rev. Paul Malayadi
Organized: 1981   Independent
MISSIONARIES IN SERVICE
(1985) 50   (1988) 85
AAGR = 19%
Foreign missionaries in 1988: 0
FIELDS OF SERVICE
India
Madhya Pradesh State Hindi, Tribal
Kerala State Malayalam, Tamil, Tribal
Maharashtra State Marathi, Hindi,
    Urdu, Tribal
Orissa State Oriya, Hindi, Tribal
Karnataka Kannada, Tamil, Tribal
*Andhra Pradesh*Telugu, Urdu, Tribal
Uttar Pradesh Hindi, Urdu, Tribal
Tamil Nadu Tamil, Malayalam, Tribal

Christ for Nagaland Ministries
Post Box 26, Kohima 797 001

Nagaland, INDIA
Joseph D. Paul
Organized: 1984   Charismatic
MISSIONARIES IN SERVICE
(1985) 12   (1988) 48
AAGR = 59%
Foreign missionaries in 1988: 8
FIELDS OF SERVICE
India
Arunachal Pradesh Territory Nissi,
    Adivasi, Tangsa
Manipur Naga Mao, Naga, Tangkhul,
    Maram, Meithei
Assam Assamese, Adivas, Karbi, (Tea
    garden workers), Boro, Kachari
Tripura Debbarma
Burma
Chin Chin, Lushai
Bhutan
Nepal

Christ the Hope Ministries
13 Sindhi Colony, Upanagar
Nasik 422 006, INDIA

Rev. M. Mohan Ram
Organized: 1984   Nondenominational
MISSIONARIES IN SERVICE
(1988) 4
AAGR = N/A
Foreign missionaries in 1988: 0
FIELDS OF SERVICE
India
Maharashtra
Tamil Nadu Sourashtra

Christ's Gospel Mission
PO Box 2018, Secunderabad 500 003
Andhra Pradesh, INDIA

C. Krupanandam
Organized: 1979   Independent
MISSIONARIES IN SERVICE
(1972) 16   (1980) 20   (1985) 24
(1988) 24
AAGR = 3%
Foreign missionaries in 1988: 0

FIELDS OF SERVICE

India
Andhra Pradesh Savara, Koya,
Lambadi, Erukala, Caste Hindu,
Prisoners, Bible Correspondence

Christian Academy for Rural Welfare & Evangelism
PO Box 5, Kotdwara
Garhwal, INDIA

Rev. Tashi Bahadur
Organized: 1980   Nondenominational

MISSIONARIES IN SERVICE

(1988) 32
AAGR = N/A
Foreign missionaries in 1988:   0

FIELDS OF SERVICE

India
Uttar Pradesh State Kumaoni,
Garhwali, Nepali, Tibetan,
Himachali, Tharu, Muslims, Urdu

Christian Endeavour for Hill Tribes
K. Kotapadu, Visakhapatnam 531 034
Andhra Pradesh, INDIA

Rev. M.S.S.K. William
Organized: 1974   Evangelical

MISSIONARIES IN SERVICE

(1975)   5   (1978) 7   (1980) 10
(1985) 15   (1988) 14
AAGR =   8%
Foreign missionaries in 1988:   0

FIELDS OF SERVICE

India
Andhra Pradesh (Visakha district)
Adivasi, Porja, Kupia, Khono

Christian Outreach Uplifting New Tribes
PO Box 1720, Secunderabad 500 017
Andhra Pradesh, INDIA

Rev. Gollapalii John
Organized: 1978   Evangelical

MISSIONARIES IN SERVICE

(1978) 5   (1980) 24   (1984) 43
(1985) 36   (1988) 36
AAGR = 22%
Foreign missionaries in 1988:   0

FIELDS OF SERVICE

India
Andhra Pradesh State Gondi,
Chenchu, Savara, Yerukala, Others
Gujarat State Bhili, Gujarat
Orissa State Savara

Church Growth Missionary Movement
PO Box 30, Madurai 625 016, INDIA

Rev. J.C. Bose Meiyappan
Organized: 1975   Evangelical

MISSIONARIES IN SERVICE

(1975) 7   (1978) 9   (1980) 11
(1988) 12
AAGR = 4%
Foreign missionaries in 1988:   0

FIELDS OF SERVICE

India
Tamil Nadu State Tamil
Maharashtra State Hindi, Marathi,
Gondi, Madi, Telugu
Gujarat State Gujarati, Vasavi, Bhili

Church of Holy Spirit
V. Fatehgarh Churian
Gurdaspur District, Teh. Batala, INDIA

Rev. Bawa Masih Zakki
Organized: 1970   Pentecostal

MISSIONARIES IN SERVICE

(1972) 34   (1980) 58   (1985) 91
(1988) 142
AAGR = 9%
Foreign missionaries in 1988:   0

FIELDS OF SERVICE

India
Himachal Pradesh State Hindus,
Muslims, Sikhs, Buddhists, Jains,
Carpenters, Christians

Punjab State Hindus, Muslims, Sikhs, Buddhists, Jains, Carpenters, Christians

Uttar Pradesh State Hindus, Muslims, Sikhs, Buddhists, Jains, Carpenters, Christians

Haryana State Hindus, Muslims, Sikhs, Buddhists, Jains, Carpenters, Christians

Jammu and Kashmir State Hindus, Muslims, Sikhs, Buddhists, Jains, Carpenters, Christians

Kerala State Hindus, Muslims, Sikhs, Buddhists, Jains, Carpenters, Christians

Compassion of Agape

Post Box No. 6
Nedumkandom 685 553, INDIA

Rev. C.P. Thomas
Organized: 1970   Nondenominational
MISSIONARIES IN SERVICE
(1972) 17   (1980) 100   (1985) 65
(1988) 85
AAGR = 11%
Foreign missionaries in 1988:   0
FIELDS OF SERVICE
India
 Kerala State Mannan, Muthuvan
 Rajasthan State Bhili

Council of Baptist Churches in Northeast India

Panbazar, Guwahati 781 001
Assam, INDIA

Rev. K. Imotemjen Aier
Organized: 1949   Baptist
MISSIONARIES IN SERVICE
(1980) 44   (1988) 89*
AAGR = N/A
Foreign missionaries in 1988: Not reported.
FIELDS OF SERVICE
Not reported.

Crusaders Prayer Centre

PO Box 1671, Secunderabad 500 003, Andhra Pradesh, INDIA

Mr. M. Krishaiah
Organized: Not reported.
MISSIONARIES IN SERVICE
(1988) 6
AAGR = N/A
Foreign missionaries in 1988:   0
FIELDS OF SERVICE
India
 Andhra Pradesh State Telugu

Diocesan Missionary Prayer Band

PO Box 629205, Santhapuram
Tamil Nadu, INDIA

Rev. M. Rajian
Organized: 1962   Denominational
MISSIONARIES IN SERVICE
(1972) 18   (1975) 23   (1978) 26
(1980) 32   (1982) 24   (1988) 29*
AAGR = N/A
Foreign missionaries in 1988: Not reported.
FIELDS OF SERVICE
Not reported.

Dipti Mission

Sahibganji 816 109, Bihar, INDIA

D. Rajkumar
Organized: 1924   Interdenominational
MISSIONARIES IN SERVICE
(1972) 7   (1975) 5   (1978) 6
(1980) 7   (1988) 7*
AAGR = N/A
Foreign missionaries in 1988: Not reported.
FIELDS OF SERVICE
Not reported.

Echo of His Call Evangelistic Programme

PO Box 2957, Madras 600 005, INDIA

Bro. S. Sam Selva Raj
Organized: Not reported.

MISSIONARIES IN SERVICE
(1972) 5   (1975) 12   (1980) 12
(1982) 28   (1984) 28   (1988) 50*
AAGR = N/A
Foreign missionaries in 1988: Not
reported.

FIELDS OF SERVICE
India
  Tamil Nadu State Hindus

Emmanuel Missionary Fellowship
D-632 Saraswati Vihar
Delhi 110 034, INDIA

Joseph D. Paul
Organized: Not reported.

MISSIONARIES IN SERVICE
(1980) 3   (1982) 20   (1984) 24
(1988) 33*
AAGR = N/A
Foreign missionaries in 1988: Not
reported.

FIELDS OF SERVICE
India
  Bihar State Hindus
  Uttar Pradesh State Hindus
  Delhi Territory Students,
    Internationals, Tamil
  Jammu and Kashmir State Hindus,
    Muslims

Evangelical Convention Church
PO Box 6, Churachandpur 795 128
Manipur, INDIA

Rev. Luai Chin Thang
Organized: Not reported.

MISSIONARIES IN SERVICE
(1984) 59   (1988) 84*
AAGR = N/A
Foreign missionaries in 1988: Not
reported.

FIELDS OF SERVICE
Not reported.

Evangelical Free Church of India
Madanriting, Shillong 793 021
Meghalaya, INDIA

Rev. R. Pakhuongte
Organized: Not reported.

MISSIONARIES IN SERVICE
(1986) 41   (1988) 49*
AAGR = N/A
Foreign missionaries in 1988: Not
reported.

FIELDS OF SERVICE
Not reported.

Evangelical Literature Service
95 A Vepery High Road
Madras 600 007, INDIA

Rev. V.M. Abraham
Organized: 1954   Evangelical

MISSIONARIES IN SERVICE
(1972) 20   (1975) 18   (1978) 26
(1980) 32   (1982) 32   (1984) 30
(1985) 27   (1988) 33
AAGR = 3%
Foreign missionaries in 1988:   0

FIELDS OF SERVICE
India
  Kerala State Malayalam, English
  Karnataka State Kannada, Telugu,
    English
  Maharashtra State Marathi, English,
    Tamil
  Tamil Nadu State Tamil, Telugu,
    Malayalam, English

Evangelical Lutheran Church in Madhya Pradesh
PO Box No. 30, Luther Bhavan
Chhindwara
Madhya Pradesh 480 001, INDIA

Bishop Rev. I.N. Roberts
Organized: 1922   Evangelical Lutheran

MISSIONARIES IN SERVICE
(1980) 10   (1988) 20*
AAGR = N/A
Foreign missionaries in 1988: Not reported.

FIELDS OF SERVICE
Not reported.

Evangelical Mission
M/186-A Station Colony Nerly-Izzat
Bareilly 243 122, Uttar Pradesh, INDIA

Mr. H.L. Sharma
Organized: Not reported.

MISSIONARIES IN SERVICE
(1988) 10
AAGR = N/A
Foreign missionaries in 1988: 0

FIELDS OF SERVICE
India
  Uttar Pradesh State Hindi

Evangelize Every Muslim in India
P.B. 420, Vellore 632 004
Tamil Nadu, INDIA

T. Babu Umar Pulavar
Organized: 1975   Interdenominational

MISSIONARIES IN SERVICE
(1978) 3   (1980) 3   (1988) 3*
AAGR = N/A
Foreign missionaries in 1988: Not reported.

FIELDS OF SERVICE
Not reported.

Federation of Evangelical Churches of India
Plot 124 Bhagirati Apts.
Shivaji Nagar, Nagpur, INDIA

Rev. Gabriel Massey
Organized: 1974   Evangelical

MISSIONARIES IN SERVICE
(1988) 61
AAGR = N/A
Foreign missionaries in 1988:   0

FIELDS OF SERVICE
India
  Tamil Nadu State Sourashtra
  Maharashtra State Mawchi
  Uttar Pradesh State Garhwali
  West Bengal State Nepali, Bhuiyali
  Madhya Pradesh State Salnami,
    Unram

Fellowship of Calvary Friends
PB Box 5, Mettupalayam 641 301, INDIA

Rev. R. George Thomas
Organized: 1986   Indepedent
                              Evangelical

MISSIONARIES IN SERVICE
(1985) 14   (1988) 20
AAGR = 13%
Foreign missionaries in 1988:   0

FIELDS OF SERVICE
India
  Kerala State Tribal People
  Tamil Nadu State Tribal People
  Karnataka State Tribal People

Fellowship of Evangelical Baptist Churches
PO Berlah Lane, Churachandpur 795 128
Manipur, INDIA

Rev. T.G. Daniel
Organized: 1987   Baptist

MISSIONARIES IN SERVICE
(1980) 2   (1988) 2
AAGR = 0%
Foreign missionaries in 1988:   2

FIELDS OF SERVICE
Burma
  Chin State Tiddim, Chin, Zomi,
India
  Manipur State Manipuri, Hindu,
    Nepali, Bengali

Fellowship of Evangelical Friends

23 Isaac Street, Nagercoil
Tamil Nadu, INDIA

D.T. Rajah
Organized: 1960   Nondenominational
MISSIONARIES IN SERVICE

(1972) 10   (1975) 20   (1978) 27
(1980) 12   (1984) 50   (1985) 12
(1988) 16
AAGR =   3%
Foreign missionaries in 1988:   0
FIELDS OF SERVICE
India
  Tamil Nadu (Madurai)
  Southern India
  Southern Hills Tribal People

Fellowship of Independent Full Gospel Churches

Veloor PO
Kottayam 686 003, Kerala, INDIA

Rev. A.A. Philpose
Organized: 1981   Pentecostal
MISSIONARIES IN SERVICE

(1972) 34   (1980) 35   (1985) 39
(1988) 52
AAGR =   3%
Foreign missionaries in 1988:   0
FIELDS OF SERVICE
India
  Kerala State Tribal People

Fellowship of the Pentecostal Churches of God India

PO Box 63
Deshbandhupura, Itarsi, INDIA

Rev. Kurian Thomas
Organized: 1966   Pentecostal
MISSIONARIES IN SERVICE

(1972) 280   (1980) 380   (1985) 540
(1988) 560
AAGR =   4%

Foreign missionaries in 1988:   0
FIELDS OF SERVICE
India
  Madhya Pradesh State
  Punjab State
  Tamil Nadu State
  West Bengal State
  Uttar Pradesh State
  Kerala State
  Bihar State
  Delhi Territory
  Gujarat State
  Andhra Pradesh State
  Orissa State
  Maharashtra State
  Rajasthan State

Followers of Christ, The

PO Box 414
Erode 638 001, Tamil Nadu, INDIA

Dhinakaran J. David
Organized: 1975   Pentecostal
MISSIONARIES IN SERVICE

(1988) 18
AAGR = N/A
Foreign missionaries in 1988:   0
FIELDS OF SERVICE
India
  Tamil Nadu State Tamil
  Kerala State Malayalam

Friends Missionary Prayer Band

No. 110 Baracca Road, Kilpauk
Madras 600 010, INDIA

Mr. M. Patrick Joshua
Organized: 1968   Nondenominational
MISSIONARIES IN SERVICE

(1972) 23   (1975) 55   (1978) 113
(1980) 170   (1982) 221   (1984) 228
(1985) 310   (1988) 439
AAGR = 20%
Foreign missionaries in 1988:   0
FIELDS OF SERVICE
India

Rajasthan State Rajasthani, Rajputs
Maharashtra State Kolami, Koli,
  Gond, Pawri, Bhil, Pakistan Refugees
Tamil Nadu State Poosali, Lingayats
Orissa State Munda
Haryana State Rajputs, Jat, Yadhava,
  Majbisikhs
Bihar State Dharu, Dubla, Kotvadi,
  Malto, Santhali, Mythili, Irkaro
Uttar Pradesh State Chammar, Kori
Madhya Pradesh State Bhili, Bhilal
Gujarat State Kakna, Vasava, Chodri,
  Varli, Gamit

Frontier Missions Center
PO Box 36
Dimapur 797 112, Nagaland, INDIA

Rev. Joseph D. Paul
Organized: 1983   Pentecostal

MISSIONARIES IN SERVICE
Further information withheld at
agency's request.

Full Gospel
Fellowship of India
PO Bhagalpur, Deoria District
Uttar Pradesh, INDIA

Rev. A.N. Jonah
Organized: Not reported.

MISSIONARIES IN SERVICE
(1972) 24   (1975) 26   (1978) 32
(1980) 32   (1984) 38   (1985) 38
(1988) 42*
AAGR = N/A
Foreign missionaries in 1988: Not
reported.

FIELDS OF SERVICE
India
  Bihar State Bhojpuri

Full Gospel Young Men's
Association
PO Box 609
Vellore 632 006, Tamil Nadu, INDIA

R. Stanley

Organized: 1971   Interdenominational

MISSIONARIES IN SERVICE
(1975) 8   (1978) 22   (1980) 27
(1988) 50*
AAGR = N/A
Foreign missionaries in 1988: Not
reported.

FIELDS OF SERVICE
Not reported.

Fundamental Independent
Baptist Church
Zotlang 796 691, INDIA

F. Lalawia
Organized: 1962   Baptist

MISSIONARIES IN SERVICE
(1972) 2   (1980) 4   (1985) 4
(1988) 2
AAGR = 0%
Foreign missionaries in 1988:   2

FIELDS OF SERVICE
Not reported.

GIFT Christian Association
Post Bag No-1
Lingampalli, Hyderabad 500 133
Andhra Pradesh, INDIA

K. Prabhudass, President
Organized: Not reported.

MISSIONARIES IN SERVICE
(1980) 1   (1984) 13   (1985) 32
(1988) 40*
AAGR = N/A
Foreign missionaries in 1988: Not
reported.

FIELDS OF SERVICE
Not reported.

Garo Baptist Convention
A B Mission Compound
West Garo Hills
Tura 794 001, Meghalaya, INDIA

Nongong Marak
Organized: Not reported.   Baptist

MISSIONARIES IN SERVICE

(1988)   3

AAGR = N/A

Foreign missionaries in 1988:   0

FIELDS OF SERVICE

India

Assam State Rabha, Katkari

Meghalaya State

Go Ye Missions

PO Box 116, Nagercoil 629 001

Tamil Nadu, INDIA

Rev. P. Kulandaivelu

Organized: 1979   Nondenominational

MISSIONARIES IN SERVICE

(1980)   7   (1982)   12   (1984)   30

(1985)   26   (1988)   32

AAGR =   21%

Foreign missionaries in 1988:   0

FIELDS OF SERVICE

India

Kerala Trichur Hindus, Backward
   Class

Coimbatore High Caste, Grounders

Periyar Hindus, Hill Tribes in Bannari
   Hills

Tamil Nadu (Kanniyakumari) Hindus

Golpara Baro Baptist Church Union

Tukrajhar Village & Post, Golpara

District 783 380, Assam, INDIA

Mr. Sulen Basumatari

Organized: Not reported.

MISSIONARIES IN SERVICE

(1988)   1

AAGR = N/A

Foreign missionaries in 1988:   0

FIELDS OF SERVICE

India

Assam State Bodo, Kachari, Tibetan,
   Burmese

Goodwill Extension Services

PO Box 10, Tilaknagar, Dombivli

Thana, Maharashtra, INDIA

Subedar R. Saran

Organized: Not reported.

MISSIONARIES IN SERVICE

(1980)   1   (1982)   2   (1984)   2

(1988)   4*

AAGR = N/A

Foreign missionaries in 1988: Not
reported.

FIELDS OF SERVICE

India

Maharashtra State Muslims

Gospel Echoing Missionary Society

13th Cross Street, Chromepet

Madras 600 044, INDIA

D. Dayanandhan

Organized: 1979   Charismatic

MISSIONARIES IN SERVICE

(1972)   3   (1975)   6   (1978) 13

(1980)   23   (1982)   39   (1984) 41

(1985)   25   (1988)   36

AAGR =   17%

Foreign missionaries in 1988:   0

FIELDS OF SERVICE

India

Uttar Pradesh State Hindi

Bihar State Bihari

Gospel Missionary Association

PO Box 962, Madras 600 012, INDIA

Rev. J. Palmer

Organized: Not reported.

MISSIONARIES IN SERVICE

(1975)   7   (1978)   9   (1980) 16

(1982)   16   (1988)   33*

AAGR = N/A

Foreign missionaries in 1988: Not
reported.

FIELDS OF SERVICE
Not reported.

Gospel Outreach
Elim Cottage, PO Jasidih District
Deoghar 811 142, INDIA

Rev. Gopal Hembrom
Organized: 1984   Independent
MISSIONARIES IN SERVICE
(1985) 7   (1988) 17
AAGR = 34%
Foreign missionaries in 1988:   0
FIELDS OF SERVICE
Not reported.

Gospel Team, The
A7 Periyar Nagar
Madras 600 082, INDIA

Mr. D. Jawahar Chelliah
Organized: Not reported.
MISSIONARIES IN SERVICE
(1988) 1
AAGR = N/A
Foreign missionaries in 1988:   0
FIELDS OF SERVICE
India
  Tamil Nadu State Tamil

Gospel for Kashmir
Batote, INDIA

Rev. K.T. Paul
Organized: 1988   Evangelical
MISSIONARIES IN SERVICE
(1988) 30
AAGR = N/A
Foreign missionaries in 1988:   0
FIELDS OF SERVICE
India
  Jammu and Kashmir State Hindus,
  Muslims

Gospel in Action Fellowship
M.C. Road
Perumbavoor 683 542, INDIA

Mr. T.S. Thomas
Organized: Not reported.
MISSIONARIES IN SERVICE
(1988) 6
AAGR = N/A
Foreign missionaries in 1988:   0
FIELDS OF SERVICE
India
  Kerala State Karimpalar, Paniyan,
  Malayalam

Henry Martyn Institute of Islamic Studies
PO Box 153, Hyderabad
Andhra Pradesh, INDIA

Rev. E.S. Isaiah
Organized: Not reported.
MISSIONARIES IN SERVICE
(1975) 17   (1978) 17   (1980) 17
(1982) 17   (1988) 17*
AAGR = N/A
Foreign missionaries in 1988: Not
reported.
FIELDS OF SERVICE
Not reported.

Himalayan Evangelical Fellowship
Kalimpon, Darjeeling 734 301, INDIA

Rev. M.H. Subba
Organized: 1976   Presbyterian
MISSIONARIES IN SERVICE
Further information withheld at
agency's request.

Himalayan Inland Mission
Lancer Lodge, Landour
Mussoorie, INDIA

Rev. Swami Sunder Singh
Organized: 1983   Charismatic
MISSIONARIES IN SERVICE
Further information withheld at
agency's request.

Hindustan Bible Institute & College

86-89 Medavakkam Tank Rpad
Kilpauk, Madras 600 010
Tamil Nadu, INDIA

Paul R. Gupta
Organized: 1952   Nondenominational

MISSIONARIES IN SERVICE

(1985) 2   (1988) 79
AAGR = 241%
Foreign missionaries in 1988:   0

FIELDS OF SERVICE

India
  Andhra Pradesh State Lambadi, Tribal
  Tamil Nadu State Telugu, Labour
    class, Poor
  Orissa State Tribal People
  Jammu and Kashmir State Urdu

Hindustan Evangelical Mission

PO Box 4989, T. Nagar
Madras 600 017, INDIA

M. George Stephenson
Organized: 1961

MISSIONARIES IN SERVICE

(1972) 12   (1975) 12   (1980) 19
(1982) 12   (1984) 12   (1985) 16
(1988) 18
AAGR =   3%
Foreign missionaries in 1988:   0

FIELDS OF SERVICE

India
  Tamil Nadu (Madras) Poor, Outcasts,
    Hindus
  Andhra Pradesh Telugu, Hill Tribes

Home Missionary Movement

Box Takou PO
Tamei 795 125, Manipur, INDIA

Rev. Kasui
Organized: 1982   Baptist

MISSIONARIES IN SERVICE

(1980) 5   (1982) 5   (1984) 9
(1985) 5   (1988) 12
AAGR = 12%
Foreign missionaries in 1988:   0

FIELDS OF SERVICE

India
  Nagaland State Naga
  Manipur State Manipuri

Independent Church of India

Sielmat PO Box 3
Churachandpur 795 128
Manipur, INDIA

Darsanglien Rvolnavl
Organized: 1930   Presbyterian

MISSIONARIES IN SERVICE

(1972) 4   (1975) 4   (1978) 15
(1980) 20   (1982) 18   (1984) 45
(1985) 34   (1988) 43
AAGR = 16%
Foreign missionaries in 1988:   0

FIELDS OF SERVICE

India
  Assam State Karbi, Cachari,
    Hrangkhol
  Manipur State Manipuri, Meithei,
    Kom, Chothe
  Tripura State Tripuri Debbarma

India National Inland Mission

V-20 Green Park Extension
New Delhi 110 016, INDIA

Dr. Paul Pillai
Organized: 1966   Evangelical

MISSIONARIES IN SERVICE

(1972) 126   (1975) 37   (1978) 48
(1980) 182   (1982) 87   (1984) 128
(1985) 243   (1988) 247
AAGR =   4%
Foreign missionaries in 1988:   0

FIELDS OF SERVICE

India

Himachal Pradesh State Purvis,
Brahmin, Kayasta, Kumbha, Kutta,
Untouchables, Hindu
Uttar Pradesh State Caste Brahmins,
Paharis, Bachnas, Jats, Yadavs,
Tribals
Punjab State Punjabi, Sikhs, Muslims
Jammu and Kashmir State Muslims
Urudu
Haryana State Jat Hindus, Hindi

India Church Growth Mission

7 Vidya Colony, K K Nagar
Madurai 625 020, INDIA

P.T. Rajan
Organized: 1978   Evangelical
MISSIONARIES IN SERVICE
(1978) 6   (1980) 9   (1985) 21
(1988) 36*
AAGR = N/A
Foreign missionaries in 1988: Not
reported.
FIELDS OF SERVICE
India
Tamil Nadu State Sourashtra

India Evangelical Crusade

60 C Ritchie Road
Calcutta 700 019, INDIA

Rev. David Dutt
Organized: 1971

MISSIONARIES IN SERVICE
(1972) 30   (1980) 99   (1985) 108
(1988) 163
AAGR = 11%
Foreign missionaries in 1988:   0
FIELDS OF SERVICE
India
Sikkim Territory Nepali, Lepcha
Uttar Pradesh State Hindi
West Bengal State Bengali, Nepali,
Tibetan, Duppa, Lepcha, Telugu
Assam State Bengali, Santhali, Boro

Bihar State Hindi, Santhali, Oraon,
Mundari

India Evangelistic Association

PO 96, Cuttack 753 008, INDIA

Rev. P.R. Parichha
Organized: 1983   Nondenominational
MISSIONARIES IN SERVICE
(1985) 12   (1988) 20
AAGR = 19%
Foreign missionaries in 1988:   0
FIELDS OF SERVICE
India
Orissa State Scheduled Castes Low
caste tribes, Konda, Poroja, State
Saura, Oriya, Bhatra

India Evangelistic and Relief Fellowship

6th Lane Cloughpet
Ongole 523 001, INDIA

Rev. K. Joseph
Organized: 1983   Presbyterian
MISSIONARIES IN SERVICE
(1972) 4   (1980) 5   (1985) 7
(1988) 12
AAGR = 7%
Foreign missionaries in 1988:   0
FIELDS OF SERVICE
India
Andhra Pradesh State Tribal People
Tamil Nadu (Madras) Backward

India Gospel Outreach Mission, Inc

House of God 4-91B, L.B. Hagar
Hyderabad 500 963
Andhra Pradesh, INDIA

Rev. P.N. Naidu
Organized: 1982   Nondenominational
MISSIONARIES IN SERVICE
Further information withheld at
agency's request.

India Gospel Outreach and Social Action
PO Box 1
Parlakhemundi 761 200, INDIA

Rev. Niranjan Bardhan
Organized: 1983   Nondenominational
MISSIONARIES IN SERVICE
(1985) 30   (1988) 17
AAGR = -16%
Foreign missionaries in 1988:   0
FIELDS OF SERVICE
India
  Andhra Pradesh State Telugu, Saura
  Orissa State Oriya, Telugu, Saura, Kui

India Nationals Evangelism Fellowship
P.O. Box 1707, Secunderabad 500 003
Andhra Pradesh, INDIA

Rev. Dr. Arthur J. Dalavai
Organized: Not reported.
MISSIONARIES IN SERVICE
(1980) 24   (1982) 23   (1984) 18
(1988) 13*
AAGR = N/A
Foreign missionaries in 1988: Not
reported.
FIELDS OF SERVICE
India
  West Bengal State Tribal People
  Andhra Pradesh State Hindus

Indian Bible Translators
Civil Aerodrome Road
Coimbatore 641 041, INDIA

S. Panneer Selvam
Organized: 1978   Nondenominational
MISSIONARIES IN SERVICE
(1988) 20
AAGR = N/A
Foreign missionaries in 1988:   0
FIELDS OF SERVICE
India

Tamil Nadu State Promotional work,
  Office Work, Sourashtra, Nilgiris,
  Badugu, Irular, Kurumbar
Madhya Pradesh State Halbi, Bhatri,
  Chattisgarhi
Bihar State Bhojpuri, Ho
Maharashtra State Gondi, Halba

Indian Evangelical Mission
38 Langford Road
Bangalore 560 025, INDIA

Dr. Theodore Williams
Organized: 1965   Interdenominational
MISSIONARIES IN SERVICE
(1972) 14   (1975) 33   (1978) 67
(1980) 160   (1982) 147   (1985) 230
(1988) 300
AAGR = 21%
Foreign missionaries in 1988:   16
FIELDS OF SERVICE
India
  Himachal Pradesh State Kului
  Karnataka State Kannada
  Gujarat State Bhili, Kukuna, Ghanasia
  Uttar Pradesh State Ghanvali
  Andhra Pradesh State Lambadi, Koya,
    Godi, Neethakami
  Maharashtra State Kolam, Korku,
    Gawri
  Madhya Pradesh State Bhakiri,
    Munda, Maria
  Tamil Nadu State Kurumba,
    Kathnpusari
Nepal
Thailand
Papau New Guinea
United Kingdom
  England
Bhutan
Middle East

Indian Evangelical Team
K 13 B Saket, New Delhi 110 017, INDIA

P.G. Vargis
Organized: 1977   Charismatic

MISSIONARIES IN SERVICE
(1972) 4   (1975) 3   (1980) 69
(1982) 118   (1984) 320   (1985) 304
(1988) 559
AAGR = 36%
Foreign missionaries in 1988:   0

FIELDS OF SERVICE

Not reported.

Indian Missionary Movement

5 Waddell Road, Kilpauk
Madras 600 010, INDIA

A. Christopher
Organized: 1973   Interdenominational

MISSIONARIES IN SERVICE

(1972) 4   (1975) 4   (1978) 6
(1980) 8   (1988) 16*
AAGR = N/A
Foreign missionaries in 1988: Not
reported.

FIELDS OF SERVICE

Not reported.

Indian Missionary Society

11 B Trivandrum High Road
Tirunelveli 627 002, Tamil Nadu, INDIA

Rev. Jason S. Dharmaraj
Organized: 1909   Denominational

MISSIONARIES IN SERVICE

(1972) 129   (1975) 133   (1978) 141
(1980) 150   (1982) 178   (1988) 216*
AAGR = N/A
Foreign missionaries in 1988: Not
reported.

FIELDS OF SERVICE

Not reported.

Indian Pentecostal Assemblies

473 Cross Cut Road
Coimbatore 641 012, INDIA

Job Gnanaprakasam
Organized: 1980   Pentecostal

MISSIONARIES IN SERVICE

(1988) 12
AAGR = N/A
Foreign missionaries in 1988:   0

FIELDS OF SERVICE

Not reported.

Indian Pentecostal Church of God, Northern Region

F-58, Green Park
New Delhi 110 016, INDIA

Rev. K.T. Thomas
Organized: 1969   Pentecostal

MISSIONARIES IN SERVICE

(1972) 80   (1980) 110   (1985) 170
(1988) 300
AAGR = 9%
Foreign missionaries in 1988:   0

FIELDS OF SERVICE

India
   Various States 14 Languages

Ishmaelite Salvation Association

PO Box 8431, St. Thomas Town
Bangalore 560 084, INDIA

Dr. T.M. Greenrose
Organized: 1974   Interdenominational

MISSIONARIES IN SERVICE

(1980) 33   (1982) 15   (1984) 20
(1985) 50   (1988) 70
AAGR = 10%
Foreign missionaries in 1988:   0

FIELDS OF SERVICE

India
   Andhra Pradesh State Muslims,
      Telugu, Urdu
   Tamil Nadu State Muslims, Tamil,
      Urdu
   West Bengal State Muslims, Bengali,
      Urdu
   Maharashtra State Muslims, Hindus,
      Hindi, Urdu
   Delhi Territory Muslims, Hindi, Urdu

Karnataka State Muslims, Kannada, Urdu

Ishmaels and Tribal Mission

PO Box 1279, Hyderabad 500 027
Andhra Pradesh, INDIA

Rev. Joseph Rutgers
Organized: 1978   Independent Baptist
MISSIONARIES IN SERVICE
(1972) 1   (1980) 38   (1985) 50
(1988) 64
AAGR = 30%
Foreign missionaries in 1988:   0
FIELDS OF SERVICE
India
  Andhra Pradesh (Amidala) Lambadi, Hindus
  Andhra Pradesh (Hyderabad) Prisoners, Orphans, Villagers
  Andhra Pradesh (Nollagonda) Muslims, Hindus
  Andhra Pradesh (Krishna) Muslims, Hindus
  Andhra Pradesh (Nezamabad) Hindus
  Andhra Pradesh (Narazamala) Lambadi
  Andhra Pradesh (Karimnagar) Koya

Jatiyo Kristiyo Prachar Samity

9/3A Ram Mohen Bera Lane
Calcutta 700 046, INDIA

Rev.John Thomas
Organized: Not reported.
MISSIONARIES IN SERVICE
(1988) 35
AAGR = N/A
Foreign missionaries in 1988:   0
FIELDS OF SERVICE
India
  Assam State Oraon, Oriya, Bengali, Assamese
  West Bengal State Boro

Jesus Lives Evangelistic Ministry

3A/ Alagar Nagar, K. Pudar
Madurai 625 007, Tamil Nadu, INDIA

Pastor Joseph Balachandran
Organized: Not reported.
MISSIONARIES IN SERVICE
(1982) 2   (1988) 3*
AAGR = N/A
Foreign missionaries in 1988: Not reported.
FIELDS OF SERVICE
Not reported.

Karbi Anglong Joint Christian Com.

Diphu 782 460, INDIA

Mr. James D. Khualluna
Organized: Not reported.
MISSIONARIES IN SERVICE
(1975) 41   (1978) 55   (1980) 58
(1982) 70   (1988) 111*
AAGR = N/A
Foreign missionaries in 1988: Not reported.
FIELDS OF SERVICE
Not reported.

Karnataka Nava Jeevara Samithi

54 II Main Road
Gangenahalli Extension
Bangalore 560 032, INDIA

Mr. G. Joseph Palangattil
Organized: Not reported.
MISSIONARIES IN SERVICE
(1988) 17
AAGR = N/A
Foreign missionaries in 1988:   0
FIELDS OF SERVICE
India
  Karnataka State Karnadigar

Kashmir Evangelical Fellowship

Mission House, Udhampur
Kashmir, INDIA

P.M. Thomas
Organized: 1980   Evangelical

MISSIONARIES IN SERVICE

(1972) 4   (1980) 33   (1985) 37
(1988) 42
AAGR = 16%
Foreign missionaries in 1988:   0

FIELDS OF SERVICE

India
  Jammu and Kashmir State Dogra,
    Hindus, Kashmiri
  Jammu and Kashmir (Ladakh)
    Ladakhi, Buddhists

Kizs Karbi Anglong Mission

PO Diphu Karbi, Anglong
Assam, INDIA

Rev. L. Kilesmo Tsamplao
Organized: Not reported.

MISSIONARIES IN SERVICE

(1988) 4
AAGR = N/A
Foreign missionaries in 1988:   0

FIELDS OF SERVICE

India
  Assam State Kharvi

Kuki Christian Church, Gospel Mission Society

PO Box 52, Imphal 795 001
Manipur, INDIA

Dr. T. Lunkim
Organized: 1979   Nondenominational

MISSIONARIES IN SERVICE

(1978) 5   (1980) 9   (1982) 23
(1984) 30   (1985) 32   (1988) 44
AAGR = 24%
Foreign missionaries in 1988:   2

FIELDS OF SERVICE

India
  Assam State Cacharis, Karbis
  Nagaland State Cacharis
  Manipur State Kuki, Meithei, Nepali
Bhutan
  Indian Border Bhutanese

Lalung Christian Mission

PO Nowgong District
Jagiroad 782 410, Assam, INDIA

Rev. N. Haolua
Organized: 1984   Evangelical

MISSIONARIES IN SERVICE

Further information withheld at
agency's request.

Madhya Kerala Diocese Parahal Mission

Chetti Street, Kottayam 686 001
Kerala, INDIA

Rev. I.C. Kurian
Organized: Not reported.

MISSIONARIES IN SERVICE

(1988) 21
AAGR = N/A
Foreign missionaries in 1988:   0

FIELDS OF SERVICE

India
  Uttar Pradesh State Hindi
  Andhra Pradesh State Telugu

Maharashtra Village Ministries

89 Kukdey Layout
Nagpur 440 027, INDIA

Rev. D.B. Kulothungan
Organized: 1982   Nondenominational

MISSIONARIES IN SERVICE

Further information withheld at
agency's request.

Manipur Presbyterian Mission

PO Imphal 795 001, Manipur INDIA

Rev. S. Lalkhuma
Organized: 1963   Presbyterian
MISSIONARIES IN SERVICE
(1972) 19   (1975) 33   (1978) 36
(1980) 44   (1982) 51   (1988) 92*
AAGR = N/A
Foreign missionaries in 1988: Not reported.
FIELDS OF SERVICE
Not reported.

Meitei Mission
c/o CBCNEI, Wangjing
Thougal, Manipur, INDIA

Rev. K.I. Aier
Organized: 1960   Denominational
MISSIONARIES IN SERVICE
(1980) 1   (1988) 2*
AAGR = N/A
Foreign missionaries in 1988: Not reported.
FIELDS OF SERVICE
Not reported.

Mission Society and Charitable Trust
1911 Hospital Road, Pulgaon Camp
Wardha 442 303, INDIA

Rev. K.V. John
Organized: 1985   Baptist
MISSIONARIES IN SERVICE
(1980) 10   (1985) 27   (1988) 27
AAGR = 13%
Foreign missionaries in 1988:   0
FIELDS OF SERVICE
India
  Maharashtra State Kolami, Gondi,
    Gawari, Narathi, Malayali
  Madhya Pradesh State
  Kerala State Banjari, Paradi

Mission for the Interior
PO Box 2, Narsapur
Andhra Pradesh, INDIA

Rev. Komanapalli
Organized: 1976   Independent
MISSIONARIES IN SERVICE
(1982) 55   (1984) 40   (1988) 68
AAGR =   4%
Foreign missionaries in 1988:   10
FIELDS OF SERVICE
India
  Madhya Pradesh State Adivasi
  Andhra Pradesh State Telugu, Koya,
    Lambadi
  Orissa State Bondas
Bangladesh
Nepal
India
Burma Burmese
Bhutan

Mission to the Unreached
Post Bag No. 7, Mandi, INDIA

Rev. Varghese Thomas
Organized: 1985   Pentecostal
MISSIONARIES IN SERVICE
Further information withheld at
agency's request.

Missionary Church
A-106 Rajajipuram, Talkatora
Lucknow 226 017, Uttar Pradesh, INDIA

Rev. P. Charles
Organized: 1980   Pentecostal
MISSIONARIES IN SERVICE
Further information withheld at
agency's request.

Nagaland Christian Revival Church
Pinny Villa Upper Circular Road
Mokokchung 798 601, Nagaland, INDIA

Rev. Shiwoto Sema
Organized: Not reported.   Pentecostal,
    Full Gospel
MISSIONARIES IN SERVICE
(1988) 40

AAGR = N/A
Foreign missionaries in 1988:   0
FIELDS OF SERVICE
India
  Manipur State Tribal People
  Assam State Tribal People
  Nagaland State Tribal People
  Arunachal Pradesh Territory Tribal
    People

Nagaland Missionary Movement
Khermahal, Dimapur 797 112
Nagaland, INDIA

Rev. Ellis Marry
Organized: Not reported.

MISSIONARIES IN SERVICE
(1988) 101
AAGR = N/A
Foreign missionaries in 1988:   0
FIELDS OF SERVICE
India
  Sikkim Territory Nepali
  Assam State Assamese
  Manipur State Manipuri
  Arunachal Pradesh Territory
    Arunachali
Nepal
Bhutan

National Missionary Society of India
206 Peters Road, Royapettah
Madras 600 014, INDIA

Rev. I.P. Andrews
Organized: 1905   Nondenominational

MISSIONARIES IN SERVICE
(1988) 127
AAGR = N/A
Foreign missionaries in 1988:   0
FIELDS OF SERVICE
India
  Various States Tribal, Hindus,
    Muslims, Buddhists, Fisherman

National Welfare Ministry
c/o K. S. Kumar
Rajahmundry 533 103
Andhra Pradesh, INDIA

Rev. K. Swatantra Kumar
Organized: 1970   Independent
MISSIONARIES IN SERVICE
(1972) 16   (1980) 23   (1985) 28
(1988) 33
AAGR =   5%
Foreign missionaries in 1988:   0
FIELDS OF SERVICE
Not reported.

New Life Center
PO Box 21, Ranipet 632 401
Tamil Nadu, INDIA

Dr. R. Chandrasekar
Organized: 1984   Nondenominational
MISSIONARIES IN SERVICE
(1985) 203   (1988) 238
AAGR =   5%
Foreign missionaries in 1988:   0
FIELDS OF SERVICE
India
  Bihar State Malto
  Gujarat State Kuknas
  Uttar Pradesh State Hindi
  Haryana State Hindi
  Delhi Territory Hindi
  Tamil Nadu State Tamil, Telugu
  Maharashtra State Vasavas

New Life Crusaders
Box 12, Imphal 795 001
Manipur, INDIA

O. Haokip
Organized: 1975   Baptist
MISSIONARIES IN SERVICE
(1980) 9   (1985) 9   (1988) 10
AAGR =   1%
Foreign missionaries in 1988:   0
FIELDS OF SERVICE
India

Manipur State Manipuri, 4 other
  dialects

New Life Ministries
PO Box 1, Churachandpur 795 128
Manipur, INDIA

Rev. C.V. John
Organized: 1979   Baptist
MISSIONARIES IN SERVICE
(1980) 9   (1985) 70   (1988) 98
AAGR = 35%
Foreign missionaries in 1988:   0
FIELDS OF SERVICE

India
  Andhra Pradesh State Harijans
  Kerala State Hindus
  Delhi Territory Hindus
  Tamil Nadu State Hindus
  Orissa State Tribal People
  Manipur State Nepali, Tribal People

North India Missionary Society, Kanyakumari District
Peruuilai PO, Peruuilai East
Assari Pallam 629 201, INDIA

Rev. C. Samuel
Organized: 1981   Independent
MISSIONARIES IN SERVICE
(1982) 2   (1984) 4   (1985) 3
(1988) 6
AAGR = 20%
Foreign missionaries in 1988:   0
FIELDS OF SERVICE

India
  Gujarat State Adivasi, Chodharis,
    Gamit

North India Pentecostal Fellowship
Berachah Prarthana Bhavan
Palampur 176 061
Himachal Pradesh, INDIA

T.C. Chacko
Organized: 1985   Pentecostal

MISSIONARIES IN SERVICE
Further information withheld at
agency's request.

Only Way, The
Plot 3876-R-25, Anna Nagar
Madras 600 040, INDIA

Mr. Winfred Jeyaraj
Organized: Not reported.
MISSIONARIES IN SERVICE
(1988) 2
AAGR = N/A
Foreign missionaries in 1988:   0
FIELDS OF SERVICE

India
  Tamil Nadu State High Caste Hindus.

Orissa Follow Up & Church Planting Ministry
PO Bag No 10, B.C. Sen Road
Balasore 756 001, Orissa, INDIA

Rev. Hrudaya Basi
Organized: 1982   Evangelical
MISSIONARIES IN SERVICE
(1988) 38
AAGR = N/A
Foreign missionaries in 1988:   0
FIELDS OF SERVICE

India
  West Bengal State Bengali, Santali,
    Muslims
  Orissa State Oriya, Santali, Ho,
    Mahanta, Mundari, Kui, Muslims

Orissa Missionary Movement
Aurbindo Nagar, Jeypore 764 001
Koraput District, Orissa, INDIA

U.C. Pattnayak
Organized: 1974   Pentecostal
MISSIONARIES IN SERVICE
(1972) 4   (1980) 11   (1985) 19
(1988) 62
AAGR = 19%

Foreign missionaries in 1988:　0

FIELDS OF SERVICE

India

Orissa State Kui Tribe, Oriya

Pawiram Baptist Mission

Council Road, Chhimtuipui District
Lawngtlai 796 891, Mizoram, INDIA

Rev. M. Lawmthanga
Organized: 1982　　　　　　　Baptist

MISSIONARIES IN SERVICE

(1972)　8　　　(1980)　10　　　(1985)　12
(1988)　13
AAGR =　3%
Foreign missionaries in 1988:　0

FIELDS OF SERVICE

Not reported.

Peniel Gospel Team

Bagdogra PO, Darjeeling 734 422
West Bengal, INDIA

Mammen Joseph
Organized: 1985　　　　　　Pentecostal

MISSIONARIES IN SERVICE

Further information withheld at
agency's request.

Pentecostal Church of God Speed-the-Good-News Crusades

3387 Christian Colony, Karol Bagh
New Dehli 110 005, INDIA

Rev. Kailash R. Rana
Organized: 1970　　　　　　Pentecostal

MISSIONARIES IN SERVICE

(1972)　3　　　(1980)　1　　　(1985)　3
(1988)　3
AAGR =　0%
Foreign missionaries in 1988:　0

FIELDS OF SERVICE

India

Northern States Hindus, Muslims,
　Sikhs, Buddhists

Pentecostal Faith Mission

PO Box 6236
New Delhi 110 015, INDIA

Cherian Thomas
Organized: 1983　　　　　　Pentecostal

MISSIONARIES IN SERVICE

(1985)　19　　　(1988)　28
AAGR =　14%
Foreign missionaries in 1988:　2

FIELDS OF SERVICE

India

Orissa State Bagat, Oriya
Darjeeling Nepali
Delhi Territory Hindi, Punjabi
Kerala State Malayalam

Prayer Partners Fellowship

Grace College
Kesavadasapuram Patton Trivandrum
695 004, Kerala, INDIA

A.J. Joseph
Organized: 1956　　　Interdenominational

MISSIONARIES IN SERVICE

(1972)　16　　　(1975)　18　　　(1978)　24
(1980)　30　　　(1988)　56*
AAGR = N/A
Foreign missionaries in 1988:　Not
reported.

FIELDS OF SERVICE

Not reported.

Prayer Temple Mission

Koottapuli, Kulappuram PO
Kaliyakkavilai
Kannyiakumari District, INDIA

S. Amos
Organized: 1979　　　Nondenominational

MISSIONARIES IN SERVICE

(1980)　6　　　(1985)　6　　　(1988)　10
AAGR =　7%
Foreign missionaries in 1988:　0

FIELDS OF SERVICE

India

Kerala State Hill Tribes, College
   Students, Harijans
Tamil Nadu State Muslims

Presbyterian Christian in Mizoram, Mission Board

PO Aizawl 796 001, INDIA

Organized: Not reported.

MISSIONARIES IN SERVICE

(1972) 54   (1975) 84   (1978) 127
(1980) 161   (1988) 301*
AAGR = N/A
Foreign missionaries in 1988: Not
reported.

FIELDS OF SERVICE

India
   Mizoram Territory

Prince of Peace Ministries

7 Arulanandam Street
Santhome Mylapore
Madras 600 004, INDIA

B.A. James Santhosam
Organized: 1974   Full Gospel Church

MISSIONARIES IN SERVICE

(1980) 3   (1988) 6
AAGR = 9%
Foreign missionaries in 1988: 0

FIELDS OF SERVICE

India
   Andhra Pradesh State Telugu
   Tamil Nadu (Madras) Tamil
   Pondicherry Territory Tamil
   Karnataka State Tamil

Quiet Corner India

3 Ramakrishnappa Road, Cox Town
Bangalore 560 005, INDIA

Thomas Samuel
Organized: 1971   Nondenominational

MISSIONARIES IN SERVICE

(1972) 5   (1975) 10   (1978) 15
(1980) 15   (1985) 14   (1988) 30
AAGR = 12%

Foreign missionaries in 1988:   0

FIELDS OF SERVICE

India
   Tamil Nadu State Kurumba, Paniyan,
      Irular
   Karnataka State Kurumba

Saviour Jesus Christ Mission

Post Box 25, Chromepet
Madras 600 044, INDIA

Rev. V. Benjamin Gnanadurai
Organized: 1971   Pentecostal

MISSIONARIES IN SERVICE

(1972) 12   (1980) 36   (1985) 43
(1988) 48
AAGR =   9%
Foreign missionaries in 1988:   3

FIELDS OF SERVICE

India
   Tamil Nadu State Villagers,
      Fishermen, Students, Patients,
      Communists, Actors
   Andhra Pradesh State Telugu
   Karnataka (Bangalore) Kanarese
Malaysia   Chinese
Singapore   Chinese

Seekers of Lost Souls

PO Aizawl, Zarkwat 796 001
Mizoram, INDIA

Mr. Chhawnzinga
Organized: 1972   Interdenominational

MISSIONARIES IN SERVICE

(1972) 7   (1975) 18   (1978) 36
(1980) 51   (1988) 95*
AAGR = N/A
Foreign missionaries in 1988: Not
reported.

FIELDS OF SERVICE

Not reported.

Shalem Gospel Ministries

Shalem House, Tanuko 534 211, West
Godavary District, INDIA

K.H. Paul

Organized: 1970   Nondenominational
MISSIONARIES IN SERVICE
(1972) 5   (1980) 15   (1985) 20
(1988) 20
AAGR = 9%
Foreign missionaries in 1988:   1
FIELDS OF SERVICE
Not reported.

Siloam Evangelical Fellowship
PO Box 128, Prakash Colony
Hubli 580 020, Karnataka, INDIA

Jesuratnam Buraga
Organized: 1952   Evangelical
MISSIONARIES IN SERVICE
(1980) 5   (1985) 15   (1988) 25
AAGR = 22%
Foreign missionaries in 1988:   0
FIELDS OF SERVICE
India
  Maharashtra State Whole State,
    Hindus, Marathi
  Tamil Nadu State Whole State,
    Hindus, Tamil
  Karnataka State Whole State, Hindus,
    Kanarese
  Andhra Pradesh State Whole State,
    Hindus, Telugu

Sion Fellowship
2-10, Hydernagar, Kukatpally
Hyderabad 500 872
Andhra Pradesh, INDIA

Y.S. John Babu
Organized: 1980
MISSIONARIES IN SERVICE
(1980) 2   (1985) 2   (1988) 2
AAGR = 0%
Foreign missionaries in 1988:   0
FIELDS OF SERVICE
Not reported.

Society of Missionaries of St. Francis Xavier
Ilhas 403 203, Goa, INDIA

Rev. Tesceino Almuda
Organized: Not reported.   Catholic
MISSIONARIES IN SERVICE
(1988) 135
AAGR = N/A
Foreign missionaries in 1988:   0
FIELDS OF SERVICE
India
  Maharashtra State Marathi, English
  Andaman Island
  Bihar State Hindi
  Goa Territory Konkani
  Punjab State Punjabi
  Karnataka State Kannada, Konkani

South India Full Gospel Revival Evangelistic Programme
Koottapuli, Kulappuram PO
Kaliyakkavilai
Kannyiakumari District, INDIA

Rev. S. Amos
Organized: Not reported.
MISSIONARIES IN SERVICE
(1980) 6   (1982) 9   (1984) 16
(1988) 43*
AAGR = N/A
Foreign missionaries in 1988: Not
reported.
FIELDS OF SERVICE
India
  Kerala State Tribal People
  Tamil Nadu State Tribal People
  Tamil Nadu (Madras) Backward
    Village

South India Soul Winners Association
PO Box 3463, Anna Nagar
Madras 600 040, INDIA

Dr. M. Prakasam

Organized: 1975   Nondenominational
MISSIONARIES IN SERVICE
(1978) 6   (1980) 28   (1982) 20
(1984) 34   (1985) 40   (1988) 55
AAGR = 25%
Foreign missionaries in 1988:   0
FIELDS OF SERVICE
India
Andaman Island Ongies, Shomalies,
  Jarawas, Bengali
Orissa State Koya
Kerala State Malayalam
Tamil Nadu State Tamil
Madhya Pradesh State Tribal People
Pondicherry Territory Tamil

Spring Valley Baptist Church
Oyoor PO, Quilon 691 510, INDIA

Dr. Vadakeattathu
Organized: Not reported.   Baptist
MISSIONARIES IN SERVICE
Further information withheld at
agency's request.

St. Thomas Evangelical Church of India
5 Tiruvalla 689 105, Kerala, INDIA

R.T. Rev T.C. Cherian
Organized: 1961   Denominational
MISSIONARIES IN SERVICE
(1975) 80   (1978) 88   (1980) 116
(1988) 210*
AAGR = N/A
Foreign missionaries in 1988: Not
reported.
FIELDS OF SERVICE
Not reported.

Tamil Villages Gospel Mission
PO Box 612, Puthur
Trichy 620 017, INDIA

P.T. Christopher

Organized: 1981   Pentecostal
MISSIONARIES IN SERVICE
(1980) 15   (1982) 10   (1984) 14
(1985) 16   (1988) 3
AAGR = -17%
Foreign missionaries in 1988:   0
FIELDS OF SERVICE
India
Tamil Nadu State Tamil

Tangkhul Baptist Convention
Mission Compound
Ukhrul 795 142, Manipur, INDIA

Rev. N. Mingyao Zimik
Organized: 1901   Baptist
MISSIONARIES IN SERVICE
(1972) 42   (1975) 12   (1978) 16
(1980) 48   (1984) 30   (1985) 74
(1988) 74
AAGR = 4%
Foreign missionaries in 1988:   0
FIELDS OF SERVICE
India
Manipur State Maram, Meithei,
  Maring, Sekmai, Andro

Tirap Mission
PO Impur 798 615, Nagaland, INDIA

Rev. I. Longsa
Organized: 1974   Denominational
MISSIONARIES IN SERVICE
(1975) 6   (1978) 12   (1980) 27
(1988) 50*
AAGR = N/A
Foreign missionaries in 1988: Not
reported.
FIELDS OF SERVICE
Not reported.

Tribal Gospel Mission
Shoppe Press, Mokokchung 798 601
Nagaland, INDIA

Rev. Bendang S. Ao

Organized: 1980   Baptist
MISSIONARIES IN SERVICE
Further information withheld at
agency's request.

Tribal Mission
Perumbavoor 683 542, INDIA

Dr. K. Muralidar
Organized: 1977   Nondenominational
MISSIONARIES IN SERVICE
(1980) 36   (1985) 32   (1988) 42
AAGR =   2%
Foreign missionaries in 1988:   0
FIELDS OF SERVICE
India
  Kerala State Irular, Mannan,
    Muthuvan, Kurumar, Kurichiya,
    Aranadan, others
  Karnataka State Lambadi
  Rajasthan State Mina

Tribal Gospel Team
Pangotil House, PO Ernakulam District
Kombanad 683 555
Kerala, INDIA

Rev. P.V. Kuriakose
Organized: 1979   Nondenominational
MISSIONARIES IN SERVICE
(1980) 14   (1982) 26   (1984) 40
(1985) 22   (1988) 26
AAGR =   8%
Foreign missionaries in 1988:   0
FIELDS OF SERVICE
India
  Kerala State Tribal People
  Tamil Nadu State Tribal People

Un-Evangelized Fields Vision
PO Box 1563
Secunderabad 500 003
Andhra Pradesh, INDIA

G.J. Yesukumar
Organized: Not reported.

MISSIONARIES IN SERVICE
(1978) 10   (1980) 10   (1982) 10
(1988) 10*
AAGR = N/A
Foreign missionaries in 1988: Not
reported.
FIELDS OF SERVICE
Not reported.

United Ministries
Post Bag No. 8
DA.329 Batu Camp 507 101
Kothagudem Collieries
Andhra Pradesh, INDIA

K. Prabhudass
Organized: Not reported.
MISSIONARIES IN SERVICE
(1985) 5   (1988) 6*
AAGR = N/A
Foreign missionaries in 1988: Not
reported.
FIELDS OF SERVICE
Not reported.

Upper Room Prayer and Evangelistic Fellowship
P.O. Box 419, Waltair-R.S.
Visakhapatnam 530 004,
Andhra Pradesh, INDIA

Rev. N. Kruparao
Organized: Not reported.
MISSIONARIES IN SERVICE
(1972) 30   (1975) 32   (1978) 25
(1980) 35   (1984) 38   (1988) 41*
AAGR = N/A
Foreign missionaries in 1988: Not
reported.
FIELDS OF SERVICE
India
  Orissa State Telugu, Oriya

Village Evangelism and Revival Crusade
8/B, Nirmal Society, Mission Area
Nadiad 387 001, Gujarat, INDIA

C.D. Pathik
Organized: Not reported.
MISSIONARIES IN SERVICE
(1984) 2   (1988) 3*
AAGR = N/A
Foreign missionaries in 1988: Not reported.
FIELDS OF SERVICE
India
Gujarat State Village people

Voice of Gospel
Trichur 680 001, Kerala, INDIA

Mr. K.V. Daniel
Organized: 1975
MISSIONARIES IN SERVICE
(1975) 4   (1978) 7   (1980) 10
(1982) 22   (1988) 24
AAGR = 15%
Foreign missionaries in 1988:   0
FIELDS OF SERVICE
India
Tamil Nadu State Tamil
Kerala State Malayalam

Worldwide Gospel Mission
Khermahal, Dimapur 797 110
Nagaland, INDIA

Dr. Phuveyi Dozo
Organized: 1964   Interdenominational
MISSIONARIES IN SERVICE
(1980) 73   (1988) 147*
AAGR = N/A
Foreign missionaries in 1988: Not reported.
FIELDS OF SERVICE
Not reported.

Zeliangrong Baptist Association of Manipur
Taminglong 796 691
Manipur, INDIA

Rev. Kaiba Riame
Organized: Not reported.

MISSIONARIES IN SERVICE
(1988) 4
AAGR = N/A
Foreign missionaries in 1988:   0
FIELDS OF SERVICE
India
Assam State Naga Zeme
Manipur State Naga Rongmei

Zoram Baptist Mission
Serkawn, Zotlang 796 691
Lunglei District, INDIA

Rev. B. Thangchina
Organized: 1939   Baptist
MISSIONARIES IN SERVICE
(1988) 408
AAGR = N/A
Foreign missionaries in 1988:   4
FIELDS OF SERVICE
India
Maharashtra State Dhowari, Halam-Kuki
West Bengal State Boro, Nepali, Rajbansi
Tripura State
Mizoram Territory Adiyan, Urali, Assamese
Madhya Pradesh State Tamaria, Riang
Assam State Bruj, Chakma, Rabha
Thailand
Chiang Rai Province Akha, Karen

Zoram Evangelical Fellowship
Chandmary Veng, Aizawl 796 007
Mizoram, INDIA

Rev. Khnanga
Organized: Not reported.
MISSIONARIES IN SERVICE
(1988) 5
AAGR = N/A
Foreign missionaries in 1988:   0
FIELDS OF SERVICE
India
Jammu and Kashmir State Kashmiri

INDONESIA

Asia Pacific Christian Mission International, Indonesia

PO Box 73
Bandung 40001, INDONESIA

Gideon Imanto Tanbunaan
Organized: 1979   Church of Christ

MISSIONARIES IN SERVICE

(1980) 10   (1985) 14   (1988) 22
AAGR = 10%
Foreign missionaries in 1988:   0

FIELDS OF SERVICE

Indonesia
  Central Java Province   Javanese, Indonesian, Chinese
  West Java Province   Convicts, Exconvicts, Prison Ministry, Sundanese, Indonesian, Chinese
  East Java Province   Javanese

Bait Allah Evangelical Foundation

PO Box 519, Medan
North Sumatra, INDONESIA

Dr. S.B. Pardede
Organized: 1972
Church of God of Prophecy

MISSIONARIES IN SERVICE

(1972) 13   (1980) 44   (1985) 60
(1988) 79
AAGR = 12%
Foreign missionaries in 1988:   5

FIELDS OF SERVICE

Indonesia
  Atjeh Territory   Achehnese, Animists
  Jakarta Region   Pelajar, Mahasiswa, Kaum, Perantall
  Maluku Province   Animists
  Lampung Province   Javanese, Transmigrants, Animists
  Java Region   Javanese, Chinese, Syncretists

  Irian Jaya Province   Animists
  Bengkulu Province   Javanese, Transmigrants, Animists
  West Kalimantan Province   Dayak, Animists
  Southeast Sulawesi Province   Toroja, Animists
  North Sumatra (Nias)   Animists
  West Sumatra (Mentawai Is.)   Animists
  South Sulawesi Province   Toroja, Bugis, Animists
  Riau Province   Chinese
  Central Kalimantan Province   Dayak, Animists
Malaysia   Chinese, Tamil

Christ The Redeemer Foundation

PO Box 23, Magelang, INDONESIA

Rev. Timothy Roy Kartiko
Organized: 1975   Pentecostal

MISSIONARIES IN SERVICE

(1985) 12   (1988) 42
AAGR = 52%
Foreign missionaries in 1988:   0

FIELDS OF SERVICE

Indonesia
  14 Provinces   Animists

Christopherus Foundation

Jl Sompok Kama 62 C, Semarang 50249
Central Java, INDONESIA

Rev. Agus Suwantoro
Organized: 1972   Evangelical

MISSIONARIES IN SERVICE

(1972) 5   (1975) 3   (1980) 7
(1982) 6   (1984) 10   (1985) 10
(1988) 13
AAGR = 6%
Foreign missionaries in 1988:   0

FIELDS OF SERVICE

Indonesia
  Central Kalimantan Province   Dayak

Convention of Indonesian Baptist Churches

PO Box 129, Manado 95001
North Sulawesi, INDONESIA

Youtie R. Legoh
Organized: 1951   Baptist
MISSIONARIES IN SERVICE
(1972) 22   (1980) 52   (1985) 74
(1988) 88
AAGR = 9%
Foreign missionaries in 1988:   0
FIELDS OF SERVICE
Indonesia
  East Java Province
  West Kalimantan Province
  Central Sulawesi Province
  Maluku Province
  North Sulawesi Province
  North Sumatra Province

Duta Sabda/Abdiel

Jl Rambutan Barat No. 11
Semarang 50249, Central Java
INDONESIA

Andreas Haryanto & Rev. Jsha
Organized: 1958   Interdenominational
MISSIONARIES IN SERVICE
(1972) 5   (1975) 2   (1978) 3
(1980) 3   (1982) 19   (1984) 22
(1988) 36*
AAGR = N/A
Foreign missionaries in 1988: Not reported.
FIELDS OF SERVICE
Indonesia
  West Java Province   Indonesian
  Kalimantan Region   Indonesian
  East-Central Indonesia   Indonesian
  Sulawesi Region   Indonesian

Evangelical Theological Seminary of Indonesia

PO Box 5/YKAP
Yogyakarta, INDONESIA

Dr. Chris Marantika
Organized: 1979
Evangelical-Nondenominational
MISSIONARIES IN SERVICE
Further information withheld at agency's request.

Fellowship of Baptist Churches of Indonesia

Tromol Pos 129
Manado, North Sulawesi, INDONESIA

Rev. Joutie Legoh
Organized: 1951   Interdenominational
MISSIONARIES IN SERVICE
(1975) 3   (1978) 15   (1980) 13
(1988) 16*
AAGR = N/A
Foreign missionaries in 1988: Not reported.
FIELDS OF SERVICE
Not reported.

Gereja Christian Jakarta

Jalan Kartini 5/16C
Jakarta Pusat, INDONESIA

Organized: Not reported.
MISSIONARIES IN SERVICE
(1980) 1   (1988) 1*
AAGR = N/A
Foreign missionaries in 1988: Not reported.
FIELDS OF SERVICE
Not reported.

Indonesian Mennonite Church (GKMI)

INDONESIA

Organized: Not reported.
MISSIONARIES IN SERVICE
(1980) 40   (1988) 50*
AAGR = N/A
Foreign missionaries in 1988: Not reported.

FIELDS OF SERVICE
Not reported.

Indonesian Missionary Fellowship
PO Box 4, Batu
Java Timur, INDONESIA

Dr. Petrus Octavianus
Organized: 1961   Evangelical
MISSIONARIES IN SERVICE
(1972) 16   (1980) 19   (1985) 31
(1988) 39
AAGR = 6%
Foreign missionaries in 1988:   10
FIELDS OF SERVICE
Indonesia
  West Kalimantan Province
  Madura
  Irian Jaya Province
  East Timor Province

India	**Brazil**
Gambia	**Pakistan**
Philippines	**Nepal**

Integrated Village Ministry
PO Box 65, Salatiga, INDONESIA

Rev. Bambang Budijanto
Organized: 1987
Evangelical-Interdenominational
MISSIONARIES IN SERVICE
(1988) 7
AAGR = N/A
Foreign missionaries in 1988:   0
FIELDS OF SERVICE
Indonesia
  Central Kalimantan Province   Dayak
  West Kalimantan Province   Dayak

Korea Mission in Indonesia
PO Box 2355, Jakarta, INDONESIA

Rev. Paul M. Suh
Organized: 1972   Interdenominational
MISSIONARIES IN SERVICE
(1972) 2   (1975) 5   (1978) 18

(1980) 32   (1988) 40*
AAGR = N/A
Foreign missionaries in 1988: Not reported.
FIELDS OF SERVICE
Not reported.

Masirey Evangelism Fellowship
PO Box 723, Jayapura
Irian Jaya, INDONESIA

Dortheis Wopari
Organized: 1988   Evangelical
MISSIONARIES IN SERVICE
(1982) 6   (1984) 35   (1985) 23
(1988) 53
AAGR = 44%
Foreign missionaries in 1988:   0
FIELDS OF SERVICE
Indonesia
  Irian Jaya Province   Animists,
    Muslims, Traditional Christians

Mennonite Board of Missions and Charities
PO Box 8/TDK, Jakarta 14001
Barat Java, INDONESIA

Rev. Yahya Chrismanto
Organized: 1965   Mennonite
MISSIONARIES IN SERVICE
(1972) 1   (1980) 49   (1985) 69
(1988) 75*
AAGR = N/A
Foreign missionaries in 1988: Not reported.
FIELDS OF SERVICE
Indonesia
  Java Region   Sundanese, Chinese,
    Javanese
  Lampung Province   Lampung, Javanese
  South Sumatra Province   Palembang,
    Javanese
  West Kalimantan Province   Dayak,
    Chinese, Javanese

Missionary Training Center

PO Box 3, Negara, Bali, INDONESIA

Rev. Luther Tubulau
Organized: 1987   Alliance

MISSIONARIES IN SERVICE

Further information withheld at
agency's request.

Open Door Mission

PO Box 97, Samarinda 75001
East Kalimantan, INDONESIA

Rev. R.A. Yohanis Sakai
Organized: 1983   Evangelical

MISSIONARIES IN SERVICE

(1972)	34	(1975)	52	(1978)	31
(1980)	67	(1982)	6	(1984)	4
(1988)	5				

AAGR = -10%
Foreign missionaries in 1988:   0

FIELDS OF SERVICE

Indonesia
  Central Kalimantan Province   Dayak
  South Kalimantan Province   Dayak

Rose of Love Ministry

Tromolpos 1 Benculuk
Banyuwangi 68481, INDONESIA

Rev. M. Tajib Moerjanto
Organized: 1973   Evangelical

MISSIONARIES IN SERVICE

(1972)	5	(1980)	15	(1985)	26
(1988)	27				

AAGR = 11%
Foreign missionaries in 1988:   0

FIELDS OF SERVICE

Indonesia
  East Java Province   Javanese Villagers
  Southeast Sulawesi Province   Javan-
    ese Transmigrants
  South Sumatra Province   Javanese
    Transmigrants
  Central Java Province   Javanese Vil-
    lagers

Rural Evangelical Ministerial Program

PO Box 62, Solo 57101, INDONESIA

Rev. Saderch Soediro
Organized: 1980

MISSIONARIES IN SERVICE

(1988) 15
AAGR = N/A
Foreign missionaries in 1988:   0

FIELDS OF SERVICE

Indonesia
  West Kalimantan Province   Dayak,
    Punan, Basap, Kenya, Tunjung,
    Benug, Iban, Barau
  South Sumatra Province   Mentawei
  Riau Province   Luhu
Malaysia 3 People Groups

Sangkakala Mission Fellowship

PO Box 262, Semarang
Central Java, INDONESIA

Adi Sutanto
Organized: 1977   Charismatic

MISSIONARIES IN SERVICE

(1978)	3	(1980)	9	(1982)	10
(1988)	2				

AAGR = -3%
Foreign missionaries in 1988:   2

FIELDS OF SERVICE

USA
  California (Pasadena)   Indonesian

JAPAN

Asia Evangelical Missionary Fellowship

PO Box 88, Nishijin, Kyoto 602, JAPAN

Rev. Kazuo Nishimoto
Organized: 1967   Evangelical

MISSIONARIES IN SERVICE

(1972)	5	(1975)	6	(1978)	5
(1980)	4	(1984)	5	(1985)	3

(1986) 3   (1988) 3
AAGR = -2%
Foreign missionaries in 1988:   3
FIELDS OF SERVICE
Taiwan   Mountain Tribe

Asian Gospel Mission
Higashi-Kagiocho
Moriguchi-shi, Osaka-Fu, JAPAN

Rev. Yoshinobu Mukarami
Organized: 1977   Pentecostal
MISSIONARIES IN SERVICE
(1986) 1   (1988) 2
AAGR = 41%
Foreign missionaries in 1988:   2
FIELDS OF SERVICE
Philippines
   Metro Manila   Local People
Taiwan
   Tainan County   Local People

Biblical Church, Overseas Mission
3-9-6 Takada, Toshima-ku 171
Tokyo, JAPAN

Rev. Yoshinobu Kobayashi
Organized: 1978   Elders Church
MISSIONARIES IN SERVICE
(1980) 2   (1983) 2   (1985) 2
(1988) 2
AAGR = 0%
Foreign missionaries in 1988:   2
FIELDS OF SERVICE
Hong Kong   Chinese
China   Chinese

Christ Gospel Mission
CPO Box 218, Yokohama 220-91, JAPAN

Rev. Minoru Hayashi
Organized: 1974   Evangelical
MISSIONARIES IN SERVICE
(1972) 4   (1975) 4   (1978) 5
(1980) 4   (1982) 2   (1984) 8
(1985) 8   (1988) 4

AAGR = 0%
Foreign missionaries in 1988:   8
FIELDS OF SERVICE
Japan   Chinese, Mangolian, Eastern
   European
Hong Kong   Chinese
USA
   California   Eastern European, English (British)

Christian Holiness Overseas Missions Department
2-20-5 Tsubakamori
Chiba City 260, Chiba Ken, JAPAN

Organized: Not reported.
MISSIONARIES IN SERVICE
(1983) 3   (1988) 3*
AAGR = N/A
Foreign missionaries in 1988: Not reported.
FIELDS OF SERVICE
Not reported.

Christian Reformed Church in Japan, Overseas Mission Com.
c/o Tokyo Kyokai, 16 Sakamachi
Shinjuku-ku 160, Tokyo, JAPAN

Sho'ichi Yauchi
Organized: Not reported.
MISSIONARIES IN SERVICE
(1983) 2   (1988) 2*
AAGR = N/A
Foreign missionaries in 1988: Not reported.
FIELDS OF SERVICE
Indonesia

Church of God
4-21 Nakasaidae-cho
Saiwaiku-Kawasaki-shi, JAPAN

Rev. Raymond Shelhone
Organized: 1951   Wesleyan

(1986) 1   (1988) 2
AAGR = 41%
Foreign missionaries in 1988:   2

FIELDS OF SERVICE

Mexico
Jalisco (Guadalajara) Mexicans,
  Americans, Koreans, Japanese

Ev. Fellowship Deaconry Church, Overseas Mission Committee

5-1 Azalgazuka, Nishiltirano, JAPAN

Rev. Michio Ebihara
Organized: 1974   Lutheran

MISSIONARIES IN SERVICE
(1980) 2   (1983) 1   (1985) 2
(1988) 2
AAGR = 0%
Foreign missionaries in 1988:   1

FIELDS OF SERVICE

USA
Minnesota Japanese

Evangelical Alliance Mission, Overseas Mission Committee

2-22-22 Gotokuji
Setagaya-ku 154, Tokyo, JAPAN

Atsuyoshi Saito
Organized: Not reported.

MISSIONARIES IN SERVICE
(1983) 8   (1988) 7
AAGR = 0%
Foreign missionaries in 1988:   9

FIELDS OF SERVICE

Thailand Thai
Canada Eskimos
Papua New Guinea Bible Translation
Taiwan Taiwanese

Evangelical Free Church of Japan

33-4 Ohno-cho, Oyama Higashi

Kita-ku 603, Kyoto Shi, JAPAN

Hisayuki Takahashi
Organized: 1962   Evangelical

MISSIONARIES IN SERVICE
(1972) 1   (1975) 1   (1978) 1
(1980) 1   (1984) 1   (1986) 1
(1988) 5
AAGR = 11%
Foreign missionaries in 1988:   0

FIELDS OF SERVICE

Singapore   **Philippines**

Group of Supporters of the Tezukas

2-14-3 Honcho
Higashi Kurume-shi 203, Tokyo, JAPAN

Masao Uenuma
Organized: Not reported.

MISSIONARIES IN SERVICE
(1988) 2
AAGR = N/A
Foreign missionaries in 1988:   0

FIELDS OF SERVICE

Spain Japanese, Portuguese, Gypsies
Portugal Japanese, Portuguese, Gypsies

Immanuel General Mission

c/o OSCC Blgd. No. 1
Kanda-Surugadai, 2 chome
Chiyoda-ku, Tokyo, JAPAN

Hiroshi Asahina
Organized: 1945   Methodist

MISSIONARIES IN SERVICE
(1972) 12   (1975) 10   (1978) 10
(1980) 14   (1985) 11   (1986) 10
(1988) 15
AAGR = 1%
Foreign missionaries in 1988:   16

FIELDS OF SERVICE

Bolivia Japanese
Kenya Kenyans, Medical Work
Jamaica Students
Taiwan

Taichu County
Philippines Students
Papua New Guinea Papuans

Japan Alliance Church
6-119 Miyake, Saeki-ku
Hiroshima-Shi, JAPAN

Rev. Hiroto Ohe
Organized: 1931   Alliance

MISSIONARIES IN SERVICE

(1972)	3	(1975)	9	(1978)	13
(1980)	1	(1985)	3	(1986)	1
(1988)	1				

AAGR = -6%
Foreign missionaries in 1988:   1

FIELDS OF SERVICE
Brazil Japanese, Brazilians

Japan Anglican Church
1-4-21 Higashi, Shibuya-ku 150
Tokyo, JAPAN

Organized: Not reported.

MISSIONARIES IN SERVICE

(1986)	3	(1988)	3*

AAGR = N/A
Foreign missionaries in 1988: Not
reported.

FIELDS OF SERVICE
Not reported.

Japan Antioch Mission
2-18 Mizumachi, Kuroiso-shi
Utsunomiya, JAPAN

Minoru Oknyama
Organized: 1977

MISSIONARIES IN SERVICE

(1978)	2	(1980)	5	(1982)	15
(1984)	14	(1986)	16	(1988)	14

AAGR = 21%
Foreign missionaries in 1988:   14

FIELDS OF SERVICE
Indonesia
Jakarta Region Leader Training
East Java (Malang) Medical Work

West Kalimantan Province Tribal
People
Sri Lanka
Western Region (Katunayake) Litera-
ture Distribution
Pakistan Medical Work
Argentina Japanese
Korea (South)
Seoul Deaf People
Nepal
Kathmandu Agricultural Training
USA Japanese

Japan Baptist Bible Fellowship, Mission Committee
2-52 Kyoshin-cho, Minami-ku
Yokohama 232, JAPAN

Toshitada Yamamiya
Organized: Not reported.

MISSIONARIES IN SERVICE

(1972)	2	(1975)	4	(1978)	4
(1980)	4	(1984)	2	(1985)	2
(1988)	2				

AAGR = 0%
Foreign missionaries in 1988:   0

FIELDS OF SERVICE
Indonesia
East Kalimantan (Batakan)

Japan Baptist Convention
7-26-24 Shinjuku
Shinjuku-ku 160, Tokyo, JAPAN

Okamura Shooji
Organized: Not reported.   Baptist

MISSIONARIES IN SERVICE

(1980)	2	(1985)	4	(1988)	6

AAGR = 15%
Foreign missionaries in 1988:   0

FIELDS OF SERVICE
Indonesia   **Thailand**

Japan Baptist Overseas Mission Society
3-18 2 Chome, Nishi-Waseda

Shinjuku-ku 169, Tokyo, JAPAN

Hideo Nagamine
Organized: 1968   Baptist
MISSIONARIES IN SERVICE
(1972)   2   (1988)   2
AAGR = 0%
Foreign missionaries in 1988:   0
FIELDS OF SERVICE
Bangladesh
  Bogra District   Medical Work

Japan Church of Jesus Christ
3-15-3 Morikawachi Hondori
Higashi 577, Osaka-shi, JAPAN

Tsuneo Koyama
Organized: Not reported.
MISSIONARIES IN SERVICE
(1988)   4
AAGR = N/A
Foreign missionaries in 1988:   0
FIELDS OF SERVICE
Taiwan   **Nepal**

Japan Evangelical Lutheran Church
1-1 Sadohard-cho, Ichijaya
Shinjuku-ku 162, Tokyo, JAPAN

Rev. Teiichi Maeda
Organized: 1893   Lutheran
MISSIONARIES IN SERVICE
(1972)   2   (1980)   2   (1983)   4
(1985)   2   (1988)   3
AAGR = 3%
Foreign missionaries in 1988:   1
FIELDS OF SERVICE
Brazil   Japanese

Japan Holiness Church
1-30-1 Mawarida
Higashi Murayama-shi, Tokyo, JAPAN

Rev. Arira
Organized: 1901   Methodist

MISSIONARIES IN SERVICE
(1986)   3   (1988)   5
AAGR = 29%
Foreign missionaries in 1988:   0
FIELDS OF SERVICE
Philippines   Filipino
Taiwan   Businessmen, Takasago Tribe

Japan Jesus Christ Church
506-1 Taga-machi
Omi-yahata-shi 523, JAPAN

Rev. Takeo Funata
Organized: 1951   Evangelical
MISSIONARIES IN SERVICE
(1972)   3   (1980)   4   (1985)   6
(1988)   6
AAGR = 4%
Foreign missionaries in 1988:   0
FIELDS OF SERVICE
Nepal
Indonesia
  Western Region
Taiwan   Buman, Taiyaru, Tsuo

Japan Liebenzelle Church Association
1933 Kawasaki Ken
Kawasaki-shi 214, JAPAN

Sugisaki Toshio
Organized: 1976
MISSIONARIES IN SERVICE
(1980)   1   (1988)   2
AAGR = 9%
Foreign missionaries in 1988:   0
FIELDS OF SERVICE
USA   Japanese

Japan Mennonite Brethren Conference, Overseas Mission Commmittee
Ikeda-shi 2-1-12, Osaka 563, JAPAN

Akiyoshi Kura
Organized: Not reported.   Mennonite

Taiwan Deaf People

Overseas Mission Committee
5-1 Aza Igasuka, Nishi Hirano
Mikage-cho, Higashinada-ku
Kobe 658, JAPAN

Pastor Tamon Ota
Organized: Not reported.
MISSIONARIES IN SERVICE
(1978) 2   (1980) 2   (1983) 2
(1984) 2   (1988) 2*
AAGR = N/A
Foreign missionaries in 1988: Not reported.
FIELDS OF SERVICE
USA Japanese
Papua New Guinea Kuwanga tribe

Pacific Broadcasting Association
2-1 Surugadai, Kanda
Chiyoda-ku 101, Tokyo, JAPAN

Rev. Akira Asuka
Organized: 1951   Chokyo
MISSIONARIES IN SERVICE
(1972) 6   (1980) 2   (1985) 4
(1986) 5   (1988) 2
AAGR = -6%
Foreign missionaries in 1988: 1
FIELDS OF SERVICE
Ecuador
  Quito Japanese

Prayer Society for Argentine Mission
2-1-10 Senea-cho
Kawagoe-shi 350, Saitasa, JAPAN

Minoiu Sasaki
Organized: Not reported.
MISSIONARIES IN SERVICE
(1983) 2   (1988) 2
AAGR = 0%
Foreign missionaries in 1988: 2

MISSIONARIES IN SERVICE
(1988) 2
AAGR = N/A
Foreign missionaries in 1988: 2
FIELDS OF SERVICE
Papua New Guinea

Japan Scripture Union
Higashi Takaido
Suginami-ku 168, JAPAN

Rev. Kiyoshi Lwai
Organized: 1953   Evangelical
MISSIONARIES IN SERVICE
(1972) 2   (1984) 2   (1985) 2
(1986) 2   (1988) 2
AAGR = 0%
Foreign missionaries in 1988: 0
FIELDS OF SERVICE
Not reported.

Living Water
PO Box 303
Shinjuku-ku 163-91, Tokyo, JAPAN

Organized: Not reported.
MISSIONARIES IN SERVICE
(1986) 10   (1988) 10*
AAGR = N/A
Foreign missionaries in 1988: Not reported.
FIELDS OF SERVICE
Not reported.

Oriental Deaf Christ Evangelistic Church
1132-1 Ozaichiba, Moroyama-machi
Irurmagun 350-04, Saitama Ken, JAPAN

Shigeru Washio
Organized: Not reported.
MISSIONARIES IN SERVICE
(1983) 1   (1986) 1   (1988) 4
AAGR = 100%
Foreign missionaries in 1988: 0
FIELDS OF SERVICE
Hong Kong Deaf People

Argentina Japanese, Pastoral Work

REAP Mission
7-39-6 Higashi Oizumi
Nerima-ku 177, Tokyo, JAPAN

Rev. Kenny Joseph
Organized: 1951   Independent

MISSIONARIES IN SERVICE
(1972) 4   (1980) 4   (1985) 4
(1988) 3
AAGR = -1%
Foreign missionaries in 1988:   0

FIELDS OF SERVICE
Indonesia
  Central Java (Solo)   Indonesian

Reformed Church in Japan
16 Saka-machi
Shinjuku-ku, Tokyo, JAPAN

Rev. Yauchi Syoji
Organized: 1946   Reformed Church

MISSIONARIES IN SERVICE
(1986) 4   (1988) 11
AAGR = 66%
Foreign missionaries in 1988:   7

FIELDS OF SERVICE
Australia Aborigines
United Kingdom
  England
Argentina   **Philippines**
Africa   **Indonesia**

Society for Support of Katsuko Ishida
2-9-7 Yagumo, Meguro-ku
Tokyo, JAPAN

Atsushi Siziki
Organized: 1972

MISSIONARIES IN SERVICE
(1983) 1   (1988) 1
AAGR = 0%
Foreign missionaries in 1988:   1

FIELDS OF SERVICE
Zaire Medical Work, Evangelism

Society for Support of Kumiko Goto
c/o Reformed Churchu in Japan
1-33-9 Ebisu Nishi
Shibuya-ku 150, Tokyo, JAPAN

Organized: 1977

MISSIONARIES IN SERVICE
(1978) 1   (1980) 1   (1988) 1
AAGR = 0%
Foreign missionaries in 1988:   0

FIELDS OF SERVICE
Indonesia

South American Mission
2-29-19 Matzubara
Setagaya-ku 156, Tokyo, JAPAN

Sadaji Ide
Organized: Not reported.

MISSIONARIES IN SERVICE
(1983) 6   (1986) 4   (1988) 4
AAGR = 0%
Foreign missionaries in 1988:   4

FIELDS OF SERVICE
Brazil
  Amazonas (Manaus)   Japanese Kin-
    dergarten
  Sao Paulo (Guarulhos)   Japanese Kin-
    dergarten

To the Ends of the Earth Mission
1-14-22 Sakura Shimachi
Setagaya-ku 154, Tokyo, JAPAN

Organized: Not reported.

MISSIONARIES IN SERVICE
(1986) 1   (1988) 1*
AAGR = N/A
Foreign missionaries in 1988: Not
reported.

FIELDS OF SERVICE
Not reported.

United Church of Christ of Japan

Rm.31 Japan Christian Center
2-13-18 Nishi-Waseda
Shinjuku-ku 161, JAPAN

Mr. Tsuji
Organized: Not reported.
Nondenominational

MISSIONARIES IN SERVICE

(1972) 46   (1980) 56   (1983) 31
(1985) 65   (1986) 68   (1988) 61
AAGR = 2%

Foreign missionaries in 1988: 61

FIELDS OF SERVICE

USA
 California Japanese
 New York Japanese
Thailand Japanese
Germany (West) German, Japanese
Brazil Japanese
India Japanese
Switzerland

West Asia Missionary Fellowship

1-60-9 Sasazuuka
Shibuya-ku 151, Tokyo, JAPAN

Organized: Not reported.

MISSIONARIES IN SERVICE

(1986) 4   (1988) 4*
AAGR = N/A
Foreign missionaries in 1988: Not
reported.

FIELDS OF SERVICE

Not reported.

West Japan Evangelical Lutheran Church

2-2-11 Nakajimadori
Chuoo-ku, Kobe 651, JAPAN

Rev. Kentaro Kubo
Organized: 1979   Evangelical Lutheran

MISSIONARIES IN SERVICE

(1980) 3   (1986) 1   (1988) 1*

AAGR = N/A
Foreign missionaries in 1988: Not
reported.

FIELDS OF SERVICE

Indonesia
 Sumatra Region Batac
 Kalimantan Region Dayac, Jawa,
  Batac

Yuzawa Bible Baptist Church

3-11 Satake-cho, Yuzawa 012
Akita, JAPAN

Rev. Kanji Torii
Organized: 1981   Baptist

MISSIONARIES IN SERVICE

(1988) 2
AAGR = N/A
Foreign missionaries in 1988:   2

FIELDS OF SERVICE

Peru Japanese

KOREA

Africa Mission Committee

187 Choong Jungro 3-Ka
Seodaemun-Ku, Seoul 120, KOREA

Rev. Kim Sung-UK
Organized: Not reported.
Nondenominational

MISSIONARIES IN SERVICE

(1985) 5   (1988) 10
AAGR = 26%
Foreign missionaries in 1988:   10

FIELDS OF SERVICE

Kenya Nationals
Zambia Nationals
Malawi Nationals
Uganda Nationals
Tanzania Nationals

Arab Mission

194-4 Insa Dong, Chongro-Ku
Seoul, KOREA

Rev. Chung Young-Kwan
Organized: Not reported.
Nondenominational

MISSIONARIES IN SERVICE

(1988)   2
AAGR = N/A
Foreign missionaries in 1988:   2

FIELDS OF SERVICE

Eygpt   Nationals

Bangladesh Pakistan Mission

130 Do Lim-Dong
Yongdeungpo-Ku, Seoul, KOREA

Rev. Kim Jong-Dae (deceased)
Organized: Not reported.
Nondenominational

MISSIONARIES IN SERVICE

(1988)   10
AAGR = N/A
Foreign missionaries in 1988:   10

FIELDS OF SERVICE

New Zealand   Koreans
Iran   Koreans
Bangladesh   Nationals
Bolivia   Koreans

Baptist Bible Fellowship of Korea

Organized: Not reported.

MISSIONARIES IN SERVICE

(1986)   2   (1988)   3*
AAGR = N/A
Foreign missionaries in 1988: Not reported.

FIELDS OF SERVICE

Not reported.

Board Foreign Missions of General Assembly of Presbyterian

277-7 Cho-up-Dong, Jin-Gu
Pusan 614-080, KOREA

Rev. Lee Kum-Cho

Organized: Not reported.   Presbyterian

MISSIONARIES IN SERVICE

(1985)   12   (1988)   68
AAGR = 78%
Foreign missionaries in 1988:   68

FIELDS OF SERVICE

Taiwan   Koreans
West Africa   Africans
Singapore   Singaporeans
Philippines   Filipinos
Germany (West)   Koreans
Brazil   Koreans
Spain   Spanish, Koreans
Japan   Japanese, Koreans
Portugal   Koreans
Africa   Africans
Indonesia   Indonesian
Hong Kong   Koreans

Foreign Mission Board of General Assembly of Presbyterian Reformed

683-25 Yuk Sam Dong
Kang Nam-Ku, Seoul, KOREA

Rev. Chang Kyung-Jae
Organized: Not reported.   Presbyterian

MISSIONARIES IN SERVICE

(1982)   10   (1988)   23
AAGR = 15%
Foreign missionaries in 1988:   21

FIELDS OF SERVICE

Japan   Nationals
Gambia   Nationals
Philippines   Nationals
Ecuador   Nationals
Germany (West)   Nationals
Hong Kong   Nationals
Brazil   Koreans
Indonesia   Nationals

Full Gospel World Missions Department

Yoido PO Box 7, Seoul, KOREA

Dr. Paul Yonggi Cho
Organized: Not reported.

Assemblies of God
MISSIONARIES IN SERVICE
(1980) 36   (1982) 60   (1984) 68
(1985) 85   (1986) 20   (1988) 97
AAGR = 13%
Foreign missionaries in 1988: 97
FIELDS OF SERVICE
Not reported.

Global Bible Translators
Recently merged with Korea Bible Translators
Yong-Dong PO Box 349
Seoul 135-603, KOREA

Kim Dong-Hwa
Organized: 1985   Nondenominational
MISSIONARIES IN SERVICE
(1984) 4   (1985) 5   (1986) 9
(1988) 19
AAGR = 48%
Foreign missionaries in 1988: 18
FIELDS OF SERVICE
Papua New Guinea   Kuot, Mongi,
   Guahatire, Waima
Indonesia
   Irian Jaya Province   Kordesi

Hallelujah World Mission
Seobu PO Box 96, Seoul, KOREA

Rev. Chung Yung-Moon
Organized: Not reported.
Nondenominational
MISSIONARIES IN SERVICE
(1988) 2
AAGR = N/A
Foreign missionaries in 1988: 2
FIELDS OF SERVICE
Japan   Koreans

Korea Bible Translators
Recently merged with Global Bible Translators
CPO Box 3476, Seoul 100, KOREA

Rev. Back Byeung-Kun

Organized: Not reported.

MISSIONARIES IN SERVICE
(1982) 4   (1986) 6   (1988) 7*
AAGR = N/A
Foreign missionaries in 1988: Not reported.
FIELDS OF SERVICE
Indonesia

Korea Christian Church of God Mission
22-1 Kae-Bong Dong San
Koru-Ku, Seoul 150-04, KOREA

Rev. Han Yong-Chul
Organized: Not reported.
MISSIONARIES IN SERVICE
(1986) 2   (1988) 3*
AAGR = N/A
Foreign missionaries in 1988: Not reported.
FIELDS OF SERVICE
Not reported.

Korea Christian Mission Society
Room 605, Youn Ji-Dong 136
Jong Ro-Ku, Seoul, KOREA

Shin-Myung Kang (deceased)
Organized: 1966   Interdenominational
MISSIONARIES IN SERVICE
(1978) 7   (1980) 7   (1988) 7*
AAGR = N/A
Foreign missionaries in 1988: Not reported.
FIELDS OF SERVICE
Not reported.

Korea Evangelical Church Mission
890-56 Daechi-Dong
Gangnam-Ku, Seoul 135, KOREA

Rev. Lee Kang-Chun
Organized: Not reported.   Evangelical

MISSIONARIES IN SERVICE
(1985) 28   (1988) 18
AAGR = -13%
Foreign missionaries in 1988:   18

FIELDS OF SERVICE
Thailand Nationals
South Africa Nationals
Philippines Nationals
Kenya Nationals
Bolivia Nationals
Cameroon Nationals
Paraguay Nationals

Korea International Mission
CPO 3476, Seoul 100, KOREA

Dr. David Cho
Organized: 1968   Nondenominational

MISSIONARIES IN SERVICE
(1972) 12   (1975) 12   (1978) 16
(1980) 24   (1982) 22   (1985) 20
(1986) 20   (1988) 28
AAGR = 5%
Foreign missionaries in 1988:   28

FIELDS OF SERVICE
Thailand Nationals
Philippines Nationals
Indonesia Nationals
Singapore
Kenya
Brazil

Korea Methodist Church, The Board of Missions
Kwanghwa Moon PO Box 285
Seoul 150, KOREA

Rev. Park Bong-Bae
Organized: Not reported.   Methodist

MISSIONARIES IN SERVICE
(1980) 4   (1982) 12   (1985) 27
(1986) 27   (1988) 27
AAGR = 27%
Foreign missionaries in 1988:   27

FIELDS OF SERVICE
Papua New Guinea
Philippines

Malaysia Koreans
United Kingdom
  England Koreans
Paraguay Koreans
Germany (West) Koreans
Bangladesh
Taiwan
Japan Koreans

Korea Mission
261 Jin Kwan Dong
Eun Pyung Ku, Seoul, KOREA

Rev. Kim Dong-Bin
Organized: Not reported.
Nondenominational

MISSIONARIES IN SERVICE
(1985) 4   (1988) 6
AAGR = 14%
Foreign missionaries in 1988:   6

FIELDS OF SERVICE
Germany (West) Koreans
Taiwan Nationals
Japan Koreans

Korean Baptist Overseas Mission Society
1-668 Yoido Dong
Yongdeungpo-Ku, Seoul 150, KOREA

Organized: Not reported.

MISSIONARIES IN SERVICE
(1980) 2   (1982) 2   (1986) 8
(1988) 13*
AAGR = N/A
Foreign missionaries in 1988: Not
reported.

FIELDS OF SERVICE
Not reported.

Mission to Moslem Area
CPO Box 4726, Seoul, KOREA

Rev. An Dong- Ki
Organized: 1975   Nondenominational

MISSIONARIES IN SERVICE
(1978) 1   (1980) 4   (1984) 4
(1988) 22

AAGR = 36%
Foreign missionaries in 1988:   22

FIELDS OF SERVICE

Nigeria Nationals
Liberia Nationals
Kenya Nationals
Middle East
Gambia Nationals
India Nationals

National Organization of the Presbyterian Women of Korea

1007-3 Daechi Dong, Kang Nam-Ku
Seoul, KOREA

Mrs. Park Soon-Hye
Organized: Not reported.   Presbyterian

MISSIONARIES IN SERVICE

(1988)   4
AAGR = N/A
Foreign missionaries in 1988:   4

FIELDS OF SERVICE

Taiwan Taiwanese

Presbyterian Church in Korea (Koryu)

PO Box 190, Busan, KOREA

Dr. Ho Jin Chun
Organized: 1955   Presbyterian

MISSIONARIES IN SERVICE

(1972)   2   (1975)   2   (1978)   4
(1980)   4   (1988)   8*
AAGR = N/A
Foreign missionaries in 1988: Not
reported.

FIELDS OF SERVICE

Not reported.

Presbyterian Church of Korea (Haptong)

1007-3 Daechi Dong
Kang Nam-Ku, Seoul, KOREA

Rev. Chun Dong-shik
Organized: Not reported.   Presbyterian

MISSIONARIES IN SERVICE

(1980) 35   (1982) 75   (1985) 108
(1986) 105   (1988) 194
AAGR = 24%
Foreign missionaries in 1988:   194

FIELDS OF SERVICE

Eygpt Nationals, Koreans
Gambia Koreans
Germany (West) Koreans
Peru Koreans
Philippines Nationals
Brazil Koreans
Kenya Koreans, Nationals
Hong Kong Koreans
Paraguay Koreans
Papau New Guinea Koreans
United Kingdom
  England Nationals, Missionary Training
Chile Koreans
Singapore Nationals
Belgium Koreans
Japan Koreans
Australia Koreans
Nigeria Koreans
India Nationals
Israel Nationals
Argentina Koreans
Bolivia Koreans
Taiwan Koreans
Turkey Koreans
Indonesia Nationals, Koreans
Ivory Coast Koreans
Uganda Nationals
Lesotho Koreans
Liberia Koreans
Thailand Nationals

Presbyterian Church of Korea, Evangelism Dept, (Tonghap)

Rm. 305 Korean Church Centennial Bldg
135 Yunji-Dong, Chongro-Ku
Seoul 110, KOREA

Rev. Rew Shi-Hong
Organized: Not reported.   Presbyterian

MISSIONARIES IN SERVICE

(1980) 36   (1982) 63   (1985) 98
(1986) 104   (1988) 136
AAGR = 18%
Foreign missionaries in 1988: 146

FIELDS OF SERVICE

Chile   Koreans, Nationals
Mexico   Nationals
Austria   Koreans
India   Nationals
Panama   Nationals
Philippines   Nationals
Nepal   Nationals
Pakistan   Nationals
Gabon   Koreans, Nationals
Indonesia   Nationals
Japan   Koreans
Hong Kong   Koreans
Kenya   Nationals
Sweden   Koreans
Brazil   Koreans, Nationals
Singapore   Koreans, Nationals
Bangladesh   Nationals
Bolivia   Koreans, Nationals
Taiwan   Koreans, Nationals
Iran   Koreans
Thailand   Koreans, Nationals
New Zealand   Koreans, Nationals
Peru   Nationals
Switzerland   Koreans
Jordan   Nationals
Germany (West)   Nationals, Koreans
Colombia   Koreans, Nationals
USA
  Guam   Koreans
United Arab Emirates   Koreans
Paraguay   Koreans

South East Asia Baptist Mission Society

Yoido PO Box 165, Seoul 150, KOREA

Rev. Yu Byung-Ki
Organized: Not reported.   Baptist

MISSIONARIES IN SERVICE

(1982) 2   (1985) 10   (1986) 10
(1988) 2

AAGR = 0%
Foreign missionaries in 1988:   2

FIELDS OF SERVICE

Taiwan   Nationals

World Mission Department of Korea Assemblies of God

222 Pyung Djong, Chongro-Ku
Seoul, KOREA

Rev. Park Jung-Keun
Organized: Not reported.
Assemblies of God

MISSIONARIES IN SERVICE

(1988) 15
AAGR = N/A
Foreign missionaries in 1988:   15

FIELDS OF SERVICE

Philippines   Koreans, Nationals
Japan   Koreans
Bangladesh   Nationals
Indonesia   Nationals
Thailand   Nationals
Macau   Nationals

World Omega Missions

Sudaemun PO Box 93
Seoul 120, KOREA

Rev. Na Chung-hee
Organized: Not reported.
Nondenominational

MISSIONARIES IN SERVICE

(1985) 17   (1988) 26
AAGR = 15%
Foreign missionaries in 1988:   26

FIELDS OF SERVICE

Belgium   Koreans
Saudi Arabia   Koreans
Eygpt   Nationals
Philippines   Koreans
Thailand   Nationals
Bangladesh   Nationals
Brunei   Koreans
Germany (West)   Koreans

MALAYSIA

Abundant Life Centre

PO Box 2134, Kuching
Sarawak, MALAYSIA

Justin Kuek
Organized: 1984   Assemblies of God
MISSIONARIES IN SERVICE
(1988) 12
AAGR = N/A
Foreign missionaries in 1988:   0
FIELDS OF SERVICE

Malaysia
  Sarawak State Iban
  Sri Aman Iban
  Kuching Chinese, Bidayuh, Iban

Full Gospel Assembly

Lot 689, Taman Goodwood
Jalan Kuchai Lama 58200
Kuala Lumpur, MALAYSIA

Roland Seow
Organized: 1982
Independent Charismatic
MISSIONARIES IN SERVICE
Further information withheld at
agency's request.

General Council of Assemblies of God, Missions Department

99 Jalan Gasing
Petaling Jaya 46710, MALAYSIA

Dr. Prince Guneratnam
Organized: Not reported.   Pentecostal
MISSIONARIES IN SERVICE
(1988) 45
AAGR = N/A
Foreign missionaries in 1988:   0
FIELDS OF SERVICE

Hong Kong	**India**
France	**Philippines**
Singapore	**United Kingdom**
Pakistan	**Thailand**

USA	**Indonesia**
Australia	

Latter Rain Church of Malaysia

2 Jalan 12/3
Petaling Jaya 46200, MALAYSIA

Dexter Low
Organized: 1976   Charismatic
MISSIONARIES IN SERVICE
Further information withheld at
agency's request.

Lutheran Church in Malaysia & Singapore

PO Box 1068, Jalan Semangat PO
Petaling Jaya 46870, MALAYSIA

Daniel Chong
Organized: 1963   Lutheran
MISSIONARIES IN SERVICE
Further information withheld at
agency's request.

Malaysia Baptist Convention Mission Board

2 Jalan 2/38
Petaling Jaya 46000, MALAYSIA

Rev. Lim Wai Ming
Organized: 1979   Baptist
MISSIONARIES IN SERVICE
(1980) 8   (1985) 6   (1988) 6
AAGR = -3%
Foreign missionaries in 1988:   0
FIELDS OF SERVICE

Malaysia
  Kedah State Tamil plantation workers
  Johor State Tamil, Chinese (Mandarin)

Malaysia Discipleship Centre

9127 Jalan Bamdar 4
Taman Melawati, Hulu Kelang 53100
Kuala Lumpur, MALAYSIA

Thomas George
Organized: Not reported.   Independent
MISSIONARIES IN SERVICE
(1988)   2
AAGR = N/A
Foreign missionaries in 1988:   2
FIELDS OF SERVICE
Philippines

Malaysia Home and World Missionary Fellowship
9 Jalan 1, Berkeley Town Center
Kelang 41300, MALAYSIA

Mr. Teh Chye Heng
Organized: 1971   Interdenominational
MISSIONARIES IN SERVICE
(1972) 2   (1980) 2   (1984) 4
(1985) 4   (1988) 6
AAGR = 7%
Foreign missionaries in 1988:   0
FIELDS OF SERVICE
Malaysia
  Kedah State   Chinese (small villages)
  Negeri Sembilan State   Chinese, Tribal
  Perak State

Malaysia India Evangelism Council
PO Box 689, Penang, MALAYSIA

Dr. Chris D. Thomas
Organized: 1976   Interdenominational
MISSIONARIES IN SERVICE
(1972) 21   (1980) 10   (1988) 5*
AAGR = N/A
Foreign missionaries in 1988: Not reported.
FIELDS OF SERVICE
Not reported.

Malaysian Care
PO Box 281, Jalan Sultan
Petaling Jaya 46370, MALAYSIA

Rev. Peter Young
Organized: 1979   Nondenominational

MISSIONARIES IN SERVICE
(1985) 1   (1988) 4
AAGR = 59%
Foreign missionaries in 1988:   4
FIELDS OF SERVICE
Thailand
  Bangkok   Child Prostitutes, Drug Addicts
Pakistan

PAKISTAN

Church of Pakistan
Diocese Office, Barah Pathar
Sialkot, PAKISTAN

George Latch
Organized: Not reported.
MISSIONARIES IN SERVICE
(1978) 4   (1980) 4   (1982) 6
(1984) 6   (1988) 8*
AAGR = N/A
Foreign missionaries in 1988: Not reported.
FIELDS OF SERVICE
Pakistan
  Punjab Province   Punjabis
  Azad Kashmir Province   Punjabis

Emmanuel's Word for the Northern Frontiers
PO Box 14
Abbottabad 22010, PAKISTAN

Akram Shakar
Organized: 1983   Pentecostal
MISSIONARIES IN SERVICE
Further information withheld at agency's request.

House of Life
A 212 Shahid Bhatti Road
Murree, PAKISTAN

Ifrahim A. Mathew
Organized: 1956   Evangelical

MISSIONARIES IN SERVICE
(1988) 8
AAGR = N/A
Foreign missionaries in 1988:   3
FIELDS OF SERVICE
Pakistan

Lahore Church Council Sharakpur

Church House, Sharakpur District
Sheikhupura, Punjab, PAKISTAN

Rev. E. Jang Bahadur
Organized: 1968   Presbyterian

MISSIONARIES IN SERVICE
(1972) 12   (1980) 20   (1985) 32
(1988) 36
AAGR = 7%
Foreign missionaries in 1988:   0
FIELDS OF SERVICE
Pakistan
  Punjab Province Illiterate, Unreached

Pakistan Gospel Assemblies

PO Box 5134, Lahore 14, PAKISTAN

Dr. William Johnson
Organized: Not reported.   Pentecostal
MISSIONARIES IN SERVICE
(1988) 10
AAGR = N/A
Foreign missionaries in 1988:   0
FIELDS OF SERVICE
Pakistan
  Sind Province
  Baluchistan Province Christian Community, Non-Christians
  Punjab Province Christian Community, Non-Christians
  Northwest Frontier Province Christian Community, Non-Christians

United Christian Fellowship

PO Box 173, Abbottabad, PAKISTAN

Samson Kurshed
Organized: Not reported.   Evangelical

MISSIONARIES IN SERVICE
(1972) 1   (1988) 5
AAGR = 11%
Foreign missionaries in 1988:   0
FIELDS OF SERVICE
Pakistan Northeastern Pakistan Region

PHILIPPINES

Action International Ministries

PO Box 110, Greenhills
Metro Manila 3113, PHILIPPINES

Doug Nichols
Organized: Not reported.

MISSIONARIES IN SERVICE
(1975) 6   (1980) 22   (1982) 26
(1984) 32   (1988) 67*
AAGR = N/A
Foreign missionaries in 1988: Not reported.
FIELDS OF SERVICE
Not reported.

Agape Evangelistic Mission

PO Box 140
Butan City 5600, PHILIPPINES

Wire Gonzalez, Sr.
Organized: 1971Independent Pentecostal
MISSIONARIES IN SERVICE
(1988) 6
AAGR = N/A
Foreign missionaries in 1988:   0
FIELDS OF SERVICE
Philippines
  Agusan del Sur Province Cebuano, Manobo
  Agusan del Norte Province Cebuano
  Southern Leyte Province Cebuano
  Surigao del Sur Province Cebuano, Manobo

Charismatic Full Gospel Ministries

PO Box 12, Surigao City 8400
Mindanao, PHILIPPINES

Ric Taboclaon
Organized: 1974
Charismatic, Pentecostal
MISSIONARIES IN SERVICE
(1988) 44
AAGR = N/A
Foreign missionaries in 1988:   0
FIELDS OF SERVICE
Philippines
  Mindanao Region Mamanwa,
    Konkista, Mandaya

Christ is Coming, Inc.

14 Visayas Avenue
Project 6, Quezon City
Metro Manila, PHILIPPINES

Gertrudo G. Aquino
Organized: 1977   Nondenominational
MISSIONARIES IN SERVICE
(1988) 6
AAGR = N/A
Foreign missionaries in 1988:   2
FIELDS OF SERVICE
Australia
Philippines
  Sorsogon Province Bicolano
  Bohol Province Boholanon

Christian & Missionary Alliance Churches of the Philippines

13 West Capitol Drive
Pasig, PHILIPPINES

Dr. Ben de Jesus
Organized: 1962   Alliance
MISSIONARIES IN SERVICE

(1972) 4	(1975) 6	(1978) 11
(1980) 2	(1982) 3	(1984) 4
(1985) 5	(1988) 11	

AAGR = 7%

Foreign missionaries in 1988:   11
FIELDS OF SERVICE
Bolivia Spanish-speaking women
Palau
  Koror Palauans
Thailand Buddhists, Thai
  Konkhan Thai
Hong Kong
  Hong Kong Island Domestic helpers
Indonesia
  South Sumatra (Palembang) Chi-
    nese, Bahasa, Indonesian
Uruguay Indigenous

Christian Fellowship Churches of the Philippines, Inc.

Box 130, Dumaguete City 6200
PHILIPPINES

Rev. Benito Pacleb
Organized: 1974   Pentecostal
MISSIONARIES IN SERVICE

(1980) 13	(1985) 22	(1988) 69

AAGR = 23%
Foreign missionaries in 1988:   0
FIELDS OF SERVICE
Philippines
  Zamboanga del Sur Province Cebu-
    ano
  Siquijor Province Cebuano
  Negros Occidental Province Ilonggo,
    Cebuano

Church of God World Missions of the Philippines, Inc.

PO Box 252, Iloilo City 5000
PHILIPPINES

Rev. Simon Valenzuela
Organized: 1977   Pentecostal
MISSIONARIES IN SERVICE

(1980) 6	(1985) 15	(1988) 19

AAGR = 16%
Foreign missionaries in 1988:   0

FIELDS OF SERVICE

Philippines
Negros Province   Cebuano
Iloilo Province   Ati

Church of the Foursquare Gospel in the Philippines

1F. Castillo St., Project 4, Quezon City
Metro Manila, PHILIPPINES

Dr. Felipe Ferrez, Jr.
Organized: 1973   Pentecostal

MISSIONARIES IN SERVICE

Further information withheld at
agency's request.

Church of the Living Christ Fellowship

E. Jacinto St., Esquina, PHILIPPINES

Rev. Leon R. Salinente, Jr.
Organized: 1986
Church of the Living Christ Fellowship

MISSIONARIES IN SERVICE

(1988) 12
AAGR = N/A
Foreign missionaries in 1988:   0

FIELDS OF SERVICE

Philippines
Cebu Province
Samar Province
Leyte Province

Conservative Baptist Association of the Philippines

PO Box 1882, Manila, PHILIPPINES

Rev. Dominador Rames
Organized: 1962   Baptist

MISSIONARIES IN SERVICE

(1978) 2   (1980) 2   (1985) 5
(1988) 3
AAGR = 4%
Foreign missionaries in 1988:   3

FIELDS OF SERVICE

United Arab Emirates

Filipino Workers
Indonesia

Door of Faith

722 BO Malaban
Binan Caguna, PHILIPPINES

Rev. Lauro T. Navarro
Organized: Not reported.   Pentecostal

MISSIONARIES IN SERVICE

(1988) 11
AAGR = N/A
Foreign missionaries in 1988:   0

FIELDS OF SERVICE

Philippines

Door of Faith Church and Bible School, Inc.

67 Zorra Cor Cabotage Sts, Quezon
City, Metro Manila, PHILIPPINES

Leopoldo Mazaredo
Organized: Not reported.   Pentecostal

MISSIONARIES IN SERVICE

(1988) 95
AAGR = N/A
Foreign missionaries in 1988:   0

FIELDS OF SERVICE

Philippines
Pampanga Province   Pampango
Bicol   Bicolano
Leyte (Tacloban)   Waray-waray
Mindanao Region   Tagalog
Bulacan Province   Tagalog
Iloilo Province   Ilonggo
La Union Province   Ilocano
Marinduque Province   Tagalog

Evangelical Presbyterian Mission, Inc.

ACPO Box 595, Quezon City 3001
Metro Manila, PHILIPPINES

Gerardo H. Kim
Organized: 1978   Presbyterian

MISSIONARIES IN SERVICE

(1978) 2   (1980) 5   (1985) 11

(1988) 20
AAGR = 26%
Foreign missionaries in 1988:   0

FIELDS OF SERVICE
Philippines
Ifugao Province Ifugao
Central Visayas Region Cebuano
Ilococ Region Ilocano
Tagalog Region Tagalog

Fellowship for Rural Evangelization & Expansion, Inc.
PO Box 2122, Manila 1099 PHILIPPINES

Rev. Ben C. Hernandez
Organized: 1983   Evangelical

MISSIONARIES IN SERVICE
(1988) 56
AAGR = N/A
Foreign missionaries in 1988:   0

FIELDS OF SERVICE
Philippines
 Laguna Province
 Pampanga Province
 Pangasinan Province
 Cavite Province
 Nueva Ecija Province
 Metro Manila
 Tarlac Province
 Batangas Province

Fellowship of Indigenous Fundamental Churches of Philippines
PO Box 4546, Manila, PHILIPPINES

Gervasio Casas, Isaac Musnic
Organized: Not reported.

MISSIONARIES IN SERVICE
(1984) 18   (1985) 27   (1988) 34*
AAGR = N/A
Foreign missionaries in 1988: Not reported.

FIELDS OF SERVICE
Philippines

Zambales Province Tagalog/Ilocano
Pangasinan Province Pangasinan
Metro Manila Tagalog
Nueva Ecija Province Tagalog,
    Ilocano
Tarlac Province Ilocano
Bataan Province Tagalog
Bulacan Province Tagalog

Full Gospel Temple Interdenominational, Inc.
PO Box 31, Surigao City 8400
Mindanao, PHILIPPINES

Rogelio Dagasdas
Organized: 1971   Pentecostal

MISSIONARIES IN SERVICE
Further information withheld at
agency's request.

Global Outreach Ministry Foundation, Inc.
Calvary Church, Tugbungan
Consolacion, Cebu, PHILIPPINES

Rev. Cornelio Pagao
Organized: Not reported.   Pentecostal

MISSIONARIES IN SERVICE
Further information withheld at
agency's request.

Grace Bible Church-Grace Bible Mission
3041 Nagtahan St.
Sampaloc, Manila, PHILIPPINES

Rev. Andrew Tenfrancia
Organized: 1950   Nondenominational

MISSIONARIES IN SERVICE
(1972) 10   (1980) 15   (1985) 14
(1988) 23
AAGR = 5%
Foreign missionaries in 1988:   0

FIELDS OF SERVICE
Philippines
 Metro Manila

Grace Evangelical Mission, Inc.

PO Box 14, Valenzuela
Metro Manila, PHILIPPINES

Rev. Hilarion Gusto
Organized: 1978   Evangelical

MISSIONARIES IN SERVICE

(1980) 6   (1982) 8   (1984) 13
(1985) 13   (1988) 27
AAGR = 21%
Foreign missionaries in 1988:   0

FIELDS OF SERVICE

Philippines
  Bulacan Province Tagalog
  Pangasinan Province Ilocano,
    Pangasinan
  Quirino Province Ilocano, Ifugao
  Cavite Province Tagalog
  Zambales Province Ilocano, Zambal
  Metro Manila Tagalog

Grace Missionary Fellowship

Socorro, Oriental Mindoro
PHILIPPINES

Romeo C. Santiago
Organized: 1983   Nondenominational

MISSIONARIES IN SERVICE

(1985) 17   (1988) 37
AAGR = 30%
Foreign missionaries in 1988:   0

FIELDS OF SERVICE

Philippines
  Metro Manila Squatters, Hotel Workers, Factory Workers
  Romblon Province Bantuanon, Sibalenon, Romblomanon, Sibuyan
  Mindoro Province San Teodoro, Mangyan, Iraya
  Bicol Sorsogon, Bicol, Waray-waray

Hda. Georgina Open Bible Church

PO Box 407, Bacolod City 6100

Negros Occidental, PHILIPPINES

Rev. Exequiel F. Guanzon
Organized: 1975   Baptist

MISSIONARIES IN SERVICE

(1972) 2   (1980) 36   (1985) 39
(1988) 40
AAGR = 21%
Foreign missionaries in 1988:   0

FIELDS OF SERVICE

Philippines
  Negros Occidental Province Tagalog, Visayan, Cebuano

Jesus Christ Deliverance Ministries, Inc.

Sampaguita Children's Learning Center
7 Sampaguita St.
General Santos City, PHILIPPINES

Marianito Hulleza
Organized: 1985   Charismatic

MISSIONARIES IN SERVICE

(1988) 40
AAGR = N/A
Foreign missionaries in 1988:   0

FIELDS OF SERVICE

Philippines
  Bukidnon Province Small farmers, Hacienda workers
  Lledo Squatters, Out of school youth
  Lansang Village (G. S. C.) Company laborers, Employees
  General Santos City Squatters, Prisoners, Students
  South Cotabato (Menanga) Small fishermen, Out of school youth
  Misamis Oriental (Cagayan) Company laborers, Office employees
  South Cotabato (Glan) Logpond Fishermen, Tenants
  Lanao del Sur Province Tenants, Muslims
  North Cotabato Province Tenants, Students, Rebels

Jesus Christ Evangelistic Team of the Philippines

Cataos Bldg, Esperanza Village
Awayan, Carcar, Cebu, PHILIPPINES

Elpedio A. Montenegro
Organized: 1988   Nondenominational
MISSIONARIES IN SERVICE
(1988) 30
AAGR = N/A
Foreign missionaries in 1988:   0
FIELDS OF SERVICE
Philippines
  Cebu Province Mamanwa, Manobo,
    Bilaan, Bagobo

Jubilee Evangelical Church, Mission Board

35 Hemady Cor., Third Street
New Manila, Quezon City
Metro Manila, PHILIPPINES

Alejandor Beltran
Organized: 1970   Interdenominational
MISSIONARIES IN SERVICE
(1972) 10   (1975) 10   (1978) 12
(1980) 13   (1988) 17*
AAGR = N/A
Foreign missionaries in 1988: Not
reported.
FIELDS OF SERVICE
Not reported.

Lift Jesus Higher Fellowship, Inc.

Zamora St.
New Escalante 6124, PHILIPPINES

Rev. Ronnie Binas
Organized: 1983   Full Gospel
MISSIONARIES IN SERVICE
(1985) 2   (1988) 12
AAGR = 82%
Foreign missionaries in 1988:   0
FIELDS OF SERVICE
Philippines

Negros Occidental Province   Ilonggo,
  Cebuano
Iloilo Province   Ilonggo

Mindanao Fellowship of Bible Churches

1260 Duterte St.
Panabo, Davao 8105, PHILIPPINES

Rev. Emmanuel Estre
Organized: 1985   Baptist
MISSIONARIES IN SERVICE
Further information withheld at
agency's request.

Northeast Luzon Baptist Fellowship

Ipil, Echaque, Isabela, PHILIPPINES

Rev. Gregg L. Rafael
Organized: 1985   Baptist
MISSIONARIES IN SERVICE
(1985) 11   (1988) 27
AAGR = 35%
Foreign missionaries in 1988:   0
FIELDS OF SERVICE
Philippines
  Cagayan Province   Atta, Ifugao
  Ifugao Province   Ifugao
  Nueva Vizcaya Province   Atta, Ifugao
  Quirino Province   Atta, Ifugao,
    Ilongot
  Isabela Province   Atta, Ifugao

Palawan Evangelistic Mission

Poblacion, Quezon 5304
Palawan, PHILIPPINES

Rev. Ernesto Dignadice
Organized: 1983   Baptist
MISSIONARIES IN SERVICE
(1988) 5
AAGR = N/A
Foreign missionaries in 1988:   0
FIELDS OF SERVICE
Philippines

Palawan Province Tagalog, Visayan

Philippine Advent Christian Conference, Inc.
32 Max Suniel St., Carmen
Cagayan de Oro City, PHILIPPINES

Graciano D. Villadolio
Organized: 1973   Adventist
MISSIONARIES IN SERVICE
Further information withheld at
agency's request.

Philippine Association of Baptists for World Evangelism
PO Box 119
Iloilo City 5000, PHILIPPINES

Dr. Antolin B. Zawar
Organized: 1957   Baptist
MISSIONARIES IN SERVICE
(1972) 11   (1975) 11   (1978) 7
(1980) 8   (1982) 8   (1984) 7
(1988) 10
AAGR = 0%
Foreign missionaries in 1988:   10

Philippine Episcopal Church, Missionary Diocese of Central
Phil. PO Box 655, Manila, PHILIPPINES

Rev. Manuel C. Lumpias
Organized: Not reported.   Episcopal
MISSIONARIES IN SERVICE
(1972) 33   (1975) 47   (1978) 54
(1980) 56   (1988) 95*
AAGR = N/A
Foreign missionaries in 1988: Not
reported.
FIELDS OF SERVICE
Not reported.

Philippine Evangelical Mission, Inc.
PO Box 4274

Manila 1099, PHILIPPINES

Rev. Cornelio R. Dalisay
Organized: 1979   Evangelical
MISSIONARIES IN SERVICE
(1980) 8   (1982) 17   (1985) 14
(1988) 10
AAGR = 3%
Foreign missionaries in 1988:   0

Philippine General Council of the Assemblies of God
PO Box 3782, Manila, PHILIPPINES

Organized: Not reported.
Assemblies of God
MISSIONARIES IN SERVICE
(1980) 1   (1988) 2*
AAGR = N/A
Foreign missionaries in 1988: Not
reported.
FIELDS OF SERVICE
Not reported.

Philippine Missionary Fellowship, Inc.
PO Box 3349, Manila, PHILIPPINES

Evangelista Siodora
Organized: 1956   Nondenominational
MISSIONARIES IN SERVICE
(1972) 14   (1980) 22   (1985) 62
(1988) 87*
AAGR = N/A
Foreign missionaries in 1988: Not
reported.
FIELDS OF SERVICE
Philippines
Aklan Province Ati, Visayan
Metro Manila
Zambales Province Zambal, Tagalog,
   Negrito
Leyte Province
Romblon Province
Mindanao Region Tagalog, Ilocano,
   Visayan
Negros Occidental (Bacolod)

Students, Town People
Negros Province
Davao (Cateel)
Palawan Province
Batangas Province
Cavite Province   Tagalog
Leyte (Tacloban)
Iloilo Province   Ilonggo
Surigao del Norte Province
    Mamanwa, Lowlanders, City People
Cotabato Province   T'Boli
Bulacan Province

Philippine Missions Association, Inc.

PO Box 1416, Manila, PHILIPPINES

Met Castillo
Organized: 1983   Evangelical
    MISSIONARIES IN SERVICE
(1988)   9
AAGR = N/A
Foreign missionaries in 1988:   5
    FIELDS OF SERVICE
Bolivia
  Cochabamba Department   Bolivians
Philippines
  Benguet Province   Kankanay, Ibaloi
Paraguay
  Central (Asuncion)   Paraguayans
Niger
  Niamey Area
Ethiopia
  Addis Ababa

Philippine Native Crusade

PO Box 121, Tuguegarao 1101
Cagayan, PHILIPPINES

Rev. Claudio R. Cortez
Organized: 1962   Nondenominational
    MISSIONARIES IN SERVICE
(1980) 207   (1988) 382*
AAGR = N/A
Foreign missionaries in 1988: Not
reported.

Not reported.

Reality of Christ, Inc.

Cacayan Village, Mangagoy
Bislig 8615, Surigao del Sur
PHILIPPINES

Joe A. Eleazar
Organized: 1983   Nondenominational
    MISSIONARIES IN SERVICE
(1985) 96   (1988) 139
AAGR = 13%
Foreign missionaries in 1988:   0
    FIELDS OF SERVICE
Philippines
  Mindanao Region   Surigaonon
  Visayas Region   Visayan
  Mindanao Region   Davaoeno, Tribal
    People, Agusanon, Muslims, others
  Luzon Region   Tagalog

Rose of Sharon International Ministries

4 Annapolis, Greenhills
San Juan, Metro Manila, PHILIPPINES

Antonio G. Sayson, Jr.
Organized: 1980   Independent
    MISSIONARIES IN SERVICE
(1988)   3
AAGR = N/A
Foreign missionaries in 1988:   0
    FIELDS OF SERVICE
Philippines
  Camarines Norte Province   Bicolano,
    Tagalog
  La Union Province   Ilocano, Tagalog,
    Pangasinan

Sambahang Kristiano Mission

13 Kasaganaan St., Marulas, Valenzuela
Metro Manila, PHILIPPINES

Miss Loida R. Abarientos
Organized: Not reported.

MISSIONARIES IN SERVICE

(1972) 4   (1975) 8   (1980) 8
(1982) 8   (1984) 5   (1988) 5*
AAGR = N/A
Foreign missionaries in 1988: Not reported.

FIELDS OF SERVICE

Philippines
Bicol (Baao) Bicolano
Pangasinan Province Pangasinan
Bicol (Iriga) Bicolano
Palawan Province (Abongan) Visaya

Translators Association of the Philippines, Inc.

PO Box 10174 (Main), Quezon City
Metro Manila, PHILIPPINES

Edmund Industan
Organized: Not reported.
Nondenominational

MISSIONARIES IN SERVICE

(1985) 39   (1988) 47
AAGR = 6%
Foreign missionaries in 1988: 0

FIELDS OF SERVICE

Philippines
Aklan Province Malay
Isabela Province Ifugao, Batad,
   Ayangan, Paranan
Davao del Norte Province Ata,
   Manobo (Talaingod
Sultan Kudarat Province Manobo,
   Cotabato
Quirino Province Ga'dang
Bukidnon Province Manobo, West-
   ern Bukidnon
Zambales Province Sambal, Tina
Zamboanga del Norte Province Sub-
   anon, Western
Davao Oriental Province Kalanga,
   Muslim
Zamboanga del Sur Province West-
   ern Subanon
Mountain (Natonin) Balangao
Romblon Province Loocnon
Davao del Norte Province

Ata, Manobo (Langilan)
Antique Province Kinaray
Kalinga Mangali
Metro Manila   Office Work
Ifugao Province   Amganad, Ifugao

Tribes and Nations Outreach

PO Box SM3, Manila, PHILIPPINES

Joseph Lee
Organized: 1985   Nondenominational

MISSIONARIES IN SERVICE

(1985) 14   (1988) 21
AAGR = 14%
Foreign missionaries in 1988:   4

FIELDS OF SERVICE

Philippines
Mindanao Region   Tribal, Non-tribal
Thailand
Chiang Mai Thai
North Eastern Region Laotians, Thai

United Church of Christ in the Philippines

PO Box 718, CPO
Manila 1099, PHILIPPINES

Bishop Estanislao Q. Abainza
Organized: 1952   Denominational

MISSIONARIES IN SERVICE

(1972) 54   (1980) 38   (1985) 35
(1988) 89
AAGR = 3%
Foreign missionaries in 1988:   0

FIELDS OF SERVICE

Philippines
Southern Luzon Region Bicolano,
   Tagalog, Mangyan
Northern Luzon Region Ilocano,
   Agta, Pampangan, Kalinga, Apayao
Mindanao Region Indonesian, Mag-
   uindanao, Subanon, Yakan,
   Manobo, Blaan, Tagakaolo, Cebuano
Visayas Region Cebuano, Leyte,
   Sama, Antique

United Evangelical Church of Philippines, Mission Board

1170 Benavidez St., Sta Cruz
Manila, PHILIPPINES

Mr. Ong Kim Peng
Organized: 1969   Evangelical

MISSIONARIES IN SERVICE

(1972) 37	(1975) 37	(1978) 38
(1980) 41	(1985) 15	(1988) 22

AAGR = -2%
Foreign missionaries in 1988:   4

FIELDS OF SERVICE

Hong Kong
  Kowloon   Cantonese
Philippines   Amoy, Tagalog
Taiwan
  Taipei County   Mandarin

SINGAPORE

Asia Evangelistic Fellowship

Maxwell Road PO Box 579 SINGAPORE

Rev. G.D. James
Organized: 1960   Nondenominational

MISSIONARIES IN SERVICE

(1972) 44	(1975) 50	(1978) 63
(1980) 80	(1982) 82	(1985) 120
(1988) 140		

AAGR = 8%
Foreign missionaries in 1988:   91

FIELDS OF SERVICE

Malaysia   Tamil
Australia   Refugees, Asian students
New Zealand   Asians, Islanders
Indonesia
  East Java Province   Javanese
India   Slum dwellers
Burma   Hidden people in rural areas
Hong Kong   Filipino Maids, Boat
  People
Philippines
  Metro Manila   Pavement dwellers,
  Beggars
Pakistan   Students, Women

Barker Road Methodist Church

48 Barker Road, SINGAPORE

Dr. Ngoei Foong Nghian
Organized: 1956   Methodist

MISSIONARIES IN SERVICE

(1988)   3
AAGR = N/A
Foreign missionaries in 1988:   0

FIELDS OF SERVICE

USA   **Hong Kong**

Bedok Methodist Church

No. 1 Lorong Pelasari, Bedok
SINGAPORE

Rev. David Wee C.S.
Organized: 1946   Methodist

MISSIONARIES IN SERVICE

(1988)   3
AAGR = N/A
Foreign missionaries in 1988:   0

FIELDS OF SERVICE

Singapore

Bethel Assembly of God

Paya Labar PO Box 46, SINGAPORE

Rev. Pang Ek Kwan
Organized: 1957   Assemblies of God

MISSIONARIES IN SERVICE

(1988)   6
AAGR = N/A
Foreign missionaries in 1988:   6

FIELDS OF SERVICE

Nepal   **Philippines**

Bethesda Brethren Co, Ltd.

15 A Jalan Rama Rama, SINGAPORE

Rev. Lauw Kim Guan
Organized: 1976   Brethren

MISSIONARIES IN SERVICE

(1988)   5
AAGR = N/A
Foreign missionaries in 1988:   5

FIELDS OF SERVICE

Singapore	Hong Kong

Bethesda Chapel
27 Lorong Melayu, SINGAPORE

Tan Kok Beng
Organized: Not reported.   Brethren

MISSIONARIES IN SERVICE
(1988) 13
AAGR = N/A
Foreign missionaries in 1988:   0

FIELDS OF SERVICE

Singapore	Australia
USA	Pakistan

Bethesda Church Bukit Arang
114 Serangoon Avenue 3, SINGAPORE

Mr. Ooi Ghee Siong
Organized: 1974   Brethren

MISSIONARIES IN SERVICE
(1988) 3
AAGR = N/A
Foreign missionaries in 1988:   0

FIELDS OF SERVICE

Singapore

Bethesda Frankel Estate Church
2-4 La Salle Street, SINGAPORE

Dr. Tan Ban Cheng
Organized: 1958   Brethren

MISSIONARIES IN SERVICE
(1988) 4
AAGR = N/A
Foreign missionaries in 1988:   2

FIELDS OF SERVICE

Japan	Singapore

Bethesda Hall
601 Ang Mo Hio Avenue 4 SINGAPORE

Mr. Lim Tian Leong
Organized: 1864   Brethren

MISSIONARIES IN SERVICE
(1988) 10
AAGR = N/A
Foreign missionaries in 1988:   3

FIELDS OF SERVICE

Singapore	Austria
United Kingdom	Africa

Bible Church Singapore
152 West Coast Road
Clementi Bible Centre, SINGAPORE

Mr. Robert Lim
Organized: 1964   Independent

MISSIONARIES IN SERVICE
(1988) 1
AAGR = N/A
Foreign missionaries in 1988:   1

FIELDS OF SERVICE

Taiwan

Calvary Charismatic Centre
Owen Road PO Box 148, SINGAPORE

Rev. Rick Seaward
Organized: 1977   Assemblies of God

MISSIONARIES IN SERVICE
(1985) 103   (1988) 130
AAGR = 8%
Foreign missionaries in 1988:   0

FIELDS OF SERVICE

Not reported.

Centre of Hope Church
Orchard Point PO Box 769, SINGAPORE

Rev. Peter Tay Yap Tong
Organized: 1987   Assemblies of God

MISSIONARIES IN SERVICE
(1988) 1
AAGR = N/A
Foreign missionaries in 1988:   1

FIELDS OF SERVICE

Netherlands
  Amsterdam

Chapel of the Resurrection
Malan Road, SINGAPORE

Dr. James Wong
Organized: 1980   Anglican

MISSIONARIES IN SERVICE
(1988)   1
AAGR = N/A
Foreign missionaries in 1988:   1

FIELDS OF SERVICE
Thailand

Charis Assembly of God
15 Lynwood Grove, SINGAPORE

Rev. Stephen Chua H.H.
Organized: 1986   Assemblies of God

MISSIONARIES IN SERVICE
(1988)   1
AAGR = N/A
Foreign missionaries in 1988:   1

FIELDS OF SERVICE
Pakistan

Chen Li Presbyterian Church
76 Guillemard Road, SINGAPORE

Mr. Phua Chee Seng
Organized: 1934   Presbyterian

MISSIONARIES IN SERVICE
(1980) 13   (1988)   5
AAGR = -10%
Foreign missionaries in 1988:   5

FIELDS OF SERVICE
Hong Kong
Malaysia
  West Malaysia Region
Singapore
Indonesia

Church of Christ of Malaya
54 Sophia Road, SINGAPORE

Ng Meng Uk
Organized: 1973   Nondenominational

MISSIONARIES IN SERVICE
(1988)   8
AAGR = N/A
Foreign missionaries in 1988:   19

FIELDS OF SERVICE
Indonesia   Indonesian
Taiwan   Chinese
Malaysia   Chinese
Thailand   Thai, Chinese

Church of Our Saviour
130 Margaret Drive, SINGAPORE

Rev. Derek Hong Tack Weng
Organized: 1950   Anglican

MISSIONARIES IN SERVICE
(1988)   7
AAGR = N/A
Foreign missionaries in 1988:   0

FIELDS OF SERVICE
Belgium   **Australia**
South Africa   **New Zealand**
Philippines

Church of Singapore
145 Marine Parade, SINGAPORE

Rev. George Ong Teng Tee
Organized: 1963   Independent

MISSIONARIES IN SERVICE
(1988)   7
AAGR = N/A
Foreign missionaries in 1988:   0

FIELDS OF SERVICE
Africa   **Guam**
Taiwan   **Philippines**
Thailand   **Hong Kong**

Emmanuel Assembly of God
165 Upper East Coast Rd., SINGAPORE

Rev. Alfred Ang
Organized: 1969   Assemblies of God

MISSIONARIES IN SERVICE
(1988)   4
AAGR = N/A

Foreign missionaries in 1988:   4

FIELDS OF SERVICE

Malaysia   **Thailand**

Evangel Assembly of God

39 Sommerville Road, SINGAPORE

Rev. Robert Lim Bak Mong
Organized: 1964   Assemblies of God

MISSIONARIES IN SERVICE

(1988)   4
AAGR = N/A
Foreign missionaries in 1988:   4

FIELDS OF SERVICE

Philippines
 Iloilo Province
 Cebu Province

Evangelize China Fellowship

74 Upper Aljunied Road, SINGAPORE

Mr. Tay Swee Lan
Organized: 1956   Independent

MISSIONARIES IN SERVICE

(1988)   1
AAGR = N/A
Foreign missionaries in 1988:   1

FIELDS OF SERVICE

Indonesia

Fairfield Methodist Church

1 Tanjong Pagar Road, SINGAPORE

Rev. Michael Wong
Organized: 1948   Methodist

MISSIONARIES IN SERVICE

(1988)   8
AAGR = N/A
Foreign missionaries in 1988:   5

FIELDS OF SERVICE

Papua New Guinea   **Singapore**
Australia

Faith Community Baptist Church

510 Thomson Road

SLF Complex #02-05, SINGAPORE

Rev. L. Khong Kin Hoong
Organized: 1986   Baptist

MISSIONARIES IN SERVICE

(1988)   2
AAGR = N/A
Foreign missionaries in 1988:   2

FIELDS OF SERVICE

Ghana

Faith Methodist Church

400 Commonwealth Drive SINGAPORE

Dr. Clarence Lim Kim Seng
Organized: 1965   Methodist

MISSIONARIES IN SERVICE

(1988)   17
AAGR = N/A
Foreign missionaries in 1988:   17

FIELDS OF SERVICE

Hong Kong
Singapore
Malaysia
 Sabah State
Australia

Galilee Bible Presbyterian Church

202 Pandan Gardens, SINGAPORE

Rev. Philip Heng Swee Choon
Organized: 1960   Presbyterian

MISSIONARIES IN SERVICE

(1988)   3
AAGR = N/A
Foreign missionaries in 1988:   3

FIELDS OF SERVICE

Indonesia

Glory Presbyterian Church

9 Pei Hwa Avenue
Bukit Timah Road, SINGAPORE

Rev. Bunyan Oey
Organized: 1881   Presbyterian

MISSIONARIES IN SERVICE

(1988)   3

AAGR = N/A
Foreign missionaries in 1988:   3
FIELDS OF SERVICE
Singapore   **Burma**

Grace (SCC) Church
14 Queen Street, SINGAPORE

Rev. Chan Fong
Organized: 1950   Independent
MISSIONARIES IN SERVICE
(1988) 17
AAGR = N/A
Foreign missionaries in 1988:   0
FIELDS OF SERVICE
United Kingdom
Burma
India
Malaysia
  West Malaysia Region
  East Malaysia Region
Indonesia
Singapore
Africa

Grace Methodist Church
65 Wishart Road, SINGAPORE

Rev. Francis Ngoi
Organized: 1969   Methodist
MISSIONARIES IN SERVICE
(1988) 2
AAGR = N/A
Foreign missionaries in 1988:   2
FIELDS OF SERVICE
United Kingdom   **Thailand**

Harvester Assembly of God
Tampines South PO Box 200
SINGAPORE

Rev. Bernard Foo
Organized: 1976   Assemblies of God
MISSIONARIES IN SERVICE
(1988) 4
AAGR = N/A
Foreign missionaries in 1988:   4

FIELDS OF SERVICE
Philippines

Hephzibah Christian Fellowship
Tanglin PO Box 0009, SINGAPORE

Dr. Augustine Tan H.H.
Organized: 1986   Independent
MISSIONARIES IN SERVICE
(1988) 1
AAGR = N/A
Foreign missionaries in 1988:   1
FIELDS OF SERVICE
Canada

Jubilee Presbyterian Church
256 Outram Road, SINGAPORE

Rev. Derek John Kingston
Organized: Not reported.   Presbyterian
MISSIONARIES IN SERVICE
(1988) 2
AAGR = N/A
Foreign missionaries in 1988:   2
FIELDS OF SERVICE
Australia   **Senegal**

Katong Presbyterian Church
42 Joo Chiat Lane, SINGAPORE

Rev. Ian Hart
Organized: 1948   Presbyterian
MISSIONARIES IN SERVICE
(1988) 5
AAGR = N/A
Foreign missionaries in 1988:   0
FIELDS OF SERVICE
Taiwan   **Philippines**
France

Kay Poh Road Baptist Church
7 Kay Poh Road, SINGAPORE

Rev. Kan Kai Ping
Organized: 1949   Baptist
MISSIONARIES IN SERVICE
(1988)   2
AAGR = N/A
Foreign missionaries in 1988:   2
FIELDS OF SERVICE
Malaysia
  Sabah State
Thailand

Lifeline Evangelism Christian Fellowship
Alexandra PO Box 7, SINGAPORE

Rev. Alan Leong Yeen Jing
Organized: 1983   Independent
MISSIONARIES IN SERVICE
(1988)   1
AAGR = N/A
Foreign missionaries in 1988:   1
FIELDS OF SERVICE
Japan

Neighbourhood Baptist Church
11 Topaz Road, SINGAPORE

Rev. James Lim
Organized: 1981   Baptist
MISSIONARIES IN SERVICE
(1988)   2
AAGR = N/A
Foreign missionaries in 1988:   2
FIELDS OF SERVICE
Japan

Newton Life Church
200 Keng Lee Road, SINGAPORE

Rev. Lee Yan Sun
Organized: 1957   Independent
MISSIONARIES IN SERVICE
(1988)   2
AAGR = N/A
Foreign missionaries in 1988:   1

FIELDS OF SERVICE
Thailand   **Singapore**

Nicay Ecclesia Centre
18 Jalan Buloh Perindu, SINGAPORE

Rev. Roland Kester Cher
Organized: 1986   Assemblies of God
MISSIONARIES IN SERVICE
(1988)   4
AAGR = N/A
Foreign missionaries in 1988:   4
FIELDS OF SERVICE
Philippines

Orchard Road Presbyterian Church
3 Orchard Road, SINGAPORE

Rev. David Chan
Organized: 1856   Presbyterian
MISSIONARIES IN SERVICE
(1988)   1
AAGR = N/A
Foreign missionaries in 1988:   1
FIELDS OF SERVICE
Thailand

Paya Lebar Chin Methodist Church
5 Boundary Road, SINGAPORE

Dr. Kang Ho Soon
Organized: 1932   Methodist
MISSIONARIES IN SERVICE
(1988)   1
AAGR = N/A
Foreign missionaries in 1988:   1
FIELDS OF SERVICE
West Africa

Pentecostal Church of Singapore
1 Tai Gin Road, SINGAPORE

Rev. R.B. Karunanandam
Organized: Not reported.   Pentecostal

MISSIONARIES IN SERVICE

(1988)   25

AAGR = N/A

Foreign missionaries in 1988:   0

FIELDS OF SERVICE

Singapore

Queenstown Baptist Church

495 Margaret Drive, SINGAPORE

Rev. Aow Kwong Bu

Organized: 1962   Baptist

MISSIONARIES IN SERVICE

(1988)   2

AAGR = N/A

Foreign missionaries in 1988:   1

FIELDS OF SERVICE

Singapore   **Hong Kong**

Salem Chapel

1 Thomson Hill Drive, SINGAPORE

Rev. Neo Ban It

Organized: 1967   Independent

MISSIONARIES IN SERVICE

(1988)   4

AAGR = N/A

Foreign missionaries in 1988:   4

FIELDS OF SERVICE

Indonesia
Malaysia
   Johor State
Philippines

Sembawang Baptist Church

88 Casuarina Road, SINGAPORE

Rev. Roger Lam

Organized: 1959   Baptist

MISSIONARIES IN SERVICE

(1988)   3

AAGR = N/A

Foreign missionaries in 1988:   3

FIELDS OF SERVICE

Pakistan   **Thailand**

Sembawang Christian Grace Church

10B Jalan Jeruju, SINGAPORE

Rev. Ling Song Cheon

Organized: Not reported.   Independent

MISSIONARIES IN SERVICE

(1988)   1

AAGR = N/A

Foreign missionaries in 1988:   1

FIELDS OF SERVICE

Africa

Singapore Baptist Church

1 Cambridge Road, SINGAPORE

Rev. John Chang

Organized: 1961   Baptist

MISSIONARIES IN SERVICE

(1988)   8

AAGR = N/A

Foreign missionaries in 1988:   0

FIELDS OF SERVICE

Africa	**Burma**
Indonesia	**Philippines**
Thailand	

Singapore Bible Baptist Church

371 Pasir Panjang Road, SINGAPORE

Rev. Eddie Ec Guan Hock

Organized: 1970   Independent

MISSIONARIES IN SERVICE

(1988)   1

AAGR = N/A

Foreign missionaries in 1988:   1

FIELDS OF SERVICE

Thailand

Singapore Gospel Church

69 Tanjong Rhu Road, SINGAPORE

Rev. Robert Sigafoose

Organized: Not reported.   Independent

MISSIONARIES IN SERVICE

(1988)   1

AAGR = N/A
Foreign missionaries in 1988:   1
FIELDS OF SERVICE
Sri Lanka

Sion Presbyterian Church
Sion Presbyterian Church, SINGAPORE

Rev. Ong Doo Ying
Organized: 1957   Presbyterian
MISSIONARIES IN SERVICE
(1988)   3
AAGR = N/A
Foreign missionaries in 1988:   3
FIELDS OF SERVICE
Taiwan   **Singapore**

Smyrna Assembly
Woodlands PO Box 346, SINGAPORE

Rev. John S Stephen
Organized: 1971   Independent
MISSIONARIES IN SERVICE
(1988)   4
AAGR = N/A
Foreign missionaries in 1988:   4
FIELDS OF SERVICE
Sri Lanka   **Sweden**
India   **Malaysia**

Tabernacle, Ltd.
RMS 210/212 Bible House
Armenian Street, SINGAPORE

Mr. Seah Hok Heng David
Organized: 1975   Nondenominational
MISSIONARIES IN SERVICE
(1975)   2   (1978)   6   (1980)   12
(1982)   13   (1988)   65*
AAGR = N/A
Foreign missionaries in 1988: Not
reported.
FIELDS OF SERVICE
Not reported.

Tao Payoh Tamil Methodist Church
480 Toa Payoh Lorong 2, SINGAPORE

Dr. Robert Solomon
Organized: 1982   Methodist
MISSIONARIES IN SERVICE
(1988)   1
AAGR = N/A
Foreign missionaries in 1988:   0
FIELDS OF SERVICE
Singapore

Toa Payoh Bible Church
Block 63
01-266 Toa Payoh East, SINGAPORE

Rev. Henry Ng T.T.
Organized: 1970   Nondenominational
MISSIONARIES IN SERVICE
(1988)   2
AAGR = N/A
Foreign missionaries in 1988:   2
FIELDS OF SERVICE
West Africa   **Liberia**

Toa Payoh Methodist Church
480 Toa Payoh Lorong 2, SINGAPORE

Rev. Sam C.P. Goh
Organized: 1970   Methodist
MISSIONARIES IN SERVICE
(1988)   1
AAGR = N/A
Foreign missionaries in 1988:   1
FIELDS OF SERVICE
Pakistan

Trinity Christian Centre, Missions Department
Tanglin PO Box 48, SINGAPORE

Rev. Eu Yat Wan
Organized: 1979   Assemblies of God
MISSIONARIES IN SERVICE
(1985)   5   (1988)   4

AAGR = -6%
Foreign missionaries in 1988:   3
FIELDS OF SERVICE
Indonesia
  Bumatra   Chinese, Indonesian, Evangelism, Church Planting
Malaysia
  Johor State   Chinese, Church Planting

World Revival Prayer Fellowship
83 Devonshire Road, SINGAPORE

Rev. P.J. Johney
Organized: 1972   Independent
MISSIONARIES IN SERVICE
(1988) 7
AAGR = N/A
Foreign missionaries in 1988:   7
FIELDS OF SERVICE
Taiwan

Yio Chu Kang Chapel
242 Yio Chu Kang Road, SINGAPORE

Mr. Freddie Ho
Organized: 1954   Brethren
MISSIONARIES IN SERVICE
(1988) 3
AAGR = N/A
Foreign missionaries in 1988:   0
FIELDS OF SERVICE
Not reported.

Zion Bible Presbyterian Church
5 Tavistock Avenue, SINGAPORE

Dr. Quek Suee Hwa
Organized: 1957   Presbyterian
MISSIONARIES IN SERVICE
(1988) 5
AAGR = N/A
Foreign missionaries in 1988:   5
FIELDS OF SERVICE
Indonesia   **Malaysia**

SRI LANKA

Good News Ministries
Good News Center
258 Matara Road, Tangalle, SRI LANKA

Rev. Premadasa Ginigalgoda
Organized: 1978   Nondenominational
MISSIONARIES IN SERVICE
(1980) 3   (1985) 5   (1988) 15
AAGR = 22%
Foreign missionaries in 1988:   0
FIELDS OF SERVICE
Sri Lanka
  Southern Province   Buddhists, Communists, Athiests

Jesus Lives Evangelical Ministry
PO Box 1044, Colombo, SRI LANKA

Rev. S. Rajandram
Organized: 1978   Evangelical
MISSIONARIES IN SERVICE
(1980) 2   (1985) 7   (1988) 12
AAGR = 25%
Foreign missionaries in 1988:   2
FIELDS OF SERVICE
Sri Lanka
  Eastern Province   Tamil
  Northern Province   Tamil
  Uva   Tamil, Sinhalese
  Tamil Nadu State   Tamil

V. Inparajah
Koddai Kallar 2, Kallar, SRI LANKA

S. Rajandram
Organized: 1981   Independent
MISSIONARIES IN SERVICE
(1988) 10
AAGR = N/A
Foreign missionaries in 1988:   0
FIELDS OF SERVICE
Sri Lanka
  Eastern Province   Tamil

TAIWAN

Chinese Baptist Convention
47-1 Huai Mein Street, Taipei, TAIWAN

Organized: Not reported.   Baptist
MISSIONARIES IN SERVICE
(1975) 1   (1980) 2   (1982) 1
(1988) 1*
AAGR = N/A
Foreign missionaries in 1988: Not reported.

FIELDS OF SERVICE
Not reported.

Chinese Mission Overseas, Inc.
PO Box 46-414, Taipei, TAIWAN

Rev. Wu Yung
Organized: 1968   Nondenominational
MISSIONARIES IN SERVICE
(1972) 6   (1980) 1   (1985) 1
(1988) 3
AAGR = -3%
Foreign missionaries in 1988:   3
FIELDS OF SERVICE
Thailand
  Chiang Mai   Miau
Indonesia
  East Java Province   Indonesian

Ling Liang World-Wide Evangelistic Mission
24 Ho-ping East Road
Sec. 2, Taipei 106, TAIWAN

Rev. Nathaniel Chow
Organized: 1976   Nondenominational
MISSIONARIES IN SERVICE
(1980) 4   (1984) 5   (1988) 6*
AAGR = N/A
Foreign missionaries in 1988: Not reported.

FIELDS OF SERVICE
Not reported.

THAILAND

Asian Gospel Mission
GPO Box 2188, Bangkok, THAILAND

Rev. Toshio Morimoto
Organized: Not reported.   Independent
MISSIONARIES IN SERVICE
(1988) 3
AAGR = N/A
Foreign missionaries in 1988:   1
FIELDS OF SERVICE
Thailand
  Bangkok   Thai
Japan   Thai

Church of Christ in Thailand
14 Pramuan Road
Bangkok 10500, THAILAND

Rev. Arun Thongdonmuan
Organized: 1934   Nondenominational
MISSIONARIES IN SERVICE
(1985) 3   (1988) 4
AAGR = 10%
Foreign missionaries in 1988:   0
FIELDS OF SERVICE
Thailand
  Phayao   Hill Tribes
  Chiang Rai Province   Chinese, Lisu, Lahu, Akha

Hope of God Ministry International
GPO Box 1390
Bangkok 10501, THAILAND

Dr. Kriengsak Chareon Wong
Organized: 1981   Charismatic
MISSIONARIES IN SERVICE
Further information withheld at agency's request.

Khelang Pantakij Church Mission
PO Box 96, Lampang 52000 THAILAND

Rev. Boonsri Glinhawn

Organized: Not reported.

MISSIONARIES IN SERVICE

(1982) 2   (1984) 2   (1988) 2*

AAGR = N/A

Foreign missionaries in 1988: Not
reported.

FIELDS OF SERVICE

Not reported.

Lampang Mission Institute

PO Box 96, Lampang 52000 THAILAND

Rev. Boonsri Glinhawm

Organized: Not reported.

MISSIONARIES IN SERVICE

(1982) 2   (1988) 3*

AAGR = N/A

Foreign missionaries in 1988: Not
reported.

FIELDS OF SERVICE

Not reported.

| ASIA TRAINING AGENCIES | ASIA NETWORKING AGENCIES |

Rajasthan Bible Institute
Mubarak Bagh, Ajmer Road
Jaipur 302 006, Rajasthan, INDIA

Dr. Anand Chudhari
Organized: Not reported.

Sharon Fellowship and Bible College
Sharon Bible College
Tiruvalla 689 101, Kerala, INDIA

P.J. Thomas
Organized: 1953   Pentecostal
MISSIONARIES IN SERVICE
(1988) 150
AAGR = N/A

Foreign missionaries in 1988:   0

Missionary Training Center
PO Box 1 Takaku
Nasu 325-03, Tochigi, JAPAN

Organized: Not reported.
MISSIONARIES IN SERVICE
(1986)   3   (1988)   3*
AAGR = N/A
Foreign missionaries in 1988: Not reported.

Asian Center for Theological Studies and Mission
187 Choong-Jungro
3-Ka Seodaemun-Ku, Seoul 120, KOREA

Organized: Not reported.

Asian Outreach International
GPO Box 3448, HONG KONG

Paul E. Kauffman
Organized: 1960   Nondenominational
MISSIONARIES IN SERVICE
(1980)   6   (1982) 7   (1984) 12
(1988) 10
AAGR =   7%
Foreign missionaries in 1988:   10
FIELDS OF SERVICE
Malaysia
 East Malaysia Region
Japan   Japanese
Hong Kong   Chinese, Filipinos

Hong Kong Association of Christian Missions
PO Box 71728, Kowloon, HONG KONG

Edmond Mok
Organized: 1973   Nondenominational

Asia Mission Research Organization
1-6 Miyashita-cho
Fukushima-shi 960, JAPAN
Organized: Not reported.

Research Group for Overseas Mission
4-34-12 Daita, Setagaya-ku 155
Tokyo, JAPAN
Organized: Not reported.

Singapore Center for Evangelism & Mission
14 Dolvey Estate, SINGAPORE
Organized: Not reported.

ASIA SERVICE AGENCIES

Asia Missionary Association in Okinawa
Okinawa, JAPAN

Organized: Not reported.
MISSIONARIES IN SERVICE
Information not reported.
FIELDS OF SERVICE
Not reported.

Japan Overseas Christian Medical Cooperation Service
JAPAN

Mikio Symiya
Organized: Not reported.
MISSIONARIES IN SERVICE
(1988)   8
AAGR = N/A
Foreign missionaries in 1988:   0
FIELDS OF SERVICE
Bangladesh   **Nepal**
Pakistan

Durano Literature Mission
16-15 Dae-Shin-Dong
Seodaemun-Ku, Seoul, KOREA

Organized: Not reported.
MISSIONARIES IN SERVICE
Information not reported.
FIELDS OF SERVICE
Not reported.

ASIA AUXILIARY AGENCIES

AFC
PO Box 41, Koru, Seoul, KOREA
Organized: Not reported.
Nondenominational

Agaphe Mission
Kwanghwa Moon PO Box 421
Seoul 110, KOREA

Chung Bong-Seuk
Organized: 1969   Nondenominational

Agaphe Music Mission Institute
34-189 Shin-Dang-Dong, Jong-Ku
Seoul 100, KOREA

Kim Doo-Wan
Organized: Not reported.
Nondenominational

Agaphe Press
Kwanghwa Moon PO Box 421
Yong San-Ku, Seoul, KOREA

Kim Young-Moo
Organized: Not reported.
Nondenominational

Algok Church
312-42 Choong Wha 1 Dong
Dong-Dae-Moon-Ku, Seoul, KOREA

Rev. Hudh Jae-Ho
Organized: Not reported.
Nondenominational

Antioch Mission
97-4 Sung Nae Dong
Choong Joo City, KOREA

Chun Yang-Woo
Organized: Not reported.
Nondenominational

Asia Gospel Mission

1005 Cho-Rang Dong
Dong-Ku, Pusan, KOREA

Rev. Choi Dong-Jin
Organized: Not reported.
Nondenominational

Asian Cultural Study Mission

CPO Box 2112, Seoul, KOREA

Rev. Kwak Sun-Hee
Organized: Not reported.
Nondenominational

Asian Gospel Mission

458-8 Mia 5 Dong
Do-Bong-Ku, Seoul, KOREA

Rev. Lee Il
Organized: Not reported.
Nondenominational

Asian Mission

465-7 Seo Kyo Dong
Mapo-Ku, Seoul, KOREA

Im Baek-Rim
Organized: Not reported.
Nondenominational

Canaan Mission

1-13 Moon-Hwa-Dong
Choong-Ku, Taejon City, KOREA

Ahn Ki-Bong
Organized: Not reported.
Nondenominational

Christian Mission Gospel for Asia

5-198 Hyo-Chang-Dong
Yong San-Ku, Seoul, KOREA

Rev. Choi Yoon-Kwon
Organized: Not reported.
Nondenominational

Christian Mission for North Korea

1641-24 Shinrim-Dong
Kwanak-Ku, Seoul, KOREA

Rev. Kil Cha-Yun
Organized: Not reported.
Nondenominational

Christian Sprouting Mission

118-82 Yong-Du, 2 Dong
Dong-Dae Moon-Ku, Seoul, KOREA

Rev. Lee Jae-Kyu
Organized: Not reported.
Nondenominational

Christian United Gospel Mission

902-5 Bong-Chun-Bon-Dong
Kwanak-Ku, Seoul, KOREA

Rev. Kim Kyung-Hee
Organized: Not reported.
Nondenominational

Council for Mission in North East Asian Churches

Dong Won Apt 8, Dong #303,
Dae Chi Dong, Kang Nam-Ku
Seoul, KOREA

Rev. Yoo Ho-Joon
Organized: Not reported.
Nondenominational

Daebang World Mission

Nam Seoul PO Box 7, Seoul, KOREA

Rev. Lim Byung-Joon
Organized: Not reported.
Nondenominational

Dongshin World Mission

PO Box 56, Daegu 630, KOREA

Rev. Kim Chang-Ryum
Organized: 1973
Nondenominational

End of the Earth Mission
Choong Wha Church, 25 Han Sung
Jung-Dong, Choong-Ku
Seoul, KOREA

Rev. Lee Sang-Hwan
Organized: Not reported.
Nondenominational

EWHA Woman's University Church
Ewha Woman's University
Seoul 120, KOREA
Organized: Not reported.
Nondenominational

Global Missionary Fellowship, Missionary Training Center
231-88 Mok 2-Dong
Yang Chun-Ku, Seoul, KOREA

Dr. Lee Tae-Ong
Organized: Not reported.
Nondenominational

Holy Land Pilgrim Mission
302 Sam Young Bldg. 6-2 San
Bando-Dong, Kang Nam-Ku
Seoul, KOREA

Rev. Lee Kil-Bu
Organized: Not reported.
Nondenominational

Institute of Mission Development
South Seoul PO Box 111, Seoul, KOREA

Park Kil-Hong
Organized: Not reported.
Nondenominational

International Audio Visual Mission
157-3 Yunhi-Dong, Mapo-Ku
Seoul, KOREA

Rev. Kim Yoon-Shin

Organized: Not reported.
Nondenominational

Joy Mission
CPO Box 4660, Seoul 100, KOREA

Rev. Moon Chung-Son
Organized: Not reported.
Nondenominational

Korea Children Education Mission
65 Euljiro 3-Ka, Choong-Ku
Seoul, KOREA

Kim Chong-Joon
Organized: Not reported.
Nondenominational

Korea Christian Child Evangelism Mission
102-19 Haoam-Dong, Yong San-Ku
Seoul, KOREA

Rev. Han Seung-Rin
Organized: Not reported.
Nondenominational

Korea Christian Mission
1378 Soong-In Dong, Chong Ro-Ku
Seoul, KOREA

Rev. Kwank Sun-Hee
Organized: Not reported.
Nondenominational

Korea Gospel Mission
5-198 Hyo-Chang-Dong, Yong San-Ku
Seoul, KOREA

Rev. Choi Yoon-Kwon
Organized: Not reported.
Nondenominational

Korea Harbor Mission
Sun-Hyang Bldg. 2F
395-153 Seokyo-Dong, Mapo-Ku
Seoul 121, KOREA

Rev. Hoon Choi
Organized: 1974

MISSIONARIES IN SERVICE

(1975) 3   (1978) 14   (1980) 25
(1982) 30   (1984) 45   (1986) 34
(1988) 63
AAGR = 26%
Foreign missionaries in 1988: 58

FIELDS OF SERVICE

Africa   Doulos Ship
Asia   Doulos Ship
Korea (South)
 Yeo Soo
 Kun San
 Incheon
 Dong Hae
 Pusan
Spain
 Premia De Mar
 Barcelona
Singapore
Netherlands
Cameroon
 Douala Area   Koreans
Cyprus
 Limassol
Belgium
 Zaventam
Libya
 Tripoli   Medical Work, Tent Making
Uganda   Medical Work
Japan
Somalia
 Mogadishi
India
 Delhi (New Delhi)   Afghan Refugees
 Uttar Pradesh (Lucknow)
Sudan
 Khartoum
Turkey
 Kizilay
Singapore
 Orchard Point
Philippines
 Quezon City
United Kingdom
 England (Coventry, West Ealing, Kent)
Pakistan
 Lahore District

South Africa
 Cape Town
Indonesia
 Jakarta Region
USA
 California
 Texas

Korea Sports Mission

58-17 Suhsomun-Dong
Choong-Ku, Seoul, KOREA

Rev. Cho Chong-Nam
Organized: Not reported.
Nondenominational

Korean Christian Education Association

1103 Yuchundo Hwoi Kwan
1-1 Yunchi-Dong, Seoul, KOREA

Rev. Lee Byung-Ho
Organized: Not reported.
Nondenominational

Korean Women's Evangelical Service

95-90 Shinkildong, Yongdeungpo-Ku
Seoul 150, KOREA
Organized: Not reported.
Nondenominational

Logos Mission

Yongdeungpo 8 Ka 74
Yongdeungpo-Ku, Seoul, KOREA

Rev. Moon Hak-Son
Organized: Not reported.
Nondenominational

Lydia Mission

1-San Dae-Hyun Dong
Seodaemun-Ku, Seoul, KOREA

Park Il-Wha
Organized: Not reported.
Nondenominational

Middle East Mission

404-1 Bando-Dong, Kang Nam-Ku

Seoul, KOREA

Do Sang-Dal
Organized: Not reported.
Nondenominational

Missionary Dentist Training Center
187 Choong Chongno 3-Ka
Seodaemun-Ku, Seoul, KOREA
Organized: Not reported.
Nondenominational

Mustard Seed Mission
493-25 Min Rak Dong, Nam-Ku
Pusan, KOREA

Mrs. Yoon Yong-Ae
Organized: Not reported.
Nondenominational

National Organization of the Presbyterian Women of Korea (Tonghap)
Rm. 212 Korean Church Centennial Bldg
135 Yunji-Dong, Chongno-Ku
Seoul 110, KOREA

Mrs. Lee Yun-ok
Organized: Not reported.   Presbyterian

New Man Mission Association
Bong-Chun-Dong, San 158, Kwanak-Ku
Seoul 151, KOREA

Rev. Cho Woo-Bang
Organized: Not reported.
Nondenominational

North Korea Mission Federation
CPO Box 5385, Seoul, KOREA

Rev. Chang-in Kim
Organized: 1977   Interdenominational
MISSIONARIES IN SERVICE
(1978) 8   (1980) 11   (1988) 39*
AAGR = N/A

Foreign missionaries in 1988: Not reported.
FIELDS OF SERVICE
Not reported.

Paidion (Children) Mission
Seoul, KOREA

Rev. Ahn Sung- Jin
Organized: Not reported.
Nondenominational

Paul Mission
6 Ahm Dong, Chunbuk Providence
Chunju City, KOREA

Rev. Lee Dong-Hwi
Organized: Not reported.
Nondenominational

Russia Mission
204 Bando Yunlip
719 Nae Bal San Dong, Kang Su-Ku
Seoul, KOREA

Rev. Kim Hong-Do
Organized: Not reported.
Nondenominational

Sae Rom Medical Mission
568-1 Myun Mok Dong
Dong-Dae-Moon-Ku, Seoul, KOREA

Rev. Lee Eung-Son
Organized: Not reported.
Nondenominational

Sam Kwang Gospel Mission
202 Na-Dong, 883-5 Bong-Chun 4 Dong
Kwanak-Ku, Seoul, KOREA

Rev. Choi Byung-Kwon
Organized: Not reported.
Nondenominational

Sejong Mission
Sejong Hotel 61-3 Choong-Moo-Ro
2-Ka Choong-Ku, Seoul, KOREA

Dr. Joo Young-ha
Organized: Not reported.

Nondenominational

Soteria World Mission
24-9 Hwa Kok Pon-Dong, Kang Su-Ku
Seoul, KOREA

Yang Dae-Sik
Organized: Not reported.
Nondenominational

Suwon Jaeil World Mission
287 Ji-Dong, Suwon
Kyungki-do, KOREA

Rev. Ahn Joon-Sup
Organized: Not reported.
Nondenominational

United Gospel Mission
902-5 Bong-Chun-Bon-Dong
Kwanak-Ku, Seoul, KOREA

Rev. Park In-Jun
Organized: Not reported.
Nondenominational

Won Chun Gospel Mission
149-11 Yunhi-3-Dong
Seodaemun-Ku
Seoul, KOREA

Rev. Moon Yung-Chul
Organized: Not reported.
Nondenominational

World Mission Association
PO Box 184, Tongdae Moon-Ku
Seoul, KOREA

Rev. Koh Whan-Kyu
Organized: Not reported.
Nondenominational

World Study Abroad Mission
Yoido PO Box 79, Seoul, KOREA

Rev. Kim Ki-Soo
Organized: Not reported.
Nondenominational

INTERNATIONAL ASIA-BASED AGENCIES

Evangelical Free Church of China, HK Overseas Missions Board
84 Waterloo Road, Cambridge Court
2/F B3 Ho Man Tin
Kowloon, HONG KONG

Rev. Peter Ho
Organized: 1965   Evangelical
MISSIONARIES IN SERVICE
(1980) 2   (1988) 6
AAGR = 15%
Foreign missionaries in 1988:   6
FIELDS OF SERVICE
Taiwan
  Chungli   Hakka
Japan
  Saitama Province   Japanese

WEC International of Hong Kong
PO Box 73261, Kowloon Central PO
Kowloon, HONG KONG

Chee Nan Pin
Organized: 1972   Nondenominational
MISSIONARIES IN SERVICE
(1985) 6   (1988) 9
AAGR = 14%
Foreign missionaries in 1988:   9
FIELDS OF SERVICE
Burkina Faso   Dioula
Ghana   Frafra
Gambia   Mandinka
Liberia   Mano

Bible Christian Fellowship Church of Indonesia

Jl Siliwangi No. 26, Manokwari 98311
Irian Jaya, INDONESIA

Rev. Noakh Rumbino
Organized: 1972   Independent

MISSIONARIES IN SERVICE

(1972) 12   (1980) 20   (1985) 24
(1988) 30
AAGR = 6%
Foreign missionaries in 1988: 0

FIELDS OF SERVICE

Indonesia
  Irian Jaya Province   Asmat, Mimika,
    Brazza, Moskona

Asian Outreach

PO Box 36, Toyonaka 560
Osaka, JAPAN

Organized: Not reported.

MISSIONARIES IN SERVICE

Information not reported.

FIELDS OF SERVICE

Singapore
  Singapore   Chinese
Hong Kong
  Hong Kong   Chinese
Indonesia
  Jakarta   Indonesians
Malaysia   Malays

Japan Assemblies of God

15-20 3chome, Komagome
Toshima-ku 170, Tokyo, JAPAN

Rev. Akiei Ito
Organized: 1949   Assemblies of God

MISSIONARIES IN SERVICE

(1978) 5   (1980) 7   (1982) 7
(1985) 4   (1986) 4   (1988) 4
AAGR = -1%
Foreign missionaries in 1988: 4

FIELDS OF SERVICE

Philippines
  Baguio City   Mountain Tribes

Israel

  Jerusalem   Jews, Arabs
Hong Kong   Chinese

Japan Wycliffe Bible Translators

4-31-7 Hamadayama, Suginami-ku 168
Tokyo, JAPAN

Shin Funaki
Organized: Not reported.   Evangelical

MISSIONARIES IN SERVICE

(1982) 23   (1986) 28   (1988) 23
AAGR = 0%
Foreign missionaries in 1988: 0

FIELDS OF SERVICE

Philippines
  Neuva Vizcaya Province   Missionary
    Children's Education, Bible Transla-
    tion
  Bukidnon Province   Bible Translation
Indonesia
  Irian Jaya Province
  Maluku Province
Papua New Guinea
  Viai Island
Nepal
  Kathmandu   Bible Translation
Australia
  Northern Territory (Berrimah)

Navigators

OSCC Bldg. Rm. 402
1-3 Kanda-Surugadai 2
Chiyoda-ku, Tokyo, JAPAN

Goro Ogawa
Organized: Not reported.

MISSIONARIES IN SERVICE

(1988) 2
AAGR = N/A
Foreign missionaries in 1988: 0

FIELDS OF SERVICE

Taiwan   Chinese University Students

Overseas Missionary Fellowship

PO Box 11, Koganei-ku 184
Tokyo, JAPAN

Rev. Tadashi Haga
Organized: Not reported.   Evangelical

MISSIONARIES IN SERVICE

(1986)   8   (1988)   7
AAGR = -5%
Foreign missionaries in 1988:   0

FIELDS OF SERVICE

Singapore   Students
Taiwan   Factory Workers

Youth With A Mission

CPO Box 1410, Osaka 530-91, JAPAN

Organized: Not reported.

MISSIONARIES IN SERVICE

(1986)   5   (1988)   5*
AAGR = N/A
Foreign missionaries in 1988: Not reported.

FIELDS OF SERVICE

Not reported.

Korea Campus Crusade for Christ

CPO Box 1042, Seoul 100-610, KOREA

Rev. Kim Joon-Gon
Organized: 1958

MISSIONARIES IN SERVICE

(1985)   12   (1988)   39
AAGR = 48%
Foreign missionaries in 1988:   39

FIELDS OF SERVICE

Philippines   **Japan**
Hong Kong

Overseas Missionary Fellowship

Kwanghwa Moon PO Box 1637
Seoul, KOREA

Rev. Peter R.M. Pattisson
Organized: 1979   Interdenominational

MISSIONARIES IN SERVICE

(1980)   2   (1988)   6*
AAGR = N/A
Foreign missionaries in 1988: Not reported.

FIELDS OF SERVICE

Philippines
 Metro Manila
 Luzon Region   Filipino
 Batangas Province   Muslim, Filipinos
Thailand
 Central Region   Thai
 Bangkok   Thai
 Southern Region   Malay
Japan
 Honshu   Japanese
 Hokkaido Province   Japanese
Singapore   Singaporean
Nepal   Nepali
Taiwan
 Taichung County   Chinese
 Taipei County   Chinese
Malaysia
 Sarawak State   Tribal People
 Sabah State   Tribal People
Hong Kong
 Hong Kong Island   Chinese

University Bible Fellowship, Inc.

54-2 Hyo Jae Dong, Chong Ro-Ku
Seoul 110-480, KOREA

Dr. John Jun
Organized: 1961   Nondenominational

MISSIONARIES IN SERVICE

(1982)   2   (1988)   149
AAGR = 105%
Foreign missionaries in 1988:   149

FIELDS OF SERVICE

Bolivia
 Santa Cruz Department   College Students
Malawi

220

Lilongwe College Students
France
Paris College Students
Taiwan
Taipei County College Students
Venezuela
Caracas College Students
USA
Chicago College Students
Germany (West)
Koln College Students
Philippines
Metro Manila College Students
Paraguay
Central (Asuncion) College Students
Sweden
Uppsala College Students
Libya
Benghazi Foreign Workers
India
Delhi (New Delhi) College Students
Bangladesh
Dhaka College Students
Saudi Arabia
Riyadh Foreign Nurses
Jeddah Foreign Nurses
Argentina
Buenos Aires College Students
Italy
Perugia College Students
Hong Kong College Students
Australia
Melbourne College Students
Mexico
Mexico City College Students
Canada
Toronto College Students
Japan
Tokyo Province College Students
Malaysia
Sabah State Foreign People

World Concern Korea

Sun-Hyang Bldg. 2F, 395-153, Seokyo-
Dong, Mapo-Ku, Seoul 121, KOREA

Rev. Chung Jin-Kyung
Organized: Not reported.

MISSIONARIES IN SERVICE
(1982) 2   (1986) 11   (1988) 26*
AAGR = N/A
Foreign missionaries in 1988: Not
reported.

FIELDS OF SERVICE
Nepal

Youth With A Mission Korea

Yeoeundo PO Box 861
Seoul 150-608, KOREA

Hong Sung-Gun
Organized: 1972   Nondenominational

MISSIONARIES IN SERVICE
(1980) 1   (1985) 14   (1988) 22
AAGR = 47%
Foreign missionaries in 1988:   14

FIELDS OF SERVICE

Philippines	**Kenya**
Indonesia	**Hong Kong**
Singapore	**India**

Overseas Misisonary Fellowship, Philippine Home Council

PO Box 458, Quezon City 3001
Metro Manila, PHILIPPINES

Dr. Isabalo Magalil
Organized: 1966   Evangelical

MISSIONARIES IN SERVICE
(1972) 12   (1980) 12   (1984) 6
(1985) 8   (1988) 12
AAGR = 0%
Foreign missionaries in 1988:   12

FIELDS OF SERVICE

Japan	Japanese
Thailand	Thai
Taiwan	Chinese
Indonesia	Indonesian
Malaysia	Malay

Navigators, Singapore

PO Box 359, Still Road PO, SINGAPORE

Jim Chew

Organized: 1964   Nondenominational

MISSIONARIES IN SERVICE
(1972) 6   (1980) 7   (1985) 5
(1988) 8
AAGR = 2%
Foreign missionaries in 1988: 8

FIELDS OF SERVICE
Australia
 Victoria   Asian Students
Southeast Africa
North Africa
South Africa

SIM East Asia
4 How Sun Drive, SINGAPORE

Tony A. Lee
Organized: Not reported.

MISSIONARIES IN SERVICE
(1980) 4   (1982) 8   (1984) 16
(1988) 64*
AAGR = N/A
Foreign missionaries in 1988: Not reported.

FIELDS OF SERVICE
Liberia
 Kolahun   Gbandi
 Sinkor   Gola
 Monrovia County   Various Groups
Kenya
 Nairobi   Seminary Students
Singapore
Nigeria
 Billiri   Tangale, Hause
Niger
 Galmi   Hausa

Youth With A Mission
PO Box 246, Bras Basah, SINGAPORE
Organized: Not reported.

MISSIONARIES IN SERVICE
Information not reported.

FIELDS OF SERVICE
Not reported.

222

AFRICA & MIDDLE EAST

CAMEROON

Presbyterian Church in Cameroon

PCC Box 19, Buea, SW Province
CAMEROON

Rev. J.C. Kangsen
Organized: 1957
Denominational, Presbyterian

MISSIONARIES IN SERVICE

(1980) 23   (1988) 51*
AAGR = N/A
Foreign Missionaries in 1988: Not reported.

FIELDS OF SERVICE

Not reported.

CENTRAL AFRICAN REPUBLIC

Baptist Church of Western C.A.R.

BP 13, Berberati
CENTRAL AFRICAN REPUBLIC

Yele-M'Baye Gilbert
Organized: 1984   Baptist

MISSIONARIES IN SERVICE

(1988) 6
AAGR = N/A
Foreign missionaries in 1988:   0

FIELDS OF SERVICE

Central African Republic

Haute-Sangha Province Foulbe (Peuls)
Sangha-Economique Province
  Pygmees
Nana-Mambere Province Foulbe
  (Peuls)

EGYPT

Apostolic Church of Christ

Shoubra, Cairo, EGYPT

Organized: Not reported.

MISSIONARIES IN SERVICE

(1980) 1   (1988) 2*
AAGR = N/A
Foreign Missionaries in 1988: Not reported.

FIELDS OF SERVICE

Not reported.

Christian Practical Service Society

Box 19, 22 Hada Sharami Street
Minia, EGYPT

Rev. Samy Hanna Ghabrial
Organized: Not reported.

MISSIONARIES IN SERVICE

(1975) 6   (1978) 37   (1980) 68
(1984) 80   (1988) 109*
AAGR = N/A
Foreign Missionaries in 1988: Not reported.

FIELDS OF SERVICE

Egypt Egyptians

Society of Salvation for Souls

12 Qotta St., Shoubra
Cairo 11231, EGYPT

Moussa Gerges
Organized: 1926   Nondenominational

MISSIONARIES IN SERVICE

(1972) 16   (1975) 13   (1978) 13
(1980) 32   (1985) 45   (1988) 59
AAGR =   9%
Foreign missionaries in 1988:   0

FIELDS OF SERVICE

Australia
  Melbourne, Sidney
Egypt   Arabs

ETHIOPIA

Faith Church of Christ
Box 796, Asmara, ETHIOPIA

Rev. Solomon T. Michael
Organized: Not reported.   Methodist

MISSIONARIES IN SERVICE

(1988)   9
AAGR = N/A
Foreign missionaries in 1988:   0

FIELDS OF SERVICE

Ethiopia
  Addis Ababa Amharic
  Eritrea Province Tigrinya, Kunama,
    Amharic

Word of Life Church
Box 5829, Addis Ababa, ETHIOPIA

Ato Berhanu Deressa
Organized: Not reported
Denominational

MISSIONARIES IN SERVICE

(1972) 100   (1975) 100   (1978) 70
(1980) 50   (1988) 25*
AAGR = N/A
Foreign Missionaries in 1988: Not
reported.

FIELDS OF SERVICE

Not reported.

GABON

Psalm David
BP 4000, Libreville, GABON

Prophet Ekang-Ngwa
Organized: 1955

MISSIONARIES IN SERVICE

(1978) 41   (1980) 29   (1988)   7*
AAGR = N/A
Foreign Missionaries in 1988: Not
reported.

FIELDS OF SERVICE

Not reported.

GHANA

Adventist Missionary
PO Box 124, Offinso, GHANA

Addai Bossman
Organized: 1979   Adventist

MISSIONARIES IN SERVICE

(1972) 44   (1980) 37   (1985) 50
(1988) 64
AAGR =   2%
Foreign missionaries in 1988:   0

FIELDS OF SERVICE

Ghana
  Eastern Region Akwapem, Kwhus
  Brong-Ahafo Region Brong
  Ashanti Region Ashanti
  Upper East Region Frafra
  Upper West Region Walla
  Western Region Nzema
  Northern Region Dagomba
  Volta Region Ewe

All Christian Spiritual Church of Ghana
PO Box A-123, Labadi, Accra, GHANA

Rev. Emmanuel O. Kodi
Organized: Not reported.

MISSIONARIES IN SERVICE

(1975)   8   (1978)   8   (1980) 13
(1982) 13   (1988) 20*
AAGR = N/A
Foreign Missionaries in 1988: Not
reported.

FIELDS OF SERVICE
Not reported.

All for Christ Mission
PO Box 3820, Accra, GHANA

Rev. Devine Amattey
Organized: 1986
Evangelical, Nondenominational

MISSIONARIES IN SERVICE
(1988) 4
AAGR = N/A
Foreign missionaries in 1988:   0

FIELDS OF SERVICE
Ghana
  Northern Region Dagbani, Frafra
  Greater Accra Region
    Ga-Adangme-Krobo

Apostles Revelation Society
PO Box 1, New Tadzewu, GHANA

Charles Kobla Nutornutsi
Organized: 1939

MISSIONARIES IN SERVICE
(1972) 48   (1975) 60   (1978) 80
(1980) 569   (1988) 860*
AAGR = N/A
Foreign Missionaries in 1988: Not reported.

FIELDS OF SERVICE
Not reported.

Army of the Cross of Christ Church
PO Box 11, Mozano, Gomoa Eshiem Via Swedru, GHANA

Miritaiah Jonah Jehu-Appiah
Organized: Not reported.

MISSIONARIES IN SERVICE
(1980) 4   (1984) 35   (1988) 43*
AAGR = N/A
Foreign Missionaries in 1988: Not reported.

FIELDS OF SERVICE
United Kingdom   Mixed Community

Sierra Leone   Africans
Liberia   Africans
Zambia   Africans
Nigeria   Africans
USA   Mixed Community
Togo   Africans
Ivory Coast   Africans

Ascension Church
PO Box 8247, Kumasi, GHANA

Rev. John Appiah
Organized: 1970   Pentecostal

MISSIONARIES IN SERVICE
Further information withheld at agency's request.

Bethesda Church Mission
PO Box 290, Kumasi, GHANA

Rev. E.N. Okla
Organized: 1966   Charismatic

MISSIONARIES IN SERVICE
(1972) 28   (1980) 16   (1985) 20
(1988) 32
AAGR = 1%
Foreign missionaries in 1988:   6

FIELDS OF SERVICE
United Kingdom
  England (London) Whites, Blacks
    (English)
Ghana
  Brong-Ahafo Region Brong
  Greater Accra Region
    Ga-Adangme-Krobo, Ewe
  Ashanti Region Akan

Blessed Redemption Outreach Ministries, Inc.
PO Box 8199, Accra-North, GHANA

William Djaba Okletey
Organized: 1983   Evangelical

MISSIONARIES IN SERVICE
(1988) 6
AAGR = N/A
Foreign missionaries in 1988:   0

FIELDS OF SERVICE
Ghana
Swedru Region Fanti, Twi
Greater Accra Region
  Ga-Adangme-Krobo, Twi, Ewe
Odumase District Ga-Adangme-Krobo
Tema District Ga-Adangme-Krobo,
  Twi
Volta Region Ewe, Twi
Somanya District Ga-Adangme-Krobo
Ivory Coast   French

Christ is the Same, Inc.
PO Box 170, Aflao, GHANA

Seth Amedetor
Organized: 1973 Evangelical Charismatic
MISSIONARIES IN SERVICE
(1972)   4   (1980) 41   (1985) 22
(1988) 28
AAGR = 13%
Foreign missionaries in 1988:   8
FIELDS OF SERVICE
Togo
Southern Region Ewe
Ghana
Greater Accra Region Ewe, Akan,
  Ga-Adangme-Krobo
Volta Region Ewe
Benin
South Ewe

Christian Faith Church
PO Box 0642, Takoradi, GHANA

Rev. Emmanuel K. Botwey
Organized: 1983   Charismatic
MISSIONARIES IN SERVICE
(1985)   5   (1988)   7
AAGR = 12%
Foreign missionaries in 1988:   0
FIELDS OF SERVICE
Ghana
Central Region Fanti
Eastern Region Akim
Western Region Twi, Fanti, Nzima,
  Wassa

Christian Living Ministries
PO Box 448, Madina, Accra, GHANA

Kwasi Asamoah-Frempong
Organized: 1988   Pentecostal
MISSIONARIES IN SERVICE
(1988)   6
AAGR = N/A
Foreign missionaries in 1988:   0
FIELDS OF SERVICE
Ghana
Eastern Region Twi
Greater Accra Region
  Ga-Adangme-Krobo
Volta Region Ewe

Christian Outreach Fellowship
PO Box 11691, Accra-North, GHANA

Delanyo Adadevoh
Organized: 1974   Interdenominational
MISSIONARIES IN SERVICE
(1980)   2   (1985)   9   (1988) 10
AAGR = 22%
Foreign missionaries in 1988:   0
FIELDS OF SERVICE
Ghana
Greater Accra Region
  Ga-Adangme-Krobo
Volta Region Ewe
Upper East Region Kasena
Western Region Nzema
Brong-Ahafo Region Muslims

Church of Pentecost
PO Box 2194, Accra, GHANA

Rev. Fred Stephen Safo
Organized: 1936   Interdenominational
MISSIONARIES IN SERVICE
(1972)   4   (1975)   6   (1978)   8
(1980)   8   (1982) 20   (1984) 22
(1988) 39*
AAGR = N/A
Foreign Missionaries in 1988: Not
reported.

FIELDS OF SERVICE

Burkina Faso
  Ougadougou Mossi
Nigeria
  Lagos State Yoruba
  Oyo State Yoruba
Benin
  Cotonou Benin
Ivory Coast
  Abidjan Ivorians
Liberia
  Monrovia County Liberians
Togo
  Lome Togolese

El Shadai Ministry
PO Box 33, Bogoso, GHANA

Rev. Matthew Twumasi Ankrah
Organized: 1982   Nondenominational
MISSIONARIES IN SERVICE
(1985) 2   (1988) 10
AAGR = 71%
Foreign missionaries in 1988:   0
FIELDS OF SERVICE
Ghana
  Brong-Ahafo Region Brong
  Ashanti Region Ashanti

Elim Evangelical Church
PO Box 5722, Abeka, Accra, GHANA

John Alex Mensah
Organized: 1987 Evangelical Charismatic
MISSIONARIES IN SERVICE
(1988) 8
AAGR = N/A
Foreign missionaries in 1988:   2
FIELDS OF SERVICE
Ghana
  Western Region Ga-Adangme-Krobo,
    Nzema, Wassa, Aowin
  Eastern Region Akim
Ivory Coast
  Abidjan French

Emmanuel
PO Box 218, Nima, Accra, GHANA

Seth Amedetor
Organized: 1970   Evangelical
MISSIONARIES IN SERVICE
(1972) 4   (1980) 8   (1985) 28
(1988) 43
AAGR = 16%
Foreign missionaries in 1988:   6
FIELDS OF SERVICE
Ghana
  Greater Accra Region Ewe,
    Ga-Adangme-Krobo, Twi
  Volta Region Ewe
Togo
  Lome Ewe

Enoch Missions
PO Box 4393, Accra, GHANA

Enoch A. Agbozo
Organized: 1980 Evangelical Pentecostal
MISSIONARIES IN SERVICE
(1980) 4   (1985) 9   (1988) 10
AAGR = 12%
Foreign missionaries in 1988:   6
FIELDS OF SERVICE
United Kingdom
  England (London) Europeans
Ghana
  Western Region Nzema
  Eastern Region Ada,
    Ga-Adangma-Krobo
Liberia
  Monrovia County
Ghana
  Northern Region Dagarti, Hausa
  Cape Palmas

Evangelical Church of Ghana
PO Box 76, Tamale, GHANA

John Kipo Mahama
Organized: 1977   Evangelical

(1985) 2   (1988) 5

AAGR = 36%

Foreign missionaries in 1988:   0

FIELDS OF SERVICE

Ghana

Northern Region Gonja, Hanga,
  Konkomba, Dagomba

Faith in God Ministry

PO Box K-294, New Town
Accra, GHANA

Rev. James Doe
Organized: 1971   Pentecostal

MISSIONARIES IN SERVICE

(1972) 1   (1980) 1   (1985) 4
(1988) 4

AAGR = 9%

Foreign missionaries in 1988:   2

FIELDS OF SERVICE

Togo

Lome French

Ghana   English

Fountain of Life Ministry

PO Box 4206, Kumasi, GHANA

Rev. Francis Boahen
Organized: 1981   Pentecostal

MISSIONARIES IN SERVICE

(1985) 4   (1988) 5

AAGR = 8%

Foreign missionaries in 1988:   1

FIELDS OF SERVICE

Ghana

Drobonso Akan
Bekwai Sefwi
Osei Kwadwokrom Brong
Kumasi Akan

Ivory Coast

Bako Aowin

Gospel Crusaders Mission

PO Box 8955, Kumasi, GHANA

Rev. John Owusu-Arko
Organized: 1980

Independent Pentecostal

MISSIONARIES IN SERVICE

(1980) 9   (1985) 15   (1988) 6

AAGR = -4%

Foreign missionaries in 1988:   0

FIELDS OF SERVICE

Ghana

Western Region Nzema
Ashanti Region Ashanti

Healing Gospel Ministry

PO Box 6068, Accra-North, GHANA

M.J. Jehu-Appiah
Organized: Not reported.

MISSIONARIES IN SERVICE

(1978) 13   (1980) 2   (1984) 12
(1988) 11*

AAGR = N/A

Foreign Missionaries in 1988: Not
reported.

FIELDS OF SERVICE

USA
Nigeria
Gambia
United Kingdom

England (London)

Ivory Coast
Liberia

Monrovia County

Sierra Leone

Freetown

Hour of Deliverance Ministry

PO Box 11192, Accra-North, GHANA

Emmanuel V. Adjei-Wiredu
Organized: 1985   Evangelical

MISSIONARIES IN SERVICE

(1985) 3   (1988) 17

AAGR = 78%

Foreign missionaries in 1988:   3

FIELDS OF SERVICE

USA

Maryland English

Ghana

Greater Accra Region
　Ga-Adangme-Krobo, Ewe, Twi,
　English
Volta Region Ewe
Eastern Region Twi
United Kingdom
　England (London) English

Islamic and Christian Studies Programme

PO Box 2063, Mamprobi
Accra, GHANA

Rocky-Bell Adatura
Organized: 1980　　　Nondenominational
MISSIONARIES IN SERVICE
(1980)　18　　　(1985)　11　　　(1988)　6
AAGR = -12%
Foreign missionaries in 1988:　0
FIELDS OF SERVICE
Ivory Coast　Local People, Muslims,
　Religious Adherents
Ghana　Local People, Muslims,
　Religious Adherents
Singapore　Local People, Muslims,
　Religious Adherents
Zimbabwe　Local People, Muslims,
　Religious Adherents
Togo　Local People, Muslims,
　Religious Adherents

Jesus Rescue Missions

PO Box B-162, Comm. 2, Tema, GHANA

Derick Rex Arthur
Organized: 1985　　　Nondenominational
MISSIONARIES IN SERVICE
(1986)　8　　　(1988)　24
AAGR = 73%
Foreign missionaries in 1988:　4
FIELDS OF SERVICE
Ivory Coast

King's Church

PO Box 4272, Kumasi, GHANA

E.R.C. Odame
Organized: 1984　　　Charismatic

MISSIONARIES IN SERVICE
(1985)　2　　　(1988)　12
AAGR = 82%
Foreign missionaries in 1988:　0
FIELDS OF SERVICE
Ghana
　Greater Accra Region
　　Ga-Adangme-Krobo
　Central Region Fanti
　Western Region Fanti
　Eastern Region Akim

Labourers Ministry

PL Box 035 UCT, Cape Coast, GHANA

Albert Saah
Organized: 1987　　　　　Evangelical
MISSIONARIES IN SERVICE
(1972)　3　　　(1980)　6　　　(1985)　8
(1988)　29
AAGR = 15%
Foreign missionaries in 1988:　11
FIELDS OF SERVICE
United Kingdom　Scottish, English
Ghana
　Southern Region Fanti, Frafra
　Upper Region Fanti, Frafra
Sierra Leone
　Freetown
Ivory Coast
　Abidjan Ghanians, Burkinabe
Liberia
　Monrovia County
Kenya
　Nairobi Bantu, Kikuyu
USA
　Maine
Burkina Faso
　Ouagadougou Gurunsi, Fratra
Togo
　Lome Ewe

Lost Souls Saving Mission

PO Box 1459, Kumasi, GHANA

Seth Kwabena Osei Tabi
Organized: 1975　　　　　Pentecostal

(1980) 7   (1985) 7   (1988) 7
AAGR = 0%
Foreign missionaries in 1988:   1
FIELDS OF SERVICE
Ghana
Greater Accra Region
  Ga-Adangme-Krobo
Eastern Region Twi
Ashanti Region Twi

New Day Mission International
PO Box 610, Koforidua, GHANA

Rev. Dan Botwe
Organized: 1981   Evangelical
MISSIONARIES IN SERVICE
(1985) 15   (1988) 24
AAGR = 17%
Foreign missionaries in 1988:   1
FIELDS OF SERVICE
Ghana
Eastern Region Ga-Adangme-Krobo,
  Larteh-Cherepon-Anum-Boso, Twi
Western Region Sefwi
Greater Accra Region
  Ga-Adangme-Krobo

New Testament Assembly
PO Box 8230, Kumasi, GHANA

Rev. James Appiah Kubi
Organized: 1979   Pentecostal
MISSIONARIES IN SERVICE
(1988) 6
AAGR = N/A
Foreign missionaries in 1988:   0
FIELDS OF SERVICE
Ghana
Eastern Region Akan
Ashanti Region Twi
Brong-Ahafo Region Brong
Central Region Fanti

Operation Andrews
PO Box 8130, Ahinsan

Kumasi, GHANA

Rev. John K. Dadzie
Organized: 1986   Pentecostal
MISSIONARIES IN SERVICE
(1985) 3   (1988) 7
AAGR = 33%
Foreign missionaries in 1988:   0
FIELDS OF SERVICE
Ghana
Eastern Region Ga-Adangme-Krobo
Ashanti Region Ashanti, Mixed Tribes

Original Church of Christ, The
PO Box 660, Tema, GHANA

Rev. Joseph Egyir
Organized: 1976   Independent
MISSIONARIES IN SERVICE
(1980) 4   (1985) 12   (1988) 6
AAGR = 5%
Foreign missionaries in 1988:   0
FIELDS OF SERVICE
Ghana
Western Region Fanti, Wassa
Central Region Fanti
Ashanti Region Ashanti

Power of Jesus Evangelistic Ministry
PO Box 234, Tarkwa, GHANA

Samuel K. Appiah
Organized: 1976   Nondenominational
MISSIONARIES IN SERVICE
(1985) 2   (1988) 7
AAGR = 52%
Foreign missionaries in 1988:   1
FIELDS OF SERVICE
Ghana
Ashanti Region Akan, Nzima
Western Region Akan, Nzima
Central Region Akan, Nzima
Sierra Leone
Freetown

Soul Winners of the African Christian Church, The

PO Box 171, Korle-Gonno
Accra, GHANA

Rev. E.N. Danso
Organized: 1972   Pentecostal
MISSIONARIES IN SERVICE
(1972) 31   (1980) 37   (1985) 43
(1988) 47
AAGR = 3%
Foreign missionaries in 1988:   6
FIELDS OF SERVICE
Ivory Coast
  Abidjan Ivorians
USA
  New York Black Americans
Canada
  Ontario Canadians
Ghana
  All Regions Ghanians
Nigeria
  Lagos State Nigerians

Standing Together Mission

PO Box 3486, Kumasi, GHANA

Yaw Asante
Organized: 1969   Charismatic
MISSIONARIES IN SERVICE
(1988) 3
AAGR = N/A
Foreign missionaries in 1988:   0
FIELDS OF SERVICE
Ghana
  Brong-Ahafo Region Ashanti, Brong
  Ashanti Region Ashanti, Brong

Torchbearers

PO Box 0654, Christianborg
Accra, GHANA

Albert Ocran
Organized: 1988   Nondenominational
MISSIONARIES IN SERVICE
(1985) 2   (1988) 7
AAGR = 52%

Foreign missionaries in 1988:   3
FIELDS OF SERVICE
Italy   Graduate Students
Mali
  Bamako Fulani
Ghana
  Greater Accra Region Frafra

United Church of the Living God (formerly Church of Jesus)

PO Box 11, Ashiaman, Ashiaman
Accra, GHANA

Brother John Sewu
Organized: 1960   Denominational
MISSIONARIES IN SERVICE
(1972) 3   (1975) 10   (1978) 15
(1980) 20   (1988) 30*
AAGR = N/A
Foreign Missionaries in 1988: Not reported.
FIELDS OF SERVICE
Not reported.

Vision for Muslims' Ministry

PO Box 3306, Kumasi, GHANA

Samuel Fosu-Mensah
Organized: 1980   Nondenominational
MISSIONARIES IN SERVICE
(1980) 13   (1985) 21   (1988) 8
AAGR = -5%
Foreign missionaries in 1988:   3
FIELDS OF SERVICE
Togo
  Lome Christians, Atheists, Muslims
Ghana
  All Regions Christians, Atheists, Muslims
USA
  Ohio (Cleveland) Christians, Athiests, Muslims
  Ohio Christians, Atheists, Muslims

Volta Evangelistic Association
PO Box 4504, Accra, GHANA

James Agbeblewu
Organized: 1965   Evangelical
MISSIONARIES IN SERVICE
(1972)   2   (1980)   4   (1985)   6
(1988)   11
AAGR =   11%
Foreign missionaries in 1988:   2

FIELDS OF SERVICE
Ghana
  Eastern Region Ewe, Akan
  Northern Region Ewe
  Volta Region Ewe, Guan
  Greater Accra Region Ewe, Akan
Togo   Ewe, Kabre

Word of God Evangelistic Ministry
PO Box 62, Asamankese, GHANA

William Adjei Darko
Organized: 1986   Pentecostal
MISSIONARIES IN SERVICE
(1988)   10
AAGR = N/A
Foreign missionaries in 1988:   6

FIELDS OF SERVICE
Liberia   **Ivory Coast**
Ghana

World Outreach Gateway
PO Box 71, Aflao, GHANA

Rev. George R. Mensah
Organized: Not reported.
MISSIONARIES IN SERVICE
(1982)   14   (1988)   19*
AAGR = N/A
Foreign Missionaries in 1988: Not reported.

FIELDS OF SERVICE
Not reported.

ISRAEL

Mount of Olives Centre
PO Box 792, Jerusalem, ISRAEL

Rev. Issam Hssen
Organized: 1984   Independent
MISSIONARIES IN SERVICE
(1988)   6
AAGR = N/A
Foreign missionaries in 1988:   0

FIELDS OF SERVICE
Israel   Arabs, Jews
  West Bank Arabs

KENYA

Africa Christ's Army
PO Box 74685, Nairobi, KENYA

Rev. Robert M. Mutambi
Organized: 1982
MISSIONARIES IN SERVICE
(1988)   6
AAGR = N/A
Foreign missionaries in 1988:   0

FIELDS OF SERVICE
United Kingdom
  North Ireland
Kenya   Samburu, Duruma, Walenguru
USA

Africa Church
PO Box 41, Machakos, KENYA

Bishop Isaac K. Vonde
Organized: Not reported.   Independent
MISSIONARIES IN SERVICE
(1988)   6
AAGR = N/A
Foreign missionaries in 1988:   1

FIELDS OF SERVICE
Kenya   Meru, Kamba, Swahili
Tanzania

Africa Church Mission
PO Box 33, Yulu, KENYA

Rev. Timothy Olwandi
Organized: 1960

MISSIONARIES IN SERVICE
(1988)   5
AAGR = N/A
Foreign missionaries in 1988:   0

FIELDS OF SERVICE
Kenya   Swahili, Teso, Luhya, Kikuyu, Kalenjin, Luo

Africa Gospel Church-Missionary Department
Box 458, Kericho, KENYA

Rev. Jonah Cheseng'eny
Organized: 1970

MISSIONARIES IN SERVICE
(1988)   12
AAGR = N/A
Foreign missionaries in 1988:   0

FIELDS OF SERVICE
Kenya   Maasai, Pokot, Multiple Tribes at Turkwell

Africa Inland Church Missionary Board
Box 45019, Nairobi, KENYA

Rev. Justus Nzau
Organized: 1960

MISSIONARIES IN SERVICE
(1980) 28   (1988) 18
AAGR = -4%
Foreign missionaries in 1988:   0

FIELDS OF SERVICE
Kenya   Pokomo, Duruma, Orma, Somali, Malekote, Luo, Pokot, Meru, Luhya

Africa Israel Ninevah Church Ministries
Box 701, Kisumu, KENYA

Rev. John M. Kivuli
Organized: 1983   Independent

MISSIONARIES IN SERVICE
(1988)   7
AAGR = N/A
Foreign missionaries in 1988:   0

FIELDS OF SERVICE
Kenya   All Peoples

African Church of Jesus Christ in Kenya
Box 47, Kerugoya, KENYA

Bishop Paul Kibuti
Organized: Not reported.

MISSIONARIES IN SERVICE
(1988)   15
AAGR = N/A
Foreign missionaries in 1988:   0

FIELDS OF SERVICE
Kenya   Kikuyu, Luo

African Evangelistic Enterprise
Box 53012, Nairobi, KENYA

Gershon Mwiti
Organized: 1976   Nondenominational

MISSIONARIES IN SERVICE
(1988)   21
AAGR = N/A
Foreign missionaries in 1988:   14

FIELDS OF SERVICE
Zimbabwe
Tanzania
Malawi
Kenya   Luhya, Luo, Kalenjin, Coastal, Kamba, Kikuyu, Masasi
Zambia
Uganda
Tanzania

Angalidom Community Health Centres
Lumbatania Castle, PO Box 142
Maragoli, KENYA

Dr. I. Angali
Organized: 1987   Independent Lutheran

MISSIONARIES IN SERVICE
(1988) 15
AAGR = N/A
Foreign missionaries in 1988:   5
FIELDS OF SERVICE
Kenya Luhya, Gusii, Maragoli, Luo
Tanzania
Uganda

Beroya Gospel Fellowship
PO Box 53170, Nairobi, KENYA

Bishop S. W. Mitsozi
Organized: 1975   Assemblies of God
MISSIONARIES IN SERVICE
(1988)   5
AAGR = N/A
Foreign missionaries in 1988:   1
FIELDS OF SERVICE
Uganda
Kenya Kikuyu, Giriama, Turkana

Bible Mission (Kenya)
PO Box 53741, Nairobi, KENYA

J. Chesoli, E. Walunywa
Organized: 1972
MISSIONARIES IN SERVICE
(1988) 40
AAGR = N/A
Foreign missionaries in 1988:   0
FIELDS OF SERVICE
Kenya Kikuyu, Luo, Kamba, Luhya

Brook Fellowship
PO Box 62112, Nairobi, KENYA

Rev. Patrick M.K. Nzuki
Organized: 1986
MISSIONARIES IN SERVICE
(1988) 10
AAGR = N/A
Foreign missionaries in 1988:   1
FIELDS OF SERVICE
Kenya Maasai, Turkana, Kamba
Tanzania
Uganda

Zimbabwe

Calvary Road Crusade
PO Box 8
Akala via Kisumu, KENYA

Enock Aloo Okech
Organized: 1980
MISSIONARIES IN SERVICE
(1988) 8
AAGR = N/A
Foreign missionaries in 1988:   0
FIELDS OF SERVICE
Kenya Luhya, Teso, Watende, Pokot

Children of God Regeneration
Box 169, Sare via Kissi, KENYA

Killion Orina Oyier
Organized: 1952   Revival Church
MISSIONARIES IN SERVICE
(1988)   6
AAGR = N/A
Foreign missionaries in 1988:   0
FIELDS OF SERVICE
Kenya Luhya, Kikuyu, Coastal People

Christ for Every Tribe Ministry
PO Box 22, Bungoma, KENYA

Rev. Jackson Maina
Organized: 1976
MISSIONARIES IN SERVICE
(1988) 10
AAGR = N/A
Foreign missionaries in 1988:   0
FIELDS OF SERVICE
Kenya Meru, Maasai, Teso, Kalenjin,
   Kikuyu

Church of Africa Sinai Mission
PO Box 154, Vihiga, KENYA

Archbishop Moses Aseri
Organized: 1974

MISSIONARIES IN SERVICE
(1988) 22
AAGR = N/A
Foreign missionaries in 1988:   0

FIELDS OF SERVICE
Kenya   Meru, Embu, Swahili, Luo

Church of God in East Africa
PO Box 21699, Nairobi, KENYA

Dr. Byran Makokha
Organized: Not reported. Church of God

MISSIONARIES IN SERVICE
(1988) 3
AAGR = N/A
Foreign missionaries in 1988:   2

FIELDS OF SERVICE
Uganda
Kenya   Maasai
Tanzania

Covenant Baptist Church Outreach
PO Box 13, Sondu, KENYA

Rev. Paul O. Obange
Organized: 1978

MISSIONARIES IN SERVICE
(1978) 4   (1980) 4   (1984) 8
(1988) 7
AAGR =   6%
Foreign missionaries in 1988:   0

FIELDS OF SERVICE
Kenya   Luo, Kisii, Maasai

Deeper Christian Life Ministry
PO Box 58541, Nairobi, KENYA

Michael Oloo
Organized: 1986

MISSIONARIES IN SERVICE
(1988) 4
AAGR = N/A
Foreign missionaries in 1988:   0

FIELDS OF SERVICE
Not reported.

Deliverance & Healing World Evangelism, Inc
PO Box 56697, Nairobi, KENYA

Israel Kyame
Organized: 1976

MISSIONARIES IN SERVICE
(1988) 30
AAGR = N/A
Foreign missionaries in 1988:   10

FIELDS OF SERVICE
USA
 California
 New York
 Texas
Zambia
Tanzania
Kenya   Kamba, Kisii, Kalenjin,
     Kikuyu, Maasai, Luya
Uganda
Zimbabwe

Deliverance Church
PO Box 28600, Nairobi, KENYA

Rev. William Tuimising
Organized: 1970   Independent

MISSIONARIES IN SERVICE
(1988) 25
AAGR = N/A
Foreign missionaries in 1988:   0

FIELDS OF SERVICE
Kenya   Kalenjin, Kikuyu, Luo, Kamba

Diocesan Missionary Association
PO Box 23031, Nairobi, KENYA

Organized: 1962
Church of the Province of Kenya

MISSIONARIES IN SERVICE
(1988) 1283
AAGR = N/A
Foreign missionaries in 1988:   0

FIELDS OF SERVICE

Kenya Taita, Duruma, Pokomo,
Giriama, Wakamba, Pokot, Turkana,
Marakwet, Duruma, Hola, Digo,
Swahili, Boran, Gabbra, Turkana,
Kamba, Maasai, Luo, Kikuyu,
Luhya, Kamba
Germany (West)

East African Divinity Church

PO Box 174, Runyenjes, KENYA

Rev. Johana Nyaga.
Organized: 1972

MISSIONARIES IN SERVICE

(1988) 4
AAGR = N/A
Foreign missionaries in 1988: 0

FIELDS OF SERVICE

Kenya Meru

Evangelical Lutheran Church in Kenya

PO Box 874, Kisii, KENYA

Organized: 1948   Evangelical Lutheran

MISSIONARIES IN SERVICE

(1988) 3
AAGR = N/A
Foreign missionaries in 1988: 0

FIELDS OF SERVICE

Kenya Kalenjin, Boran, Gabra

Evangelistic Association

Box 28118, Nairobi, KENYA

Andrew O. Olala
Organized: 1984

MISSIONARIES IN SERVICE

(1988) 6
AAGR = N/A
Foreign missionaries in 1988: 2

FIELDS OF SERVICE

Kenya Luo, Kamba, Luhya, Kikuyu
Uganda

Tanzania

Evangelistic Fellowship of Africa

PO Box 69, Kitale, KENYA

Rev. Daniel Chege
Organized: 1966

MISSIONARIES IN SERVICE

(1988) 7
AAGR = N/A
Foreign missionaries in 1988: 3

FIELDS OF SERVICE

Tanzania
Kenya Kalenjin, Baluhya, Pokot,
Turkana
Uganda
USA

Evangelistic Sponsors Association

PO Box 85574, Mombasa, KENYA

Joseph Charo
Organized: 1968   Nondenominational

MISSIONARIES IN SERVICE

(1988) 8
AAGR = N/A
Foreign missionaries in 1988: 0

FIELDS OF SERVICE

Kenya Maasai, Kalenjin, Pokomo,
Orma, Taita, Taveta, Giryama,
Duruma

Free Baptist Church

PO Box 33, Kambu via Kibwezi, KENYA

Rev. Richard M Muumbi
Organized: 1975

MISSIONARIES IN SERVICE

(1988) 6
AAGR = N/A
Foreign missionaries in 1988: 3

FIELDS OF SERVICE

Tanzania
Kenya Maasai, Kikuyu, Taita

Fulfilment of God's Work

Box 96, Mitaboni-Machakos, KENYA

David K. Ndullwah
Organized: 1967

MISSIONARIES IN SERVICE

(1988) 25
AAGR = N/A
Foreign missionaries in 1988:   0

FIELDS OF SERVICE

Kenya   Kikuyu, Embu, Meru, Maasai

Gatanga Area Team of Evangelists

PO Box 1106, Nairobi, KENYA

Daniel Mbarathi
Organized: 1984

MISSIONARIES IN SERVICE

(1988) 6
AAGR = N/A
Foreign missionaries in 1988:   0

FIELDS OF SERVICE

Kenya
  North Eastern Province Muslims

Gjet International, Inc.

PO Box 1567, Meru, KENYA

Rev. Gichuru Jeremy
Organized: 1983   Nondenominational

MISSIONARIES IN SERVICE

(1985) 9   (1988) 29
AAGR = 48%
Foreign missionaries in 1988:   9

FIELDS OF SERVICE

India
  Andhra Pradesh State Telugu
Kenya
  Rift Valley Province Samburu
  North Eastern Province Somali
  Eastern Province Meru
Uganda
  Entebbe Baganda
Tanzania
  Dar Es Salaam Region Swahili
Zaire

Kivu Region Lingala

Good News Church of Africa

PO Box 72708, Nairobi, KENYA

Rev. S. M. Matonoi
Organized: 1968

MISSIONARIES IN SERVICE

(1988) 3
AAGR = N/A
Foreign missionaries in 1988:   0

FIELDS OF SERVICE

Kenya   Giriama, Kamba, Meru

Good News Outreach Church

PO Box 238, Busia, KENYA

C.J. & E. Itubo
Organized: 1982

MISSIONARIES IN SERVICE

(1988) 4
AAGR = N/A
Foreign missionaries in 1988:   0

FIELDS OF SERVICE

Kenya   Luhya, Teso, Luo, Kikuyu

Gor Okech

PO Box 84941, Mombasa, KENYA

Rev. Hezekiah O. Gor
Organized: 1980

MISSIONARIES IN SERVICE

(1988) 6
AAGR = N/A
Foreign missionaries in 1988:   6

FIELDS OF SERVICE

Zaire	Uganda
Zimbabwe	Tanzania

Holy Trinity Church in Africa, Central Diocese of Masogo

PO Box 81, Rabuor via Kisumu, KENYA

Rev. H. O. Njera
Organized: 1975

MISSIONARIES IN SERVICE
(1980)   3   (1988)   43
AAGR = 39%
Foreign missionaries in 1988:   4
FIELDS OF SERVICE
Kenya   Luo, Luhya, Abagusii, Kamba,
   Kikuyu, Kuria, Kipsigi
Tanzania

Independent Presbyterian Church, Missionary Board
PO Box 37, Mwingi
Kitui District, KENYA

Organized: 1964

MISSIONARIES IN SERVICE
(1988)   5
AAGR = N/A
Foreign missionaries in 1988:   0
FIELDS OF SERVICE
Kenya   Kikuyu, Swahili, Teso, Kisii,
   Nairobi mixed groups

Kenya Evangelism Team & Crusades
PO Box 1895, Kitale, KENYA

Rev. Sylvester M. Okango
Organized: 1975

MISSIONARIES IN SERVICE
(1988)   20
AAGR = N/A
Foreign missionaries in 1988:   4
FIELDS OF SERVICE
Uganda
Kenya   Turkana, Luhya, Teso, Saboti,
   Kikuyu, Swahili, Kalenjin

Methodist Church in Kenya, Mission and Evangelism Department
PO Box 47633, Nairobi, KENYA

Rev. Lawi Imathiu
Organized: 1978   Methodist
MISSIONARIES IN SERVICE
(1988)   21

AAGR = N/A
Foreign missionaries in 1988:   2
FIELDS OF SERVICE
Kenya   Boran, Meru, Luo, Maasai,
   Mijikenda, Kikuyu
Uganda
Tanzania

Missionary Fellowship of Kenya
PO Box 1190, Bungoma, KENYA

Rev. Patrick Okumu
Organized: 1978

MISSIONARIES IN SERVICE
(1988)   9
AAGR = N/A
Foreign missionaries in 1988:   9
FIELDS OF SERVICE
Tanzania
Zaire
Uganda
United Kingdom
   England

Musanda Holy Ghost Church of East Africa
PO Box 10, Ahero, KENYA

Rev. S.K. Ahando
Organized: 1948

MISSIONARIES IN SERVICE
(1980)   3   (1988)   7
AAGR = 11%
Foreign missionaries in 1988:   0
FIELDS OF SERVICE
Tanzania   **Uganda**

Nabii Church Mission
Box 23412, Nairobi, KENYA

Tabson S.N. Walubengo
Organized: 1983

MISSIONARIES IN SERVICE
(1988)   3
AAGR = N/A
Foreign missionaries in 1988:   0

FIELDS OF SERVICE

Kenya　Various Groups

Pentecostal Assemblies of God, Missions Department

PO Box 671, Kisumu, KENYA

Rev. Jacton Nditi
Organized: 1982
Pentecostal Assemblies of God

MISSIONARIES IN SERVICE

(1988)　8
AAGR = N/A
Foreign missionaries in 1988:　0

FIELDS OF SERVICE

Kenya　Turkana, Samburu, Tugen,
　Njemps, Orma, Pokomo, Kamba,
　Somali,

Pentecostal Christian Universal Church

Box 50258, Nairobi, KENYA

Godfrey Masinde Mechumo
Organized: 1981

MISSIONARIES IN SERVICE

(1988)　11
AAGR = N/A
Foreign missionaries in 1988:　2

FIELDS OF SERVICE

Kenya　Luhya, Luo, Kikuyu, Kisii,
　Kamba
Uganda

Pentecostal Church of Africa

PO Box 28809, Nairobi, KENYA

Bishop Peter Phillips Ngungu
Organized: 1985　　　　Pentecostal

MISSIONARIES IN SERVICE

(1988)　3
AAGR = N/A
Foreign missionaries in 1988:　0

FIELDS OF SERVICE

Kenya　Taita, Giriama, Luo, Kuria

Pentecostal Crusade Ministry

PO Box 46127, Nairobi, KENYA

Justus Wanjala Kisiangani
Organized: 1986　　　　Pentecostal

MISSIONARIES IN SERVICE

(1988)　9
AAGR = N/A
Foreign missionaries in 1988:　8

FIELDS OF SERVICE

Tanzania
Europe
Kenya　Maasai
Uganda
India
USA

Pentecostal Evangelism Team

PO Box 282, Tiriki, KENYA

Organized: 1976

MISSIONARIES IN SERVICE

(1984)　31　　　(1988)　8
AAGR = -28%
Foreign missionaries in 1988:　0

FIELDS OF SERVICE

Kenya　Luhya, Kikuyu, Kalenjin, Luo

Pentecostal Gospel Centre, Churches and Mission of E.A.

PO Box 1852, Eldoret, KENYA

Rev. Zacharias K. Karanja
Organized: 1984　　　　Pentecostal

MISSIONARIES IN SERVICE

(1988)　5
AAGR = N/A
Foreign missionaries in 1988:　2

FIELDS OF SERVICE

Kenya　Kalenjin, Kikuyu, Turkana,
　Luhya
Tanzania

Power of Jesus Around the World Church
PO Box 991, Kisumu, KENYA

Bishop Washington O. Ngede
Organized: 1980

MISSIONARIES IN SERVICE
(1988) 6
AAGR = N/A
Foreign missionaries in 1988:   0

FIELDS OF SERVICE
Kenya   Kalenjin, Meru, Luhya, Maasai, Taita, Kikuyu, Pokomo, Giriama

Power of the Holy Trinity Church
PO Box 209, Homa Bay, KENYA

Rev. Tobias Owiti
Organized: 1975

MISSIONARIES IN SERVICE
(1988) 10
AAGR = N/A
Foreign missionaries in 1988:   1

FIELDS OF SERVICE
Kenya   Nyeri, Coastal Areas, Turkana, Suk, Keiyo.
Tanzania

Presbyterian Church of East Africa
PO Box 48268, Nairobi, KENYA
Organized: 1967   Presbyterian

MISSIONARIES IN SERVICE
(1988)   6
AAGR = N/A
Foreign missionaries in 1988:   1

FIELDS OF SERVICE
Tanzania
Kenya   Maasai, Turkana, Kamba, Samburu, Kalenjin

Redeemed Gospel Church-Sirende
PO Box 1761, Kitale, KENYA

Arthur Kitonga
Organized: 1988

MISSIONARIES IN SERVICE
(1988) 9
AAGR = N/A
Foreign missionaries in 1988:   5

FIELDS OF SERVICE
Uganda
Tanzania
Kenya   Kikuyu, Luhya, Kamba, Maasai, Kalenjin, Kisii, Coastal Areas

Scriptural Holiness Mission
PO Box 85, Kipkelion, KENYA

Rev. Gilbert M. Mulaha
Organized: 1948

MISSIONARIES IN SERVICE
(1988) 12
AAGR = N/A
Foreign missionaries in 1988:   0

FIELDS OF SERVICE
Kenya   Maasai

Soul Winning Evangelistic Church
PO Box 57329, Nairobi, KENYA

Rev. Charles Ouma Ogweno
Organized: 1986   Evangelical

MISSIONARIES IN SERVICE
(1988) 5
AAGR = N/A
Foreign missionaries in 1988:   0

FIELDS OF SERVICE
Kenya   Kikuyu, Luhya

Strategizing Penetrating Equipping for Africa's Redemption
PO Box 45178, Nairobi, KENYA
Organized: 1989   Churches of Christ

MISSIONARIES IN SERVICE
(1988) 6
AAGR = N/A
Foreign missionaries in 1988:   6

Uganda	Tanzania

United International Life Ministry of Churches

PO Box 1019, Kisumu, KENYA

Maurice Arao
Organized: 1984   Apostolic Faith

MISSIONARIES IN SERVICE

(1988)   4
AAGR = N/A
Foreign missionaries in 1988:   0

FIELDS OF SERVICE

Kenya   Luo, Kuria, Kisii, Kamba,
    Kikuyu, Luyha, Teso, Taite, Maasai

Voice of Salvation and Healing Church

PO Box 582, Kisumu, KENYA

Javan Aggrey S. Owiti
Organized: 1957

MISSIONARIES IN SERVICE

(1988) 20
AAGR = N/A
Foreign missionaries in 1988:   19

FIELDS OF SERVICE

USA	Sweden
Tanzania	Norway
Uganda	

World Independent Lutheran Church

c/o Angali Loyalist Missionary Agency
PO Box 142, Lumbatania Castle
Maragoli, KENYA

Dr. Angali - I
Organized: 1961   Lutheran

MISSIONARIES IN SERVICE

(1975) 4   (1978) 4   (1980) 2
(1985) 171   (1988) 221*
AAGR = N/A
Foreign Missionaries in 1988: Not
reported.

FIELDS OF SERVICE

Australia
   Victoria Latvians
Kenya
   Nyanza Province Baluhia, Luo
Uganda
   Western (Masindi) Teso

World Revival Mission

PO Box 1410, Eldoret, KENYA

John Kisuli
Organized: 1984   Revival Church

MISSIONARIES IN SERVICE

(1988)   6
AAGR = N/A
Foreign missionaries in 1988:   0

FIELDS OF SERVICE

Kenya   Kikuyu, Luhya, kalenjin,
    Kamba, Luo

LIBERIA

African Christian Fellowship

PO Box 4655, Monrovia, LIBERIA

Rev. T. Edward Kofi
Organized: 1986   Independent

MISSIONARIES IN SERVICE

(1988) 270
AAGR = N/A
Foreign missionaries in 1988:   0

FIELDS OF SERVICE

Liberia
   Rivercess County Bassa, Kru
   Nimba County Gio, Mano
   Grand Gedeh County Krahn
   Montserrado County Kru, Bassa,
      Krahn, Gio, Mano, Loma, Kissi
   Sino County Kru
   Grand Bassa County Bassa, Kpelle

World Wide Missions of Liberia

PO Box 2581, Monrovia, LIBERIA

Rev. Chauncey Karnga
Organized: 1961   Nondenominational

MISSIONARIES IN SERVICE
(1988) 10
AAGR = N/A
Foreign missionaries in 1988:   0
FIELDS OF SERVICE
Liberia
  Bong County Mano, Kpelle
  Nimba County Gio, Krahn

MADAGASCAR

Malagasy Protestant Church
V. B-48, Ialana Ratsimilaho
Antananarivo, MADAGASCAR

Rev. Dr. Ratovonarivo
Organized: 1893   Nondenominational
MISSIONARIES IN SERVICE
(1980) 9   (1988) 20*
AAGR = N/A
Foreign Missionaries in 1988: Not reported.
FIELDS OF SERVICE
Not reported.

Renewed Malagasy Lutheran Church
PO Box 1006
Antananarivo, MADAGASCAR

Rev. Pr. Ernest Rakotondrats
Organized: 1970   Lutheran
MISSIONARIES IN SERVICE
(1972) 24   (1975) 20   (1978) 19
(1980) 21   (1988) 18*
AAGR = N/A
Foreign Missionaries in 1988: Not reported.
FIELDS OF SERVICE
Not reported.

MALAWI

African Gospel Assemblies
PO Box 849, Blantyre, MALAWI

Rev. Jerry P. Chitakata
Organized: 1961   Assemblies of God
MISSIONARIES IN SERVICE
(1972) 15   (1980) 25   (1985) 30
(1988) 40
AAGR = 6%
Foreign missionaries in 1988:   15
FIELDS OF SERVICE
Mozambique
  Zambezia Province Sena
Zambia
  Lusaka Province Bemba, Lunda
Zaire
  Shaba (Lumbumbashi) Swahili

Chisomo Church of Pentecost
PO Box 30231, Capitol City
Lilongwe 3, MALAWI

Bishop Thaulo Phiri
Organized: 1983   Pentecostal
MISSIONARIES IN SERVICE
Further information withheld at agency's request.

Christ Deliverance Ministries
PO Box 459, Lilongwe, MALAWI

Rev. Moses Makhaya
Organized: 1975   Pentecostal
MISSIONARIES IN SERVICE
Further information withheld at agency's request.

Christian Movers for Lost Souls Ministry
PO Box 51, Mikolongwe, MALAWI

Rev.C.B. Kanyaoa Phiri
Organized: 1969   Nondenominational
MISSIONARIES IN SERVICE
(1972) 19   (1980) 41   (1985) 59
(1988) 87
AAGR = 10%
Foreign missionaries in 1988:   27

FIELDS OF SERVICE

Mozambique

Zambezia Province Portuguese,
Chichewa, Lomwe

Malawi

All Three Regions Nyanja
Southern Region Sena, Chichewa,
Lomwe
Central Region Yao, Muslims
Northern Region Tumbuka, Chichewa,
Chitonga

Church of Disciples Mission in Malawi

PO Box 34, Nsanje, MALAWI

Hamard S. Chakanza
Organized: 1978   Pentecostal
MISSIONARIES IN SERVICE
(1988) 46
AAGR = N/A
Foreign missionaries in 1988:   29
FIELDS OF SERVICE

Malawi

Northern Region Tonga, Tumbuka,
Sena
Central Region Chewa, Yao, Lomwe,
Sena
Southern Region Chewa, Yao, Lomwe,
Sena

Mozambique

Manica Province Portuguese, Shona,
Ndau, Chopi, Shangaan
Zambezia Province Portuguese, Sena,
Shona, Ndau
Cabo Delgado Province Portuguese,
Shona, Ndau, Chopi, Shangaan
Maputo Province Portuguese, Shona,
Ndau, Chopi, Shangaan
Nampula Province Portuguese, Sena,
Shona, Ndau
Tete Province Portuguese, Sena,
Shona, Ndau
Sofala Province Portuguese, Sena,
Shona, Ndau

Church of Pentecost Free Mission

Kapenuka Mission, Box 12, Jali
Zomba, MALAWI

B.A. Khobili
Organized: 1977   Pentecostal
MISSIONARIES IN SERVICE
(1988) 10
AAGR = N/A
Foreign missionaries in 1988:   0
FIELDS OF SERVICE

Malawi

Southern Region Nyanja, Tumbuka,
Lomwe, Yao, Tonga

Evangelical Baptist Church

Box 121, Liwonde, MALAWI

Rev. M.J. Munyewe
Organized: 1973   Baptist
MISSIONARIES IN SERVICE
(1980) 3   (1983) 3   (1984) 4
(1985) 5   (1986) 10   (1988) 27
AAGR = 32%
Foreign missionaries in 1988:   0
FIELDS OF SERVICE
Malawi
Southern Region Yao

Free Love Ministries

PO Box 488, Zomba, MALAWI

Dave Gama
Organized: 1985   Pentecostal
MISSIONARIES IN SERVICE
(1988) 45
AAGR = N/A
Foreign missionaries in 1988:   11
FIELDS OF SERVICE
Nigeria
Anambra (Onitsha) Ibo
Mozambique
Southern Region Chewa, Lomwe, Yao
Ghana
Takoradi English
Zimbabwe

North Matabeleland Province Shona,
Ndebele
Zambia
Northern Province Wemba, Lozi

God's Ministries Worldwide
PO Box 2662, Blantyre, MALAWI

Rev. Damson J. Mchenga
Organized: 1986   Pentecostal
MISSIONARIES IN SERVICE
(1988) 17
AAGR = N/A
Foreign missionaries in 1988:   2
FIELDS OF SERVICE
Malawi
Southern Region Lomwe, Mang'anja
Northern Region Tumbuka, Tonga,
Ngoni
Zimbabwe
Mashonaland East (Harare City) All
Peoples
Namibia
Windhoek City Coloured

Revival Church of God
PO Box 40105, Kanengo
Lilongwe, MALAWI

Rev. L.F. Mbewe
Organized: Not reported.
Revival Church of God
MISSIONARIES IN SERVICE
(1988) 74
AAGR = N/A
Foreign missionaries in 1988:   5
FIELDS OF SERVICE
Mozambique   Sena, Yao, Lomwe,
Nyanja, Tumbuka

World Wide Missions
PO Box 3, Mikolongwe, MALAWI

Rev. J.B. Chaphidza
Organized: 1975   Evangelical
MISSIONARIES IN SERVICE
(1972) 26   (1980) 30   (1985) 36
(1988) 52

AAGR =   4%
Foreign missionaries in 1988:   0
FIELDS OF SERVICE
Malawi
Southern (Chiradzulu) Lomwe
Southern (Mulanje) Lomwe
Southern (Nsanje) Sena
Southern (Machinga) Yao
Southern (Thyolo) Chewa

NAMIBIA

Bethesda Sending Mission
PO Box 3050, Vineta 9000, NAMIBIA

Rev. C.M. Pieterse
Organized: 1979   Pentecostal
MISSIONARIES IN SERVICE
(1980) 9   (1985) 8   (1988) 13
AAGR =   5%
Foreign missionaries in 1988:   10
FIELDS OF SERVICE
Belgium
Brussels Dutch, Flamish
South Africa
Transvaal Province Blacks, Whites,
Afrikaans, English
Cape Province Blacks, Whites,
Afrikaans, English
Netherlands
Amsterdam Dutch, Flamish
Namibia   Damara, Ovambo,
Bushmen, Nama, Coloured

NIGERIA

Advent Christian Mission
471 Kot Ekpene Rd., Uyo, NIGERIA

Paul Etukarpan
Organized: 1966
MISSIONARIES IN SERVICE
(1972) 2   (1975) 1   (1978) 2
(1980) 5   (1984) 15   (1988) 29*
AAGR = N/A
Foreign Missionaries in 1988: Not
reported.

FIELDS OF SERVICE

Not reported.

Apostles Revival Crusaders' Ministry, Inc

PO Box 59, Gombe, NIGERIA

Rev. Charles I. Okonkwo
Organized: 1976   Pentecostal

MISSIONARIES IN SERVICE

(1985) 3   (1988) 12
AAGR = 59%
Foreign missionaries in 1988:   2

FIELDS OF SERVICE

Nigeria
  Gangola State Fulfulde, Fulani
  Borno State Kanuri
  Bauchi State Muslims, Hausa
Cameroon
  Baminda Cameroonians

Arise Gospel Mission

PO Box 1047, Apapa, NIGERIA

Rev. Raphael Ologundf
Organized: 1979   Pentecostal

MISSIONARIES IN SERVICE

(1980) 11   (1985) 13   (1988) 15
AAGR =   4%
Foreign missionaries in 1988:   0

FIELDS OF SERVICE

Nigeria
  Kwara (Offa) Yoruba
  Imo (Aba) Igbo, English
  Ogun (Ijebu Obe) Yoruba
  Oyo (Ibadan) Yoruba
  Kaduna (Kaduna) Hausa, English
  Federal Capitol Territory Gwari,
    Hausa
  Niger (Minna) Yoruba, Hausa, English
  Lagos (Baagry) Yoruba, English

Arm of the Lord Ministry

Box 2866, Owerri, Imo State, NIGERIA

Rev. S.E. Gbazie
Organized: 1979   Pentecostal

MISSIONARIES IN SERVICE

(1980) 8   (1985) 27   (1988) 31
AAGR = 18%
Foreign missionaries in 1988:   12

FIELDS OF SERVICE

Liberia   English, Pegen
Kenya   English, Swahili
Nigeria   Igbo, Ifik, Tiv, Ichekin
Cameroon   Douala, French, English

Bible Believing Christian Ministry

PO Box 1280, Ilorin
Kwara State, NIGERIA

Rev. Akinola Ayoola
Organized: 1984   Pentecostal

MISSIONARIES IN SERVICE

(1985) 3   (1988) 16
AAGR = 75%
Foreign missionaries in 1988:   0

FIELDS OF SERVICE

Nigeria
  Kaduna State Hausa, Fulani, Muslims
  Oyo State Yoruba, Muslims, Idol
    Worshippers
  Ondo State Yoruba, Idol Worshippers
  Kwara State Yoruba, Muslims

Bible Faith Mission, The

PO Box 2775, Jos
Plateau State, NIGERIA

Wilson Ezeofor
Organized: 1979   Charismatic

MISSIONARIES IN SERVICE

(1980) 4   (1985) 10   (1988) 14
AAGR = 17%
Foreign missionaries in 1988:   0

FIELDS OF SERVICE

Nigeria
  Plateau State Rukuba, Anaang,
    Mauhuul Bassa-Kontagora, Berom,
    Hausa
  Gangola State Bachama, Hausa

Bible Way Mission
PO Box 13, Ehime, Imo State, NIGERIA

Nwachukwu F.C.
Organized: 1979   Pentecostal
MISSIONARIES IN SERVICE
(1980) 8   (1985) 17   (1988) 25
AAGR = 15%
Foreign missionaries in 1988:   0
FIELDS OF SERVICE
Nigeria
  Imo State Igbo
  Rivers State Kalabari, Italo, Ikwerre
  Anambra State Igbo
  Northern States Hausa, Nupe
  Cross River State Efik
  Bendel State Benin, Ido

Calvary Christian Talent Development Centre, Inc.
Calvary Grace Faith Village
PO Box 234, Port Harcourt
Rivers State, NIGERIA

Dr. Godwin O.C. Obia
Organized: 1977   Nondenominational
MISSIONARIES IN SERVICE
(1972) 30   (1980) 34   (1985) 40
(1988) 66
AAGR = 5%
Foreign missionaries in 1988:   54
FIELDS OF SERVICE
Korea (South)   English
India
  Delhi (New Delhi) English
Niger
  Niamey Area Fulani, Hausa
Uganda
  Kampala English
USSR   Third World Students
USA   Third World Students
Nigeria
  Rivers State Ijaw, Huasa, Fulani, Kanuri
Ghana
  Tema District Fanti, Ashanti, English

Sierra Leone
  Freetown English
Cameroon
  Douala Area French, English

Calvary Evangelistic Ministry, Inc.
GPO Box 4390, Ibadan, NIGERIA

Dr. David A. Anjorin
Organized: 1967   Evangelical
MISSIONARIES IN SERVICE
(1988) 76
AAGR = N/A
Foreign missionaries in 1988:   0
FIELDS OF SERVICE
Nigeria
  Ondo State Yoruba
  Ogun State Yoruba
  Oyo State Yoruba
  Benue State Yoruba, Tiv, Hausa

Calvary Love Foundation
PO Box 1802, Ilorin
Kwara State, NIGERIA

Rev. J.M. Uloegbulem
Organized: 1986   Evangelical
MISSIONARIES IN SERVICE
(1988) 10
AAGR = N/A
Foreign missionaries in 1988:   0
FIELDS OF SERVICE
Nigeria   Muslims, Rural Pagans,
    Prisoners, Youth, Roman Catholics

Calvary Ministries
PO Box 6001, Jos, NIGERIA

Dr. S.K. Oni
Organized: Not reported.
MISSIONARIES IN SERVICE
(1988) 85
AAGR = N/A
Foreign missionaries in 1988:   0
FIELDS OF SERVICE
Not reported.

Calvary Productions (CAPRO)

Capro International Office
PO Box 144, Kafanchan
Kaduna, NIGERIA

J. 'Bayo Famonure
Organized: Not reported.

FIELDS OF SERVICE

Not reported.

Child Evangelism Training Institute

PO Box 513, Bauchi, NIGERIA

Rev. Okafor T. Emfesi
Organized: 1980   Nondenominational

MISSIONARIES IN SERVICE

(1980) 8   (1985) 72   (1988) 87
AAGR = 35%
Foreign missionaries in 1988: 5

FIELDS OF SERVICE

Nigeria
  Cross River State Ogoja, Boki
  Kaduna State Hausa, Fulani
  Anambra State Ibo
  Benue State Idoma, Tiv, Igala
  Plateau State Berom
  Gangola State Mambila, Bachama
  Bauchi State Tangale, Hausa
  Imo State Ibo
  Kwara State Yoruba
Ghana
  Eastern Region Asene
Cameroon
  North Western Province Bamileke

Christ Apostolic Crusaders Gospel Church

PO Box 3971, Ikeja, Lagos, NIGERIA

Rev. Gabriel A. Shobayo
Organized: 1977   Brethren

MISSIONARIES IN SERVICE

(1988) 51
AAGR = N/A
Foreign missionaries in 1988:   0

FIELDS OF SERVICE

Not reported.

Christ Church Mission

PO Box 43, Oboi Etoi, Uyo, NIGERIA

Rev. O.M. Akpan
Organized: Not reported.
Interdenominational

MISSIONARIES IN SERVICE

(1980) 88   (1982) 67   (1988) 30*
AAGR = N/A
Foreign Missionaries in 1988: Not reported.

FIELDS OF SERVICE

Nigeria
  Kwara State
  Lagos State
  Kano State Hausa
  Oyo State Ibibio
  Bendel State Yoruba

Christ Disciple Ministries

Box 173, Mubi, NIGERIA

James Ogunshola
Organized: Not reported.

MISSIONARIES IN SERVICE

(1988)   5
AAGR = N/Λ
Foreign missionaries in 1988:   0

FIELDS OF SERVICE

Not reported.

Christ Gospel Church Mission, Inc.

PO Box 322, Sapele, NIGERIA

Rev. Gabriel Okorodudu
Organized: 1963   Charismatic

MISSIONARIES IN SERVICE

(1972) 54   (1980) 48   (1985) 44
(1988) 56
AAGR = 0%
Foreign missionaries in 1988:   0

FIELDS OF SERVICE

Nigeria

Bendel State Urhobo, Isekiri, Benin,
Ibo, Kwale, Yoruba, Hausa

Christ Temple, Pentecostal Churches

PO Box 76, Abak
Akwa Ibom State, NIGERIA

Rev. Imeh John Akpan
Organized: 1967   Independent

MISSIONARIES IN SERVICE

(1972) 14	(1975) 11	(1978) 11
(1980) 18	(1982) 8	(1984) 8
(1985) 7	(1988) 14	

AAGR = 0%
Foreign missionaries in 1988:   4

FIELDS OF SERVICE

Kenya
Nairobi English
St. Vincent English
United Kingdom
England (Reading, Berks) English
Nigeria
Lagos State Yoruba

Christ United Missionary Organization

PO Box 2113, Akure, NIGERIA

Rev. Tom O. Awodele
Organized: 1983   Evangelical

MISSIONARIES IN SERVICE
(1985) 7   (1988) 9
AAGR = 9%
Foreign missionaries in 1988:   0

FIELDS OF SERVICE
Nigeria
Ondo State Ebira, Ogoja, Yoruba, Akoko
Ogun State Yoruba, Ijebus

Christ for Rural Areas Ministries

PO Box 2226, Ilorin, NIGERIA

Rev. S.O. Olanrewaju
Organized: 1978   Pentecostal

MISSIONARIES IN SERVICE
(1988) 10
AAGR = N/A
Foreign missionaries in 1988:   0
FIELDS OF SERVICE
Nigeria
Kaduna State Gwari, Hausa
Kwara State Owe, Yagba, Kemberi, Batonu
Plateau State Ibrom, Hausa

Christ for the Whole World

PO Box 39, Agbedek
Bendel State, NIGERIA

Rev. Llayi Ejiwoye
Organized: Not reported.   Evangelical
MISSIONARIES IN SERVICE
(1988) 9
AAGR = N/A
Foreign missionaries in 1988:   0
FIELDS OF SERVICE
Nigeria
Bendel State Ishan, Etsako
Ondo State Yoruba
Oyo State Yoruba

Christ the Redeemer's Ministries

PO Box 172, Ebute-Metta
Lagos, NIGERIA

Pastor E.A. Adeboye
Organized: 1977   Evangelical
MISSIONARIES IN SERVICE
(1988) 14
AAGR = N/A
Foreign missionaries in 1988:   3
FIELDS OF SERVICE
Nigeria
Benue State Tiv
Rivers State Ijaw, Kalabari
Ondo State Yoruba, Igalls
Lagos State Yoruba, Awari
Ivory Coast
Ghana
Ashanti Region Akan

Eastern Region Akan

Christ's Followers Mission, Inc.

PO Box 171, Satellite Town
Lagos, NIGERIA

Bishop Jacob A.F. Akeredolu
Organized: 1974   Pentecostal

MISSIONARIES IN SERVICE

(1988) 34
AAGR = N/A
Foreign missionaries in 1988:   0

FIELDS OF SERVICE

Nigeria
  Oyo State Yoruba
  Ogun State Yoruba
  Lagos State Yoruba, English
  Kaduna State Hausa
  Anambra State Ibo
  Bendel State Benin

Christian Evangelical & Missionary Society, Inc.

PO Box 50, Orerokpe, NIGERIA

Rev. Edmund Dolor
Organized: 1975   Nondenominational

MISSIONARIES IN SERVICE

(1972) 10   (1980) 16   (1985) 16
(1988) 25
AAGR = 6%
Foreign missionaries in 1988:   0

FIELDS OF SERVICE

Nigeria
  Bendel (Okpe) Ugolo, Urholo
  Kaduna State Muslims, Hausa
  Bendel (Akoko) Ojeramic, Ugbo
  Bendel (Bomadi) Riverine communities
  Benue State Tiv, Rural Dwellers

Christian Growth Ministry, Inc.

PO Box 5181, Aba, Imo State, NIGERIA

Dr. I.U. Godwin
Organized: 1976   Nondenominational

MISSIONARIES IN SERVICE

(1980) 17   (1985) 30   (1988) 41
AAGR = 12%
Foreign missionaries in 1988:   2

FIELDS OF SERVICE

Nigeria
  Niger State Gwari
  Imo State Igbo
  Kano State Hausa
  Lagos State Yoruba
  Bauchi State Hausa
  Sokoto State Hausa
  Plateau State Hausa
  Benue State Tiv
  Federal Capital Territory Hausa,
    Gwari
  Ondo State Yoruba
  Gangola State Hausa
  Kaduna State Hausa
  Rivers State Kalabari
Kenya
  Eastern Province Kiswahili
Ghana
  Ashanti Region Ashanti

Christian Missionary Foundation

UIPO Box 9890, Ibadan, NIGERIA

Rev. Reuben E. Ezemadu
Organized: 1982   Nondenominational

MISSIONARIES IN SERVICE

(1985) 39   (1988) 34
AAGR = -3%
Foreign missionaries in 1988:   11

FIELDS OF SERVICE

Gambia
  Serrekunda Mandinka, Dyola, Wolof
Nigeria
  Benue State Igala
  Rivers State Ijaw, Izom
  Federal Capitol Territory Gbagyi,
    Ganagana, Gwandara
  Niger State Kemberi
Cameroon
  Northern Province Mandara
Benin

Atlantique Fon-Gbe
Kenya
Meru District Kimeru

Christian Missionary Out-Reach Ministry

PO Box 1987, Aduwana
Benin City, NIGERIA

Rev. A. Edosomwan
Organized: 1979   Pentecostal
MISSIONARIES IN SERVICE
(1988)   9
AAGR = N/A
Foreign missionaries in 1988:   0
FIELDS OF SERVICE
Nigeria
Bendel State Esan, Bini, Urhobo,
    Yoruba, Bini
Ondo State Yoruba

Christian Redemption Evangelical Ministries

PO Box 5775, Benin City, NIGERIA

Rev. Moses Amakhabi
Organized: 1979   Pentecostal
MISSIONARIES IN SERVICE
(1980)   9   (1985)   12   (1988)   20
AAGR =   11%
Foreign missionaries in 1988:   0
FIELDS OF SERVICE
Nigeria
Bendel State Edo, Urhobo, Etsako
Imo State Ibo
Ondo State Yoruba
Ogun State Yoruba
Kaduna State Hausa
Lagos State Yoruba
Anambra State Ibo

Church of Christ in the Sudan Among the Tiv., Mission Board

P.A. Mkar, P.O., Gboko
Benue State, NIGERIA

Dr. S. Yakobu
Organized: 1975   Denominational
MISSIONARIES IN SERVICE
(1978) 20   (1980) 18   (1988) 12*
AAGR = N/A
Foreign Missionaries in 1988: Not
reported.
FIELDS OF SERVICE
Not reported.

Cocim Community Mission

Cocim Hats, PMB 2127, Jos
Plateau State, NIGERIA

Rev. Dayou Gyang
Organized: 1937   Evangelical
MISSIONARIES IN SERVICE
(1972) 22   (1980) 50   (1985) 64
(1988) 80
AAGR =   8%
Foreign missionaries in 1988:   0
FIELDS OF SERVICE
Nigeria
Bauchi State Hausa, Muslims
Borno State Karmuri
Sokoto State Hausa, Muslims
Niger State Muslims

Day of Deliverance Ministry, The

PO Box 387, Ahoada, NIGERIA

Rev. Moses O. Ewoh
Organized: 1975   Pentecostal
MISSIONARIES IN SERVICE
(1980) 21   (1985) 39   (1988) 61
AAGR =   14%
Foreign missionaries in 1988:   2
FIELDS OF SERVICE
Equatorial Guinea
Malabo
Nigeria
Rivers State Ijaw
Anambra State Ibo, Ekpeye
Ghana
Greater Accra Region

Disciples of Christ Mission, Inc.

PO Box 2576, Aba, NIGERIA

Rev. I.D. Nwagbugbo
Organized: 1978   Pentecostal

MISSIONARIES IN SERVICE

(1980) 2   (1985) 11   (1988) 15
AAGR = 29%
Foreign missionaries in 1988:   0

FIELDS OF SERVICE

Nigeria
  Imo State Ibo, Ngwa, Cobioma, Isiala
  Imo (Umuhaia, Ikwuano) Oloko

Emmanuel Church Mission of Nigeria Inc.

PO Box 108, Uyo, NIGERIA

Bishop S.O.E. Umoh
Organized: 1957   Mennonite

MISSIONARIES IN SERVICE

(1972) 4   (1980) 6   (1985) 10
(1988) 13
AAGR = 8%
Foreign missionaries in 1988:   0

FIELDS OF SERVICE

Nigeria
  Akwa Ibom State Ibibio
  Imo State Igbo
  Lagos State Yoruba
  Cross River State Efik

Evangelical Missionary Society

PO Box 63, Jos, NIGERIA

Rev. Maikudi Kure
Organized: 1948   Evangelical

MISSIONARIES IN SERVICE

(1972) 190   (1975) 240   (1978) 260
(1980) 428   (1982) 485   (1984) 575
(1985) 645   (1986) 618   (1988) 729
AAGR = 9%
Foreign missionaries in 1988:   29

FIELDS OF SERVICE

Nigeria
  Sokoto State Hausa, Dukawa,
    Zabarmawa, Arawa
  Niger State Dukawa, Erena, Gbagyin,
    Yamma
  Borno State Kerikeri, Ngizum
  Gangola State Koma, Dirim
  Plateau (Benue District) Gade,
    Gwandara, Gbagyi, Bassa-Komu,
    Agatu
  Imo State Ibo
  Kano State Hausa, Maguzawa
  Bendel State
  Cross River State Obundu, Betti
  Kaduna State Numana, Gwandara,
    Hausa, Gbagyi, Kuturmi, Kadara
  Bauchi State Palchi, Jarawan, Dutse,
    Guruntawa
  Bauchi (Gombe District) Beriberi,
    Bolawa, Tera
  Lagos State Hausa, Yoruba
  Kastina Hausa, Fulani
  Kwara State Boko, Kambari, Dukawa,
    Agatu, Yoruba, Ebira
  Bauchi (Tangale District) Fulani,
    Bolawa
  Plateau (Plateau District) Chikobo,
    Limoro, Amawa, Morto, Kurama
  Oyo State Yoruba
  Anambra State Ibo
Chad   Musai, Ngambai, Ndam,
    Kananbu
Niger   Hausa
Benin   Boko

Full Gospel Bible Church Apostolic

Anan Ikono HQ, Uyo
Akwa Ibom State, NIGERIA

Rev. K.E. Nice
Organized: 1972
Full Gospel Bible Church Apostolic

MISSIONARIES IN SERVICE

(1972) 6   (1980) 8   (1985) 10
(1988) 12

AAGR =   4%
Foreign missionaries in 1988:   0
FIELDS OF SERVICE
Nigeria
Ikono Ibibio
Cross River (Uyo) Ibibio
Akwa Ibom State Ibibio, Anaang
Cross River State Efik

Gabriel Olasoji World Evangelism
PO box 9351, University of Ibadan
Ibadan, Oyo State, NIGERIA

Dr. Gabriel K. Olasoji
Organized: 1979   Evangelical
MISSIONARIES IN SERVICE
(1985)   6   (1988)   8
AAGR =   10%
Foreign missionaries in 1988:   0
FIELDS OF SERVICE
Nigeria
Borno State Beriberi, Fulani
Niger (Minna) Gwari
Gangola State Mosomgwari, Fulani
Plateau State Fulani, Tiv
Benue State Tiv, Fulani, Ibibio
Kano State Hausa

Gospel Defenders Mission
PO Box 258, Somolu
Lagos State, NIGERIA

Rev. Israel A. Aina
Organized: 1982   Pentecostal
MISSIONARIES IN SERVICE
(1972)   2   (1980)   2   (1985)   4
(1988)   6
AAGR =   7%
Foreign missionaries in 1988:   0
FIELDS OF SERVICE
Nigeria
Ondo State Yoruba

Gospel Missionary Foundation International, Inc.
PO Box 55207, Ikeja, Lagos, NIGERIA

Rev. I.O. Obioha
Organized: 1984   Nondenominational
MISSIONARIES IN SERVICE
(1985)   10   (1988)   31
AAGR =   46%
Foreign missionaries in 1988:   2
FIELDS OF SERVICE
Nigeria
Rivers State Ikwerre, Ogoni
Kaduna State Hausa, Muslims
Anambra State Igbo, Idol worshippers
Imo State Igbo, Idol worshippers
Ogun State Yoruba, Idol Worshippers
Cross River State Ibibio
Kastina Hausa, Muslims
Lagos State Yoruba, Idol Worshippers
Sokoto State Hausa, Muslims
Cameroon
South Western Province Muslims

Gospel Promoters' Mission, The
PO Box 1183, Surulere
Lagos State, NIGERIA

Dr. E.W.A. Kukoyi
Organized: 1977   Pentecostal
MISSIONARIES IN SERVICE
(1980)   6   (1985)   6   (1988)   12
AAGR =   9%
Foreign missionaries in 1988:   5
FIELDS OF SERVICE
Ghana
All Regions English, French
Nigeria
Ondo State English, Yoruba
Oyo State English, Yoruba
Ogun State English, Yoruba
Netherlands   English, French
Benin   English, French
France   English, French

Harvest Time Mission
PO Box 882, Enugu, NIGERIA

Rev. Godwin Ekpe
Organized: 1983   Pentecostal
MISSIONARIES IN SERVICE
(1988)   7
AAGR = N/A
Foreign missionaries in 1988:   0
FIELDS OF SERVICE
Not reported.

His Grace Evangelical Movement, Inc.
GPO Box 1550, Ibadan, NIGERIA

Rev. Nicholas D. Osameyan
Organized: 1975   Pentecostal
MISSIONARIES IN SERVICE
(1980)   4   (1985) 11   (1988) 22
AAGR = 24%
Foreign missionaries in 1988:   4
FIELDS OF SERVICE
Nigeria
  Oyo State Yoruba
  Ondo State (Riverine) Ijaw
  Ondo State Yoruba
  Kwara State Yoruba
  Bauchi State Hausa
Brazil
USA
  Florida English
Benin
  Save Yoruba, French

His Grace Mission
Box 119, Awka
Anambra State, NIGERIA

Rev. Ephraim Ndife
Organized: 1978   Pentecostal
MISSIONARIES IN SERVICE
(1988) 18
AAGR = N/A
Foreign missionaries in 1988:   0
FIELDS OF SERVICE
Nigeria

Anambra State Ibo
Rivers State Ikwerre

Holiness Assembly
PO Box 3149, Festac Town PO
Lagos, NIGERIA

Michael A. Adeoye
Organized: 1982   Pentecostal
MISSIONARIES IN SERVICE
(1985)   6   (1988) 16
AAGR = 39%
Foreign missionaries in 1988:   1
FIELDS OF SERVICE
USA
  New York Blacks
Nigeria
  Oyo State Oyo
  Akwa Ibom State Anaang, Efik
  Ogun State Ijebu, Egba, Awori
  Rivers State Ikwerre, Ijaw, Ibibio
  Ondo State Akure, Ekiti, Ondo

John 3:16 Ministries
PO Box 1508, Aba, NIGERIA

Rev. Samuel Ajayi
Organized: 1980   Pentecostal
MISSIONARIES IN SERVICE
(1980)   2   (1985)   7   (1988) 18
AAGR = 32%
Foreign missionaries in 1988:   5
FIELDS OF SERVICE
Ghana
Liberia
Nigeria
  Northwestern States Hausa, Yoruba
Kenya

Koma Hills Mission
PO Box 748, Yola, NIGERIA

Rev. I.T. Micah
Organized: 1983   Pentecostal
MISSIONARIES IN SERVICE
(1988) 10
AAGR = N/A
Foreign missionaries in 1988:   0

FIELDS OF SERVICE
Nigeria
Gangola State Koma, Umon, Verre

Last Days Messengers Mission, Inc.
PO Box 196, Okigwe
Imo State, NIGERIA

Dr. Gabriel E. Nwokoro
Organized: Not reported.   Pentecostal
MISSIONARIES IN SERVICE
(1972)   8   (1980) 34   (1985) 64
(1988) 86
AAGR = 16%
Foreign missionaries in 1988:   1
FIELDS OF SERVICE
Nigeria
Lagos State Yoruba
Imo State Igbo
Bendel State Idaw
Benue State Tiv
Niger State Nupe, Ginari, Hausa
Bauchi State Hausa
Kaduna State Hausa
Cameroon

Life Transformers' Mission
PO Box 10910, Okpoko Via Onitsha
Anambra State, NIGERIA

Rev. Jeol C. Anisiji
Organized: 1982   Pentecostal
MISSIONARIES IN SERVICE
(1988) 10
AAGR = N/A
Foreign missionaries in 1988:   0
FIELDS OF SERVICE
Nigeria
Anambra State Ibo, Edo
Bendel State Ikwo

Life and Light Apostolic Mission
PO Box 90, Ikot Ekpene, NIGERIA

Brother N.A. Umoh
Organized: 1960   Nondenominational

MISSIONARIES IN SERVICE
(1972) 40   (1975) 40   (1978) 90
(1980) 90   (1988) 203*
AAGR = N/A
Foreign Missionaries in 1988: Not reported.
FIELDS OF SERVICE
Not reported.

NKST Mission Board
PA, Mkar, Bendel State, NIGERIA

Rev. Gberihwa
Organized: Not reported.
MISSIONARIES IN SERVICE
(1980) 14   (1982) 20   (1984) 25
(1988) 45*
AAGR = N/A
Foreign Missionaries in 1988: Not reported.
FIELDS OF SERVICE
Not reported.

National Evangelical Mission
PO Box 34, Aguata
Anambra State, NIGERIA

Rev. Benjamin Ogbuozobe
Organized: 1971   Pentecostal
MISSIONARIES IN SERVICE
(1972) 4   (1980) 30   (1985) 120
(1988) 150
AAGR = 25%
Foreign missionaries in 1988:   1
FIELDS OF SERVICE
Nigeria
Borno State Kanuri, Hausa
Niger State Gwari, Hausa
Benue State Tiv
Bendel State Benin, Ido
Kano State Hausa
Cross River State Efik, Calabar
Gangola State Hausa, Kutepu, Jukum
Akwa Ibom State Efik, Ibibio
Equatorial Guinea
Malabo Spanish

National Evangelistic Crusade, Inc.
PO Box 935, Yaba, Lagos, NIGERIA

Rev. Emmanuel Aderdtimi
Organized: 1973
Independent Evangelical
MISSIONARIES IN SERVICE
(1988)   6
AAGR = N/A
Foreign missionaries in 1988:   0
FIELDS OF SERVICE
Nigeria
  Ogun State Muslims, Idol
     Worshippers, Christians
  Lagos State Muslims, Idol
     Worshippers, Christians
  Kwara State Muslims, Idol
     Worshippers, Christians
  Ondo State Muslims, Idol
     Worshippers, Christians
  Oyo State Muslims, Idol Worshippers,
     Christians

Nigeria for Christ Revival
PO Box 35, Ilesa, NIGERIA

Rev. A. Ola Adewale
Organized: 1985   Evangelical
MISSIONARIES IN SERVICE
(1985) 13   (1988) 26
AAGR = 26%
Foreign missionaries in 1988:   0
FIELDS OF SERVICE
Nigeria
  Northern States Hausa
  Eastern States Ibo
  Western States Yoruba

Nigerian Baptist Convention
PMB 5113, Ibadan, NIGERIA

Rev. Ola Akande
Organized: 1914
MISSIONARIES IN SERVICE
(1972) 10   (1975) 16   (1978) 10
(1980) 14   (1988) 20*

AAGR = N/A
Foreign Missionaries in 1988: Not
reported.
FIELDS OF SERVICE
Not reported.

Nigerian Christian Ministries
PO Box 2168, Mushin, Lagos, NIGERIA

Rev. Canon C. Obasi
Organized: 1985   Nondenominational
MISSIONARIES IN SERVICE
Further information withheld at
agency's request.

Pentecostal Faith Church
Edem Idim Ibakesi
Nung Ubim, Ikot Ekpene, NIGERIA

Rev. O. Ekanem
Organized: 1972   Pentecostal
MISSIONARIES IN SERVICE
(1972)   4   (1980)   6   (1985) 10
(1988) 14
AAGR =   8%
Foreign missionaries in 1988:   0
FIELDS OF SERVICE
Nigeria
  Itu Ikpe, Ikot, Nkon, Eupene
  Akwa Ibom State Ibaesi
  Cross River (Calabar) Calabar, Hyo
  Ikono Akpeyak, Ikpe, Ikono,
     Mbiabong, Hkaan
  Cross River State Nungu, Hkaan

Pentecostal Mission
PO Box 225, Uyo
Akwa Ibom State, NIGERIA

Rev. E. Jackson
Organized: 1964   Pentecostal
MISSIONARIES IN SERVICE
(1988) 36
AAGR = N/A
Foreign missionaries in 1988:   12
FIELDS OF SERVICE
Cameroon

Douala Area Ibibio, Ibo, Ube

Rescue Team Evangelistic Ministries
PO Box 39, Obiaruku
Bendel State, NIGERIA

Rev. B.F. Umukoro
Organized: 1980   Evangelical
MISSIONARIES IN SERVICE
(1988)   6
AAGR = N/A
Foreign missionaries in 1988:   0
FIELDS OF SERVICE
Nigeria
  Bendel State Ibo, Urhobo, Benin,
    Ukwuani-Aboh

Revival Mission Inc., The
PO Box 1984, Calabar
Cross River State, NIGERIA

Rev. M. Imaikop
Organized: 1984   Nondenominational
MISSIONARIES IN SERVICE
Further information withheld at
agency's request.

Sowers for Christ Ministries
UIPO Box 9044, Ibadan, NIGERIA

Rev. Lawrence A. Fadeyi
Organized: 1975   Evangelical
MISSIONARIES IN SERVICE
(1980)   7   (1985)   10   (1988)   8
AAGR =   2%
Foreign missionaries in 1988:   3
FIELDS OF SERVICE
Not reported.

Thy Word is Truth Ministries
PO Box 1782, Sokoto
Sokoto State, NIGERIA

Nmeribe E. Elisha
Organized: 1982   Pentecostal
MISSIONARIES IN SERVICE
(1985)   7   (1988)   9

AAGR =   9%
Foreign missionaries in 1988:   6
FIELDS OF SERVICE
Ghana
  Volta Region Ewe
  Eastern Region Akan, Twi
  Greater Accra Region
    Ga-Adangme-Krobo
Nigeria
  Rivers State Ijaw, Kalabari
  Imo State Ibo, Igbo
  Sokoto State Hausa

United Evangelical Mission
PO Box 2037, Calabar
Cross River State, NIGERIA

Rev. E.J. Usoroh
Organized: 1985   Pentecostal
MISSIONARIES IN SERVICE
(1985)   2   (1988)   4
AAGR =   26%
Foreign missionaries in 1988:   0
FIELDS OF SERVICE
Nigeria
  Cross River State Ekoi
  Akwa Ibom State Ibibio

United Missionary Church of Africa, Missions Board
PO Box 171, Ilorin
Kwara State, NIGERIA

Rev. Olu Peters
Organized: 1987   Evangelical
MISSIONARIES IN SERVICE
(1988)   1
AAGR = N/A
Foreign missionaries in 1988:   0
FIELDS OF SERVICE
Nigeria
  Niger State Kamuku

Universal Missions International
PO Box 1680, Uyo
Akwa Ibom State, NIGERIA

Dr. Joseph Sam
Organized: 1970   Interdenominational
MISSIONARIES IN SERVICE
Further information withheld at agency's request.

West African Episcopal Church Mission
St. Stephen Cathedral
76 Adeniji Adele Road
Lagos, NIGERIA

Patriarch Daniel Olarimiwa
Organized: 1903   Episcopal
MISSIONARIES IN SERVICE
(1972) 72   (1975) 76   (1978) 80
(1980) 84   (1988) 98*
AAGR = N/A
Foreign Missionaries in 1988: Not reported.
FIELDS OF SERVICE
Not reported.

Word of God Mission International
PO Box 562, Calabar
Cross River State, NIGERIA

Rev. Felix Esinwang
Organized: 1982   Evangelical
MISSIONARIES IN SERVICE
(1985) 3   (1988) 3
AAGR = 0%
Foreign missionaries in 1988:   0
FIELDS OF SERVICE
Nigeria
Cross River State Ejagham, Bekwarra
Akwa Ibom State Ibibio, Anaang

Word of Life Mission
GPO Box 2312, Dugba
Ibadan, NIGERIA

Rev. David Oyedeji
Organized: 1984   Pentecostal
MISSIONARIES IN SERVICE
(1985) 3   (1988) 5

AAGR = 19%
Foreign missionaries in 1988:   0
FIELDS OF SERVICE
Nigeria
Ogun State Ijebu, Egba, Yoruba

SIERRA LEONE

Bread of Life Mission
PO Box 1166
Freetown, SIERRA LEONE

Rev. D.W. Spaine-Young
Organized: 1971   Pentecostal
MISSIONARIES IN SERVICE
(1972) 29   (1980) 41   (1985) 34
(1988) 64
AAGR = 5%
Foreign missionaries in 1988:   0
FIELDS OF SERVICE
Sierra Leone
Southern Province Mende
Western Area Creole
Eastern Province Mende, Kono
Northern Province Temne, Loko

Faith Baptist Church
PO Box 47, Makeni, SIERRA LEONE

Rev. A.A. Bangura
Organized: 1986   Baptist
MISSIONARIES IN SERVICE
(1985) 21   (1988) 25*
AAGR = N/A
Foreign missionaries in 1988: Not reported.
FIELDS OF SERVICE
Sierra Leone
Northern Province Limba

New Life Challenge Ministry
PO Box 522, Freetown, SIERRA LEONE

Rev. Osman Mansaray
Organized: 1985   Assemblies of God
MISSIONARIES IN SERVICE
(1985) 9   (1988) 14

AAGR = 16%
Foreign missionaries in 1988: 0
FIELDS OF SERVICE
Sierra Leone
  All Provinces Creole, Temne, Mende, Limba, Kissi, Loko
  Western Area Creole, Temne, Mende, Limba, Kissi, Loko

SOUTH AFRICA

Africa Evangelical Fellowship
Rowland House, Montrose Ave.
Claremont 7700, SOUTH AFRICA

Rev. L.E. Glass
Organized: 1946   Interdenominational
MISSIONARIES IN SERVICE
(1980) 22   (1988) 35*
AAGR = N/A
Foreign missionaries in 1988: Not reported.
FIELDS OF SERVICE
Not reported.

Apostolic Faith Mission of South Africa
PO Box 89187
Lyndhurst 2106, SOUTH AFRICA

Dr. F.P. Moller
Organized: 1907   Denominational
MISSIONARIES IN SERVICE
(1972) 60   (1975) 72   (1978) 80
(1980) 83   (1988) 115*
AAGR = N/A
Foreign missionaries in 1988: Not reported.
FIELDS OF SERVICE
Not reported.

Bet-el Evangelistic Action
PO Box 23227
Innesdale 0031, SOUTH AFRICA

Rev. Robbie Engelbrecht

Organized: 1974   Evangelical
MISSIONARIES IN SERVICE
(1980) 23   (1985) 26   (1988) 34
AAGR = 5%
Foreign missionaries in 1988: 6
FIELDS OF SERVICE
South Africa
  Cape Province Ciskei, Transkei
  Transvaal Province Northern Sotho, Venda
  Natal Province Zulu
Lesotho Leshoto

Evangelical Bible Seminary of South Africa
SOUTH AFRICA

Organized: Not reported.
MISSIONARIES IN SERVICE
(1980) 2   (1982) 5   (1984) 9
(1988) 41*
AAGR = N/A
Foreign missionaries in 1988: Not reported.
FIELDS OF SERVICE
Not reported.

Frontline Fellowship
PO Box 74, Newlands 7725
Cape Town, SOUTH AFRICA

Rev. Peter Hammond
Organized: 1982   Evangelical
MISSIONARIES IN SERVICE
(1985) 6   (1988) 8
AAGR = 10%
Foreign missionaries in 1988: 6
FIELDS OF SERVICE
Zimbabwe
  Manicaland Province Shona
Mozambique
  Manica Province Sena, Shona, Chindau
  Zambezia Province Sena, Lomwe, Makua
Namibia Ovambo, Afrikaans, Kavango

Angola
Southern Area Chokwe, Ovimbundu
South Africa
Venda District Venda

Full Gospel Church of God in South Africa
PO Box 40, Irene 1675, SOUTH AFRICA

M.L. Badenhorst
Organized: 1910   Denominational
MISSIONARIES IN SERVICE
(1972) 21   (1975) 29   (1978) 29
(1980) 29   (1988) 40*
AAGR = N/A
Foreign missionaries in 1988: Not reported.
FIELDS OF SERVICE
Not reported.

Leprosy Mission, The
PO Box 890527
Lyndhurst 2106, SOUTH AFRICA

Rev. L.A. Wiseman
Organized: 1949   Nondenominational
MISSIONARIES IN SERVICE
(1972) 15   (1980) 21   (1985) 48
(1988) 69
AAGR = 10%
Foreign missionaries in 1988:   6
FIELDS OF SERVICE
South Africa
Transkei District Xhosa
Transvaal Province English, Afrikaans, Southern Sotho, Zulu, Tswana, Pedi
Kwazulu District Zulu
Ciskei District Xhosa
Cape Province English, Afrikaans
Natal Province English, Afrikaans
Orange Free State English, Afrikaans, Southern Sotho
Swaziland Siswati

Reformed Independent Churches Association
PO Box 32309
Braamfontein 2017, SOUTH AFRICA

Rev. Isaac P.B. Moko
Organized: 1970   Interdenominational
MISSIONARIES IN SERVICE
(1980) 407   (1988) 643*
AAGR = N/A
Foreign missionaries in 1988: Not reported.
FIELDS OF SERVICE
Not reported.

SWAZILAND

Africa's Hope Crusade
PO Box 868, Mbabane, SWAZILAND

Rev. Aaron B. Gamedze
Organized: 1955   Nondenominational
MISSIONARIES IN SERVICE
(1972) 2   (1975) 4   (1978) 4
(1980) 4   (1984) 16   (1985) 24
(1988) 28
AAGR = 18%
Foreign missionaries in 1988: 28
FIELDS OF SERVICE
Zimbabwe
Bulawayo Shona, Ndebele
Mashonaland East (Harare City) Shona, Ndebele
Swaziland Swazi
Mozambique
Six provinces Four Tribes
South Africa
Zululand Province Zulu
Zambia
Lusaka Province Two main tribes

TANZANIA

Africa Mission International
PO Box 2664, Arusha, TANZANIA

Rev. Nixon N. Issangya

Organized: Not reported.
Nondenominational
MISSIONARIES IN SERVICE
(1972) 46   (1980) 52   (1985) 64
(1988) 70
AAGR = 3%
Foreign missionaries in 1988: 20
FIELDS OF SERVICE
Tanzania
 Arusha Area Arusha, Meru, Maasai

Christ Ambassadors Evangelistic Team
PO Box 2678, Arusha, TANZANIA

Rev. Odrick Nassary
Organized: 1986   Nondenominational
MISSIONARIES IN SERVICE
(1988) 24
AAGR = N/A
Foreign missionaries in 1988: 0
FIELDS OF SERVICE
Tanzania
 Mbulu Mangati
 Dodoma Region Wagogo
 Arusha Area Residents, Schools
 Ngorongoro Massai
 Kiteto Massai

Evangelical Lutheran Church of Tanzania
PO Box 3033, Arusha, TANZANIA

Rev. Uswege Mwakalinga
Organized: Not reported.
Interdenominational, Lutheran
MISSIONARIES IN SERVICE
(1980) 2   (1988) 3*
AAGR = N/A
Foreign missionaries in 1988: Not reported.
FIELDS OF SERVICE
Not reported.

House to House Evangelical and Prayer Ministry
PO Box 22274
Dar es Salaam, TANZANIA

Cyprian Sallu
Organized: 1972   Evangelical
MISSIONARIES IN SERVICE
(1988) 30
AAGR = N/A
Foreign missionaries in 1988: 0
FIELDS OF SERVICE
Tanzania
 Zanzibar Kiswahili, English
 Tanga Kiswahili, English
 Morogoro Kiswahili, English
 Njombe Kiswahili, English
 Dar Es Salaam Region Kiswahili, English
 Mbeya Region Kiswahili, English
 Dodoma Region Kiswahili, English
 Iringa Kiswahili, English
 Mwanza Kiswahili, English

Redemption Gospel Team
PO Box 72, Arusha
USA River, TANZANIA

Rev. Michael P. Nnko
Organized: 1983   Pentecostal
MISSIONARIES IN SERVICE
(1985) 24   (1988) 24
AAGR = 0%
Foreign missionaries in 1988: 0
FIELDS OF SERVICE
Tanzania
 All Provinces All Peoples

Stewards of the Gospel Team, The
PO Box 2692, Arusha, TANZANIA

Rev. Nuhu Mkirumi
Organized: 1983   Pentecostal
MISSIONARIES IN SERVICE
(1985) 13   (1988) 17

AAGR = 9%
Foreign missionaries in 1988: 0

FIELDS OF SERVICE

Tanzania
Southern Area Makonde, Makua, Yao
Coastal Area Students at University of
Dar Es Salaam

UGANDA

All Nations Mobile Bible Training Centres
PO Box 30825
Nakivubo-Kampala, UGANDA

Ponsiano S. Lwakatale
Organized: 1985　Nondenominational

MISSIONARIES IN SERVICE
(1988) 10
AAGR = N/A
Foreign missionaries in 1988: 0

FIELDS OF SERVICE

Uganda
Western Province Rukiga, Runyakole
West Nile Province Ruo
Kasese Rukotzo
Hoima Runyoro, Rutoro

Back to the Bible Truth Evangelistic Team, Inc.
PO Box 15100, Kampala, UGANDA

Rev. Alex Willy Mitala
Organized: 1979　Nondenominational

MISSIONARIES IN SERVICE
(1980) 24　　(1985) 34　　(1988) 48
AAGR = 9%
Foreign missionaries in 1988: 2

FIELDS OF SERVICE
Not reported.

Eastern Orthodox Church
PO Box 1487, Kampala, UGANDA

Rev. S.K. Kasasa
Organized: 1929　Interdenominational

MISSIONARIES IN SERVICE
(1972) 86　　(1975) 135　　(1980) 22
(1988) 6*
AAGR = N/A
Foreign missionaries in 1988: Not
reported.

FIELDS OF SERVICE
Not reported.

Gospel Mission of Uganda
PO Box 2560, Kampala, UGANDA

Rev. J.K. Musoke
Organized: 1961　　　　Pentecostal

MISSIONARIES IN SERVICE
(1988) 406
AAGR = N/A
Foreign missionaries in 1988: 136

FIELDS OF SERVICE

Uganda
All Provinces Luganda, Shahili, Luo,
Runyoro, Rutoro, Runyankole,
Rukiga

Holy Gospel Mission
PO Box 1368, Kampala, UGANDA

Bishop G.W. Mubiru
Organized: 1981　Holy Gospel Mission

MISSIONARIES IN SERVICE
(1985) 29　　(1988) 42*
AAGR = N/A
Foreign missionaries in 1988: Not
reported.

FIELDS OF SERVICE

Uganda
Western Province Ankute, Toro
Central Province Baganda

Messengers of God International Foundation
PO Box 8637, Kampala, UGANDA

Rev. Charles Kato
Organized: 1986　　　　Pentecostal

MISSIONARIES IN SERVICE
(1988) 25

AAGR = N/A
Foreign missionaries in 1988:   0
FIELDS OF SERVICE
Uganda
  Central Province Luganda
  Eastern Province Soga
  Western Province Nvoro, Nkope
  Eastern Province Tororo

Triumphant Christian Centre
PO Box 936, Kampala, UGANDA

Sewava-Kigozi
Organized: 1985   Pentecostal
MISSIONARIES IN SERVICE
(1985) 53   (1988) 249
AAGR = 67%
Foreign missionaries in 1988:   2
FIELDS OF SERVICE
Uganda
  Central Province Kampala City
  Eastern Province Basoga, Bagwere,
    Banyore
  Northern Province Lwo, Lugbara,
    Gulu, Arua
  Western Province Nyankole, Kiga,
    Nyoro, Toro

ZAIRE

21st Evangelical Episcopalian Church of Zaire
BP 216, Kisangani, Region du
Haute-Zaire, ZAIRE

Bishop Eveque Assani Baraka
Organized: Not reported.
MISSIONARIES IN SERVICE
(1972) 20   (1975) 40   (1980) 60
(1982) 80   (1984) 100   (1988) 149*
AAGR = N/A
Foreign missionaries in 1988: Not
reported.
FIELDS OF SERVICE
Zaire
  Ubundu Balengola

Nord Shaba Region Baluba
Shaba Region Baluba
Kipushi Baluba
Haut-Zaire Region Bahema
Basok Bakumu
Sud Shaba Region Baluba
Aketi Bangelema, Babenza
Kisangani Balendu
Kanyama Baluba

Africa Missionary Evangelistic Committee
BP 2881, Lubumbashi, ZAIRE

Bishop Hitshika Mayuke
Organized: 1978   Pentecostal
MISSIONARIES IN SERVICE
(1988) 31
AAGR = N/A
Foreign missionaries in 1988:   8
FIELDS OF SERVICE
Tanzania
  Arusha Area Massai
France   French
Zaire
  Kivu Region Babemba
  Kasai Region Baluba
  Kinshasa Region Bayaka
  Shaba Region Luena
Zambia
  Lusaka Province Balenje
  Kitwe Babemba

African Baptist Episcopal Church (CEBA)
BP 3866, Lubumbashi
Lubumbashi, Shaba, ZAIRE

Bishop Kabwe-Ka-Leza
Organized: 1956   Interdenominational
MISSIONARIES IN SERVICE
(1980) 4   (1988) 9*
AAGR = N/A
Foreign missionaries in 1988: Not
reported.
FIELDS OF SERVICE
Not reported.

Baptist Church of Kinshasa
BP 9855, Kinshasa, ZAIRE

Rev. Nkuba Kalunda
Organized: 1976   Baptist
MISSIONARIES IN SERVICE
(1985) 12   (1988) 6
AAGR = -20%
Foreign missionaries in 1988:   2
FIELDS OF SERVICE
Zaire
  Kasai Occidental Region Kanyoka
  Shaba Region Lamba

Christian Association for World Evangelism
BP 18503, Kinshasa 13, ZAIRE

Rev. Ngoy Yanghuba Safi
Organized: 1984   Pentecostal
MISSIONARIES IN SERVICE
(1988) 15
AAGR = N/A
Foreign missionaries in 1988:   4
FIELDS OF SERVICE
Cameroon
  Douala Area (Yaounde)
Zaire
  Kasai Oriental Region Luba
  Kivu Region Swahili
  Kasai Occidental Region Luba
  Bas-Zaire Region Kongo
  Shaba Region Swahili
Zambia
  Lusaka Province
Nigeria
  Lagos State
Ivory Coast
  Abidjan
Central African Republic
  Bangui-Bangoran (Mbaiki)

Christian Community of Pentecostal Assemblies in Zaire
Rue Mabwa No. 4, Qyartier Manenga, Zone de Ngaliema, ZAIRE

Mwimba Tsasa
Organized: Not reported.
MISSIONARIES IN SERVICE
(1972) 98   (1975) 66   (1980) 464
(1982) 464   (1984) 464   (1988) 670*
AAGR = N/A
Foreign missionaries in 1988: Not reported.
FIELDS OF SERVICE
Zaire
  Bas-Zaire Region C.C.A.P.Z.
  Kinshasa Region C.C.A.P.Z.

Church Union of the Zairean Baptist Churches (CUEBZ)
BP 78, Kikwit 2, Bandunda, ZAIRE

Rev. Wai-Wai Dibudi
Organized: 1960   Denominational
MISSIONARIES IN SERVICE
(1980) 2   (1988) 4*
AAGR = N/A
Foreign missionaries in 1988: Not reported.
FIELDS OF SERVICE
Not reported.

Church of Christ in the World
BP 10963, Kinshasa 1, ZAIRE

Nzolele Nluengisi-Nkuka
Organized: 1986   Independent
MISSIONARIES IN SERVICE
Further information withheld at agency's request.

Churches of Christ of Zaire, Sankuru Region
BP 24, Kole via Lodja, ZAIRE

Rev. Elembe Iwuwd
Organized: 1936   Denominational
MISSIONARIES IN SERVICE
(1980) 5   (1988) 11*
AAGR = N/A
Foreign missionaries in 1988: Not reported.
FIELDS OF SERVICE
Not reported.

Community of Christian Unity of Zaire
BP 20139, Kinshasa 21, ZAIRE

Rev. Lukwikila Nsambu
Organized: 1970   Nondenominational
MISSIONARIES IN SERVICE
(1988) 38
AAGR = N/A
Foreign missionaries in 1988:   1
FIELDS OF SERVICE
Zaire

Evangelical Church of Central Africa
BP 143, Bunia, ZAIRE

Rev. Uchanda Polepole
Organized: Not reported.
MISSIONARIES IN SERVICE
(1984) 2   (1988) 3*
AAGR = N/A
Foreign missionaries in 1988: Not reported.
FIELDS OF SERVICE
Not reported.

Evangelical Church of Christ in Shaba
BP 4296, Lubumbashi, Shaba, ZAIRE

Organized: Not reported.

MISSIONARIES IN SERVICE
(1975) 4   (1978) 4   (1980) 6
(1982) 10   (1988) 22*
AAGR = N/A
Foreign missionaries in 1988: Not reported.
FIELDS OF SERVICE
Not reported.

Evangelical Church of Zaire
BP 36, Luozi, ZAIRE

Rev. Ntontolo L. Kitete
Organized: 1881   Evangelical
MISSIONARIES IN SERVICE
(1972) 44   (1975) 37   (1978) 24
(1980) 109   (1988) 242*
AAGR = N/A
Foreign missionaries in 1988: Not reported.
FIELDS OF SERVICE
Zaire

Evangelical Church of the Deuvres Saints (CEDS)
BP 10963, Kinshasa 1, ZAIRE

Nzolele Nluengisi Nku
Organized: 1963   Denominational
MISSIONARIES IN SERVICE
(1980) 10   (1982) 141   (1984) 250
(1988) 373*
AAGR = N/A
Foreign missionaries in 1988: Not reported.
FIELDS OF SERVICE
Not reported.

Evangelical Community of Zaire
Eglise Du Christ Au Zaire, B.P. 36 Louzi, Bas, ZAIRE

L.K. Ntontolo
Organized: Not reported.
MISSIONARIES IN SERVICE
(1972) 4   (1975) 4   (1980) 4

(1982) 4   (1984) 4   (1988) 4*
AAGR = N/A
Foreign missionaries in 1988: Not
reported.

FIELDS OF SERVICE

Congo
Zanaga Pygmees

Evangelical Episcopal Church of Zaire

BP 1520, Lubumbashi, Shaba, ZAIRE

Yumba Kitna Musoya K
Organized: 1932   Denominational

MISSIONARIES IN SERVICE

(1980) 8   (1988) 18*
AAGR = N/A
Foreign missionaries in 1988: Not
reported.

FIELDS OF SERVICE

Zaire

Evangelical Free Church of Zaire

BP 3020, Kinshasa-Gombe, ZAIRE

Muhung Mwanana Ndumba Tembo
Organized: 1969   Denominational

MISSIONARIES IN SERVICE

(1980) 12   (1984) 90   (1988) 134*
AAGR = N/A
Foreign missionaries in 1988: Not
reported.

FIELDS OF SERVICE

Zaire
 Bandundu Region
 Kinshasa Region
 Shaba Region
 Kasai Occidental Region

Evangelical Mission

BP 12763, Kinshasa 1, ZAIRE

Thipoy Tsitang
Organized: 1980   Evangelical

MISSIONARIES IN SERVICE

(1988) 12

AAGR = N/A
Foreign missionaries in 1988:   4

FIELDS OF SERVICE

Ivory Coast
 Abidjan Plusiens, Ethnics
Zaire
 Bandundu Region
 Shaba Region

Holy Spirit Church in Africa

BP 10172, ZAIRE

Rev. Mangitukwa Lukombo
Organized: 1961   Denominational

MISSIONARIES IN SERVICE

(1972) 20   (1975) 22   (1978) 22
(1980) 28   (1988) 39*
AAGR = N/A
Foreign missionaries in 1988: Not
reported.

FIELDS OF SERVICE

Not reported.

Light Church in Zaire

BP 10498, Kinshasa 1, ZAIRE

Patriarche Kayuwa
Organized: 1966   Church of Christ

MISSIONARIES IN SERVICE

(1988) 40
AAGR = N/A
Foreign missionaries in 1988:   0

FIELDS OF SERVICE

Zaire Tshiluba, Lingala, Swahili,
 Kikongo

Lutheran Church in Zaire

BP 12575, Kinshasa 1, ZAIRE

Rev. Matuta Lulenda
Organized: 1966   Lutheran

MISSIONARIES IN SERVICE

(1988) 126
AAGR = N/A
Foreign missionaries in 1988:   1

FIELDS OF SERVICE

Zaire

Kinshasa Region Bangala, Bayaka,
  Mono
Bas-Zaire Region Bakongo, Bapende,
  Bangala, Banbunda

New Life Evangelization Association

BP 245, Mbujimayi, ZAIRE

Rev. Kabangu-Kapepula Wak
Organized: 1984   Evangelical

MISSIONARIES IN SERVICE
(1988) 24
AAGR = N/A
Foreign missionaries in 1988:   0

FIELDS OF SERVICE
Zaire
  Shaba Region Bemba, Sanga, Lunda,
    Luba, Shaba
  Bas-Zaire Region Kongo
  Haut-Zaire Region Lokele, Mongo
  Kasai Occidental Region Lulua, Kuba,
    Kete, Tshiokue, Lualua, Bindi
  Kinshasa Region Bateke, Yaka
  Equatuer Region Mongo, Gbande
  Kasai Oriental Region Luba, Songe,
    Tetela, Kanyoka
  Bandundu Region Shilele, Sakata
  Kivu Region Bashi, Bareka, Bakusu

Pentecost Christian Church of Zaire

BP 10679, Kinshasa 1, ZAIRE

Rev. Tsassa Dinasa D.
Organized: 1976   Denominational

MISSIONARIES IN SERVICE
(1980) 278   (1988) 617*
AAGR = N/A
Foreign missionaries in 1988: Not
reported.

FIELDS OF SERVICE
Not reported.

Rama Full Gospel Center

BP 1231, Likasi, ZAIRE

Majila Lukama

Organized: 1981   Pentecostal

MISSIONARIES IN SERVICE
(1988) 10
AAGR = N/A
Foreign missionaries in 1988:   6

FIELDS OF SERVICE
Zaire
  Shaba Region
  Kasai Region
  Kinshasa Region

S/P Siforzal Masina Nganguele

BP 10064, Kinshasa 21, ZAIRE

Rev. Matuka Sumbulangongo
Organized: 1983   Assemblies of God

MISSIONARIES IN SERVICE
(1988)   8
AAGR = N/A
Foreign missionaries in 1988:   0

FIELDS OF SERVICE
Zaire

United Church of the Holy Spirit

BP 11763, Kinshasa 1, ZAIRE

M'Panya Mamba
Organized: Not reported.
Nondenominational

MISSIONARIES IN SERVICE
(1988) 16
AAGR = N/A
Foreign missionaries in 1988:   0

FIELDS OF SERVICE
Zaire
  Kinshasa Region

ZAMBIA

Apostolic Church in Zambia

PO Box 250092, Ndola, ZAMBIA

Hans Peter Pedersen
Organized: 1957   Interdenominational

MISSIONARIES IN SERVICE
(1972) 4   (1975) 6   (1978) 9
(1980) 8   (1982) 15   (1988) 33*
AAGR = N/A
Foreign missionaries in 1988: Not reported.

FIELDS OF SERVICE

Zambia
  Copper Belt Province Africans

Apostolic Faith Holy Gospel Church (ARONI)
PO Box 71339, Ndola, ZAMBIA

Rev. Z. Limbango
Organized: 1946   Interdenominational

MISSIONARIES IN SERVICE
(1975) 9   (1980) 12   (1982) 12
(1988) 15*
AAGR = N/A
Foreign missionaries in 1988: Not reported.

FIELDS OF SERVICE

Zambia
  Northwestern Region Luchazi, Luvale

Baptist Convention of Zambia
PO Box 730127, Kawambua, ZAMBIA

Rev. A.P. Chali
Organized: 1982   Baptist

MISSIONARIES IN SERVICE
(1988) 15
AAGR = N/A
Foreign missionaries in 1988: 0

FIELDS OF SERVICE

Zambia
  Lusaka Province Nyanja
  Copper Belt Province
  Central Province Bemba
  Northern Province Lala, Kaonde
  Western Province

Baptist Urban Outreach
Lusaka Baptist Church, Box 30636
Lusaka, ZAMBIA

Rev. Joe M. Simfukwe
Organized: 1987   Baptist

MISSIONARIES IN SERVICE
(1978) 4   (1980) 4   (1988) 17
AAGR = 16%
Foreign missionaries in 1988:   0

FIELDS OF SERVICE

Zambia
  Eastern Province Nsenga, Tumbuka,
    Ceba, English
  Luapula Province Bemba, English
  Southern Province Tonga, English
  Copper Belt Province Lamba, Bemba,
    English
  Lusaka Province Nyanja, English

Christ Liveth Mission
PO Box 71954, Ndola, ZAMBIA

Rev. Patterson Kajimalwendo
Organized: 1982   Evangelical

MISSIONARIES IN SERVICE
(1985) 19   (1988) 19
AAGR = 0%
Foreign missionaries in 1988:   0

FIELDS OF SERVICE

Zambia
  Copper Belt Province Bemba
  Northwestern Province Kaonde
  Central Province Kaonde, Ila

Christian Tract Distributors
PO Box 40859, Mufulira, ZAMBIA

Rev. Peter S. Kiboko
Organized: 1976   Nondenominational

MISSIONARIES IN SERVICE
(1980) 12   (1985) 12   (1988) 6
AAGR = -7%
Foreign missionaries in 1988:   8

FIELDS OF SERVICE

Angola
  Luanda Province Luvale
Zambia
  Northwestern Province Kaonde,
    Lunda, Luvale

Copper Belt Province Bemba, Kaonde,
  Lambe
Zaire Swahili
Tanzania
  Mbeya Region Swahili

Churches of Christ
PO Box 22297, Kitwe, ZAMBIA

Organized: 1910   Church of Christ
        MISSIONARIES IN SERVICE
(1972) 4   (1980) 16   (1985) 33
(1988) 42
AAGR = 16%
Foreign missionaries in 1988:   14
           FIELDS OF SERVICE
United Kingdom
  England English, Asians
  Wales Welsh
Angola
Zambia
  Southern Province Tonga
  Western Province Lozi
  Northern Province Bemba
  Central Province Nyanja
  Eastern Province Nyanja
  Northwestern Province Lunda,
    Luvale, Kaonde
  Several Provinces All Peoples
Zimbabwe
  Matabeleland Province Matabele
Zaire
  Shaba Region Bemba, Lunda

Dorthea Mission
PO Box 32696, Lusaka, ZAMBIA

H. Von Staden
Organized: 1942   Interdenominational
        MISSIONARIES IN SERVICE
(1980) 5   (1988) 10*
AAGR = N/A
Foreign missionaries in 1988: Not
reported.
           FIELDS OF SERVICE
Not reported.

Evangelical Church in Zambia
PO Box 31981, Lusaka, ZAMBIA

Enoch Masuhwa
Organized: Not reported.   Evangelical
        MISSIONARIES IN SERVICE
(1980) 2   (1985) 4   (1988) 8
AAGR = 19%
Foreign missionaries in 1988:   2
           FIELDS OF SERVICE
Namibia
  Kavango Luchazi
Zambia
  Central Province Lamba
  Northwestern Province Lunda
  Northern Province Bemba

International Gospel Crusaders Ministries
PO Box 70329, Ndola, ZAMBIA

Rev. Christopher Muliokela
Organized: 1985   Pentecostal
        MISSIONARIES IN SERVICE
(1985) 12   (1988) 28
AAGR = 33%
Foreign missionaries in 1988:   1
           FIELDS OF SERVICE
Zambia
  Copper Belt Province
Zaire
  Shaba Region Lingala, Swahili

Operation Rescue Group Ministry
PO Box 35202, Lusaka, ZAMBIA

Rev. G.M. Simwinga
Organized: 1982   Evangelical
        MISSIONARIES IN SERVICE
(1988) 15
AAGR = N/A
Foreign missionaries in 1988:   1
           FIELDS OF SERVICE
Tanzania

Tunduma Area Mwachusa
Zambia
Eastern Province Nsenga, Chewa
Southern Province Tonga
Northern Province Bemba, Namwanga

Pentecostal Fellowship Association of Zambia

PO Box 31337, Lusaka, ZAMBIA

John H. Mambo
Organized: 1987   Pentecostal

MISSIONARIES IN SERVICE

(1972) 15   (1980) 25   (1985) 34
(1988) 49
AAGR = 8%
Foreign missionaries in 1988:   9

FIELDS OF SERVICE

Zambia   Nationals
Angola   Nationals
Australia   Nationals
Tanzania   Nationals
Mozambique   Nationals

Pentecostal Holiness Church

PO Box 1751, Kitine, Lusaka, ZAMBIA

Bishop J. Wilhan
Organized: 1955   Denominational

MISSIONARIES IN SERVICE

(1975) 4   (1978) 4   (1980) 4
(1988) 4*
AAGR = N/A
Foreign missionaries in 1988: Not reported.

FIELDS OF SERVICE

Not reported.

Salvation Pentecostal Church

PO Box 240213, Ndola, ZAMBIA

Rev. P.B. Khagalo
Organized: 1981   Pentecostal

MISSIONARIES IN SERVICE

(1988) 90

AAGR = N/A
Foreign missionaries in 1988:   4

FIELDS OF SERVICE

Kenya
Nairobi Kiswahili, English
Tanzania
Dar Es Salaam Region Swahili
Mbeya Region Swahili
Zambia
Ndola Bemba, English
Lusaka Province Bemba, English

Voice of Miracle Healing and Soul Winning Evangelism

PO Box 36077, Lusaka, ZAMBIA

N. Svosve Mangini
Organized: 1980   Pentecostal

MISSIONARIES IN SERVICE

(1980) 7   (1985) 21   (1988) 41*
AAGR = N/A
Foreign missionaries in 1988: Not reported.

FIELDS OF SERVICE

Zaire
Shaba Region Swahili, Luba, Lingala
Zimbabwe
Matabeleland Province Ndebele, Tonga, Venda
Midlands Province Shona, Ndebele
Zambia
Copper Belt Province Bemba, Lamba, Kaonde
Central Province Nyanja, Soli, Lenje, Ila
Southern Province Tonga, Ila, Tokeleya
Eastern Province Nyanja, Senga, Chewa, Tumbuka

ZIMBABWE

Back to God Crusade

PO Box 110, Bulawayo, ZIMBABWE

Rev. Geoffrey Mkwanzai
Organized: 1959   Assemblies of God

MISSIONARIES IN SERVICE
(1988) 49
AAGR = N/A
Foreign missionaries in 1988:   4

FIELDS OF SERVICE
Zimbabwe
  Mashonaland Province Shona, Rural,
    Town People
  Matabeleland Province Ndebele,
    Rural People
  Zambezi Valley Tonga, Tribal People

Christ Ministries
PO Box 6497, Harare, ZIMBABWE

Rev. Cuthbert Makoni
Organized: Not reported.   Independent

MISSIONARIES IN SERVICE
(1988) 7
AAGR = N/A
Foreign missionaries in 1988:   0

FIELDS OF SERVICE
Zimbabwe
  Midlands Province Ndebele, Shona
  Victoria Province (Masringo) Shona
  Matabeleland Province Ndebele
  Manicaland Province Shona

Christian Marching Church
PO Box 9038, Mbane
Harare, ZIMBABWE

Rev. Philip M. Gobvu
Organized: 1956   Charismatic

MISSIONARIES IN SERVICE
(1972) 2   (1975) 3   (1978) 4
(1980) 9   (1988) 5
AAGR = 6%
Foreign missionaries in 1988:   0

FIELDS OF SERVICE
Zimbabwe   Shona, Ndebele, Blacks

Church of Central Africa, Harare Synod
PO Box 533, Harare, ZIMBABWE

Organized: Not reported.

MISSIONARIES IN SERVICE
(1972) 10   (1975) 10   (1978) 8
(1980) 6   (1988) 4*
AAGR = N/A
Foreign missionaries in 1988: Not
reported.

FIELDS OF SERVICE
Not reported.

Disciples in Action, International
Box 481, Harare, ZIMBABWE

Rev. Richmond Chiundiza
Organized: 1982   Assemblies of God

MISSIONARIES IN SERVICE
(1988) 4
AAGR = N/A
Foreign missionaries in 1988:   0

FIELDS OF SERVICE
Zimbabwe
  Matabeleland Province Ndebele
  Manicaland Province Manyika, Ndau

Dutch Reformed Mission, Harare Synod
PO Box C R 32, Cranborne
Harare, ZIMBABWE

Rev. A.J. Viljoen
Organized: Not reported.

MISSIONARIES IN SERVICE
(1972) 10   (1975) 8   (1980) 7
(1982) 4   (1984) 6   (1988) 5*
AAGR = N/A
Foreign missionaries in 1988: Not
reported.

FIELDS OF SERVICE
Zimbabwe
Malawi   Migratory Laborers

Forward in Faith Ministries, International
Box UA 346, Harare, ZIMBABWE

Ezekiel H. Guti
Organized: 1960

MISSIONARIES IN SERVICE

(1972) 300   (1980) 450   (1985) 1050
(1988) 1275
AAGR = 9%
Foreign missionaries in 1988:   20

FIELDS OF SERVICE

Malawi
Blantyre Chewa, Nyanja, Ngoni
Zaire
Bandundu Region Luwa, Lingala,
   Kilongo
Botswana
Gaborone Tswana
Ghana
Greater Accra Region
   Ga-Adangme-Krobo, Twi
Tanzania
Mbeya Region Swahili
South Africa
Pretoria Zulu, Ndebele, Sutu
Mozambique
Sofala Province (Beira) Sena, Ndau,
   Portuguese
Zambia
Lusaka Province Bemba, Nyanja,
   Chewa

Independent African Church

PO Box 9027, Harare, ZIMBABWE

Rev. S.C. Machinguria
Organized: 1946   Interdenominational

MISSIONARIES IN SERVICE

(1980) 24   (1988) 67*
AAGR = N/A
Foreign missionaries in 1988: Not
reported.

FIELDS OF SERVICE

Not reported.

Methodist Church, Pakame Circuit

PO Box 121, Shurugwi, ZIMBABWE

Rev. C.M. Matsikiti
Organized: 1986   Methodist

MISSIONARIES IN SERVICE

(1988) 13
AAGR = N/A
Foreign missionaries in 1988:   0

FIELDS OF SERVICE

Zimbabwe
   Midlands Province Shona, Ndebele

United Assemblies in Africa

PO Box 4442, Harare, ZIMBABWE

R.M.G. Kupara
Organized: 1984   Pentecostal

MISSIONARIES IN SERVICE

(1985) 2   (1988) 4
AAGR = 26%
Foreign missionaries in 1988:   2

FIELDS OF SERVICE

Mozambique   **Zambia**
Malawi

Zion Christian Church

PO Mbungo, Mbungo Estates
Masvingo, ZIMBABWE

Bishop Nehemia Mutendi
Organized: 1923
Independent Charismatic

MISSIONARIES IN SERVICE

(1988) 107
AAGR = N/A
Foreign missionaries in 1988:   18

FIELDS OF SERVICE

Mozambique
   Sofala Province (Beira) Portuguese
   Manica Province (Chimoio)
      Portuguese
Zambia   Zambian
Zimbabwe   Shona, Ndebele, English

AFRICA TRAINING AGENCIES

Christian Service College
PO Box 3110, Kumasi, GHANA

Dr. D.O. Gyane
Organized: 1973   Evangelical

AFRICA SERVICE AGENCIES

Lost Israelites of Kenya
PO Box 699, Kitale, KENYA

William Misiko Waswa
Organized: 1960   Denominational

MISSIONARIES IN SERVICE
(1980) 28   (1988) 55*
AAGR = N/A
Foreign missionaries in 1988: Not reported.

FIELDS OF SERVICE
Not reported.

AFRICA AUXILIARY AGENCIES

Gospel Bankers, Inc.
PO Box 1890
Warri, Bendel State, NIGERIA

Rev. F.J. Toritse
Organized: 1974   Nondenominational

INTERNATIONAL AFRICA-BASED SENDING AGENCIES

Youth With A Mission — African Relief Ministries
PO Box 8138, Comm. 7, Tema, GHANA

Loren Cunningham
Organized: Not reported.
Nondenominational
MISSIONARIES IN SERVICE
(1988) 12
AAGR = N/A
Foreign missionaries in 1988:   0
FIELDS OF SERVICE
Ghana
  Eastern Region   Ga-Adangme-Krobo

Life Ministry
PO Box 21417, Nairobi, KENYA

Rev. Wellington Mutiso
Organized: Not reported.
Interdenominational
MISSIONARIES IN SERVICE
(1988) 60
AAGR = N/A
Foreign missionaries in 1988:   5
FIELDS OF SERVICE
Somalia
Kenya   Luo, Turkana, Somali, Boran,
    Orma, Rendille, Samburu
USA

Nairobi Lighthouse Church
PO Box 34011, Nairobi, KENYA

Donald Matheny
Organized: 1987
MISSIONARIES IN SERVICE
(1988)   1
AAGR = N/A
Foreign missionaries in 1988:   0

FIELDS OF SERVICE

Kenya Bajun

Navigators, Kenya

PO Box 47300, Nairobi, KENYA

Mutua Mahiaini
Organized: 1985

MISSIONARIES IN SERVICE

(1988) 4
AAGR = N/A
Foreign missionaries in 1988: 4

FIELDS OF SERVICE

Zimbabwe   **Zambia**
USA

African Enterprise

PO Box 647
Pietermaritzburg 3200, SOUTH AFRICA

Michael Cassidy
Organized: 1962   Nondenominational

MISSIONARIES IN SERVICE

(1975) 15   (1978) 22   (1980) 30
(1984) 76   (1988) 14
AAGR = 0%
Foreign missionaries in 1988: 14

FIELDS OF SERVICE

Not reported.

Fishers of Men, Ltd.

PO Box 16702, Kampala, UGANDA

Micheal Watt
Organized: 1985   Nondenominational

MISSIONARIES IN SERVICE

(1985) 7   (1988) 20
AAGR = 42%
Foreign missionaries in 1988: 0

FIELDS OF SERVICE

Zaire
  Beni   Swahili, French
Uganda
  West Central Province   Baganda,
  Banyore

Good News Foundation, Inc.

PO Box 4130, Kampala, UGANDA

Rev. Kulwazi Musisi John
Organized: 1982   Evangelical

MISSIONARIES IN SERVICE

(1980) 1   (1985) 9   (1988) 19
AAGR = 44%
Foreign missionaries in 1988: 4

FIELDS OF SERVICE

Uganda
  Eastern Province   Basoga, Gishu
  Western Province   Nyankole, Toro,
    Kiga
  Central Province   Baganda, Luganda
  Northern Province   Arua, Lugwara,
    Acholi
Zambia
  Mfulira   Ndola
Kenya
  Nyanza Province   Dholuo, Kisi
Zaire
  Haut-Zaire (Boga)   Lingala

LATIN AMERICA

ARGENTINA

Apostolic Christian Nazarene Church
Codigo Postal 3170
Basavilbaso, ARGENTINA

Omar Gava
Organized: 1900   Nazarene
MISSIONARIES IN SERVICE
(1988)   3
AAGR = N/A
Foreign missionaries in 1988:   1
FIELDS OF SERVICE
Paraguay   Guarani
Argentina
  Buenos Aires   Laotians

Argentine Missionary Association of the Church of God
Codigo Postal 3315
Misiones Province, ARGENTINA

Arturo Uberman
Organized: 1927   Church of God
MISSIONARIES IN SERVICE
(1988)   3
AAGR = N/A
Foreign missionaries in 1988:   3
FIELDS OF SERVICE
Paraguay   German
Dominican Republic
  Santo Domingo

Assemblies of God
Codigo Postal 1161
Don Torcuato, ARGENTINA

Miguel Silva
Organized: 1988   Pentecostal
MISSIONARIES IN SERVICE
(1988)   1
AAGR = N/A
Foreign missionaries in 1988:   1
FIELDS OF SERVICE
Pakistan

Association of Evangelical Nazarene Churches
Codigo Postal 3613
La Primavera, ARGENTINA

Juan Chumba
Organized: 1919   Nazarene
MISSIONARIES IN SERVICE
(1988)   4
AAGR = N/A
Foreign missionaries in 1988:   0
FIELDS OF SERVICE
Argentina
  Formosa Department

Association of Church of God
Codigo Postal 1408
Buenos Aires, ARGENTINA

Gabriel O. Vaccaro
Organized: 1952   Pentecostal
MISSIONARIES IN SERVICE
(1988)   4
AAGR = N/A
Foreign missionaries in 1988:   0
FIELDS OF SERVICE
Argentina
  Chaco Department   Toba

Formosa Department   Mataco

Baptist Church of Quilmes

Codigo Postal 1878
Buenos Aires, ARGENTINA

Nicolas Paganini
Organized: 1965   Baptist

MISSIONARIES IN SERVICE
(1988)   1
AAGR = N/A
Foreign missionaries in 1988:   1

FIELDS OF SERVICE
Spain   Muslims

Biblical Seminary of Faith

Codigo Postal 1408
Buenos Aires, ARGENTINA

Milton Pope
Organized: 1988   Nondenominational

MISSIONARIES IN SERVICE
(1988)   2
AAGR = N/A
Foreign missionaries in 1988:   2

FIELDS OF SERVICE
Spain

Christian Evangelical Church, Free Brethren

Calle Brasil
Buenos Aires, ARGENTINA

Organized: Not reported.   Free Brethren

MISSIONARIES IN SERVICE
(1988)   4
AAGR = N/A
Foreign missionaries in 1988:   4

FIELDS OF SERVICE
Zaire

Christian and Missionary Alliance

Codigo Postal 1428
Buenos Aires, ARGENTINA

Rogelio Nonini
Organized: Not reported.

MISSIONARIES IN SERVICE
(1988)   2
AAGR = N/A
Foreign missionaries in 1988:   2

FIELDS OF SERVICE
Paraguay

Evangelical Baptist Convention of Argentina

Codigo Postal 1203
Buenos Aires, ARGENTINA

Carlos Caramutti
Organized: 1909   Baptist

MISSIONARIES IN SERVICE
(1988)   15
AAGR = N/A
Foreign missionaries in 1988:   2

FIELDS OF SERVICE
Argentina
  Santiago del Estero   Quechua
  Chaco Department   Guarani, Toba
  Neuquen Department   Mapuche
  Formosa Department   Guarani, Toba
Peru

Evangelical Mennonite Church of Argentina

Codigo Postal 1407
Buenos Aires, ARGENTINA

Dan Nuesch, Raul O. Garcia
Organized: 1919   Mennonite

MISSIONARIES IN SERVICE
(1988)   6
AAGR = N/A
Foreign missionaries in 1988:   0

FIELDS OF SERVICE
Argentina
  Formosa Department   Toba

Evangelical Pentecostal and Missionary Church

Codigo Postal 1615
Grand Bourg, ARGENTINA

Joel I. Stefanini

Organized: 1983   Pentecostal
MISSIONARIES IN SERVICE
(1988)   2
AAGR = N/A
Foreign missionaries in 1988:   2
FIELDS OF SERVICE
Paraguay Guarani
Bolivia Quechua

Evangelical Union in Argentina
Codigo Postal 7406
La Madrid, ARGENTINA

Osvaldo Romano
Organized: 1988   Evangelical
MISSIONARIES IN SERVICE
(1988)   1
AAGR = N/A
Foreign missionaries in 1988:   1
FIELDS OF SERVICE
Africa Muslims

BELIZE

Kekchi and Mayan Churches of Belize
Box 55, Toledo District, Laguna Village
Punta Gorda, BELIZE

Rev. Pedro Shol
Organized: Not reported.   Pentecostal
MISSIONARIES IN SERVICE
(1988) 10
AAGR = N/A
Foreign missionaries in 1988:   0
FIELDS OF SERVICE
Not reported.

BOLIVIA

Evangelical Missionary Association of Bolivia
Casilla 1043, BOLIVIA

Rev. Nilson Mendoza Chavez
Organized: Not reported.   Evangelical

MISSIONARIES IN SERVICE
(1985) 15   (1988) 15
AAGR =   0%
Foreign missionaries in 1988:   0
FIELDS OF SERVICE
Bolivia
El Beni Department Peasant farmers

BRAZIL

Alabama (Baptist Missionary Alliance of Amazonia)
C. Postal 1067, CEP 66000
Belem, P.A., BRAZIL

Gidalfo Sales Figueira
Organized: 1976   Denominational
MISSIONARIES IN SERVICE
(1978) 20   (1980) 25   (1988) 61*
AAGR = N/A
Foreign missionaries in 1988: Not reported.
FIELDS OF SERVICE
Not reported.

Amazon Evangelical Mission
C. Postal 154, CEP 69300
Boa Vista, R.R., BRAZIL

Enoque Ozorio de Faria
Organized: Not reported. Interdenominational
MISSIONARIES IN SERVICE
(1988) 46
AAGR = N/A
Foreign missionaries in 1988:   0
FIELDS OF SERVICE
Brazil
  Amazonas State Atruahi
  Roraima State Waiwai, Ingariko,
    Yanomami, Macusa

Amazon Methodist Mission
Rua Raul de Castro, 38 J. Chapadao
Campinas, S.P., BRAZIL

Messias Andrino
Organized: Not reported.   Methodist
MISSIONARIES IN SERVICE
(1980)   4   (1985)   6   (1988) 14
AAGR = 17%
Foreign missionaries in 1988:   0
FIELDS OF SERVICE
Brazil
  Rondonia (Cacoal)
  Para (Belem)
  Para (Altamira)
  Acre (Rio Branco)
  Rondonia State
  Parana State

Antioch Mission
C. Postal 582, CEP 01051
Sao Paulo, S.P., BRAZIL

Jonathan F. dos Santos
Organized: 1974   Interdenominational
MISSIONARIES IN SERVICE
Further information withheld at
agency's request.

Assemblies of God in the Amazon
C. Postal 22, 69000
Manaus, Amazonas, BRAZIL

Pr. A.P. Vasconcelos
Organized: 1973   Assemblies of God
MISSIONARIES IN SERVICE
(1980) 21   (1988) 43*
AAGR = N/A
Foreign missionaries in 1988: Not
reported.
FIELDS OF SERVICE
Not reported.

Assemblies of God - National Missions Board
Estrado Vicente de Carvalho 1003
Rio de Janeiro, R.J., BRAZIL

Isael Cortaz Teixeira
Organized: Not reported.

Assemblies of God
MISSIONARIES IN SERVICE
(1980) 82   (1988) 123
AAGR =   5%
Foreign missionaries in 1988:   86
FIELDS OF SERVICE
Argentina
  Buenos Aires
  Cordoba
  Misiones
  Patagonia
  Entre Rios (Concordia)
  Santiago del Estero
Peru
  Arequipa Department
  Piura Department
Uruguay
  Montevideo
  Mercedes
Mozambique
Paraguay
  Central (Asuncion, Ita)
Macau
  Lima Department
USA
  Virginia
  Florida (Miami)
  Illinois (Chicago)
  California (Riverside)
Italy
  Veneza
Ecuador
  Guayas (Machala)
  Los Rios (Babahoyo)
  Manabi (Portoviejo)
  Santo Domingo
  Pichincha Department
Senegal
Guinea-Bissau
Angola
Chile
  Antofagasta Region
  Valparaiso
  Biobio (Concepcion, Tome)
Bolivia
  Santa Cruz Department

Cochabamba Department
Swaziland
Spain
 Madrid Region
Colombia
 Cucuta
Japan
 Tokyo Province
United Kingdom
 England
Brazil
 Brasilia
 Sao Paulo State
 Rondonia State
 Mato Grosso State
Canada
Portugal
 Braga District

Associacao Religiosa Milad
C. Postal 6101, CEP 01051
Sao Paulo, S.P., BRAZIL

Nelson Pinto Jr.
Organized: 1985   Interdenominational
MISSIONARIES IN SERVICE
(1988) 10
AAGR = N/A
Foreign missionaries in 1988:   0
FIELDS OF SERVICE
Not reported.

Avante
C. Postal 1261, CEP 01051
Sao Paulo, S.P., BRAZIL

Ken Kudo
Organized: 1987   Interdenominational
MISSIONARIES IN SERVICE
(1988) 20
AAGR = N/A
Foreign missionaries in 1988:   20
FIELDS OF SERVICE
Spain
 Malaga (Velez) Spanish
Uruguay
 Florida (Cardal) Uruguayans

Florida Department Uruguayans

Board of Foreign Missions
Rua Miguel Teles Junio 382-394
CEP 01540, Sao Paulo, S.P., BRAZIL

Rev. Evandio da Silva
Organized: 1968   Presbyterian
MISSIONARIES IN SERVICE
(1988) 27
AAGR = N/A
Foreign missionaries in 1988:   24
FIELDS OF SERVICE
Germany (West)
 Berlin Muslims
Guinea-Bissau Africans
Ecuador
 Quito Ecuadorians
Spain
 Barcelona Spaniards
Portugal
 Carnide Portuguese
 Lisboa District Portuguese
Paraguay
 Concepcion Department Paraguayans
 San Lorenzo Paraguayans
 Central (Asuncion) Paraguayans
 Concepcion (Belen) Paraguayans
USA
 California (Milpitas) Americans
Bolivia Bolivians
France
 Etienne du Rouvray French

Brazil Outreach for Christ
C. Postal 2277, CEP 20001
Rio de Janeiro, R.J., BRAZIL

Julio de Barcellos Pinto
Organized: 1979   Interdenominational
MISSIONARIES IN SERVICE
(1980) 21   (1985) 22   (1988) 28
AAGR = 4%
Foreign missionaries in 1988:   3
FIELDS OF SERVICE
Brazil
 Paraiba State Brazilians

Mato Grosso State Brazilians
Rio de Janeiro State Brazilians
Bolivia
Santa Cruz Department Bolivians, Indians
Guinea-Bissau Pasteu

Brazil and Portugal Gospel Mission

Rua Alexandre Mackenzie
CEP 20221, Rio De Janeiro, R.J., BRAZIL

David Basilio da Costa
Organized: 1890
Evangelical Congregational

MISSIONARIES IN SERVICE
(1988) 12
AAGR = N/A
Foreign missionaries in 1988:   6

FIELDS OF SERVICE
Portugal
Ponte do Rol
Brazil
Espirito Santo State
Sao Paulo State
Rio de Janeiro State

Brazilian Baptist Convention - Mission Board

Rua Senador Furtado 56 Pca de
Bandeira, CEP 20270
Rio de Janeiro, R.J., BRAZIL

Waldemiro Tymchak
Organized: 1906   Baptist

MISSIONARIES IN SERVICE
(1975) 45   (1978) 62   (1980) 70
(1982) 75   (1984) 98   (1988) 104
AAGR =   7%
Foreign missionaries in 1988:   104

FIELDS OF SERVICE
Chile
Curico
Talca
Antofagasta Region
Bolivia
Montero

Santa Cruz Department
El Beni (Trinidad)
Guayaramerin
South Africa
Germiston
Cape Town
Johannesburg
Zimbabwe
Gueru
Peru
Ica Department
Lima Department
Macau
Colombia
Huila (Colombia)
Spain
Valladolid
Jerez de la Frontera
Portugal
Lisboa District
Porto District
Barcelos
Matosinhos
Braga District
Angra do Heroismo District
Santarem (Caldas da Rainha)
Canada
Oakwille
Hamilton
Strathroy
Toronto
Ecuador
Guayaquil
Paraguay
Neembucu (Pilar)
Concepcion Department
Pedro Juan Caballero
Puerto Presidente Stroessner
Guarambare
Central (Asuncion)
Argentina
Viedma
Rio Tercero
Buenos Aires
Obera
Charata
Ecuador

Quito
Venezuela
  Puerto Ordaz
  Puerto la Cruz
Mozambique
  Sofala Province (Beira)
  Maputo Province
Uruguay
  Durazno Department
  Pando
  Trinidad
Colombia
  Bucaramanga
Angola
  Lobito

Brazilian Baptist Convention, Home Mission Board

Rua Barao do Bom Retiro, 1241
CEP 20000, Rio de Janeiro, R.J., BRAZIL

Paulo Roberto Seabra
Organized: 1906   Baptist

MISSIONARIES IN SERVICE
(1980) 300   (1988) 431*
AAGR = N/A
Foreign missionaries in 1988: Not reported.

FIELDS OF SERVICE
Not reported.

Brazilian Bethel Department of World Missions

C. Postal 194, CEP 58000
Joao Pessoa, P.B., BRAZIL

Lidia Almeida de Menezes
Organized: 1972   Interdenominational

MISSIONARIES IN SERVICE
(1972) 1   (1975) 6   (1980) 9
(1982) 7   (1984) 10   (1985) 11
(1988) 7
AAGR = 13%
Foreign missionaries in 1988:   17

FIELDS OF SERVICE
United Kingdom
  England (London, Nottingham)   Muslims, English
Peru
  Piura Department
    Peruvians, Quechuas
  Ayacucho Department   Peruvians, Quechuas
Japan
  Osaka Province   Japanese
Portugal
  Ovar   Portuguese, Cigano People
  Porto District   Portuguese, Cigano People
Italy
  Rome   Italians
France
  Massy   French
Germany (West)
  Freiburg   German
Brazil
  Rondonia State   Aikana

Brazilian Methodist Church

Rua Visconde de Porto Seguro, 442
Santa Amaro, S.P., BRAZIL

Rev. Francisco Antonio Corre
Organized: Not reported.   Methodist

MISSIONARIES IN SERVICE
(1980) 30   (1988) 62*
AAGR = N/A
Foreign missionaries in 1988: Not reported.

FIELDS OF SERVICE
Not reported.

Caiua Evangelical Mission

C. Postal 04, CEP 79800
Douados, M.S., BRAZIL

Beijamim Benedito Bernardes
Organized: 1928   Presbyterian

MISSIONARIES IN SERVICE
(1980) 30   (1988) 81
AAGR = 13%

Foreign missionaries in 1988:   3

FIELDS OF SERVICE

Paraguay

Pyssiry   Guarani

Brazil

Mato Grosso do Sul (Tacuru)   Caiua, Guarani

Mato Grosso do Sul (Ramada)   Caiua, Guarani

Mato Grosso do Sul (Caarapo)   Caiua, Guarani

Mato Grosso do Sul (Iguatemi)   Guarani

Mato Grosso do Sul (Taquari)   Caiua, Guarani

Mato Grosso do Sul State   Terena, Caiua, Guarani

Mato Grosso do Sul (Amambai)   Caiua, Guarani

Commandos for Christ

C. Postal 2277, CEP 20001
Rio de Janeiro, R.J., BRAZIL

Julio Cesar de Barcellos
Organized: Not reported.
Interdenominational

MISSIONARIES IN SERVICE

(1980)   21   (1985)   22   (1988)   28
AAGR =   4%
Foreign missionaries in 1988:   3

FIELDS OF SERVICE

Not reported.

Convention of Independent Baptist Churches

C. Postal 13532, CEP 03399
Sao Paulo, S.P., BRAZIL

Jose T.R. Lima
Organized: Not reported.

MISSIONARIES IN SERVICE

(1985)   101   (1988)   116*
AAGR = N/A
Foreign missionaries in 1988: Not reported.

FIELDS OF SERVICE

Not reported.

Evangelical Linguistic Missionary Association

C. Postal 6101, CEP 70359
Brasilia, D.F., BRAZIL

Ricardo Barbosa de Souza
Organized: 1982   Interdenominational

MISSIONARIES IN SERVICE

(1988)   12
AAGR = N/A
Foreign missionaries in 1988:   0

FIELDS OF SERVICE

Brazil

Amazonas State

Kama,   Maku-Yahup

Rondonia State   Tupari

Para State   Anambe, Kayabi, Kaxarari

Amazonas (Jaruara)   Jaruara

Evangelical Mission for Assistance to Fishermen

Rua Marechal Pego Junior 21
CEP 11013, Santos, S.P., BRAZIL

Marcos Garcia Alonso
Organized: 1986   Interdenominational

MISSIONARIES IN SERVICE

(1988)   9
AAGR = N/A
Foreign missionaries in 1988:   0

FIELDS OF SERVICE

Brazil

Sao Paulo State   Fishermen

Parana State   Fishermen

Evangelical Mission to the Indians of Brazil

C. Postal 3030, CEP 66041
Belem, P.A., BRAZIL

Zacarias Matos Monteiro
Organized: 1971   Alliance

MISSIONARIES IN SERVICE

(1972)   3   (1975)   6   (1978)   6

(1980) 11   (1985) 13   (1988) 12
AAGR = 9%
Foreign missionaries in 1988:   0

FIELDS OF SERVICE

Brazil
  Para State Kayapo
  Maranhao State Guajajara

First Baptist Church of St. Andrew

C. Postal 49, CEP 09000
Santo Andre, S.P., BRAZIL

Consecho Missionario
Organized: Not reported.

MISSIONARIES IN SERVICE

(1984) 33   (1988) 47*
AAGR = N/A
Foreign missionaries in 1988: Not reported.

FIELDS OF SERVICE

Macau Portuguese
Brazil
  Rio Grande do Sul State Brazilians
  Piaui Brazilians
  Belem Indigenous
  Sao Paulo State Satare-Mogue
Bolivia
  Sucre Bolivians
Angola
  Huambo Region Angolans

Gipsy Missionary Work in Brazil

Rua das Acacias 193 (Pituga)
Salvador 40000, Bahia, BRAZIL

Dr. Evaldo A. dos Santos
Organized: Not reported.
Interdenominational

MISSIONARIES IN SERVICE

(1980) 1   (1988) 2*
AAGR = N/A
Foreign missionaries in 1988: Not reported.

FIELDS OF SERVICE

Not reported.

Intervarsity Christian Fellowship of Brazil

C. Postal 30505, CEP 01051
Sao Paulo, S.P., BRAZIL

Dr. Ross Alan Douglas
Organized: 1963   Interdenominational

MISSIONARIES IN SERVICE

Further information withheld at agency's request.

Kairos

Rua Mal Renato 270
Sao Paulo, S.P., BRAZIL

Waldemar Carvalho
Organized: 1988   Interdenominational

MISSIONARIES IN SERVICE

Further information withheld at agency's request.

Logos Evangelical Mission

C. Postal 414, CEP 12940
Atibaia, S.P., BRAZIL

Paulo Cesar da Silva
Organized: 1981   Interdenominational

MISSIONARIES IN SERVICE

(1988) 6
AAGR = N/A
Foreign missionaries in 1988:   0

FIELDS OF SERVICE

Brazil

Missionary Aviation Fellowship

C. Postal 184, CEP 77100
Anapolis, G.O., BRAZIL

Eldon Larsen
Organized: 1958   Nondenominational

MISSIONARIES IN SERVICE

(1980) 4   (1985) 7   (1988) 15
AAGR = 18%
Foreign missionaries in 1988:   2

FIELDS OF SERVICE

Bolivia

Missao Rincon   Spanish
Brazil
Goias (Anapolis)   Portuguese
Amazonas (Eirunepe)   Portuguese
USA

Missionary Expansion Fund
Estrada do Itamarati 313, C. Postal 421
Petropolis 25600, R.J., BRAZIL

Rev. Gesse Teixeira de Carva
Organized: Not reportedDenominational
MISSIONARIES IN SERVICE
(1980) 23   (1988) 48*
AAGR = N/A
Foreign missionaries in 1988: Not reported.

FIELDS OF SERVICE
Not reported.

Morumbi Baptist Church
Rua None de Jullio, 230 Santo Amaro
Sao Paulo 04739, S.P., BRAZIL

Pr. Guilherme Kerr Neto
Organized: Not reported.
MISSIONARIES IN SERVICE
(1982) 2   (1984) 6   (1988) 54*
AAGR = N/A
Foreign missionaries in 1988: Not reported.

FIELDS OF SERVICE
Uruguay
Cardal   Uruguayans
Brazil
Sao Paulo State   Television Ministry
Roraima State   Yanomami tribe
Rio Grande do Sul State   Bible Institute

Philadelphia Mission
C. Postal 5101, Vemda Nova 31.611
Belo Horizonte, M.G., BRAZIL

Klaas van de Raa
Organized: 1979   Pentecostal
MISSIONARIES IN SERVICE
(1988) 21

AAGR = N/A
Foreign missionaries in 1988:   2
FIELDS OF SERVICE
Not reported.

Project Andes
C. Postal 1027, CEP 29001
Vitoria, E.S., BRAZIL

Marcos Martins Dias
Organized: 1986   Presbyterian
MISSIONARIES IN SERVICE
(1988) 62
AAGR = N/A
Foreign missionaries in 1988:   30

FIELDS OF SERVICE
Brazil
Minas Gerais State
Peru
Trujillo
Chile
Bolivia
Cochabamba Department
Paraguay
Central (Asuncion)
Ecuador
Quito

Seara Group
C. Postal 50014, Carioca, R.J., BRAZIL

Victor Sales
Organized: 1985   Interdenominational
MISSIONARIES IN SERVICE
(1985) 5   (1988) 6
AAGR = 6%
Foreign missionaries in 1988:   0
FIELDS OF SERVICE
Brazil
All States

Union of Evangelical Congregational Churches of Brazil
Rua Sao Luiz Gonzaga 1132
CEP 20910, Sao Cristovao, R.J., BRAZIL

Nilson Ferreira Braga
Organized: 1932   Congregational
MISSIONARIES IN SERVICE
(1972) 20   (1980) 31   (1985) 22
(1988) 32
AAGR = 3%
Foreign missionaries in 1988:   0
FIELDS OF SERVICE
Brazil
  Espirito Santo State
  Rio Grande do Norte State
  Para State
  Bahia
  Maranhao State
  Acre (Rio Branco)
  Roraima State
  Mato Grosso State

Victors Through Christ
C. Postal 21324, CEP 04698
Sao Paulo, S.P., BRAZIL

Luiz Antonio F. Caseira
Organized: 1968   Interdenominational
MISSIONARIES IN SERVICE
(1972) 9   (1980) 10   (1985) 9
(1988) 8
AAGR = -0%
Foreign missionaries in 1988:   0
FIELDS OF SERVICE
Brazil

Word of Life Organization
C. Postal 43, CEP 12940
Atibaia, S.P., BRAZIL

John Harold Reimer
Organized: 1957   Interdenominational
MISSIONARIES IN SERVICE
(1988) 120
AAGR = N/A
Foreign missionaries in 1988:   2
FIELDS OF SERVICE
Brazil
  Pernambuco (Recife)
  Parana (Curitiba)
  Sao Paulo State

Amazonas (Porto Alegre)
Portugal
  Lisboa District

COLOMBIA

Christian Brethren
Apartado Aereo 4248
Cartagena, COLOMBIA

Carlos Machacon
Organized: 1976   Denominational
MISSIONARIES IN SERVICE
(1980) 4   (1988) 4*
AAGR = N/A
Foreign missionaries in 1988: Not reported.
FIELDS OF SERVICE
Not reported.

Colombian Baptist Convention
Apartado Aereo 51687
Bogota, COLOMBIA

Ricardo Rolfe
Organized: 1979   Baptist
MISSIONARIES IN SERVICE
(1988) 10
AAGR = N/A
Foreign missionaries in 1988:   0
FIELDS OF SERVICE
Colombia
  La Guajira (Riohacha, Maicao)   Professionals, All People
  Lerida   Lower Middle Class, Injured People
  San Andres   Spanish
  Ibague   Lower Middle Class, Injured People
  Bogota   Lower Class

Colombian Christian Alliance
Apartado Aereo 678
Armenia, Quindio, COLOMBIA

Jose Rafael Lopez H.

Organized: 1942   Denominational
MISSIONARIES IN SERVICE
(1978) 10   (1980) 8   (1988) 3*
AAGR = N/A
Foreign missionaries in 1988: Not
reported.

FIELDS OF SERVICE
Not reported.

Foursquare Gospel Church
Apartado Aereo 40
Barrancabermeja, COLOMBIA

Sigilfredo Silva
Organized: 1948   Pentecostal
MISSIONARIES IN SERVICE
(1972) 6   (1980) 2   (1985) 2
(1988) 2
AAGR = -6%
Foreign missionaries in 1988: 5
FIELDS OF SERVICE
Spain
  Avila
Peru
  Cusco Department Families

Mission of the Motilone Indians
COLOMBIA

Bruce E. Olson
Organized: Not reported.

MISSIONARIES IN SERVICE
(1980) 3   (1988) 3*
AAGR = N/A
Foreign missionaries in 1988: Not
reported.

FIELDS OF SERVICE
Not reported.

Missionary Project 1985
Apartado Aereo 2700, Meta
Villavicencio, Meta, COLOMBIA

Leonel M. Ortiz V.
Organized: Not reported.

MISSIONARIES IN SERVICE
(1980) 5   (1982) 9   (1984) 8
(1988) 13*
AAGR = N/A
Foreign missionaries in 1988: Not
reported.

FIELDS OF SERVICE
Colombia
  Vaupes Department Indigenous, Mestizos

COSTA RICA

Costa Rican Evangelical Missions Federation
1307-1000, San Jose, COSTA RICA

Rev. Alberto Pozo
Organized: 1986   Interdenominational
MISSIONARIES IN SERVICE
Further information withheld at
agency's request.

ECUADOR

Ecuadorian Evangelical Missionary Association
Casilla 5185, Quito, ECUADOR

Rev. Washington Leon C.
Organized: 1968   Nondenominational
MISSIONARIES IN SERVICE
(1972) 5   (1975) 5   (1978) 11
(1980) 12   (1982) 14   (1984) 22
(1988) 36*
AAGR = N/A
Foreign missionaries in 1988: Not
reported.

FIELDS OF SERVICE
Not reported.

EL SALVADOR

Miramonte Baptist Church
EL SALVADOR

Organized: Not reported.   Baptist

MISSIONARIES IN SERVICE
(1985) 2   (1988) 3*
AAGR = N/A
Foreign missionaries in 1988: Not reported.
FIELDS OF SERVICE

Mexico   **Ecuador**

Salvadorean Evangelical Mission
Apartado 05-12
San Salvador, EL SALVADOR

Francisco Choriego
Organized: 1984   Evangelical
MISSIONARIES IN SERVICE
(1985) 5   (1988) 12
AAGR = 34%
Foreign missionaries in 1988:   2
FIELDS OF SERVICE
El Salvador
  San Salvador   Deaf People
Guatemala
  El Quiche (San Juan Cotzal)   Ixil

GUATEMALA

Baptist Convention of Guatemala
Apartado 322
Guatemala City, GUATEMALA

Jose Angil Samol
Organized: Not reported.   Baptist
MISSIONARIES IN SERVICE
Further information withheld at agency's request.

Calvary (El Calvario)
Av. Ferrocarril Y 2a. C., Zona 9
Guatemala City, GUATEMALA

Pr. Eliu Castillo
Organized: 1962   Denominational
MISSIONARIES IN SERVICE
(1980) 18   (1988) 26*
AAGR = N/A

Foreign missionaries in 1988: Not reported.
FIELDS OF SERVICE
Not reported.

Christian Calvary Mission
33 Calle A 2-19, Zone 8
Guatemala City, GUATEMALA

Abraham Castillo
Organized: 1947   Pentecostal
MISSIONARIES IN SERVICE
(1985) 13   (1988) 3
AAGR = -38%
Foreign missionaries in 1988:   0
FIELDS OF SERVICE
Honduras
  San Pedro Sula   Hondurans
USA
  California (Los Angeles)   Hispanics
  New York (New York City)   Hispanics
  Florida (Miami)   Hispanics
Mexico
  Federal District   Mexicans
  Acapulco   Mexicans
Peru
Colombia

Christians in Action
GUATEMALA

Miguel Toledo
Organized: Not reported.
MISSIONARIES IN SERVICE
(1985) 1   (1988) 1*
AAGR = N/A
Foreign missionaries in 1988: Not reported.
FIELDS OF SERVICE
Ecuador   Shuar

Church of God Full Gospel
Zone 12
Guatemala City, GUATEMALA

Roberto Aldana
Organized: Not reported.   Pentecostal

MISSIONARIES IN SERVICE

(1988)   2

AAGR = N/A

Foreign missionaries in 1988:   2

FIELDS OF SERVICE

Ecuador
  Bolivar (Guacanda)

Church of God of Universal Prophecy

Apartado 1001
Guatemala City, GUATEMALA

Jorge Marrero
Organized: Not reported.   Pentecostal

MISSIONARIES IN SERVICE

(1985)   4   (1988)   5*

AAGR = N/A

Foreign missionaries in 1988: Not reported.

FIELDS OF SERVICE

Bolivia   **Costa Rica**

Church of the Nazarene

Calle Marizcal 12-22, Zone 11
Guatemala City, GUATEMALA

Jerry Porter
Organized: Not reported.   Nazarene

MISSIONARIES IN SERVICE

(1988)   2

AAGR = N/A

Foreign missionaries in 1988:   1

FIELDS OF SERVICE

Honduras
  San Pedro Sula   Local Church

El Camino Bible Center

29 Calle 13-11, Zone 12
Guatemala, GUATEMALA

Dr. Abel Morales
Organized: 1984   Independent

MISSIONARIES IN SERVICE

(1985)   11   (1988)   20

AAGR =   22%

Foreign missionaries in 1988:   5

FIELDS OF SERVICE

Europe   Logos Ship
Spain   Spaniards

Elim Christian Mission

48 Av. 4-21, Zona 7, Colonia El Rosario
Guatemala City, GUATEMALA

Dr. Otoniel Rios P.
Organized: 1967   Denominational

MISSIONARIES IN SERVICE

(1980)   6   (1988)   9*

AAGR = N/A

Foreign missionaries in 1988: Not reported.

FIELDS OF SERVICE

Not reported.

Evangelical Church of El Aposento Alto

4a. Calle 10-65, Zone 11
Colonia Roosevelt
Guatemala City, GUATEMALA

Fredy Cisneros Z.
Organized: 1981   Assemblies of God

MISSIONARIES IN SERVICE

(1988)   1

AAGR = N/A

Foreign missionaries in 1988:   1

FIELDS OF SERVICE

Peru
  Cusco Department   Indigenous
  Lima Department   Spanish

Missionary Evangelical Agency

Apartado 55 "A"
Guatemala, GUATEMALA

Fredy Gularte
Organized: 1984   Evangelical

MISSIONARIES IN SERVICE

(1988)   2

AAGR = N/A

Foreign missionaries in 1988:   0

FIELDS OF SERVICE
Guatemala
  Huehuetenango (Coatan)   Chuj Indians

Prince of Peace National Association
Apartado 786
Guatemala City, GUATEMALA

Rev. Jose A. Coellar
Organized: 1955   Denominational
MISSIONARIES IN SERVICE
(1980)   3   (1988)   4*
AAGR = N/A
Foreign missionaries in 1988: Not reported.
FIELDS OF SERVICE
Not reported.

Verbo Christian Church
Av. Reforma 3-00 Zone 9
Guatemala City, GUATEMALA

Rev. Carlos Ramirez
Organized: Not reported.   Charismatic
MISSIONARIES IN SERVICE
(1988)   10
AAGR = N/A
Foreign missionaries in 1988:   8
FIELDS OF SERVICE
USA
  Louisiana (New Orleans)   Immigrants
  Florida (Miami)   Immigrants
Ecuador
  Quito

HONDURAS

Hondurean Mission to the Unreached
Apartado 164, La Ceiba, HONDURAS

Ambrosio Cordova
Organized: 1988   Baptist
MISSIONARIES IN SERVICE
(1988)   7

AAGR = N/A
Foreign missionaries in 1988:   0
FIELDS OF SERVICE
Honduras   Garifuna

World Reach, Honduras
Apartado 14, Siguatepeque
Comayagua, HONDURAS

Ezequiel Martinez
Organized: Not reported.
MISSIONARIES IN SERVICE
(1984)   8   (1988)   10*
AAGR = N/A
Foreign missionaries in 1988: Not reported.
FIELDS OF SERVICE
Honduras
  San Pedro Sula   Lower Clase, Middle Clase

MEXICO

Apostolic Church of the Faith in Jesus Christ
Apartado 1-1122
Guadalajara 44100, MEXICO

Rev. Miguel Agustin Reyes
Organized: 1907   Pentecostal
MISSIONARIES IN SERVICE
(1988)   26
AAGR = N/A
Foreign missionaries in 1988:   4
FIELDS OF SERVICE
Colombia
Belize
Mexico
  Sonora State   Seri
  Jalisco State   Huichol
  Chiapas State   Tzotzil
  Sinaloa State   Huichol
  Sinaloa State   Cora
  Chihuahua State   Tarahumara

Assemblies of God General Council

Nicolas Leon 118, Colonia Jardin
Balbuena, Mexico D.F. 15900, MEXICO

Alfonso de los Reyes
Organized: Not reported.
Assemblies of God
MISSIONARIES IN SERVICE
(1988)   2
AAGR = N/A
Foreign missionaries in 1988:   2
FIELDS OF SERVICE
Guatemala

Bible Church of Venustiano Carranza

Apartado 17, Guadalajara, MEXICO

Javier Sanchey Pulido
Organized: 1980   Evangelical
MISSIONARIES IN SERVICE
(1988)   2
AAGR = N/A
Foreign missionaries in 1988:   2
FIELDS OF SERVICE
Morocco

Chiapas Mission

c/o Reformed Church in America
Apt 8, San Cristobal de las Casas
Chipas, MEXICO

Rev. Harold Brown
Organized: 1942   Denominational
MISSIONARIES IN SERVICE
(1972) 18   (1975) 20   (1978) 18
(1980) 16   (1988) 14*
AAGR = N/A
Foreign missionaries in 1988: Not
reported.
FIELDS OF SERVICE
Not reported.

Church of God of Prophecy

Apartado 67-559
Delegacion Venustiano

Mexico D.F. 07910, MEXICO

Ruben Carmona Avila
Organized: Not reported.   Pentecostal
MISSIONARIES IN SERVICE
(1988) 22
AAGR = N/A
Foreign missionaries in 1988:   4
FIELDS OF SERVICE
Mexico
Chihuahua State
Chiapas State   Chol
Durango State
Mexico City   Mazahua
Baja California State
Yucatan State   Mayans
Sinaloa State
Oaxaca State   Mixe
Ecuador
Guayaquil
Panama
Panama City

Church of the Nazarene

Apartado 6-118
Guadalajara 44600, MEXICO

Samuel Orando
Organized: Not reported.   Nazarene
MISSIONARIES IN SERVICE
(1988) 2
AAGR = N/A
Foreign missionaries in 1988:   0
FIELDS OF SERVICE
Mexico
Mexico City   Mazahua

Covenant Evangelical Church

Gorriones 41
Parque Residencial Coacales
Mexico 55700, MEXICO

Fernando Marcin
Organized: 1974   Evangelical
MISSIONARIES IN SERVICE
(1988) 2

AAGR = N/A
Foreign missionaries in 1988:   2
FIELDS OF SERVICE
Mexico
Oaxaca State   Mixe
USA
California

Fraternity of the Churches of God in Mexico
Tipografia 45
Colonia 20 de Noviembre
Mexico D.F. 1530, MEXICO

Hilario Jimenez
Organized: Not reported.   Pentecostal
MISSIONARIES IN SERVICE
(1988)   1
AAGR = N/A
Foreign missionaries in 1988:   0
FIELDS OF SERVICE
Mexico
Mexico City   Mazahua

Independent Pentecostal Christian Church Movement
Javier Rojo Gomez 209
Colonia Sta. Julia
Pachuca 42080, MEXICO

Sr. Aroldo Espinoza
Organized: 1925   Pentecostal
MISSIONARIES IN SERVICE
(1988)   42
AAGR = N/A
Foreign missionaries in 1988:   0
FIELDS OF SERVICE
Mexico
Chiapas State   Chamula
Quintana Roo Territory   Guatemalan
    Immigrants
San Luis Potosi State   Nahuatl
Michoacan State   Tarasco
Puebla State   Otomi
Mexico City
Oaxaca State   Mixteco
Hidalgo State   Otomi

Hidalgo State   Nahuatl
Chiapas State   Lacandon
Veracruz State   Nahuatl

Legaspia Church
Apartado 5-1124
Guadalajara 5, Jalisco, MEXICO

Jose Luis Garcia
Organized: Not reported.   Quaker
MISSIONARIES IN SERVICE
(1988)   8
AAGR = N/A
Foreign missionaries in 1988:   4
FIELDS OF SERVICE
Mexico
Jalisco State (El Briseno)
Michoacan State   Jiquilpan
Pakistan
Peshawar District   Pathan
Morocco   Fes

Magreb Project
c/o Church of Guadalajara
P.O. Box 5-1124
Guadalajara, Jalisco, MEXICO

Pablo Carrillo
Organized: Not reported.

MISSIONARIES IN SERVICE
(1984)   3   (1988)   4*
AAGR = N/A
Foreign missionaries in 1988: Not
reported.
FIELDS OF SERVICE
Not reported.

Messiah Baptist Church
Apartado 13-G, Merida, MEXICO

Victor F. Villanueva A.
Organized: Not reported.   Baptist
MISSIONARIES IN SERVICE
(1988)   5
AAGR = N/A
Foreign missionaries in 1988:   0

FIELDS OF SERVICE
Mexico
  Yucatan State Mayans

Methodist Church of Mexico

Apartado 13-538
Mexico D.F. 03570, MEXICO

Bishop Raul Ruiz
Organized: Not reported.   Methodist
  MISSIONARIES IN SERVICE
(1988) 2
AAGR = N/A
Foreign missionaries in 1988: 2
  FIELDS OF SERVICE
Guatemala

Mexican Church of the Gospel of Christ

Apartado 606
Mexico D.F. 15000, MEXICO

Sra. Gracielasparza
Organized: Not reported.   Pentecostal
  MISSIONARIES IN SERVICE
(1988) 9
AAGR = N/A
Foreign missionaries in 1988: 3
  FIELDS OF SERVICE
Mexico
  Oaxaca State Trique
  Chiapas State Chamula
Japan
Nicaragua

Mission of the Evangelical Alliance

Apartado 415, Satelite 53100
EDO de Mexico, MEXICO

Dr. Gerardo Reed
Organized: Not reported.
  MISSIONARIES IN SERVICE
(1975) 4   (1980) 8   (1982) 10
(1984) 14   (1988) 24*
AAGR = N/A

Foreign missionaries in 1988: Not
reported.
  FIELDS OF SERVICE
Mexico
  Oaxaca State Indigenous
  Mexico City Middle Class
  Oaxaca State Indigenous

Missionary Revival Crusade

Membrillos 33, Colonia de Granjas
Chalco 56600, MEXICO

Timoteo Ost
Organized: 1967   Pentecostal
  MISSIONARIES IN SERVICE
(1988) 14
AAGR = N/A
Foreign missionaries in 1988:   0
  FIELDS OF SERVICE
Mexico
  Oaxaca State
  Aguascalientes State
  San Luis Potosi State
  Chiapas State
  Tamaulipas State Soto la Marina

National Baptist Convention of Mexico

Vizcainas 16 altos, Colonia Centro
Mexico D.F. 06080, MEXICO

Daniel Rangel Ramos
Organized: Not reported.   Baptist
  MISSIONARIES IN SERVICE
(1988) 24
AAGR = N/A
Foreign missionaries in 1988:   6
  FIELDS OF SERVICE
Mexico
  Chiapas State Chontal, Chol
  Campeche State Escarcega, Paraiso
  Tamaulipas State Various Groups
  Puebla State Mixteco
  Nuevo Leon State Various Groups
  San Luis Potosi State Nahuatl
  Oaxaca State Miahuatlan
  Oaxaca State Mazateco

Tabasco State   Chontal, Chol
Sonora State   Mayo
Hidalgo State   Nahuatl
Veracruz State   Nahuatl
Chihuahua State   Tarahumara
Honduras
Olancho Department   Various Groups
Capacamas   Various Groups
Spain
Alicante (Denia)   Various Groups

Potter's House

Apartado 6-640, Colonia Juarez
Mexico D.F. 06600, MEXICO

Ernesto Cary Renault
Organized: 1985   Charismatic
MISSIONARIES IN SERVICE
(1988) 12
AAGR = N/A
Foreign missionaries in 1988:   0
FIELDS OF SERVICE
Mexico
Morelos State
Chiapas State   Tzeltal
Michoacan State
Guanajuato State
Guerrero State
Puebla State

PERU

AMEN

Apartado 5342, Lima, PERU

Obed Alvarez M.A.
Organized: 1946   Nondenominational
MISSIONARIES IN SERVICE
(1972) 7   (1980) 134   (1985) 130
(1988) 140
AAGR = 21%
Foreign missionaries in 1988:   47
FIELDS OF SERVICE
Netherlands
Rotterdam   Dutch, Portuguese, Spanish
Costa Rica   Costa Ricans

USA
Texas   Americans
California   Hispanics, Americans
New York   Hispanics, Americans
Puerto Rico   Americans
Brazil
Sao Paulo State   Brazilians
United Kingdom
England (London)   British, Spaniards, Hispanics
Colombia
Bogota   Colombians
France
Paris   French, Spanish

Indigenous Missionary Committee of Peru

Apartado 6185, Lima 100, PERU

Rev. Victor Laguna G.
Organized: 1983   Assemblies of God
MISSIONARIES IN SERVICE
(1985) 4   (1988) 8
AAGR = 26%
Foreign missionaries in 1988:   0
FIELDS OF SERVICE
Peru
Puno Department   Aymara
La Sierra Region   Quechua

Malaquias Missionary Group

Apartado 115, Sicuani, PERU

Valentin Sumine Hanco
Organized: 1985   Evangelical
MISSIONARIES IN SERVICE
(1985) 5   (1988) 6
AAGR = 6%
Foreign missionaries in 1988:   0
FIELDS OF SERVICE
Peru
Cusco Department   Quechua
Arequipa Department   Quechua

PUERTO RICO

Bethel Mission of Puerto Rico

Calle 13, S.O. 824
Caparra Terrace 00921, PUERTO RICO

Rev. Edwards J. DePree
Organized: Not reported.

MISSIONARIES IN SERVICE

(1972) 15   (1975) 21   (1980) 36
(1982) 29   (1984) 34   (1988) 45*
AAGR = N/A
Foreign missionaries in 1988: Not reported.

FIELDS OF SERVICE

USA
  Puerto Rico (Durado)
  Puerto Rico (Capparra Terrace)
  Puerto Rico (San Juan)

VENEZUELA

Evangelical Free Church Mission

Apartado 4713
Maracay Aragua, VENEZUELA

Juan Olson
Organized: Not reported.

MISSIONARIES IN SERVICE

(1972) 58   (1975) 58   (1980) 66
(1982) 56   (1984) 60   (1988) 61*
AAGR = N/A
Foreign missionaries in 1988: Not reported.

FIELDS OF SERVICE

Not reported.

Evangelical Service Mission

Apartado 419
Barquisimeto, VENEZUELA

Julio Hidalgo
Organized: Not reported.

MISSIONARIES IN SERVICE

(1980) 3   (1982) 3   (1984) 3

(1988) 3*
AAGR = N/A
Foreign missionaries in 1988: Not reported.

FIELDS OF SERVICE

Venezuela
  Tronador
  Apure Yarurd

LATIN AMERICA TRAINING AGENCIES

Evangelical Center of Missions
C. Postal 53, CEP 36570
Vicosa, M.G., BRAZIL

Elben M. Lenz Csar
Organized: 1983   Presbyterian
MISSIONARIES IN SERVICE
(1984)   6   (1988)   9*
AAGR = N/A
Foreign missionaries in 1988: Not reported.

Missionary Training Program
Apartado 5-1124
Guadalajara, Jalisco, MEXICO
Organized: Not reported.

LATIN AMERICA NETWORKING AGENCIES

Association of Transcultural Missions of Brazil
C. Postal 1269, CEP 04004
Sao Paulo, S.P., BRAZIL

Jonathan F. de Souza
Organized: 1978   Nondenominational

Brazilian Center for Missionary Information
C. Postal 108388, CEP 24400
Sao Goncalo, R.J., BRAZIL

Paulo Roberto Barbosa
Organized: 1979   Interdenominational

MISSIONARIES IN SERVICE
(1988)   1
AAGR = N/A
Foreign missionaries in 1988:   0
FIELDS OF SERVICE
Not reported.

COMIBAM
C. Postal 1269
Bernardino de Campos, BRAZIL

Jonathan F. dos Santos
Organized: 1986   Interdenominational

INTERNATIONAL LATIN AMERICA-BASED SENDING AGENCIES

Campus Crusade for Christ, International
Codigo Postal 1127
Buenos Aires, ARGENTINA

Mario Bloise
Organized: Not reported.
Nondenominational
MISSIONARIES IN SERVICE
(1988)   2
AAGR = N/A
Foreign missionaries in 1988:   2
FIELDS OF SERVICE
Italy

Operation Mobilization in Argentina
C.C. 65, Sue 48
Buenos Aires 1448, ARGENTINA

Luis Perfetti
Organized: Not reported.
MISSIONARIES IN SERVICE
(1984)   12   (1988)   14*
AAGR = N/A

Foreign missionaries in 1988: Not reported.

FIELDS OF SERVICE
Not reported.

Project Magreb
Castilla 711, Santa Fe, ARGENTINA

Organized: 1984   Nondenominational
MISSIONARIES IN SERVICE
(1988)   6
AAGR = N/A
Foreign missionaries in 1988:   6
FIELDS OF SERVICE
Africa   Muslims

Youth with A Mission
Castilla 595
Buenos Aires 1000, ARGENTINA

Alejandro Rodriguez
Organized: Not reported.
Nondenominational
MISSIONARIES IN SERVICE
Information not reported.
FIELDS OF SERVICE
Not reported.

Youth with A Mission
Castilla 20566, La Paz, BOLIVIA

Oscar Lima Castano
Organized: 1983   Interdenominational
MISSIONARIES IN SERVICE
(1985)   13   (1988)   32
AAGR = 35%
Foreign missionaries in 1988:   1
FIELDS OF SERVICE
Israel   Jews
Bolivia
  Cochabamba Department   City
    Youth, Drug Addicts
  Tarija Department   Southern Towns
  La Paz Department   Children,
    Aymara, Residents

Africa Inland Mission International-Brazil
C. Postal 277, CEP 17500
Marilia, S.P., BRAZIL

Antonio Carlos Nasser
Organized: Not reported.
Interdenominational
MISSIONARIES IN SERVICE
(1988)   1
AAGR = N/A
Foreign missionaries in 1988:   1
FIELDS OF SERVICE
Mozambique
  Sofala Province (Beira)

Operation Mobilization
Rua da Constituicao 14, CEP 20060
Rio De Janeiro, R.J., BRAZIL

Decio Sanches de Carvalho
Organized: Not reported.
Interdenominational
MISSIONARIES IN SERVICE
Further information withheld at agency's request.

Youth With A Mission
C. Postal 2024, CEP 30161
Belo Horizonte, M.G., BRAZIL

James Robert Stier
Organized: 1976   Interdenominational
MISSIONARIES IN SERVICE
(1980)   61   (1985) 150   (1988) 255
AAGR = 20%
Foreign missionaries in 1988:   18
FIELDS OF SERVICE
Netherlands
  Amsterdam
Brazil   Poor People, Needy Children
  Rio Grande do Sul State   Children
  Northeast Region   Plantation Workers, Street People
  Para State   Children
  Minas Gerais (Belo Horizonte)   Urban Dwellers

Amazonas State Maui, Ribeirinho, Benjamia, Constant, Macaroca, Tapaua, Parauari, Palmari, Satere-Mawe

Minas Gerais (North Contagem) Poor People

Minas Gerais (Belo Horizonte) Abandoned Children

Minas Gerais (Contagem) Orphans

Rio de Janeiro State Urban Dwellers

Parana (Curitiba) Urban Dwellers

Canada

Ontario Urban Dwellers

USA

Texas (Tyler) Urban Dwellers

Uruguay Urban Dwellers

Peru Urban Dwellers

Youth With A Mission

Casilla 10161, Correo Central
Santiago, CHILE
Organized: Not reported.

MISSIONARIES IN SERVICE

Information not reported.

FIELDS OF SERVICE

Not reported.

New Tribes Mission of Colombia

Apartado Aereo 16569
Bogota, COLOMBIA

Dan Germann
Organized: 1967   Interdenominational

MISSIONARIES IN SERVICE

(1988) 157
AAGR = N/A
Foreign missionaries in 1988:   0

FIELDS OF SERVICE

Colombia

Vaupes Department Guanano

Guainia Department Piapoco

Amazonas Department Miranas

Guaviare Region Macusa, Guaviare

Narino Department Epena

Guainia Department Puinave

Vichada Department Guahibo

Central American Mission

Apartado 213, 32 Calle 4-46, Zone 3
Guatemala City, GUATEMALA

Armando Osorio
Organized: Not reported.

MISSIONARIES IN SERVICE

(1988) 1
AAGR = N/A
Foreign missionaries in 1988:   1

FIELDS OF SERVICE

Nicaragua

Managua Local Church

Operation Mobilization

Apartado 3-632, Colonia Guerrero
Mexico D.F. 06300, MEXICO

Dario Grassman
Organized: Not reported.   Evangelical

MISSIONARIES IN SERVICE

(1988) 9
AAGR = N/A
Foreign missionaries in 1988:   0

FIELDS OF SERVICE

Italy

South America Doulos Ship

Turkey

Mexico

Hidalgo State

Chihuahua State

Spain

Barcelona

Cyprus

Reapers

Apartado 1710, Lima 100, PERU

Rev. Peter Hocking
Organized: 1963   Nondenominational

MISSIONARIES IN SERVICE

(1972) 6   (1975) 6   (1980) 10
(1982) 11   (1984) 11   (1985) 11
(1988) 10
AAGR = 3%
Foreign missionaries in 1988:   0

FIELDS OF SERVICE

Peru

Junin Department   Quechua
Pasco Department   Amuesha
Huanuco Department   Quechua

INTERNATIONAL LATIN-AMERICA SENDING AGENCIES

Project Magreb

Proyecto Magreb
Apartado 573
Granada 18080, SPAIN

Ing. Pablo Carrillo Luna
Organized: 1984   Interdenominational

MISSIONARIES IN SERVICE

Further information withheld at agency's request.

LATIN AMERICA NON-REPORTING AGENCIES

Evangelical Methodist Church of Argentina

240, 10B, Buenos Aires, ARGENTINA
Organized: Not reported.

MISSIONARIES IN SERVICE

Information not reported.

FIELDS OF SERVICE

Not reported.

Laguna Yacre Evangelical Mission

Bacacay 3450, Capital Federal
ARGENTINA
Organized: Not reported.

MISSIONARIES IN SERVICE

Information not reported.

FIELDS OF SERVICE

Not reported.

Missionary Association of the Aymaro Indians

La Paz, BOLIVIA
Organized: 1976

MISSIONARIES IN SERVICE

Information not reported.

FIELDS OF SERVICE

Not reported.

Brazil's Korean Church

C. Postal 18861-Aeroporto
Sao Paulo 0100, S.P., BRAZIL
Organized: Not reported.

MISSIONARIES IN SERVICE

Information not reported.

FIELDS OF SERVICE

Not reported.

Brazilian Council of African Evangelical Fellowship

Rua Alexandre MacKenzie 60
Rio de Janiero, R.J., BRAZIL
Organized: Not reported.

MISSIONARIES IN SERVICE

Information not reported.

FIELDS OF SERVICE

Not reported.

Brazilian Presbyterian Church, Board of Foreign Missions

c/o Calvary Presb. Church
CEP 18106, Sorocaba, S.P., BRAZIL
Organized: Not reported.

MISSIONARIES IN SERVICE

Information not reported.

FIELDS OF SERVICE

Not reported.

Christ Is Salvation Evangelistic Ministry

Praca Apogitaguaras 67
CEP 02970, Sao Paulo, S.P., BRAZIL

Benedito P. de Oliveira
Organized: 1986   Interdenominational

MISSIONARIES IN SERVICE

Information not reported.

FIELDS OF SERVICE

Brazil
 Sao Paulo State
Chile
 Various Departments   Spanish

Edward Lane Bible Institute

C. Postal 12, CEP 38740
Parocinio, M.G., BRAZIL

Roberto Brasileiro Silva
Organized: 1933   Presbyterian

MISSIONARIES IN SERVICE

Information not reported.

FIELDS OF SERVICE

Brazil
 Parana State   Dutch Immigrants
 Mato Grosso do Sul State   Terena
 Para State   Arara, Caiua
South Africa
Paraguay
 Concepcion (Belen)
 Central (Asuncion)

Evangelical Church of Lutheran Confession in Brazil

C. Postal 2876, CEP 90000. Porto Alegre
Rio Grande do Sul, BRAZIL

Rev. P. Heimberto Kunkel
Organized: Not reported.   Lutheran

MISSIONARIES IN SERVICE

Information not reported.

FIELDS OF SERVICE

Not reported.

Independent Presbyterian Church, Board of Missions

C. Postal 300, CEP 01000
Sao Paulo, S.P., BRAZIL
Organized: Not reported.

MISSIONARIES IN SERVICE

Information not reported.

FIELDS OF SERVICE

Not reported.

Missionary Church, Board of Missions

C. Postal 618, Maringa, Parana, BRAZIL
Organized: Not reported.

MISSIONARIES IN SERVICE

Information not reported.

FIELDS OF SERVICE

Not reported.

National Baptist Convention

C. Postal 400
Belo Horizonte, M.G., BRAZIL
Organized: Not reported.

MISSIONARIES IN SERVICE

Information not reported.

FIELDS OF SERVICE

Not reported.

PAS (Project South America)

C. Postal 30548
Sao Paulo 404, S.P., BRAZIL
Organized: Not reported.

MISSIONARIES IN SERVICE

Information not reported.

FIELDS OF SERVICE

Not reported.

Priscilla and Aquilla Mission

Travessa Ipatinga, 30, CEP 39800
Teofilo Otonia, M.G., BRAZIL
Organized: Not reported.

MISSIONARIES IN SERVICE

Information not reported.

FIELDS OF SERVICE
Not reported.

Pro-Redemption of the Indians Mission
C. Postal 4, Dourados
Mato Grosso do Sul, BRAZIL
Organized: Not reported.

MISSIONARIES IN SERVICE
Information not reported.

FIELDS OF SERVICE
Not reported.

REMI
C. Postal 68, CEP 35100
Gov. Valdares, M.G., BRAZIL
Organized: Not reported.

MISSIONARIES IN SERVICE
Information not reported.

FIELDS OF SERVICE
Not reported.

Transmission
C. Postal 1206, CEP 30000
Belo Horizonte, M.G., BRAZIL
Organized: Not reported.

MISSIONARIES IN SERVICE
Information not reported.

FIELDS OF SERVICE
Not reported.

Faith Christian Missions
Apartado Aero 1505
Barranquilla, Atlantico, COLOMBIA
Organized: Not reported.

MISSIONARIES IN SERVICE
Information not reported.

FIELDS OF SERVICE
Not reported.

Pan American Mission of Colombia
Apartado Aereo 53425
Bogota, COLOMBIA
Organized: Not reported.

MISSIONARIES IN SERVICE
Information not reported.

FIELDS OF SERVICE
Not reported.

Church of God of the Prophecy
Apartado 1792, Santo Domingo
DOMINICAN REPUBLIC
Organized: Not reported.

MISSIONARIES IN SERVICE
Information not reported.

FIELDS OF SERVICE
Not reported.

O.C.S.
Casilla 4829, Quito, ECUADOR
Organized: Not reported.

MISSIONARIES IN SERVICE
Information not reported.

FIELDS OF SERVICE
Not reported.

SI Amen
Casilla 8507, Guayaquil, ECUADOR
Organized: Not reported.

MISSIONARIES IN SERVICE
Information not reported.

FIELDS OF SERVICE
Not reported.

Great Final Day
Apartado 1213
Guatemala City, GUATEMALA

Rev. Hernandez
Organized: Not reported.

MISSIONARIES IN SERVICE
Information not reported.

FIELDS OF SERVICE
Not reported.

Mount Sinai
Apartado 1213
Guatemala City, GUATEMALA

Rev. Antonio Lima
Organized: Not reported.

MISSIONARIES IN SERVICE
Information not reported.

FIELDS OF SERVICE
Not reported.

Strict English Baptist
Jacmel, HAITI
Organized: Not reported.

MISSIONARIES IN SERVICE
Information not reported.

FIELDS OF SERVICE
Not reported.

Church of the Golden Covenant
Apartado 451 CD
Satelite 53100, MEXICO
Organized: Not reported.

MISSIONARIES IN SERVICE
Information not reported.

FIELDS OF SERVICE
Not reported.

Fraternity of Independent Pentecostal Churches
Vasco de Quiroga 1724
Colonia Santa Fe
Mexico D.F. 01201, MEXICO

Juan Figueroa Contreras
Organized: Not reported.   Pentecostal

MISSIONARIES IN SERVICE
Information not reported.

FIELDS OF SERVICE

Mexico
Mexico City   Mazahua
Oaxaca State   Otomi
Veracruz State   Totonaca
Michoacan State   Tarasco

JUMIME (Junta Miskionera Mexicana)
Apartado M 10244
Mexico D.F. 06000, MEXICO
Organized: Not reported.

MISSIONARIES IN SERVICE
Information not reported.

FIELDS OF SERVICE
Not reported.

Spiritual Christian Evangelical Church
Necaxa 196, Colonia Portales
Mexico D.F. 03300, MEXICO

Cesar Garcia Benavides
Organized: Not reported.

MISSIONARIES IN SERVICE
Information not reported.

FIELDS OF SERVICE

Mexico
Oaxaca State   Xochitonalco, Huautla
   de Jimenez

OCEANIA

OCEANIA SENDING AGENCIES

FIJI

Anglican Church, Diocese of Polynesia
Box 35, Suva, FIJI
Organized: Not reported.

MISSIONARIES IN SERVICE
(1975) 136   (1978) 132   (1980) 128
(1982) 158   (1988) 180*
AAGR = N/A
Foreign missionaries in 1988: Not reported.

FIELDS OF SERVICE
Not reported.

Assemblies of God of Fiji
PO Box 13142, Suva, FIJI

Rev. Filimoni K Waqa
Organized: 1926   Assemblies of God

MISSIONARIES IN SERVICE
(1972) 12   (1980) 8   (1985) 4
(1988) 2
AAGR = -10%
Foreign missionaries in 1988: 2

FIELDS OF SERVICE
Australia
  Queensland   Thursday Islanders

Methodist Church in Fiji Overseas Mission
GPO Box 357, Suva, FIJI

Rev. Josateki Koroi
Organized: 1874   Methodist

MISSIONARIES IN SERVICE
(1972) 17   (1980) 17   (1985) 19
(1988) 20
AAGR = 1%
Foreign missionaries in 1988: 20

FIELDS OF SERVICE
Australia
  Melbourne   English
  Darwin   Aborigines
Belize   English, Spanish
Panama   Dutch
New Zealand
  Auckland   English
  Wellington   English
Papua New Guinea
  Highlands Region   Tari, Hagen, Huli, Mendi
  Bougainville Island   Bougainvilleans
United Kingdom
  England (London)   English
Costa Rica   Spanish

PAPUA NEW GUINEA

Assemblies of God in Australia Papua New Guinea Mission
PO Box 34, Maprik, East Sepik Province
PAPUA NEW GUINEA

Rev. John Sweeney
Organized: Not reported.

MISSIONARIES IN SERVICE
(1984) 41   (1988) 38*
AAGR = N/A
Foreign missionaries in 1988: Not reported.

FIELDS OF SERVICE
Papua New Guinea
  Southern Highlands Province   Various Tribal Groups
  Central Province

Various Tribal Groups
Enga Province   Various Tribal Groups
East Sepik Province   Various Tribal Groups
North Solomons Province   Various Tribal Groups
Morobe Province   Various Tribal Groups
West New Britain Province   Papuans
Western Highlands Province   Various Tribal Groups

Evangelical Lutheran Church of Papua New Guinea

Box 80, Lae, PAPUA NEW GUINEA

Rev. Getake S Gam
Organized: Not reported.   Lutheran
MISSIONARIES IN SERVICE
(1980) 45   (1988) 4
AAGR = -25%
Foreign missionaries in 1988: 4
FIELDS OF SERVICE
Germany (West)
  Bavaria   German
USA   Americans
Australia
  Queensland   Aborigines

Good News Lutheran Church

PO Box 111, Wabag, Enga Province
PAPUA NEW GUINEA

Mr. Mark Yapao
Organized: 1960   Lutheran
MISSIONARIES IN SERVICE
(1972) 28   (1975) 27   (1978) 22
(1980) 24   (1988) 21*
AAGR = N/A
Foreign missionaries in 1988: Not reported.
FIELDS OF SERVICE
Not reported.

Highland Christian Mission

Okapa via Goroka
PAPUA NEW GUINEA

Dr. Stuart H. Merriam
Organized: 1964   Interdenominational
MISSIONARIES IN SERVICE
(1972) 5   (1975) 6   (1978) 12
(1980) 12   (1988) 29*
AAGR = N/A
Foreign missionaries in 1988: Not reported.
FIELDS OF SERVICE
Not reported.

United Church in Papua New Guinea & Solomon Islands

United Church, Assembly Office
PO Box 1401
Port Moresby, PAPUA NEW GUINEA

Rev. Edea Kidu
Organized: 1980
MISSIONARIES IN SERVICE
Further information withheld at agency's request.

SOLOMON ISLANDS

Church of Melanesia, Board of Mission

PO Box 19
Honiara, SOLOMON ISLANDS

B.J. LePine-Williams
Organized: 1979   Denominational
MISSIONARIES IN SERVICE
(1978) 100   (1980) 120   (1988) 249*
AAGR = N/A
Foreign missionaries in 1988: Not reported.
FIELDS OF SERVICE
Not reported.

South Sea Evangelical Church

PO Box 16
Honiara, SOLOMON ISLANDS

Rev. Jezreel Filoa
Organized: 1903   Denominational
MISSIONARIES IN SERVICE
(1978) 12   (1980) 10   (1988) 5*
AAGR = N/A
Foreign missionaries in 1988: Not reported.
FIELDS OF SERVICE
Not reported.

TONGA

Methodist Church in Tonga

Box 57, Nukualota, TONGA

Sione Amanaki Havea
Organized: 1824   Methodist
MISSIONARIES IN SERVICE
(1988) 14
AAGR = N/A
Foreign missionaries in 1988:   0
FIELDS OF SERVICE
Not reported.

WESTERN SAMOA

Samoa Congregational Church

Tamaligl, WESTERN SAMOA

Rev. Elder Tuuau
Organized: 1830
Interdenominational Congregational
MISSIONARIES IN SERVICE
(1972) 5   (1975) 4   (1978) 6
(1980) 10   (1988) 20*
AAGR = N/A
Foreign missionaries in 1988: Not reported.
FIELDS OF SERVICE
Not reported.

INTERNATIONAL OCEANIA-BASED SENDING AGENCIES

Youth With A Mission American Samoa

Youth With A Mission American Samoa
P.O. Box 2608
Pago Pago, AMERICAN SAMOA

Larry Anderson
Organized: 1975   Nondenominational
MISSIONARIES IN SERVICE
(1988) 18
AAGR = N/A
Foreign missionaries in 1988:   0
FIELDS OF SERVICE
Western Samoa   Samoans
American Samoa   Samoans

NON-REPORTING OCEANIA AGENCIES

First Church of God

PO Box 20850, Gmf 96921, GUAM

Organized: Not reported.
MISSIONARIES IN SERVICE
Information not reported.
FIELDS OF SERVICE
Not reported.

General Baptist Church of Guam

PO Box 595, Agana 96910, GUAM
Organized: Not reported.
MISSIONARIES IN SERVICE
Information not reported.

FIELDS OF SERVICE
Not reported.

Palau Evangelical Church
PO Box 3664, Agana 96910, GUAM
Organized: Not reported.
MISSIONARIES IN SERVICE
Information not reported.
FIELDS OF SERVICE
Not reported.

Boroko Baptist Church
PO Box 333
Port Moresby, PAPUA NEW GUINEA
Organized: Not reported.
MISSIONARIES IN SERVICE
Information not reported.
FIELDS OF SERVICE
Not reported.

C.L.T.C.
PO Box 382
Mt. Hagen, Western Highland Province
PAPUA NEW GUINEA
Organized: Not reported.
MISSIONARIES IN SERVICE
Information not reported.
FIELDS OF SERVICE
Not reported.

Global Prayer Warriors
PO Box 4017
Boroko, PAPUA NEW GUINEA

Walo Ani
Organized: Not reported.
MISSIONARIES IN SERVICE
Information not reported.
FIELDS OF SERVICE
Not reported.

QUESTIONAIRE

This questionaire primarily concerns the indigenous missionary sending agencies in *AFRICA, ASIA* and *LATIN AMERICA,* who <u>send</u> missionaries from their own country, state, or *"people"* to another. It is very important that you fill in as much information as you can and return it within two weeks if at all possible. In any case, please **DO** return it as soon as possible.

THANK YOU FOR YOUR HELP!

NAME, ADDRESS AND HISTORY OF YOUR MISSION:

1. Official Name:_____
2. Name in English: _____
3. Postal Address: _____
4. Street Address:_____
5. Country:_____ 6. Telephone: _____
7. Name of leader, president, or head of mission today:
   Name:_____ Title: _____
8. When was the mission organized (date):_____
9. Choose the theological position which best describes this organization (choose only one and circle it, please):

Adventist	Alliance	Anglican	Assemblies of God	Baptist
Brethren	Charismatic	Church of Christ		Episcopal
Evangelical	Indepedent	Lutheran	Mennonite	Methodist
Nondenominational		Pentecostal	Presbyterian	Other: _____

INFORMATION ABOUT MISSIONARIES

10. How many active missionaries are there with the mission, organization, or agency (include those on temporary leave)?

Year	Couples	Unmarried Men	Unmarried Women	Total*
This Year				
1985				
1980				
1972				

*When counting totals, please count each couple as two people.

11. How many of your missionaries usually minister in a language other than their mother tongue in their place of service? _____
    This is an: ( ) Estimate; ( ) Actual Count   (Please tick one.)

12. What is the most common language spoken in the community where the sending base is located?_____.
    How many of your missionaries minister in a language other than that one?_____

13. How far away from their sending base do your missionaries usually minister? Fill in the number of missionaries in each catagory:
    _____ Outside their own country, on another <u>continent</u>*.
    _____ Outside their own coutnry, on same <u>continent</u>*.
    _____ Inside their own country, more than 300 kilometers away from the sending base.
    *If "continent" does not fit your situation use "region" instead.

14. Where are your missionaries working? Among what peoples?
    (Indicate on the following chart)

Country	State/Province	Target People, tribe, or language group	Number of Missionaries

(If needed attach additional paper)

PARTNERSHIP INFORMATION

15. Do ANY of your missionaries work through a partnership arranged with ANOTHER mission agency, board or society?   ( ) Yes   ( ) No
    If yes, please complete the following:

PARTNER MISSION AGENCY		YOUR MISSIONARIES WORKING IN PARTNERSHIP		
Name	Address	Number	%Supported by THEIR Mission	Target People, Tribe or Language

NAMES OF NEW THIRD WORLD INDIGENOUS MISSIONARY SOCIETIES OR AGENCIES.

16. Please list the names and addresses of other missionary agencies which you consider to be indigenous in your country:

Name: _____
Address: _____

Name: _____
Address: _____

Please return this questionaire within two weeks to:

Reverend Larry D. Pate
25 Corning Avenue
Milpitas, CA 95035   USA

308

Mission Information Update

APPENDIX B

This book includes the best information available on the missionary movement in latin America, Africa, Asia and Oceania. But we know there are corrections which could be made and additional missionary organizations for which we have no information. Please use this form to help us! If you know of additional information, corrections or other sources of data which should be included in the second phase of this research, please complete this form. You may duplicate it and send information on more than one mission organization or source. Your help will be greatly appreciated. It will also go a long way toward making the next publication of this type more accurate. Thank You!

Larry D. Pate
Emerging Missions
25 Corning Avenue
Milpitas, CA 95035 USA

1. The mission agency or person referred to in this report is:

   Address (if known):   **Telephone:**

   _____   **Cable or FAX:**

   _____   **Other:**

2. The information I wish to report is:
   - ☐ An up-date of information already listed
   - ☐ A new listing
   - ☐ A corrective suggestion
   - ☐ A personal comment
   - ☐ _____

3. The information I am reporting is based upon: (please tick one or more)
   - ☐ Personal, first hand knowledge of facts
   - ☐ Personal experience and understanding

☐ Written information of which I am enclosing a copy
☐ I heard this from people who know
☐ _____

4. Information:

_____
_____
_____
_____
_____
_____
_____
_____
_____
_____
_____
_____
_____
_____
_____
_____
_____
_____
_____
_____
_____

Your name: _____
Position: _____
Address: _____
_____
Telephone: _____
Cable or FAX: _____
Other: _____

THANK YOU FOR HELPING US UPDATE THIS INFORMATION